# FINANCIAL STABILITY, ECONOMIC GROWTH,
## AND THE ROLE OF LAW

Financial crises have become an all-too-common occurrence over the past twenty years, largely as a result of changes in finance brought about by increasing internationalization and integration. As domestic financial systems and economies become more interlinked, weaknesses can significantly impact not only individual economies but also markets, financial intermediaries and economies around the world. This volume addresses the twin objectives of financial development in the context of financial stability and the role of law in supporting both. Financial stability (frequently seen as the avoidance of financial crisis) has become an objective of the international financial architecture as well as individual economies and central banks. At the same time, financial development is now seen to play an important role in economic growth. In both financial stability and financial development, law and related institutions have a central role.

Douglas W. Arner is the Director of the Asian Institute of International Financial Law (www.AIIFL.com) and an Associate Professor at the Faculty of Law of the University of Hong Kong (HKU). In addition, at HKU, he is Director of the LLM (Corporate and Financial Law) Program and Co-Director of the Duke University–HKU Asia-America Institute in Transnational Law. Prior to his appointment at HKU, Dr. Arner was the Sir John Lubbock Support Fund Fellow at the Centre for Commercial Law Studies at Queen Mary, University of London, and Director of Research of the London Institute of International Banking, Finance and Development Law (a think-tank consultancy).

Specializing in economic and financial law, regulation and development, he is author, co-author or editor of eight books, including *Financial Markets in Hong Kong: Law and Practice* (Oxford University Press), and is author or co-author of more than fifty articles, chapters and reports on related subjects.

Dr. Arner has served as a consultant with, among others, the World Bank, Asian Development Bank, Asia Pacific Economic Cooperation (APEC) Forum, European Bank for Reconstruction and Development, and Development Bank of Southern Africa. He has lectured, co-organized conferences and seminars and been involved with financial sector reform projects in more than twenty economies in Africa, Asia and Europe, and has been a visiting professor or visiting fellow at the National University of Singapore, the University of Melbourne, Shanghai University of Finance and Economics, Southern Methodist University and the University of Reading.

He holds a B.A. in literature, economics and political science from Drury University, a J.D. (cum laude) from Southern Methodist University, an LL.M. (with distinction) in banking and finance law from the University of London (Queen Mary College) and a Ph.D. from the University of London.

# Financial Stability, Economic Growth, and the Role of Law

## DOUGLAS W. ARNER

University of Hong Kong

CAMBRIDGE
UNIVERSITY PRESS

CAMBRIDGE UNIVERSITY PRESS
Cambridge, New York, Melbourne, Madrid, Cape Town, Singapore, São Paulo

Cambridge University Press
32 Avenue of the Americas, New York, NY 10013-2473, USA

www.cambridge.org
Information on this title: www.cambridge.org/9780521870474

First published 2007

Printed in the United States of America

*A catalog record for this publication is available from the British Library.*

*Library of Congress Cataloging in Publication Data*

Arner, Douglas W.
Financial stability, economic growth, and the role of law / Douglas W. Arner.
    p.   cm.
Includes bibliographical references and index.
ISBN-13: 978-0-521-87047-4 (hardback)
ISBN-10: 0-521-87047-X (hardback)
ISBN-13: 978-0-521-69056-0 (pbk.)
ISBN-10: 0-521-69056-0 (pbk.)
1. Financial crises.   2. Economic development.   3. Finance – Law and legislation.
I. Title.
HB3722.A76   2007
332'.042 – dc22      2006039199

ISBN   978-0-521-87047-4 hardback
ISBN   978-0-521-69056-0 paperback

*To Pearline, Becky and Chantal*

# Contents

# Introduction

The research underlying this volume began with a question: why do financial crises occur and what can be done to prevent such crises and reduce their impact when they do occur? Today, following a series of financial crises around the world over the past fifteen years, this question to some extent has been answered through the establishment of a system of international standards directed towards the overall goal of financial stability. If one is interested in financial crises, it follows that one is also interested in the broader role of the financial system: clearly, financial crises are deleterious to economic growth, but can the financial system also have positive effects? Likewise, this question is now generally answered in the affirmative: an effectively functioning financial system is important for economic growth, though (as demonstrated by the existence of financial crises) finance also brings risks. The question then becomes how to develop a financial system which supports economic growth (and thereby economic development) in the context of financial stability. The purpose of this volume is to address this question.

In the past fifteen years, the recognition of the importance of law in an economy has increased greatly. It is now commonly accepted that property rights, enforcement of contracts and the rule of law are significant for economic development. Unfortunately, in most cases, the literature – especially the economic literature – has still not progressed significantly beyond this basic realization. The question arises: what do these ideas mean in practice? More precisely, if law is important, what sort of legal infrastructure and institutions are best?

This volume attempts to answer this question in the context of the financial sector – arguably the area of an economy in which law has the greatest importance. Specifically, this volume discusses the relationship among law, finance, and economic growth and development. It argues that law and the related institutional framework are fundamental to economic development generally.

Further, it argues that an effective financial sector is essential to economic growth. On this basis, the volume addresses the question of how laws and institutions should be designed in order to support financial sector development to underpin economic growth in the context of financial stability.

In order to do this, the volume analyses international responses to financial crises in developing, emerging and transition economies[1] at the end of the twentieth and beginning of the twenty-first centuries. The volume argues that financial crises since the Mexican crisis in 1994 have caused a fundamental re-evaluation of the role of financial law and institutions, with the consequent development for the first time of a comprehensive framework of internationally acceptable standards delineating minimum requirements for financial stability.

The author argues, on the basis of recent research, that law has a fundamental role in both financial stability and financial market development, both of which, in turn, are significant for economic growth. The volume analyses the international consensus (formalized through a series of international standards) respecting financial stability which developed following the series of financial crises around the world at the end of the twentieth century. It combines the elements of the key standards which have been developed with research respecting financial development in an effort to provide an understanding of the main legal and institutional elements supporting financial sector stability and development.

The volume discusses whether the international financial architecture, as currently structured, addresses the risks inherent in moving from a closed domestic financial system to an open system integrated into the global financial system. It suggests that the current structure of the international financial architecture has developed as a response to the risks inherent in financial liberalization, domestic restructuring and globalization of finance. However, unlike the structure developed at Bretton Woods at the end of World War II or in the European Union, the current structure of the international financial architecture fails to explicitly link domestic restructuring (addressed by

---

[1] Throughout, this volume will use the terms "developed", "emerging", "transition" and "developing" economies. Herein, "developed" countries or economies are the advanced nations of North America, Europe and East Asia (Japan, Hong Kong and Singapore). "Emerging economies" are market-based economies which are in the process of moving to "developed" status through integration into the global economic and financial systems. "Transition economies" are formerly centrally planned economies which are in the process of transitioning to market-based economic systems. "Developing" countries or economies are poorer states which are in the process of building economies and financial systems. These general terms reflect related terminology used by the International Monetary Fund.

the current matrix of international financial standards) with financial liberalization (especially in the context of both capital account liberalization and the role of the World Trade Organization [WTO]) and globalization of financial markets (and the role of the international financial institutions in this process). Further, it fails to move coherently beyond the requirements of stability to the requirements of development.

The volume concludes by suggesting that individual governments, regional arrangements and development organizations should take an active interest in the legal and institutional design of financial systems, much in the way that one would pursue major construction or technological development projects, to support financial stability in the context of financial development and in order to enhance economic growth and development.

Following this introduction, the volume proceeds through ten chapters organized into four parts.

## FINANCIAL MARKETS AND THE INTERNATIONAL FINANCIAL ARCHITECTURE

The first part discusses the relationship among law and institutions, financial sector development and economic growth, and the international financial architecture.

The part begins, in the first chapter, with a discussion of theories of economic development, suggesting that there is an emerging consensus relating to the importance of an economy's institutional framework, including law and legal infrastructure, in economic growth and development; presents research addressing the role of law in an economy; and argues that law and legal infrastructure have an important role in economic growth, development and finance. The chapter highlights three aspects: first, the fundamental role of law and institutions in economic growth and development; second, the growing body of research suggesting that an effective financial system is necessary to support economic growth; and third, the role of law and institutions in an effective financial system. Second, the chapter discusses the role of finance in economic growth and development, suggesting that the role is both positive and negative. Financial crises and research have highlighted weaknesses in both domestic and international financial systems, as well as the significance of the financial sector – both positive and negative – in economic growth and development more generally. In order to discuss the role of law in financial development, it is first necessary to have a general understanding of the financial sector, what it does, and how it works. The chapter therefore includes a brief introduction to financial systems. This picture of financial systems, however, is only a stylized description, both of domestic and international financial systems. Finally, the chapter also looks at the function of law in finance, and concludes by suggesting that law plays an essential role in financial development, which, in turn, is significant for economic growth and development generally.

The second chapter of this volume discusses the developing international framework addressing the potential negative impact of finance on economic development – namely, the concepts of financial stability and the international financial architecture. It addresses financial stability, its role and the central issue of whether the international financial architecture as currently structured addresses the risks of participation of individual economies, especially developing, emerging and transition economies, in the global financial system. It argues that appropriate law and legal infrastructure are a necessary but not sufficient component of financial stability, economic growth and development. Specifically, Chapter Two discusses financial stability and the significant but incomplete international consensus that has developed in the past decade. This consensus is often discussed in the context of the "new international financial architecture". With this international framework in mind, the remainder of the volume addresses the mechanics of legal infrastructure in finance.

The chapter first looks at the post–World War II design for international financial stability and economic development: the Bretton Woods international economic system and its objectives (financial stability and economic development, based on three pillars: money, finance and investment, and trade). Second, it briefly discusses the changes in the international financial system between the creation of Bretton Woods and the end of the twentieth century: the process of financial market globalization.

The onset of the Mexican financial crisis in 1994 signaled the return of a sort of financial crisis not seen since before the establishment of the Bretton Woods system and its structure of fixed relationships among closed domestic financial systems. Prior to 1944, however, such crises were not uncommon and, in fact, one goal of the design of the Bretton Woods system was to eliminate the possibility of similar financial crises in the future. In many ways, it was remarkably successful; however, following the break up of the fixed exchange rate system in 1973, the gradual return to free movement of capital and the increasing re-integration of financial systems, the stage was set for a return to the sorts of crises common during the nineteenth and early twentieth centuries. Financial crises in emerging economies around the world over the past fifteen years highlight the dangers inherent in financial liberalization without adequate domestic restructuring in the context of participation in increasingly an globalized financial system.

Third, the chapter analyses the international response to the string of financial crises over the past fifteen years: discussions regarding the international financial architecture and the development of a system of international financial standards, comprising the political framework, international financial standards themselves, standard setters and setting, implementation, and monitoring. As a direct result of the Mexican and east Asian crises, the Group of Seven (G-7) and the Group of Ten (G-10) (among others) analysed the causes of and appropriate responses to similar situations in the future. The G-7 issued directions based on the analysis to the international financial organizations and institutions – a pattern that has since solidified into a methodology, perhaps even a system. In regard to financial stability, the G-7 issued directions to international financial organizations (e.g., the Basel Committee on Banking Supervision) to develop standards to address domestic financial sector weaknesses, which were a significant underlying factor in the various crises of the 1990s. The international financial institutions (especially the Bretton Woods institutions) are charged with supporting implementation and monitoring of those standards. In addition, the international financial institutions were directed to implement emergency measures to be used in future crises. The result is the only development respecting the international financial architecture which can really be called "new": a system of international financial standards under which political decisions are taken by the G-7; standards are formulated by international financial organizations; coordinated by the new Financial Stability Forum; and international financial institutions develop mechanisms of implementation, monitoring and response to crises, with the result being translation of international standards into domestic legal systems.

In essence, a system of international financial soft law based on implementation and monitoring of nonbinding standards has been added to the existing international financial architecture. Unfortunately, the system of international financial standards, while significant, does not form a coherent system in the same way as the Bretton Woods system as designed (though not as implemented). The system is designed to address the same issues as the Bretton Woods system (stability and development), but does so in an incomplete manner and, thus, the existing international financial architecture needs to be reviewed in order to appropriately address all three pillars in a coherent and integrated system. The chapter concludes that the current structure of the international financial architecture fails to adequately address the realities of globalized financial markets and that individual countries should undertake coherent reform processes as part of the process of financial integration and development, albeit using the system of international financial standards as a starting point.

From this background, the second and third parts of the volume analyse the specific elements of the legal and institutional framework for a stable and effective financial sector. Specifically, parts two and three discuss the main issues to be considered in financial stability and development, on the basis of international standards and related research. The system of international standards focuses on fifteen "key standards for sound financial systems", organized under three broad headings and twelve key subject areas. The first broad heading, macroeconomic policy and data transparency, is the responsibility of the International Monetary Fund; the second and third (institutional and market infrastructure, and financial regulation and supervision) are the responsibility of a wide variety of different standard-setting organizations. The chapters look at the main elements of the consensus respecting financial stability and summarize research addressing the role of law and institutions in financial market development in an effort to outline the appropriate institutional framework for finance, reflecting current international best practices.

## FOUNDATIONS OF FINANCIAL SECTOR DEVELOPMENT

Part II discusses the foundations of financial stability and development. Specifically, we look in Chapter Three at the preconditions for finance – the fundamental elements necessary for finance to develop and function, namely: (1) foundations of financial development and economic growth and (2) institutional underpinnings of finance. Chapter Four, in turn, deals with the role of central banks in financial, monetary and macroeconomic stability. While the system of international financial standards addresses the third area (reflecting an immense amount of research outside the scope of this volume), it does not address the first and second, even though, in fact, foundations and institutional underpinnings may be of at least as great, if not greater, significance for finance and development than macroeconomic policy.

Building on recent research, Chapter Three argues that financial systems require certain legal and institutional elements to be in place in order to function. These include property rights, collateral frameworks and company law, which, in turn, must be set in a framework supporting effective governance providing for enforcement of contracts and commercial dispute resolution. In addition to these institutional foundations, financial sector development occurs best in the context of a stable macroeconomic setting, including appropriate monetary, financial and fiscal policies and frameworks (Chapter Four). In addition, Chapter Four addresses certain responsibilities of central banks and financial authorities, including payment and settlement and government bond markets.

Chapter Five discusses the elements of institutional and market infrastructure which are essential to support the development of an effective, functional financial system. These elements – all addressed by international financial standards – build upon the underpinnings discussed in Chapters Three and Four and are necessary for the financial regulatory systems and structures discussed in Part III to function properly in a market economy. Building on these foundations, Chapter Five looks to the many sorts of legal infrastructure necessary for sophisticated financial systems to function properly what could be called essential financial infrastructure. It therefore considers the supporting institutional and market infrastructure which is necessary for sophisticated financial systems to develop. Aspects include insolvency regimes, corporate governance, and accounting and auditing systems ("financial information"). These are supported by appropriate measures to protect market integrity and thus confidence in the financial system. It is only when both the foundations and the supporting infrastructure are in place that financial liberalization, regulation and supervision can function properly.

### FINANCIAL REGULATION AND SUPERVISION

Part III discusses a central focus of recent international efforts: financial regulation, supervision and liberalization. Specifically, it investigates the primary areas addressed by the system of international financial standards: banking (Chapter Six), nonbank finance (Chapter Seven), and financial liberalization and related issues such as financial conglomerates and financial regulatory structure (Chapter Eight). International financial standards, however, generally only address stability and not the role of development. The volume attempts to take both into account and to consider other areas meriting further attention.

### LOOKING FORWARD

Part IV discusses deficiencies in the international financial architecture as currently structured and in the process through which economies address their financial sector legal and institutional frameworks. The volume concludes, first, that international financial standards constitute a necessary but not sufficient requirement for financial stability. Second, the current pseudo-system is inadequately structured to deal with the central issue presented at the outset – that is, the relationships among the requirements for development (namely, liberalization, restructuring and integration), especially as the system discussed interacts with the WTO and its constituent financial services provisions. Third, the current structure of the international financial architecture does not adequately address the issue of crisis resolution.

The final two chapters thus look forward and address the reform of the international financial architecture and financial systems. They focus on the role of the international financial architecture discussed in preceding chapters, including weaknesses of the current system and a brief agenda for possible reform, and discuss issues which need to be considered in developing fully effective financial systems but to date have not been adequately treated by the international financial architecture, including development (especially competition and its relationship to the international framework of the WTO), the interaction between liberalization and regulation, and the systemic context.

Chapter Nine suggests, first, that the system of international financial standards (with its focus on financial stability) does not adequately address certain issues, especially those related to development. It argues that although the system of international standards addresses financial stability comprehensively, it does not address the issue of development to any great extent. In this regard, as standards are revised, developmental issues should be addressed in addition to stability requirements. Further, at present, international standards do not adequately address issues of competition. Especially significant is the fact that the WTO framework governing financial services access has not been incorporated into the system of international financial standards.

Second, chapters nine and ten suggest that, unlike the Bretton Woods or EU structures, the current system of international standards does not adequately address the interlinkages between finance and the international architecture. Specifically, they argue, first, that the current system of financial standards does not address the important issue of the relationship between financial liberalization and financial stability, even though this relationship is addressed by the more formal structure of the EU single financial market project. In addition, as discussed previously, financial systems today have the added complication of their interaction with one another. As a result, economies must consider issues respecting interaction and integration with global and regional financial systems. Unfortunately, the current system of financial standards does not address the important issue of the relationship between financial liberalization and financial stability at a global level. However, this relationship has been addressed at a regional level by the more formal structure of the European Union, which may provide a model for both international and other regional arrangements. Second, the international financial architecture still does not address adequately issues of crisis resolution.

The final chapter discusses financial sector design, including financial and regulatory structure, and a suggestion that individual economies proactively support financial sector development and stability by addressing the legal and institutional framework of their financial and economic systems on a holistic basis in order to achieve the desired results of financial stability and development. Governments may consider a variety of models available for domestic financial structure and for regulatory systems. If law and institutions are important for stable and effective finance, how can officials take advantage of research and best practices in their own systems and what can development professionals and organizations do to assist? The chapter suggests that financial sector development indeed can be influenced and recommends careful analysis and planning by governments and their advisors in order to appropriately address issues of legal infrastructure in financial development in order to secure economic development.

Unfortunately, despite much effort, financial crises continue, with dramatic consequences for development. The volume argues that the current framework provides an important starting point but that significant deficiencies remain. In order to support financial stability, economic growth and economic development, a fresh look should be taken at the international financial architecture in the context of the realities of today's global financial system.

This book has been supported by my interactions with a wide range of individuals and organizations around the world. While it is impossible to acknowledge all of these influences (and I am vastly appreciative of all those I have worked with on related issues over the years), I would like to especially thank the following for their input, support and/or thoughts on related issues: Ernesto Aguirre, Noritaka Akamatsu, James Barth, David Bernstein, William Blair, Charles Booth, Ross Buckley, Joao Farinha, Stefan Gannon, Say Goo, Jorge Guira, Christos Hadjiemmanuil, Vanndy Hem, Angela Itzikowitz, Lolette Kritzinger-van Niekirk, Rosa Lastra, Jing Leng, Julia Leung, José de Luna, Donald McIsaac, Matthew Morgan, Christopher Olive, Jae-Ha Park, Anita Ramasastry, Keith Reid, Gerard Sanders, Norbert Seiler, Heba Shams, Andrew Sheng, Marc Steinberg, Tull Traisorat, George Walker, Wei Wang, Mamiko Yokoi-Arai, Said Zaidansyah, and Zhongfei Zhou.

I would also like to thank the present and former staff of the Asian Development Bank, European Bank for Reconstruction and Development, International Monetary Fund and World Bank, as well as my present and former colleagues at the University of London and the University of Hong Kong.

In addition, I would like to thank Mads Andenas, Charles Chatterjee, Ross Cranston, Chantal Hébert, Paul Lejot, Joseph Norton and Michael Taylor for comments on various drafts. Finally, I would like to thank John Berger, Mary Cadette, Linda Smith and the staff of Cambridge University Press for their highly professional support and production.

All errors of course are my own.

Douglas W. Arner
January 2007

PART ONE

# FINANCE AND THE INTERNATIONAL FINANCIAL ARCHITECTURE

# 1

# Law, Finance and Development

Until the mid-1990s, the role of the financial sector in economic development was largely ignored. Today, research increasingly focuses on the central role of the financial sector in economic growth and therefore in economic development more generally.[1] Further, the importance of law in economic development prior to the early 1990s was largely ignored by most economists. Today, it is very difficult to avoid statements highlighting the importance of law and other institutional structures in economic development. Moreover, it is only more recently that the role of law in the financial sector is beginning to be carefully evaluated and understood. These are all significant developments and underscore the theme of this volume: law, legal institutions and regulatory systems ("legal infrastructure") are fundamental to financial stability and financial sector development, which, in turn, are essential to economic growth and development.

This chapter discusses the changing understanding of the role of law and the financial sector in economic growth and development. It begins with a discussion of theories of economic growth and development, suggesting that

---

[1] Economic development is a term about which much has been written but about which there is no general agreement. See G. Meier and J. Stiglitz (eds), *Frontiers of Development Economics: The Future in Perspective* (Washington DC: World Bank and New York: Oxford University Press, 2001). Today, it is generally agreed that economic development encompasses a range of factors, as indicated by the United Nations Millennium Development Goals ("MDGs") – see United Nations (UN), *United Nations Millennium Declaration, General Assembly Resolution 55/2*, 8 Sep. 2000; UN General Assembly, *Road Map Towards the Implementation of the United Nations Millennium Declaration: Report of the Secretary General*, UN General Assembly 56th Session, A/56/326, 6 Sep. 2001; see also www.developmentgoals.org. Among the most significant factor affecting economic development is economic growth. See World Bank, *2004 Annual Review of Development Effectiveness: The Bank's Contribution to Poverty Reduction*, 2005. As a result, this volume will focus primarily on economic growth.

there is an emerging consensus relating to the importance of institutions, including law and legal institutions, in economic growth and development.

Second, the chapter discusses the role of finance in economic growth and development as highlighted by a series of financial crises over the past decade and a half, suggesting both positive and negative aspects. In order to discuss the role of law in financial development, it is first necessary to have a general understanding of the financial sector, what it does, and how it works. This picture of the financial system, however, is only a stylized description, of both domestic and international financial systems.

Third, we look at the function of law in the financial system. The chapter concludes by suggesting that law plays an essential role in financial development which, in turn, is significant for economic growth and development generally.

### 1.1. LAW, INSTITUTIONS AND ECONOMIC DEVELOPMENT

Since the early 1990s, the factors supporting economic development have received increasing attention from a variety of sources. Generally speaking, theories of economic development today focus on the roles of geography (or "endowments"), policies and institutions. Geography-based theories arguably explain much of early development, but are less useful in relation to more advanced stages. Theories based upon policies dominated from World War II, culminating in the predominance of market economics and the policies of the Washington Consensus, to the Asian financial crises in the late 1990s. Following the series of financial crises beginning in the mid-1990s, attention has focused on the role of institutions in economic development, with research suggesting that institutions, in fact, may be the dominant underlying factor.

### 1.1.1. *Geography and Endowments*

Theories based upon geography suggest that economic development results from the essential physical endowments present in a given location, including such things as flora, fauna, climate and geography. Jared Diamond has reinvigorated analysis about the role of physical endowments and their influence on economic development by drawing together the various strands of the biological and physical sciences, anthropology and archaeology, and linking their discoveries to economic development.[2] Arguably, factors relating to endowments were determinative of much of economic development prior to

---

[2] See J. Diamond, *Guns, Germs, and Steel: The Fates of Human Societies* (New York: W.W. Norton, 1997).

the twentieth century, but are less relevant to contemporary development. At the same time, with global climate change, some of these factors may become increasingly relevant as the twenty-first century progresses.

### 1.1.2. *Policies*

Since the end of World War II and the creation of the International Monetary Fund (IMF) and the International Bank for Reconstruction and Development ("World Bank") at Bretton Woods, New Hampshire in 1944, the focus of development theory and professionals largely has been on design and implementation of appropriate policies supported through aid and assistance, culminating in pre-eminence of the so-called Washington Consensus of stabilization, liberalization and privatization.[3]

William Easterly, in the most accessible account to date, outlines a number of "waves" of development theories focusing on a variety of policies since World War II:

(1) foreign aid to bridge the gap between savings and investment[4],
(2) investment in technology[5],
(3) investment in education[6],
(4) population control[7],
(5) official loans to induce policy reforms[8], and
(6) debt forgiveness to support policy reforms.[9]

Overall, Easterly suggests that all of these have failed because they missed the main goal: aligning incentives to support economic growth which, in turn, reduces poverty.[10] Instead, Easterly in effect argues that the new paradigm must be the creation and maintenance of incentives through effective institutionalization of appropriate policies, thus highlighting the roles of incentives and

---

[3] See P. Krugman, "Dutch Tulips and Emerging Markets", For. Affairs, Jul./Aug. 1995, p. 28. Krugman describes the so-called "Washington Consensus" regarding economic policies that developed in the early 1990s as:

> Liberalize trade, privatize state enterprises, balance the budget, peg the exchange rate, and one will have laid the foundations for an economic takeoff; find a country that has done these things, and there one may confidently expect to realize high returns on investments.

Id., p. 29.

[4] See W. Easterly, *The Elusive Quest for Growth: Economists' Adventures and Misadventures in the Tropics* (Cambridge, MA: MIT Press, 2001), ch. 2.

[5] See id., ch. 3.

[6] See id., ch. 4.

[7] See id., ch. 5.

[8] See id., ch. 6.

[9] See id., ch. 7.

[10] See id., Prologue and ch. 1.

institutions in economic growth, which, in turn, underlies development more generally. He argues for focus on institutionalization of policies and incentives in a number of areas highlighted by recent research, including:

(1) Government action is needed to escape the trap of poverty: bad government policies must be removed and all forms of knowledge and capital accumulation, especially technological innovation and research and development, should be subsidized through a fiscal system that does not discourage knowledge accumulation.[11]

(2) Macroeconomic policy is important: governments should avoid creating poor incentives for growth through the elimination of high inflation, black markets, excessive budget deficits, strongly negative real interest rates, restrictions on free trade, excessive red tape, and inadequate public services.[12]

(3) An appropriate institutional framework is vital, especially for reducing corruption: this includes the elimination of red tape, establishment of rules under which governments honour contracts and do not expropriate unjustly, and creation of a meritocratic civil service.[13]

(4) The institutional framework also extends to political arrangements, supporting a stable and public-interested political system, which reduces political polarization and extreme inequality.

Policies thus continue to be important, as they impact on incentives; however, the way in which policies are implemented rests on devising and implementation of the institutional framework.

### 1.1.3. *Institutions*

The role of institutions in economic development began to receive significant attention in the early 1990s, largely as a result of the requirements of transition from state-ownership and control to market-based economies in the countries of the former Soviet Bloc, combined with the failure of policy-based approaches to achieve significant results.

By the late 1980s, the communist experiment was rapidly coming to an end around the world. With the demise of communism in most economies, the question became how to move from total state ownership and control to a functioning market economy. Followers of Friedrich Hayek, Milton Friedman and the Chicago school of economics focused on "shock therapy": the idea

---

[11] Id., pp. 168–9 and 192.
[12] Id., pp. 237–9.
[13] Id., p. 252.

that if everything was liberalized and privatized as rapidly as possible (following initial monetary and fiscal stabilization), then a market economy would naturally develop. Unfortunately, this did not work quite as planned; quickly, reformers began to realize the importance of institutions, including law and property rights, in the functioning of a market economy and the complexity of developing these in the context of the transition economies, with implications for development in developing and emerging economies more generally.

It was at this time that theory and experience came together in the "new institutional economics". For Douglass North, institutions are fundamental to economic development. Property rights are embedded in institutions, and institutions provide an incentive structure for economic activity. Economic development will take place if property rights are embedded in institutions designed to provide appropriate incentives. Needless to say, there are many potential pitfalls to success in this simple formulation, which are discussed throughout this volume.

North's theories have been most comprehensively expressed in 1990 in *Institutions, Institutional Change and Economic Performance*[14]; however, his ideas had developed over the previous two decades. In 1973, in *The Rise of the Western World*[15], North and Robert Thomas argued[16]:

> Economic organization is the key to growth; the development of an efficient economic organization in Western Europe accounts for the rise of the West. Efficient organization entails the establishment of institutional arrangements and property rights that create an incentive to channel individual economic effort into activities that bring [economic growth].

In 1981, in *Structure and Change in Economic History*[17], North analysed the structure of economies over time and developed a theory to account for stability and change in those structures.[18] The theory of institutions which he develops is based on three pillars[19]:

(1) a theory of property rights that describes the individual and group incentives in the system;

(2) a theory of the state, since it is the state that specifies and enforces property rights; and

[14] D. North, *Institutions, Institutional Change and Economic Performance* (Cambridge: Cambridge University Press, 1990).

[15] D. North and R. Thomas, *The Rise of the Western World: A New Economic History* (Cambridge: Cambridge University Press, 1973).

[16] Id., p. 1.

[17] D. North, *Structure and Change in Economic History* (New York: W.W. Norton, 1981).

[18] Id., p. 3.

[19] Id., pp. 7–8.

(3) a theory of ideology that explains how different perceptions of reality affect the perceptions of individuals regarding the changing "objective" situation.

In 1990, in *Institutions, Institutional Change and Economic Performance*[20], North[21]:

> provides an outline of a theory of institutions and institutional change. . . . The specification of exactly what institutions are, how they differ from organizations, and how they influence transaction and production costs is the key to much of the analysis. . . . The evolution of institutions that create an hospitable environment for cooperative solutions to complex exchange provides for economic growth.

The question arises as to the meaning of institutions. According to North[22]:

> Institutions are the rules of the game in a society or, more formally, are the humanly devised constraints that shape human interaction. In consequence, they structure incentives in human exchange, whether political, social, or economic. Institutional change shapes the way societies evolve through time and hence is the key to understanding historical change.

Building on this, North sums up the role of institutions[23]:

> Institutions provide the basic structure by which human beings throughout history have created order and attempted to reduce uncertainty in exchange. Together with the technology employed, they determine transaction and transformation costs and hence the profitability and feasibility of engaging in economic activity. They connect the past with the present and the future so that history is a largely incremental story of institutional evolution in which the historical performance of economies can only be understood as a part of a sequential story. And they are the key to understanding the interrelationship between the polity and the economy and the consequences of that interrelationship for economic growth (or stagnation and decline).

### 1.1.4. *Recent Empirical Evidence*

The results of a 2002 study are striking: Easterly and Ross Levine test the endowment, institution and policy views against each other using cross-country evidence and find, first, evidence that endowments affect development through

---

[20] North (1990), op. cit., n. 14.
[21] Id., p. vii.
[22] Id., p. 3.
[23] Id., p. 118.

institutions; and second, no evidence that endowments affect country incomes directly other than through institutions, nor do they find any effect of policies on development after controlling for institutions.[24]

Similarly, Dani Rodrik, Arvind Subramanian and Francesco Trebbi test the respective contributions of institutions, endowments and trade in determining cross-country income levels.[25] Their results indicate that the quality of institutions is most important: controlling for institutions, endowments have at best weak direct effects on incomes, although they have a strong indirect effect through institutions; similarly, trade has a positive impact on institutions.

Importantly, both sets of authors agree on two points: their results, while very significant, do not provide much guidance for policy makers and therefore much remains to be done in teasing out exactly what sorts of institutions are most significant and how to implement these in the context of the widely varying circumstances of individual economies.

### 1.1.5. *The Role of Law*

As discussed earlier, development theory has gone through a number of stages. Development assistance, including that relating to law, has tracked theory.

Thomas Heller suggests that theories relating to the role of law in development have progressed through a series of waves.[26] The first wave, roughly from 1950–65, focused on building national legal systems, in the context of newly independent states. The second wave, the "law and development" movement, developed roughly from 1960–75. The law and development movement focused on enabling technocracy and disabling established elites. After the gradual erosion of law and development, the third wave, roughly from 1985–2000, focused on human rights and constitutionalism. The fourth wave, beginning from around 1990 and still on-going, focuses on the interactions among law, markets and economics. Founded upon Max Weber's ideas of legal certainty, its leading exponents have been North and Mancur Olson. Today, this wave looks at increasingly diverse areas, including intellectual property, corporate governance and competition.

---

[24] W. Easterly and R. Levine, "Tropics, Germs, and Crops: How Endowments Influence Economic Development", NBER Working Paper No. 9106 (Aug. 2002).

[25] D. Rodrik, A. Subramanian and F. Trebbi, "Institutions Rule: The Primacy of Institutions over Integration and Geography in Economic Development", IMF Working Paper WP/02/189 (Nov. 2002).

[26] See E. Jensen and T. Heller, *Beyond Common Knowledge: Empirical Approaches to the Rule of Law* (Palo Alto: Stanford University Press, 2004).

## 1.1.6. *The Way Forward*

We began this section with an analysis of the various theories of economic development. Two related quotations from Niall Ferguson and William Easterly sum up the consensus today.

According to Ferguson[27]:

> A country's economic fortunes are determined by a combination of natural endowments (geography, broadly speaking) and human action (history for short): this is economic history's version of the nature-nurture debate. While a persuasive case can be made for the importance of such 'given' factors as the mean temperature, humidity, the prevalence of disease, soil quality, proximity to the sea, latitude and mineral resources in determining economic performance, there seems strong evidence that history too plays a crucial part. In particular, there is good evidence that the imposition of British-style institutions has tended to enhance a country's economic prospects, particularly in those settings where indigenous cultures were relatively weak because of thin (or thinned) population, allowing British institutions to dominate with little dilution. Where the British, like the Spaniards, conquered already sophisticated, urbanized societies, the effects of colonization were more commonly negative, as the colonizers were tempted to engage in plunder rather than to build their own institutions. Indeed, this is perhaps the best available explanation of that 'great divergence' which reduced India and China from being quite possibly the world's most advanced economies in the sixteenth century to relative poverty by the early twentieth.

Easterly goes further[28]:

> We have learned once and for all that there are no magical elixirs to bring a happy ending to our quest for growth. Prosperity happens when all the players in the development game have the right incentives. It happens when government incentives induce technological adaptation, high-quality investment in machines, and high-quality schooling. It happens when donors face incentives that induce them to give aid to countries with good policies where aid will have high payoffs, not to countries with poor policies where aid is wasted. It happens when the poor get opportunities and incentives, which requires government welfare programs that reward rather than penalize earning income. It happens when politics is not polarized between antagonistic

---

[27] N. Ferguson, *Empire: The Rise and Demise of the British World Order and the Lessons for Global Power* (New York: Basic Books, 2002), pp. 360–1.

[28] Easterly (2001), op. cit., n. 4, p. 289. In his second book, Easterly takes this forward with discussion of methodologies to achieve this goal, focusing on small-scale results. W. Easterly, *The White Man's Burden: Why the West's Efforts to Aid the Rest Have Done So Much Ill and So Little Good* (New York: Penguin Press, 2006).

interest groups, but there is a common consensus to invest in the future. Broad and deep development happens when a government that is held accountable for its actions energetically takes up the task of investing in collective goods like health, education, and the rule of law.

To apply today's consensus on development, David Landes suggests that the "ideal growth-and-development society" would have the following character-istics[29]:

(1) knowledge of how to operate, manage and build the instruments of production, and to create, adapt, and master new techniques on the technological frontier;

(2) ability to impart this knowledge and know-how to the young, whether by formal education or apprenticeship training;

(3) selection of people for jobs by competence and relative merit, and pro-motion and demotion on the basis of performance;

(4) provision of opportunity to individual or collective enterprise, and encouragement of initiative, competition and emulation; and

(5) allowance for people to enjoy and employ the fruits of their labour and enterprise.

Such a society would also possess the kind of political and social institutions that favour the development of these larger goals, for example[30]:

(1) secure rights of private property, the better to encourage savings and investment;

(2) secure rights of personal liberty, against both the abuse of tyranny and private disorder (e.g., crime and corruption);

(3) enforceable rights of contract, explicit and implicit;

---

[29] D. Landes, *The Wealth and Poverty of Nations: Why Some Are So Rich and Others So Poor* (London: Little, Brown, 1998), p. 217.

[30] Id., pp. 217–18. Niall Ferguson suggests that the British Empire was beneficial for economic growth in its constituent economies. Ferguson (2002), op. cit., n. 27. According to Ferguson, the British Empire disseminated a number of important features:

(1) the English language,
(2) English forms of land tenure,
(3) Scottish and English banking,
(4) the Common Law,
(5) Protestantism,
(6) team sports,
(7) the limited or "night watchman" state,
(8) representative assemblies, and
(9) the idea of liberty.

Id., p. xxv.

(4) stable government, not necessarily democratic, but itself governed by publicly known rules (i.e., a government of laws rather than men – the "rule of law");

(5) responsive government, that will hear complaints and make redress;

(6) honest government, such that economic actors are not moved to seek advantage and privilege inside or outside the marketplace (i.e, no rents to favour and position); and

(7) moderate, efficient, ungreedy government, holding down taxes, reducing government's claim on the social surplus and avoiding privilege.

These ideas have been adopted and developed by, inter alia, the World Bank.[31] Thus, one can say that there is now a consensus that law and related institutions play a fundamental role in economic growth and development.

## 1.2. FINANCIAL CRISES IN THE 1990S

In addition to changing views of the role of law and institutions in economic growth and development, the role of the financial sector has also received increasing attention. Two sets of events at the end of the twentieth century changed the way in which the financial sector is viewed: the process of transition from centrally planned to market-based economies (discussed earlier in the context of its importance for analysis of the role of institutions) and a series of financial crises around the world in the 1990s.

Financial crises in Latin America from the end of 1994 and in Asia from mid-1997 have drawn increased attention to the potential dangers of globalization of the international financial system. In order to prevent the collapse of the economies involved and reduce the risk of potential contagion throughout the international financial system, international financial rescues of unprecedented proportions were organized for Mexico, Thailand, Indonesia and South Korea.[32] Including contributions from multilateral and bilateral creditors, these financing packages totaled US$48.8 billion for Mexico in 1995, US$17 billion for Thailand, US$40 billion for Indonesia and US$57 billion for South Korea in 1997. In these respective packages, the contribution of the IMF alone totaled US$52.8 billion: US$17.8 billion for Mexico, US$4 billion for Thailand, US$10 billion for Indonesia and US$21 billion for South Korea.

---

[31] See World Bank, *World Development Report 2002: Building Institutions for Markets* (New York: Oxford University Press, 2002).

[32] See generally D. Arner, "An Analysis of International Support Packages in the Mexican and Asian Financial Crises", J. Bus. L. 380 (1998).

In addition, subsequent crises and/or international rescues occurred in Russia and Brazil in 1998, Turkey in 2000 and Argentina in 2002.

The magnitude of these international financial rescue packages and their impact on international finance underlines a number of on-going changes in the international financial system. These changes can be seen in respect of the potential dangers to developing, emerging and transition economies of international capital flows, the importance of financial regulation, and in the changing role of the IMF. This section, however, only highlights the basic causes of the crises and the nature of the international rescues organized in order to give the reader a greater understanding of the underlying factors and responses involved in this broader context of change.

### 1.2.1. *Prelude: 1990–95*

A number of financial crises occurred during the late 1980s and the first half of the 1990s, including in the United States and the Nordic countries (domestic banking crises in developed economies), Europe (an international crisis involving developed country currencies participating in the European Exchange Rate Mechanism – the precursor to the development of the European currency, the euro), and Mexico (an international crisis in an emerging economy, with contagious impact on other emerging economies, especially in Latin America). These crises foreshadowed the sorts of crises that occurred in the second half of the 1990s in developed, emerging, developing and transitioning economies[33] and held important lessons for the crises that occurred around the world in the second half of the 1990s and into the twenty-first century, with recent examples including in Argentina and Turkey.

In many ways, the experiences of the United States in liberalizing its financial system in the 1970s and 1980s as a reaction to the internationalization of financial markets are similar to the crises experienced in other countries throughout the 1990s, not only in developing, emerging and transition economies, but also in the developed economies of western Europe and Japan. The crisis in Mexico and subsequent contagion were largely similar to those which occurred in east Asia, beginning in Thailand in 1997. Crises in Russia, Brazil, Argentina and Turkey followed similar patterns. In other words, the writing was on the wall, but no one outside of the immediately affected countries was reading it. At the same time, however, these crises were considerably different from the developing country debt crisis of the early 1980s, which was largely caused by

---

[33] See generally D. Arner, M. Yokoi-Arai and Z. Zhou (eds), *Financial Crises in the 1990s: A Global Perspective* (London: British Institute of International and Comparative Law, 2001).

over-borrowing by countries, over-lending by international banks and interest volatility resulting from US efforts to control inflation.[34] Instead, these crises have had much more in common with financial crises prior to the establishment of the Bretton Woods international economic system at the end of World War II.[35]

### 1.2.2. *The Mexican Financial Crisis: 1994–95*

The first "post-modern" financial crisis, now commonly described as the Mexican peso crisis, erupted in Mexico in 1994 and continued to deepen into 1995.[36] During the 1994–95 crisis, Mexico faced a temporary liquidity crisis due to a large number of intertwined factors, some caused by problems within or exacerbated by Mexico, but others not – for example, increases in US interest rates. As a result of the crisis and the perceived need to protect the international financial system, the United States organized an international response to the crisis. However, following the Mexican crisis, the United States and other leading industrialized economies placed the leading role in addressing future crises on the shoulders of the IMF. As a result, when similar circumstances struck in Thailand, Indonesia and South Korea, among others, in 1997, the IMF led the response, albeit one based very closely on the experiences garnered in Mexico in 1994–95.

The evidence suggests that the origins of the crisis can be found in the interplay of a number of complex financial, economic and political factors that developed in the period prior to December 1994.[37] According to an analysis by the US General Accounting Office[38], Mexico's financial crisis originated

---

[34]  See generally J. Frieden, *Debt, Development and Democracy: Modern Political Economy and Latin America, 1965–1985* (Princeton, NJ: Princeton University Press, 1991).

[35]  The Bretton Woods system is discussed in more detail in Chapter 2.

[36]  See generally D. Arner, "The Mexican Peso Crisis of 1994–95: Implications for the Regulation of Financial Markets", 2 NAFTA L. & Bus. Rev. 28 (1996).

[37]  See generally IMF, *International Capital Markets: Developments, Prospects, and Policy Issues*, Aug. 1995, pp. 53–64; W. Lovett, "Lessons from the Recent Peso Crisis in Mexico", 4 Tul. J. Int'l & Comp. L. 143 (1996); E. Truman, "The Mexican Peso Crisis: Implications for International Finance", 82 Fed. Res. Bull. 199 (Mar. 1996); M. Kornis, "The Peso Crisis Revisited", 5 No. 4 Mex. Trade & L. Rep. 14 (1 Apr. 1995); idem, "Financial Crisis in Mexico", 5 No. 2 Mex. Trade & L. Rep. 5 (1 Feb. 1995).

[38]  As a result of the US commitments resulting from the Mexican crisis, the US General Accounting Office (GAO) prepared a comprehensive report on Mexico's 1994–95 financial crisis at the request of the then-Chairman of the US House of Representatives Committee on Banking and Financial Services, James A. Leach. See US General Accounting Office, *GAO Report: Mexico's Financial Crisis: Origins, Assistance, and Initial Efforts to Recover*, GAO/GGD-96–56, 23 Feb. 1996 ("GAO Mexico Report"). In preparing the report, the GAO interviewed all major participants from all entities involved, as well as significant private participants, and reviewed substantially every available piece of information regarding its mandate.

in the growing inconsistency in 1994 between Mexico's monetary and fiscal policies and its exchange rate system. Due in part to an upcoming presidential election, Mexican authorities were reluctant to take actions in the spring and summer of 1994, such as raising interest rates or devaluing the peso, that could have reduced these inconsistencies. These fundamental policy inconsistencies were exacerbated by the Mexican government's responses to several economic and political events that created investor concerns about the likelihood of a currency devaluation and generally reduced investor confidence in the political and economic stability of Mexico. In response to these investor concerns, the Mexican government issued large amounts of short-term, dollar-indexed notes (*tesobonos*), so that by the end of November 1994[39], Mexico had become particularly vulnerable to a financial crisis because its foreign exchange reserves had fallen to US$12.9 billion[40], while it had *tesobono* obligations of US$28.7 billion maturing in 1995.[41]

**The Rescue Package.** Although the US Treasury, the US Federal Reserve and the IMF purportedly did not anticipate the magnitude of the crisis, they soon concluded that outside assistance was required to prevent Mexico's financial collapse and to prevent the spread of the crisis to other emerging economies. Beyond its direct impact on other emerging economies, officials viewed the crisis as a threat to market-oriented economic reforms that the IMF and the United States had urged such countries to adopt.[42]

As a result, then–US President Bill Clinton announced a package of loan guarantees of up to US$40 billion for Mexico on 12 January 1995; however, doubts regarding approval by the US Congress led to its ineffectiveness and withdrawal. Subsequently, on 31 January 1995, Clinton announced a

[39] During October and November, high-level US officials cautioned Mexican officials that the peso seemed overvalued and indicated that it was risky to continue the existing exchange rate policy. US officials, however, were undecided about the extent to which the peso was overvalued and if and when financial markets might force Mexico to take action. Moreover, Federal Reserve and Treasury officials apparently did not foresee the magnitude of the crisis that eventually unfolded. See id., pp. 77–109.

[40] IMF International Capital Markets (1995), op. cit., n. 37, p. 56.

[41] Id. at 61, Table 1.3.

[42] According to the then-US Secretary of the Treasury, as well as government and industry analysts, Mexico had been a paradigm for countries striving to put inward-looking, state-controlled models of economic development behind them and move to free market models. The Secretary also noted that new prosperity, based on open markets, encouraging investment, and privatization of state-controlled industries, was beginning to be realized in these emerging markets economies. Other US government officials stated that they believed a spread of Mexico's financial difficulties to other emerging markets could have halted or even reversed the global trend toward market-oriented reform and democratization. GAO Mexico Report (1996), op. cit., n. 38, pp. 110–14.

US$48.8 billion multilateral assistance package. Under this package, the United States would provide up to US$20 billion to Mexico through the use of the Exchange Stabilization Facility and the Federal Reserve swap network.[43] On 1 February, the IMF approved an eighteen-month stand-by arrangement for Mexico of up to US$17.8 billion. In addition, other countries, under the auspices of the Bank for International Settlements (BIS), agreed to provide a short-term facility of US$10 billion[44], in addition to which Canada had already provided US$1 billion in December 1994.[45]

The US and international response to the Mexican crisis was one of the largest multilateral economic assistance packages ever extended to any one country. The objectives of the US and IMF assistance packages, following the December devaluation and the subsequent loss of confidence in Mexico's currency, were twofold: first, to help Mexico overcome its short-term liquidity crisis, and second, to limit the adverse effects of the Mexican crisis spreading to other economies.[46] Some observers opposed any US financial assistance to Mexico, arguing that investors should not be shielded from financial losses, and that neither the danger posed by the spread of Mexico's crisis to other nations nor the risk to US trade, employment and immigration was sufficient to justify the assistance.[47] As can be seen by the US response, US officials disagreed. At the same time, similar arguments have been raised in relation to each subsequent crisis, although not always with the same result (e.g., Russia and Argentina were not rescued in 1998 and 2002 respectively, while rescues were organized for Brazil in 1998 to prevent a crisis from occurring and for Turkey in 2000).

**Domestic Structural Reforms.** As part of the terms and conditions of the rescue package, the government of Mexico released an economic plan on 9 March 1995 to address the required economic criteria in the agreements with the United States and the IMF.[48] Overall, the goals of the plan were to restore

---

[43] A swap arrangement provides for temporary exchanges of currencies between participating countries. Partners in the arrangement can draw on one another's currency by supplying their own currency up to an agreed amount. The swap is usually reversed within a short period of time, but may be rolled over.

[44] In early January, the BIS announced a US$5 billion faculty, later increased to US$10 billion. These funds were short-term and were not drawn upon by Mexico.

[45] Argentina, Brazil and a group of international commercial banks were also to provide funds; however, none of these funds materialized, due – in the cases of Argentina and Brazil – to the "tequila effect".

[46] GAO Mexico Report (1996), op. cit., n. 38, pp. 110–14; see US-Mexico Framework Agreement for Mexican Economic Stabilization, 21 Feb. 1995, art. I ("US-Mexico Agreement").

[47] See GAO Mexico Report (1996), op. cit., n. 38, pp. 117–18.

[48] See id., pp. 128–31, 133–6; P. Wertman, "Economic Recovery: Mexico's 1995 Economic Program and the IMF", 5 No. 6 Mex. Trade & L. Rep. 4 (1 Jun. 1995); idem, "Peso Crisis: Mexico's

financial stability, strengthen public finances and the banking sector, regain confidence, and reinforce the groundwork for long-term sustainable growth. In general terms, the plan addressed monetary policy, exchange rate policy, fiscal policy, banking policy[49], income and social policy, and improved transparency.[50] This approach was consistent with the then-existing approach of IMF conditionality[51], based upon the policy approach to economic development described in the first section of this chapter.

Although the government of Mexico had taken steps to improve the Mexican banking system prior to the onset of the crisis, the banking sector continued to be a significant weakness throughout the liquidity crisis and was burdened by a nonperforming loan level estimated by the World Bank to be about 27 per cent of total loans as of 30 September 1995.[52] The government of Mexico took several measures designed to assist the banking sector deal with the problems associated with Mexico's financial difficulties; several of these were initiated unilaterally by Mexico, while others were undertaken with the direct support of the international financial community.[53]

### 1.2.3. *The East Asian Financial Crisis: 1997–98*

Unfortunately, the lessons from Mexico were not taken on board outside of the country, with most dramatic consequences for Asia. Over the several decades prior to 1997, numerous economies in east Asia experienced an extended period of growth that ended abruptly in 1997, with the onset of the east Asian financial crisis.[54] The east Asian financial crisis began in Thailand in the summer of 1997 and spread to Malaysia, Indonesia, Philippines, South Korea and Hong Kong. Fundamentally, these were all international crises involving emerging economies that in many ways were foreshadowed by the crises discussed in

---

1995 Economic Program and the IMF", 5 No. 3 Mex. Trade & L. Rep. 7 (1 Mar. 1995). Mexico actually proposed an initial economic plan in January 1995; however, without the international rescue package in place, it was largely ignored.

[49] The World Bank, the Inter-American Development Bank (IADB), and other sources agreed to provide up to US$3 billion to strengthen Mexican banks.

[50] The plan included a promise by Mexico that information on foreign currency reserves and domestic credit conditions should be announced on a weekly basis. Such disclosure was also mandated by the US-Mexico Agreement (1995), op. cit., n. 46, Annex D.

[51] Id., Annex B. See GAO Mexico Report (1996), op. cit., n. 38, pp. 133–6.

[52] Id., pp. 143–6.

[53] See id.

[54] For a discussion, see World Bank, *The East Asian Miracle: Economic Growth and Public Policy* (Oxford: Oxford University Press, 1993). This is typically attributed to a number of factors, including policies directed towards macroeconomic stabilization, strong savings and investment performance, openness of their economies, and an emphasis on human capital formation.

the previous two sections, the lessons of which were unfortunately largely ignored both at the domestic level and at the international level, with direct and significant consequences for hundreds of millions of people in east Asia.

Despite the significant analyses of and international reactions to the Mexican crisis[55], the scenario was repeated in all too similar a fashion in Thailand in 1997, with contagion severely impacting numerous countries in east Asia, resulting in international rescues for first Thailand, followed by Indonesia and South Korea. The immediate cause of the onset of the crisis in Thailand, followed by Indonesia and South Korea, was a reversal of capital flows, upon which the economies of all three countries had become dependent. According to estimates by the Institute of International Finance[56], net private in-flows to the five east Asian countries hardest hit by the crisis (Indonesia, South Korea, Malaysia, Philippines and Thailand) decreased from US$93 billion to −US$12.1 billion, a reversal of US$105 billion on a combined pre-shock gross domestic product (GDP) of approximately US$935 billion or approximately 11 per cent of GDP. Of that US$105 billion decline, US$77 billion was in the form of commercial bank lending, US$24 billion in portfolio equity and US$5 billion in nonbank lending, while direct investment remained constant at approximately US$7 billion. Unfortunately, as currencies were defended, foreign exchange reserves were exhausted to the point where they were insufficient to cover the large stock of short-term foreign debt coming due. As a result, international rescues became necessary in Thailand, Indonesia and South Korea. Including contributions from multilateral and bilateral creditors, these financing packages totaled US$17 billion for Thailand, US$40 billion for Indonesia and US$57 billion for South Korea. (Rather than seeking international assistance, Malaysia instead chose to seek to detach its domestic financial system from the international financial system through capital and currency controls.)

As with the crises in the first half of the 1990s, the east Asian financial crises occurred in individual countries as a result of the exposure of idiosyncratic domestic systems to the international financial system. In all cases, reform should have preceded liberalization but did not. This must be seen as a central lesson from the crises and one to which we will return in detail in Chapter Eight. Further, the experiences of the countries involved demonstrated the inadequacies of the framework applied by the IMF in the various east Asian countries and the need for analysis and action with respect to the international financial architecture (discussed in Chapters Three and Nine).

---

[55]  Discussed in Chapter Two.
[56]  See www.iif.org.

While it is impossible to produce a completely accurate picture of the causes of the Asian crisis, various causes can be delineated.[57] First, the immediate cause of the onset of the crisis in Thailand, followed by Indonesia, Malaysia and South Korea, was a reversal of capital flows, upon which the economies of all four countries had become dependent. In contrast to the situation in Mexico, these flows had not been used to fund domestic consumption, but rather to fund extraordinarily high rates of investment (much of which was in speculative areas such as real estate, which created an exaggerated asset price bubble).[58] This reversal of flows can be attributed to a number of factors, of which the pegging of exchange rates to the US dollar and the resulting decline in competitiveness after the strengthening of the US dollar in mid-1995 probably is central.[59]

The decline in external capital flows brought certain structural problems to the surface which had been previously ignored due to strong economic growth. Of most importance were financial sector weaknesses.[60] These weaknesses included: (1) lack of proper prudential regulation and supervision, (2) the development of equity and property price bubbles through inappropriate lending encouraged by external capital flows, (3) public guarantees and/or rescues of politically important financial institutions, and (3) excessive foreign borrowing through the banks and other financial institutions for on-lending in domestic currencies, with financial institutions facing loan problems as local currencies and exports declined. Beyond the financial sector, other structural

---

[57] Two distinct viewpoints seem to have emerged: one blaming the countries afflicted, the other blaming panic among international investors. See M. Wolf, "Capital Punishment", *Financial Times*, 17 Mar. 1998, p. 22. These views can be clearly seen in the writings of Paul Krugman and Jeffrey Sachs, respectively. See P. Krugman, *The Return of Depression Economics* (New York: W.W. Norton, 1999); S. Radelet and J. Sachs, The Onset of the East Asian Financial Crisis (Harvard Institute for International Development, 1998, mimeographed). The reality is probably some combination of the two – much as in many of the emerging markets financial crises of the nineteenth century. See J. Norton, "'Are Latin America and East Asia an Ocean Apart?' The Connecting Currents of Asian Financial Crises", 4 NAFTA L. & Bus. Rev. 5 (1998). See generally C. Kindleberger, *Manias, Panics and Crashes: A History of Financial Crises*, 3rd ed. (Houndmills: Macmillan, 1996). The standard line from the IMF and World Bank generally leans toward the second line of thought in its focus on the countries involved, rather than international panic. See, inter alia, IMF, *World Economic Outlook: Interim Assessment*, Dec. 1997, pp. 1–19. See also S. Sugisaki, "Economic Crisis in Asia", Address at the 1998 Harvard Asia Business Conference, Harvard Business School, 30 Jan. 1998; World Bank, "Responding to the Crisis: Backing East Asia's Social and Financial Reforms – World Bank Announces Visit by its President, James D. Wolfensohn, to East Asia", Press Statement, 27 Jan. 1998.

[58] IMF, *World Economic Outlook: Interim Assessment*, Dec. 1997, pp. 3–4 and box 1, pp. 10–11.

[59] Contrary to early accusations, especially from Malaysian officials, hedge funds and other international speculators did not play a significant role in the capital outflows. Id., p. 41.

[60] See World Bank, *Are Financial Sector Weaknesses Undermining the East Asia Miracle?* Sep. 1997.

problems included trade restrictions, inconsistent and imprudent capital policies, excessive links among government, banks and corporations (subsequently
termed "crony capitalism"), and lack of transparency and effective governance,
both private and public.

Beyond specific causes, a number of common underlying factors can be
identified. Significant domestic factors included: first, the failure to dampen
overheating pressures which became manifest in large external deficits and
property and stock market bubbles; second, the maintenance of pegged
exchange regimes, thereby encouraging external borrowing and leading to the
assumption of excessive foreign exchange risk; and third, ineffective prudential regulation and supervision in the financial sector combined with implicit
government support for financial intermediaries, allowing a deterioration of
financial intermediary balance sheets to take place without appropriate remedial measures.[61]

**The Asian Financial Rescue Packages.** In approving the requests of Thailand,
Indonesia and South Korea for stand-by credits, the IMF made use of accelerated procedures established following the Mexican crisis. The intention was
that loans from bilateral lenders would be disbursed in proportion to the IMF

---

[61] IMF *World Economic Outlook*, Dec. 1997, op. cit., n. 58, p. 40; S. Fischer, "The Asian Crisis:
A View from the IMF", Address at the Midwinter Conference of the Bankers' Association
for Foreign Trade, Washington, DC, 22 Jan. 1998. Similar underlying problems can also be
attributed to Japan, whose own economic problems (and especially attempts to use easy credit
to grow out of those problems) bear some of the responsibility for the onset of the crisis in the
region. See IMF *World Economic Outlook*, Dec. 1997, op. cit., n. 58, box 2, p. 26.

Not surprisingly, the World Bank came to similar conclusions to the IMF. According to
World Bank analysis, four factors, appearing in different degrees across the region, contributed
to the vulnerability of the Asian economies: first, a build-up of short-term debt exceeding
foreign exchange reserves, which rendered countries vulnerable to sudden outflows; second,
heavy unhedged foreign currency borrowing by banks and companies reduced the ability of
the authorities to devalue in a timely fashion without putting the private sector under great
financial pressure; third, high levels of debt and low-quality bank loan portfolios meant banks
and companies were vulnerable to rises in interest rates or economic slowdowns, thus further
restricting the authorities' ability to respond to significant currency pressures; and fourth, a
more traditional vulnerability of the external sector, with some economies facing exchange
rate appreciation, thereby slowing export revenues.

In addition, there were five root causes of these problems: first, moral hazards in financial
sectors, leading to overinvestment in financial assets; second, crony capitalism covering up
unprofitable business transactions; third, lax regulation and supervision of the financial system
aggravated by a general lack of reliable information about banks; fourth, rigid exchange rate
regimes led to perceptions that the risk of devaluation was low, while the linkage to an appre-
ciating dollar curbed exports; and fifth, partial and ill-sequenced financial and capital account
liberalization programs had eased restrictions on foreign borrowing while restricting foreign
ownership of the domestic banking sector. See S. Fidler, "Latin America Looks Fit Enough to
Fend Off Crisis", Financial Times, 16 Mar. 1998, p. 7 (discussing World Bank analysis of the
vulnerability of Latin America to a crisis similar to that in Asia).

facility. These proceeds were intended solely to assist in financing the balance of payments gap and to rebuild the official reserves of the respective central banks, in accordance with the IMF Articles of Agreement.

**The Asian Structural Reform Programs.** According to IMF officials, the programs in Thailand, Indonesia and South Korea reflected a change in the traditional design of IMF programs, placing much less emphasis on austerity measures designed to ensure macroeconomic equilibrium and focusing instead on structural measures to establish conditions for sustainable growth in the context of globalization.[62] Specifically, the objective was to re-establish confidence, with emphasis placed on: (1) temporary tightening of monetary policy; (2) immediate action to correct obvious banking weaknesses; and (3) implementing structural reforms to remove impediments to growth such as rigidities, monopolies and governance problems.[63] As can be seen from the earlier discussion, the notes of the Mexican package were being replayed, albeit in a more coherently packaged format.

All three programs called for a substantial rise in interest rates to halt currency depreciation, and all three programs called for action to put the financial system in order. The centrepiece of each program was a set of structural reforms aimed at restoring confidence through (1) strengthening financial systems, (2) increasing transparency and (3) opening markets.[64] Mechanisms included: first, the closure of nonviable financial institutions; second, restructuring and recapitalization of viable institutions to meet internationally accepted best practices, including international capital adequacy standards and internationally accepted accounting practices and disclosure rules; and third, institutional reforms to strengthen financial sector regulation and supervision, increase transparency in the corporate and government sectors, create a more level playing field for private sector activity, and increase competition.[65]

While issues of moral hazard are often raised, in fact, the IMF-supported programs did not provide for any support to nonfinancial firms, and where possible, shareholders and creditors of insolvent financial intermediaries were to bear similar losses to those which would have occurred in the context of liquidation. In regard to insolvent financial intermediaries, no liquidity support was to be given, no special treatment was provided for shareholders of intermediaries

---

[62] See M. Camdessus, "Reflections on the Crisis in Asia", IMF Speech 98/3, Address to the Extraordinary Ministerial Meeting of the Group of 24, Caracas, Venezuela, 7 Feb. 1998.

[63] M. Camdessus, "Opening Statement", Press Conference, Kuala Lumpur, Malaysia, 16 Jan. 1998.

[64] M. Camdessus, "The Role of the IMF: Past, Present, and Future", IMF Speech 98/4, Remarks at the Annual Meeting of the Bretton Woods Committee, Washington, DC, 13 Feb. 1998.

[65] Id.

that lost their capital, and in cases where governments granted guarantees prior to entering negotiations with the IMF, the domestic authorities were to ensure that any such recourse could be met while still maintaining a sustainable medium-term fiscal position.[66] In regard to undercapitalized but solvent financial intermediaries, liquidity support could be provided. However, such support was conditional upon the intermediary(ies) being restructured and recapitalized; in cases where public resources were involved, previous owner capital was to be utilized first and management replaced; and potential public costs were to be minimized through measures to (1) improve intermediaries' financial health and capacity for repayment and (2) strengthen the economy so that creditors would have less reason to seek to unwind their exposures.[67]

### 1.2.4. *International Contagion: 1995 and 1998–99*

In addition to individual crises, international contagion was a characteristic of both the Mexican crisis in 1995 and the east Asian crises in 1998–99. While, in each case, contagion may have been the triggering cause of a crisis (or near crisis, in the case of Brazil in both 1995 and 1998), underlying domestic weaknesses in effect allowed the trigger of the contagion. In other words, domestic weaknesses were exposed by international reactions to problems in another economy viewed to have similar circumstances.

In the context of the Mexican crisis, by the end of the first week of January 1995, it became clear to the then–Mexican Secretary of Finance that the situation was much graver than first anticipated. News that some Mexican banks were unable to renew their certificates of deposit held by foreign investors triggered another wave of flight from the Mexican currency (peso), and the exchange rate of the peso continued to deteriorate. Investors panicked, not only those with Mexican securities holdings, but also investors in similar instruments issued by borrowers from countries in the same part of the world or perceived to be in similar circumstances. Thus began the so-called "tequila effect". The tequila effect was induced by two types of factors. First, as perceived risks rose and expected returns fell, individual investors determined to divest. Second, institutional holders, such as mutual funds, faced with actual or threatened redemptions, liquefied their holdings not only of Mexican investments but also of investments in other emerging economies, especially if they could do so while limiting their capital losses.[68]

---

[66] IMF, "IMF Bail Outs: Truth and Fiction", IMF Factsheet (Jan. 1998).

[67] Id.

[68] See E. Truman, "The Risks and Implications of External Financial Shocks: Lessons from Mexico", Board of Governors of the Federal Reserve System No. 535 (1996), p. 19.

Immediately after the Mexican devaluation, most of the larger Western hemisphere developing and emerging economies experienced varying degrees of turbulence in their foreign exchange markets and registered significant declines in their equity markets.[69] Equity markets in Argentina and Brazil in particular suffered heavy trading losses immediately after the Mexican crisis.[70] Once the international assistance package was announced and the initial reaction subsided, investors began to discriminate significantly against emerging economies such as Argentina and Brazil which were viewed as having the same general characteristics that afflicted Mexico; namely: (1) low savings rates, (2) large current account deficits, (3) weak banking systems, and (4) significant volumes of short-term debt. While overall international efforts were significant in reducing the ultimate contagion effect, the resulting lessons taught by international investors are instructive for future policy directions.

Contagion following the onset of the crisis in Thailand in 1997 followed a similar pattern, eventually impacting not only emerging economies in east Asia but also Russia, Brazil and the United States through the near collapse and US Federal Reserve–orchestrated private sector rescue of Long Term Capital Management (LTCM) – a large, leverged investment fund or "hedge fund". However, contagion following the crisis in Turkey in 2000 and the crisis in Argentina in 2002 was quite limited.

In relation to contagion, research confirms both the vital causative role of domestic weaknesses and the triggering effect of contagion from external events. The experiences also suggest that the interaction between external contagion through the international financial system and problematic domestic structural conditions can at least to some extent be seen as a result of policies encouraged by the international community and the United States, reflected in the Washington Consensus. At present, the most significant result of the experiences of the contagion-affected economies may be a new focus on the importance of domestic restructuring through development of appropriate legal infrastructure in order to better equip economies to weather the risks of contagion apparently inherent in participation in the international financial system (discussed in the following chapters).

The collective interconnection of major emerging economies into the international financial system implies that disturbances in any other market, whether developed or emerging, can be rapidly translated in the form of financial contagion into developed or emerging economies. Empirical investigations by the IMF and other international organizations have confirmed

---

[69] GAO Mexico Report (1996), op. cit., n. 38, pp. 112–13, tables 4.1–4.2. See IMF, International Capital Markets (1995), op. cit., n. 37, pp. 64–9.
[70] GAO Mexico Report, op. cit., n. 38, pp. 112–13, tables 4.1–4.2.

that the increase in cross-border capital flows over the past twenty years, most notably through portfolio investment, has bound national capital markets more closely together and that the cross-border translation of disturbances can occur with unnerving speed. This concept was reinforced by the ensuing contagion from the Mexican and east Asian crises extending to other countries in the region and world-wide, as most countries in these regions, even those with fundamentally sound economic indicators, experienced temporary exchange and equity market disturbances during the respective crises.

According to Alan Greenspan, vicious crisis cycles such as that in Mexico in 1994 and Asia in 1997–98, in fact, may be "a defining characteristic" of today's international financial system.[71] As a result, while human panic reactions may not be controllable, at least the imbalances that exacerbate them can be addressed, preferably in advance.

According to Stanley Fischer, in order to avoid crises, a country needs both sound macroeconomic policies and a strong financial system.[72] A sound macroeconomic policy framework is one that promotes growth by keeping inflation low, the budget deficit small and the current account sustainable. This reflects the traditional IMF focus on policies.

The focus on the importance of the financial system, however, is a more recent development. The critical role of the strength of the financial system was becoming clear before the Mexican crisis; it was crystal clear in that crisis and its aftermath; and it has been equally clear in the east Asian crises and their aftermath. In this respect, Greenspan notes eight factors that have been present in international and economic disruptions, but which appear in more stark relief today, namely[73]: excessive leverage[74]; interest rate and currency risk[75];

---

[71] A. Greenspan, Remarks by Chairman Alan Greenspan before the Annual Financial Markets Conference of the Federal Reserve Bank of Atlanta, Miami Beach, 27 Feb. 1998.

[72] S. Fischer, "How to Avoid International Financial Crises and the Role of the International Monetary Fund", 15th Annual Cato Institute Monetary Conference, Washington DC, 14 Oct. 1997.

[73] Greenspan, op. cit., n. 71.

[74] Exceptionally high leverage is often a symptom of excessive risk taking that leaves financial systems and economies vulnerable to loss of confidence. This concern is particularly relevant to banks and other financial intermediaries, whose assets typically are less liquid than their liabilities and so depend on confidence in the payment of liabilities for their continued viability. Further, excessive leverage can create problems for lenders that can, in turn, spread to other borrowers that rely on those lenders. This is particularly the case in South Korea and in Japan.

[75] Banks, because of their nature, lend long and fund short, thereby incurring interest rate or liquidity risk. This exposes them to shocks, especially those with low capital-asset ratios. These problems are exacerbated when financial intermediaries borrow in unhedged foreign currency, with the result of potential bank runs following the collapse of the domestic currency.

weak banking systems[76]; interbank funding, especially in foreign currencies[77]; moral hazard[78]; weak central banks[79]; underdeveloped securities markets[80]; and inadequate legal structures.[81] All of these problems are financial sector issues and relate to legal and institutional factors, and must be addressed in that context.

## 1.3. THE ROLE OF THE FINANCIAL SECTOR

The past two decades have driven home the lesson that a well-functioning, stable financial sector is vital to a nation's economic growth and development. This lesson has been conveyed by two teachers. The first has been the succession of financial crises that have stifled economic growth and development, and burdened countries with huge fiscal and social costs. The second is research showing that when finance functions well, it fuels economic growth. Growth resulting from a broad, deep and liquid financial system provides goods, services and jobs benefiting all members of society.

### 1.3.1. *Lessons from Financial Crises*

As discussed in the previous section, the harsh teacher has been the succession of financial crises over the past fifteen years. One significant result of this series

[76] When banks are undercapitalized, have lax lending standards, and are subject to weak supervision and regulation, they become a source of systemic risk, both domestically and internationally.

[77] Despite its importance for distributing savings to their most valued use, short-term interbank funding, especially cross-border, may turn out to be the "Achilles' heel" of an international financial system that is subject to wide variations in confidence.

[78] The expectation that monetary authorities or international financial institutions will come to the rescue of failing financial systems and unsound investments has clearly engendered a significant element of moral hazard and excessive risk taking. Further, the dividing line between public and private liabilities too often becomes blurred. Interest and currency risk taking, excessive leverage, weak financial systems, and inappropriate interbank funding are all encouraged by the existence of a excessive safety net (e.g., US savings and loan crisis) or perceptions of the existence of an excessive safety net (e.g., east Asia).

[79] To effectively support a stable currency, central banks need to be independent, that is, their monetary policy decisions are not subject to the dictates of political authorities. See Chapter Four.

[80] Adverse banking experiences have emphasized the problems that can arise if banks are almost the sole source of financial intermediation. Their breakdown induces a sharp weakening in economic growth. Therefore, a wider range of nonbank institutions, including viable debt and equity markets, are important safeguards of economic activity when banking fails. See Chapter Seven.

[81] An effective competitive market system requires a rule of law that severely delimits government's arbitrary intrusion into commercial disputes. While defaults and restructuring are, in some circumstances, unavoidable and, in fact, a beneficial element of renewal in a market economy, an efficient bankruptcy statute is required to aid in this process, including in the case of cross-border defaults. See Chapter Five.

of financial crises is the recognition of the importance of financial stability.[82] Further, the role of legal and financial infrastructure in financial stability was recognized, and for the first time an international consensus is developing on exactly what is necessary in the way of legal and financial infrastructure to support that goal.[83]

This emerging financial consensus can be seen to be the result of two separate series of events since the collapse of the Bretton Woods system in 1973. These series of events can be classified along two axes, one based on the experience of the developed economies and one based on experiences in emerging, transition and developing economies. First, the growth of international cooperation and the establishment of minimum standards in the area of regulation of financial intermediaries have come to be viewed as essential in order to maintain and strengthen the confidence and integrity of the international financial system. This trend is reflected, for example, in the development of the Basel Committee on Banking Supervision as a response to various crises involving international financial intermediaries since the 1970s and the increasing importance and effectiveness of its pronouncements in the area of financial institution regulation and supervision.[84] Further, international cooperation in this area continues to be of increasing importance to the developed economies as financial and technological innovation and internationalization continue at a rapid rate, as demonstrated by recent intense focus on the areas of derivatives and payment and settlement systems throughout the world.[85]

The second strand of developing consensus is the realization of the importance of financial stability for both the international financial system and for developed, developing, emerging and transition economies, especially given their potential vulnerabilities to changes in capital flows within the international financial system. In many ways, this emerging consensus is the result of the combined lessons of the 1980s debt crisis, the transition process, the Mexican financial crisis, the east Asian financial crises, and the

---

[82] This consensus was initially detailed in Group of Ten (G-10), *Report of the Group of Ten (G-10) Working Party on Financial Stability in Emerging Markets, Financial Stability in Emerging Market Economies: A Strategy for the Formulation, Adoption and Implementation of Sound Principles and Practices to Strengthen Financial Systems*, Apr. 1997.

[83] See J. Norton, "International Cooperative Efforts in the Realm of Financial Crises in Developing Countries", in R. Lastra and H. Schiffman (eds), *Bank Failures and Bank Insolvency Law in Economies in Transition* (London: Kluwer, 1999).

[84] See J. Norton, *Devising International Bank Supervisory Standards* (Dordrecht: Martinus Nijhoff, 1995).

[85] See J. Norton and C. Olive, "The On-going Process of International Bank Regulatory and Supervisory Convergence: A New Regulatory-Market 'Partnership'", 16 B. U. Ann. Rev. Bnkg. L. 227 (1997).

subsequent crises in, inter alia, Russia, Brazil, Turkey and Argentina. The consensus in this area is that in order to develop economically, emerging economies must have in place appropriate structures to guarantee financial stability, especially given the increasing mobility of international capital and the reliance of emerging economies on that capital to fund their own development processes.[86]

Today, these two strands are increasingly coming together as the line between developed and emerging, transition and developing economies continues to blur and as all become more closely integrated into the international financial system. An effective financial infrastructure is as necessary to a developed economy as to an emerging economy, although it can be easier for a developed economy to successfully extricate itself from problems than for an emerging economy. Beyond this intertwining, this consensus can be seen to have developed in a similar fashion to most regulatory developments: as a response to a significant crisis that exposed the weaknesses in the then-existing system, weaknesses that generally only became evident with technological and financial innovation.

In reading through case studies of financial crises in the 1990s, one cannot avoid a number of lessons. First, in order to become full participants in the international financial system while at the same time maintaining both domestic and international financial stability requires careful domestic restructuring as part of any process of liberalization. Throughout financial crises, liberalization without appropriate restructuring often has been followed by crisis, and those crises have sometimes had international or even global impact. Second, the policies and systems advocated by the Bretton Woods and other international financial organizations during the 1990s did not adequately take into account the risks inherent in financial sector liberalization and likewise provided insufficient guidance on the requirements necessary to implement domestically in the context of restructuring. Third, developments in one country are no longer restricted to its own borders in today's increasingly globalized financial system and therefore there is an imperative need to readdress the Bretton Woods system and to have in place an appropriate international financial architecture, designed to deal with today's realities in much the same manner that was employed originally at Bretton Woods to deal with the realities at the end of World War II. Fourth, all of these systems, whether domestic or international, need to be based upon transparent, rule-based structures. The implication is that if these central issues are not addressed, financial crises similar to those

---

[86] These ideas are being increasingly formalized: see IMF, *Financial Stability in Emerging Markets*, Dec. 1997.

common in the past decade (and, in fact, likewise in the nineteenth century) will continue to be commonplace in the twenty-first century.

### 1.3.2. *The Financial System and Economic Growth*

The second teacher, more benign than the first, is a growing body of research into the positive role of finance. A substantial body of work, often labeled "finance and growth", now suggests that well-functioning financial intermediaries and markets promote economic growth.[87] The financial development and growth literature has established that finance matters for growth both at the macroeconomic and the microeconomic levels.[88] It is now generally agreed that financial development is important for economic growth.[89]

The genesis for these ideas came from theoretical work by Ronald McKinnon[90], Edward Shaw[91] and Raymond Goldsmith.[92] In the 1990s, especially following the Mexican and east Asian financial crises, empirical research confirmed the link. The empirical research has taken two strands – macro[93] and micro (firm level)[94] – with both showing that financial development is significant.

Asli Demirgüç-Kunt and Ross Levine[95], address three questions[96]: (1) What happens to national financial systems as countries develop? (2) Does overall

---

[87] R. Levine, "Law, Finance, and Economic Growth", J. Fin'l Intermediation 17 (1999).

[88] R. King and R. Levine, "Finance and Growth: Schumpeter Might Be Right", 108 Quarterly J. Econometrics 717 (1993); R. Levine, "Financial Development and Growth", 35 J. Econ. Lit. 688 (1997).

[89] See T. Beck and R. Levine, "Legal Institutions and Financial Development", World Bank Policy Research Working Paper 3136 (Sep. 2003).

[90] R. McKinnon, *Money and Capital in Economic Development* (Washington, DC: Brookings Institution Press, 1973).

[91] E. Shaw, *Financial Deepening in Economic Development* (Oxford: Oxford University Press, 1973).

[92] R. Goldsmith, *Financial Structure and Development* (New Haven, CT: Yale University Press, 1969).

[93] See R. Levine and S. Zervos, "Stock Markets, Banks and Economic Growth", 88 Amer. Econ. Rev. 537 (1998); R. King and R. Levine, "Financial Intermediation and Economic Development", in C. Mayer and X. Vives (eds), *Financial Intermediation in the Construction of Europe* (London: Centre for Economic Policy Research, 1993).

[94] See T. Beck, A. Demirguc-Kunt and V. Maksimovic, "Financing Patterns around the World: The Role of Institutions", World Bank Policy Research Working Paper 2905 (Oct. 2002); A. Demirguc-Kunt and V. Maksimovic, "Law, Finance and Firm Growth", 53 J. Fin. 2107 (1998); R. Rajan and L. Zingales, "Financial Dependence and Growth", 88 Amer. Econ. Rev. 559 (1998).

[95] A. Demirgüç-Kunt and R. Levine (eds), *Financial Structure and Economic Growth: A Cross-Country Comparison of Banks, Markets, and Development* (Cambridge, MA: MIT Press, 2001).

[96] A. Demirgüç-Kunt and R. Levine, "Financial Structure and Economic Growth: Perspectives and Lessons", in Demirgüç-Kunt and Levine, op. cit., n. 95, p. 11.

financial development influence economic growth and firm performance? (3) Does the structure of the financial system – bank-based or market-based – influence economic growth and firm performance? Significantly, they conclude: (1) national economic systems tend to become more developed overall and more market-oriented as they become richer; (2) overall financial development tends to accelerate economic growth, facilitate new firm formation, ease firm access to external financing, and boost firm growth; and (3) financial structure is not an analytically very useful way to distinguish among national financial systems.[97] Further, they find that the evidence strongly suggests that legal systems that effectively protect the rights of outside investors and enforce contracts efficiently improve the operation of financial markets and intermediaries with positive ramifications for long-run growth.[98]

Research also suggests that an effective financial system increases exports.[99] While significant research has demonstrated the role of the financial sector in economic growth, recent research is also supporting the view that financial development reduces poverty. Specifically, Thorsten Beck, Demirguc-Kunt and Levine have found that "financial intermediary development reduces income inequality by disproportionately boosting the income of the poor and therefore reduces poverty."[100]

Raghuram Rajan and Luigi Zingales summarize the emerging consensus very well[101]:

> Capitalism, or more precisely the free market system, is the most effective way to organize production and distribution that human beings have found. While free markets, particularly free financial markets, fatten people's wallets, they have made surprisingly few inroads into their hearts and minds. Financial markets are among the most highly criticized and least understood parts of the capitalist system. The behavior of those involved in recent scandals like the collapse of Enron only solidifies the public conviction that these markets are simply tools for the rich to get richer at the expense of the general public. Yet, as we argue, healthy and competitive financial markets

[97] Id., pp. 11–12.

[98] Id., p. 12.

[99] See B. Becker and D. Greenberg, "The Real Effects of Finance: Evidence from Exports", (May 2004, mimeographed) (available at http://home.uchicago.edu~dbgreenb/beckergreenberg.pdf).

[100] T. Beck, A. Demirguc-Kunt and R. Levine, "Finance, Inequality and Poverty: Cross-Country Evidence", World Bank Working Paper (May 2004). See P. Honohan, "Financial Development, Growth and Poverty: How Close Are the Links?", World Bank Policy Research Working Paper 3203 (Feb. 2004).

[101] R. Rajan and L. Zingales, *Saving Capitalism from the Capitalists: Unleashing the Power of Financial Markets to Create Wealth and Spread Opportunity* (New York: Crown Business, 2003), p. 1.

are an extraordinarily effective tool in spreading opportunity and fighting poverty. Because of their role in financing new ideas, financial markets keep alive the process of 'creative destruction' – whereby old ideas and organizations are constantly challenged and replaced by new, better ones. Without vibrant, innovative financial markets, economies would invariably ossify and decline.

From this, they argue that[102]:

because free markets depend on political goodwill for their existence and because they have powerful political enemies among the establishment, their continued survival cannot be taken for granted, even in developed countries.

### 1.3.3. *The Role of the Financial Sector*

The financial system is one of the most complex and also one of the most regulated aspects of any economy (whatever its level of development). A financial system, whether purely domestic (very rare today) or fully integrated into the global financial system (still rare today), is very complex and therefore difficult both to describe and to understand. This section seeks to present a stylized picture of the financial system (domestic or international) in order to provide a framework for the discussion in the rest of this volume.

As a first point, and one hinted at earlier, financial markets are often described as "globalized", with references to the "global financial system" common. It is, in fact, true that some segments of the financial sector are among the most globalized markets in existence – for instance the currency markets. Nonetheless, at present, outside of specific globalized segments, financial markets remain a mixture of domestic and international. Nonetheless, the discussion that follows attempts to present a picture of the financial system generally, whether domestic, internationally integrated or truly global in nature.

**Functions of the Financial System.** In a review of recent research on the role of the financial sector, Patrick Honohan suggests four primary functions of finance[103]:

(1) mobilizing savings (thereby creating concentrations of capital that allow exploitation of economies of scale),
(2) allocating capital (and thereby helping to judge where returns are most likely to be obtained through economically beneficial endeavours),

---

[102] Id., p. 3.
[103] Honohan (2004), op. cit., n. 101, p. 9.

(3) monitoring the use of financial resources (thereby increasing their like-lihood of generating economic benefit), and

(4) transforming and redistributing risk to those most interested and best able to bear it.

These functions in turn underlie the role of the financial system in economic growth.

**Supply and Demand: Allocation and Pricing.** Most importantly, financial markets serve a pricing and allocation function: the financial system should serve to allocate financial resources, with allocation taking place on the basis of pricing of risk. Efficient allocation of financial resources, by means of price, equates with financial development. Financial development serves to support economic growth, which in turn supports economic development more generally. However, at the same time that finance brings great benefits, it also brings great risks, especially in the context of financial crises, which can result in huge costs to an economy.

At the most basic level, a financial system should serve to match supply and demand for finance in an economy. In general terms, a financial system comprises the interactions of two elements: the supply of financial resources and the demand for financial resources.[104] Supply of finance results from the existence of lenders, savers and/or investors with financial assets excess to their current requirements. Lenders, savers and investors take a variety of forms, including individuals, firms (including financial intermediaries) and governments. Supply of finance can be seen as potentially coming from two sources: domestic and foreign. Domestic finance is a function of domestic savings, whether privately motivated or government mandated (i.e., through manda-tory pension schemes). Foreign finance comes from a number of potential sources, including institutional and private investment, whether for portfolio or speculative purposes; direct financing by international financial institutions or by venture capitalists and strategic investors; and (potentially quite impor-tant in some cases) repatriation of flight capital. Demand for funds comes from borrowers and/or spenders which require additional financial resources. Borrowers and spenders include individuals, firms (including financial inter-mediaries), governments and international financial institutions such as the World Bank.

---

[104] See W. Philbrick, "The Paving of Wall Street in Eastern Europe: Establishing the Infrastructure for Stock Markets in the Formerly Centrally Planned Economies", 25 Law & Pol'y Int'l Bus. 565 (1994), p. 576.

While generally commercial lending has declined in importance as a source of capital for developed economies, equity investment from foreign investors, whether in the form of foreign direct investment (FDI) or of portfolio investment, continues to increase, even despite the string of financial crises around the world of the past fifteen years. While an analysis of FDI would be beyond the scope of this chapter, it should be emphasized that the existence of a functioning domestic financial system can encourage foreign investment in a number of ways. Such a system provides a channel for external portfolio investment. Foreign investors, especially institutional investors[105], are much more likely to invest in countries where effective securities laws and well-disciplined securities exchanges which provide them with the infrastructure and the information necessary to analyse and implement prospective investments. This ensures additional capital for domestic enterprises. Given the volatility of portfolio-type investment, however, this may not be so important a benefit as once thought. In addition, the financial system permits the eventual "exit" of foreign investment, since such investment providers typically do not wish to stay involved with an enterprise for the long term, but prefer to exit and take profits. Even in the case of long-term or strategic investors, who are brought in for the purpose of exercising permanent, or at least longer-term, control of an enterprise, the possibility of potential disengagement can make involvement more attractive. Accordingly, such investors require a mechanism which makes possible the eventual liquidation of their holdings. This mechanism can be provided through the creation of functioning equity markets and securities exchanges, which for this reason encourage primary capital investment by private investors, and possibly even by multilateral development institutions.

In allocating financial resources, the financial sector serves the role of a transmission mechanism, transferring supply to meet demand on the basis of price. There are a variety of transmission mechanisms. In an ideal world, supply of and demand for financial resources could be matched directly, with suppliers effortlessly and costlessly locating appropriate opportunities for their excess resources. However, the real world is considerably different. In an ideal financial system, information is perfect, participants are rational and there are no transaction costs. In reality, none of these conditions applies in even the most sophisticated financial systems.

In terms of transmission mechanism, there are two main forms: direct finance and indirect finance. Direct finance occurs through direct investment and also

---

[105] For a discussion of the increasing role of institutional investors in the international financial system, see B. Steil, *The European Equity Markets: The State of the Union and an Agenda for the Millennium* (London: Royal Institute of International Affairs, 1996), pp. 147–84.

through financial markets (though in both cases usually with the assistance of various types of financial intermediary). Indirect finance involves financial intermediation of some form – in other words, an intermediary of some form steps in to assist in matching supply and demand.

Financial markets take a variety of forms, with four main categorizations: currency, money and interbank, capital, and insurance. In addition to these four market segments, there are also markets for derivatives, which overlap with the other markets. Currency markets are markets for actual currencies and behave in many ways more like commodities markets than other sorts of financial markets. The currency markets are both the largest and the most globalized segment of financial markets, with turnover exceeding US$1.8 trillion on a daily basis.[106] The money and interbank markets are markets for very short-term money, with initial duration to maturity of less than one year.

The capital markets are markets for financial resources with initial duration to maturity of one year or more – that is, capital. Capital markets are one of the most significant external sources of long-term funding for enterprises and governments within any market-based system. The capital markets include two main segments: equity and debt. Capital markets (i.e., markets for longer-maturity financial assets, including equity and debt) can be subdivided on the basis of the different legal relationships and forms of legal claims represented by the traded securities. At the most basic level, one could distinguish between equity markets, which focus on the issuance and trading of instruments representing ownership participations in business enterprises and creating residual claims on their assets, and long-term debt markets, which deal in instruments documenting fixed nominal-value, interest-bearing claims on such enterprises. Equity capital markets are markets for ownership interests, typically evidenced by shares of companies. By its nature, equity investment is generally of potentially unlimited duration. As a subset of capital markets, then, equity markets are composed of the supply of equity investment opportunities and demand for equity ownership. The supply of equity can be viewed as a portion of the demand for capital, while the demand for equity can be viewed as related to the supply of capital. Debt capital markets, on the other hand, represent debt claims on a borrower. The most common forms are loans and bonds or related debt securities. Bonds and equity both typically take the form of securities – freely tradable financial instruments.

Insurance markets are markets for protection against specific risks, whether certain (e.g., death) or uncertain (e.g., property damage). Derivatives markets are related to other financial markets. Specifically, a derivative is a financial

---

[106] See www.bis.org.

instrument the value of which is derived from something else, often a financial asset or market, criss-crossing and interlinking market segments.

There are a range of intermediaries which assist in the transmission of financial resources in the financial system. Common forms of intermediary include banks, insurance companies, pension funds, investment institutions such as unit trusts, mutual funds or hedge funds, investment banks or merchant banks, and international financial institutions. Generally speaking, intermediaries can be characterized as deposit institutions (e.g., banks), contractual savings/risk protection (e.g., insurance companies) or investment institutions (e.g., hedge funds).

As noted earlier, indirect finance arises because financial markets are not perfect markets. Their imperfections arise from two main sources: first, transaction costs (e.g., enforcement), and second, asymmetric information (i.e., imperfect information, imperfectly distributed). Asymmetric information also results in adverse selection (e.g., the worst opportunities are the ones most likely to be presented) and moral hazard (e.g., incentives to take excessive or insufficient risk). In addition, an increasing amount of research indicates that market participants are not always rational – an especially important consideration in finance.

Financial markets take a variety of forms in providing direct finance. First, financial markets can be centred on an exchange or exist in an over-the-counter (OTC) structure (e.g., the global derivatives market). Second, they can be primary or secondary.

Direct finance is most familiar in the context of securities exchanges.[107] A securities exchange may be defined as "a body that provides a centralized forum in which [securities] trades are undertaken."[108] As such, a securities exchange provides the means by which the market prices of securities can be openly established and through which price information can be produced and disseminated to users of the market.[109] OTC markets are distinguished from organized exchanges, in that an OTC market traditionally refers to trading done outside of an organized exchange; however, as technology has developed, the distinction between exchanges and OTC markets has become blurred.[110] While historically observers have often viewed securities exchanges as philanthropic

---

[107] See J. Macey and H. Kanda, "The Stock Exchange as a Firm: The Emergence of Close Substitutes for the New York and Tokyo Stock Exchanges", 75 Cornell L. Rev. 1007 (1990), p. 1008.

[108] Id., p. 1008 n. 5.

[109] Id.

[110] Id. In the United States, the OTC markets have increasingly come to resemble the securities exchanges, especially as prices of securities are increasingly quoted and traded on various electronic exchanges, such as NASDAQ – the "National Association of Securities Dealers

institutions organized to act in the public interest, this is not, in fact, the case.[111] Instead, exchanges are self-interested economic organizations which supply services to companies and other organizations listing their securities in exchange for fees, which typically come in the form of an initial listing fee and an annual fee, as well as trading fees.[112] Firms are not required to have their securities listed on an exchange, but firms with publicly traded securities have shown a strong interest in having their securities traded on an exchange, thus indicating that exchanges, in fact, offer something of value to listing firms for the fees charged and the various costs (e.g., compliance and disclosure) incurred.[113]

In view of the various aspects of the financial system, the policy discussion should focus on the determination of the most appropriate path for supporting the achievement of its primary purposes.

### 1.3.4. *Financial Sector Development*

Developing a financial system requires an expansion of both the supply of and the demand for finance. The primary policy concern is the design of systems with a view to encouraging participation by domestic and foreign participants and increasing the efficiency of their functioning.

A financial system can be basic, functioning, developed or sophisticated.

A "basic" financial system typically comprises simple currency, simple payment, simple banking, and simple insurance activities. David Beim and Charles Calomiris suggest that[114]:

> [t]he most primitive function of a financial system is to issue and safeguard money. The next function to evolve is a payments mechanism, typically a check-clearance system, which enables parties to transfer money among each other without taking the risk of delivering it in coin or currency. These basic functions are the domain of banks, which are invariably the first financial institutions to evolve in a developing country.

A "functioning" financial system provides financing functions beyond the basic level – namely currency, payment, banking and interbank, insurance, simple securities, and simple derivatives transactions. Such a system will also provide a basic level of risk management.

---

Automated Quotations". This is also an increasingly important development in the European Union.

[111] Id., p. 1009.

[112] Id.

[113] Id.

[114] D. Beim and C. Calomiris, *Emerging Financial Markets* (New York: McGraw-Hill, 2001), p. 44.

A "developed" financial system provides for effective allocation of resources via market pricing, as well as a variety of instruments and risk management functions. According to Beim and Calomiris[115]:

> In a fully developed, competitive economy the financial system includes not only banks but also securities firms, specialized financial intermediaries such as finance companies and mortgage brokers, as well as institutional investors such as insurance companies, pension funds, and mutual funds. Such a financial system plays a large and sophisticated role: It encourages and mobilizes private saving and investment, and channels the capital so created into its most productive uses. It creates a diverse menu of saving and investment options for individuals – some at higher risk, some at lower risk, some for the long term, and some for a shorter term.

A "sophisticated" financial system will provide a full and ever-changing range of products and services; truly sophisticated systems, however, to date have only developed in a few major financial centres around the world (e.g., London, New York, Hong Kong).

Rajan and Zingales make four proposals to support financial market development[116]:

(1) ensure that control of productive assets is not concentrated in a few hands and that those who do control also have the ability to use the assets well (competition and efficiency)[117],

(2) creation of a safety net to protect the losers (financial stability and consumer protection)[118],

(3) open borders (competition and liberalization)[119], and

(4) public awareness of the benefits of the financial system (education).

In achieving these, the focus today is on the role of law in the financial sector.

## 1.4. LAW, THE FINANCIAL SECTOR AND ECONOMIC GROWTH

It is now agreed that the financial sector plays a central role in supporting economic growth and development: first, a sound financial system facilitates

---

[115] Id.

[116] Rajan and Zingales (2003), op. cit., n. 103, p. 294.

[117] Tools include competition/antitrust law, property taxes, better corporate governance and inheritance taxes. Id., pp. 294–300.

[118] Tools include supporting individuals rather than firms and designing the system before it is needed. Id., pp. 300–6.

[119] Tools include open goods and capital markets, and regional trading blocs. Id., pp. 306–9.

financial intermediation and resource allocation, which, in turn, support economic growth and development; and second, a sound financial system reduces the risks of financial crises. A sound financial system therefore is essential for both financial stability and financial sector development. Specifically, following the financial sector crises of the 1990s around the world, international efforts have focused on the causes of the crises, their resolution and prevention of future crises. A principal lesson to emerge is the importance of the institutional, legal and regulatory framework for financial sector stability, financial development and financial crisis resolution.

First, a reliable framework is essential to provide the rules of the game for financial transactions and to support financial sector development. Without an appropriate legal and institutional context based on law, developed financial markets cannot function.

Second, weak financial sectors have been a significant cause of many financial crises. An adequate regulatory and supervisory framework is necessary to strengthen financial intermediaries and to help prevent the occurrence of crises.

Third, in the context of distress or crisis, an adequate framework supports the resolution of difficulties. In the absence of such a framework, crisis resolution becomes much more difficult, time-consuming and expensive.

As a result of both the growth of institutional economics and the experiences of financial crises in economies around the world from the early 1990s to the present, attention has increasingly turned to the role of institutions in economic development, with recent research suggesting that institutions may, in fact, be the most significant factor. One aspect of institutional development is law, legal institutions and regulatory and supervisory structures. Institutions, especially legal infrastructure, are fundamental to a sound financial system. A consensus is emerging with respect to the supporting institutions necessary for a sound financial sector, both domestically and internationally, focused around the international financial architecture, discussed in the following chapter.

Today, the interaction between law and financial market development is characterized by the on-going development of "law and finance" theory.

Law and finance is, in many ways, a development of institutional economics and finance and growth research. The leading writers in the area of law and finance are Hernando de Soto and Andrei Shleifer. For de Soto (whose ideas are discussed further in Chapter Three), property rights underlie finance which, in turn, makes economic development possible. For Shleifer and others, the focus has been on the role of law in financial development ("law and finance").

This second strand of research attempts to analyse differences between different institutional models of a market economy. Simeon Djankov, Edward Glaeser, Rafael La Porta, Florencio Lopez-de-Silanes and Andrei Shleifer have called this the "New Comparative Economics."[120] One aspect of this research focuses on the role of law and legal institutions in financial development.[121] From the theoretical basis developed by North, in the late 1990s a burgeoning empirical literature developed as North's theories were modeled and tested. The most influential has been a series of studies by La Porta, Lopez-de-Silanes, Shleifer and Robert Vishny, usually collectively referred to as "LLSV."[122]

According to Thorsten Beck and Ross Levine[123]:

> [T]he first part of the law and finance theory holds that in countries where legal systems enforce property rights, support private contractual arrangements, and protect the legal right of investors, savers are more willing to finance firms and financial markets flourish. In contrast, legal institutions that neither support property rights nor facilitate private contracting inhibit corporate finance and stunt financial development. The second part of the law and finance theory emphasizes that different legal traditions that emerged in Europe over previous centuries and were spread internationally through conquest, colonization, and imitation help explain cross-country differences in investor protection, the contracting environment, and financial development today.

Beck and Levine suggest that there are two mechanisms through which the second strand may function: the "political" mechanism and the "adaptability" mechanism.[124] Essentially, the political explanation suggests that different legal systems embed differing relationships between the state and private property[125], while the adaptability mechanism suggests that different legal systems have differing levels of flexibility and reactive ability to changes in economic circumstances and needs. Unlike finance and growth theory, law and finance theory has not been generally agreed, especially in relation to the second line respecting the role of legal origin. At present, it is generally agreed (per North) that law and legal institutions have an important role in economic growth and financial development; however, beyond the agreed importance of governance and property rights, significant divisions remain.

---

[120] S. Djankov et al., "The New Comparative Economics", J. Comp. Econ. (Dec. 2003).

[121] See T. Beck and R. Levine, "Legal Institutions and Financial Development", World Bank Policy Research Working Paper 3136 (Sep. 2003).

[122] See R. La Porta et al., "Legal Determinants of External Finance", 52 J. Fin. 1131 (1997); idem, "Law and Finance", 106 J. Pol. Econ'y 1113 (1998); and idem, "Investor Protection and Corporate Governance", 58 J. Fin'l Econ. 3 (2000).

[123] Beck and Levine (2003), op. cit., n. 123, p. 1.

[124] Id., p. 2.

[125] See E. Glaeser and A. Shleifer, "Legal Origins", Quarterly J. Economics (Nov. 2002).

Nonetheless, important elements to date include:

(1) Finance is better developed in countries with strong legal frameworks.[126]
(2) National differences in financial development may be explained by a range of factors, including the origins of the legal system, exemplified in the treatment of investor or property rights, or how legal systems adapt to commercial circumstances.
(3) Empirical research indicates that both the legal system brought by colonizers and the initial endowments in former colonies are important determinants of financial development.
(4) The spread of legal traditions had enduring influences on national approaches to private property rights and financial development.[127]
(5) Differences in endowments shaped initial institutions and these institutions have had long-lasting repercussions on private property rights protection and financial development.[128]

Generalizing from the basis of these various strands, Stijn Claessens and Luc Laeven address firm-level issues, arguing that[129]:

> the existence of an environment with poorly developed financial systems and weak property rights has two effects on firms: first, it reduces the access of firms to external financing; and second, it leads firms to allocate resources in a suboptimal way.

They find:

(1) the effect of insecure property rights on the asset mix of firms (the "assets allocation" effect) is economically as important as the lack of financing effect as it impedes the growth of firms to the same quantitative magnitude;
(2) the asset allocation effect is particularly important in hindering the growth of new firms; and

---

[126] La Porta et al. (1998), op. cit., n. 124.
[127] Id.
[128] D. Acemoglu, S. Johnson and J. Robinson, "The Colonial Origins of Comparative Development: An Empirical Investigation", 91 Am. Econ. Rev. 1369 (2001).
[129] S. Claessens and L. Laeven, "Financial Development, Property Rights, and Growth", World Bank Policy Research Working Paper 2923 (Nov. 2002), p. 38.

(3) the degree to which firms allocate resources in an optimal way will depend on the strength of a country's property rights and that that allocation effect is an important channel of the effect of property rights on firm growth.

They suggest that these results may have the implication that a functioning legal system is just as important to property rights protection and protection of returns to different types of assets as it is to the establishment of a good financial system.[130]

The conclusion to emerge is that law is, in fact, important for financial development; however, the exact mechanics are not yet fully understood nor agreed.

### 1.5. CONCLUSION

This chapter has reviewed and integrated the literature respecting the role of law and institutions in financial sector development and economic growth and development. In that review and integration, the chapter argues that it is now clear that an appropriate legal and institutional framework underlie both financial sector stability and development and economic growth and development. What, then, are the most significant principles underlying financial stability and development, and how is a robust supporting legal system to be developed?

The following chapters attempt to answer these questions, arguing that the minimum content of the requisite financial laws and the necessary elements of the legal system that makes those laws effective can be discerned through analysis of the demands of the role of law in the context of finance and through recognizing that internationally acceptable minimum financial standards can be distilled from a developing consensus on underlying principles necessary to support the requisite elements of financial systems. Of particular importance are the pronouncements of those international bodies concerned with promoting financial stability and development.

---

[130] Id., p. 39.

# 2

# Law, Financial Stability and the International Financial Architecture

By the mid-1990s, both the theoretical understanding of finance and the actual nature of international and domestic financial systems had changed radically from those at the end of World War II. In that context, this chapter looks at the changing nature of the international financial architecture in response to those changes.

This chapter addresses five main areas. Section I presents an overview of the Bretton Woods international economic system and its development to the early 1990s – at the time of the Mexican financial crisis. It also discusses the changing roles of the Bretton Woods institutions in the context of financial globalization and the series of financial crises over the past decade. Section II looks at changes to the international financial architecture arising from events of the 1990s – including the new role of international financial standards, the only element of the international financial architecture which (along with the related Financial Stability Forum) can truly be classified as new. Section III discusses the specific aspect of the international financial architecture of most concern to this volume: the system of international standards and standard setting. However, while an important development, to be effective these standards must be implemented by individual economies – an issue discussed throughout the following chapters. Section IV therefore discusses international efforts to monitor and support the domestic process of implementation. Finally, section V concludes that the current structure of the international financial architecture does not amount to a coherent regime in the same manner as the Bretton Woods system as designed. Rather, today's "system" is more of a non-system.

## 2.1. THE BRETTON WOODS SYSTEM AND GLOBALIZATION
## OF FINANCIAL MARKETS

Designed at the end of World War II by the United States and the United Kingdom, the purpose of the Bretton Woods system was to prevent international economic instability of the sort seen in the interwar period (1914–44) and to support economic development through reintegration of domestic economies. Its design was based on three elements. First, its structure was formal and institutional, based on an interlinked set of international treaties and institutions. Second, it was based on the premise of closed national financial markets, with limited capital flows, but open markets for trade in goods. Third, relationships among closed national systems were structured through an international institutional framework.

The Bretton Woods system as designed included three interlinked international institutions: the International Monetary Fund (IMF), the International Bank for Reconstruction and Development (IBRD, commonly known as the World Bank) and the International Trade Organization (ITO). These three institutions were designed to address the three main elements of the international economic system: money, finance and investment, and trade.

Unfortunately, the Bretton Woods system as designed never actually functioned: the ITO was still-born (though ultimately reincarnated as the WTO in 1994 after fifty years in the limbo of the General Agreement on Tariffs and Trade [GATT]). Likewise, the role of the World Bank was quickly usurped in many ways by the bilateral efforts of the United States through the Marshall Plan and related reconstruction initiatives, leaving the Bank to focus on developing (often post-colonial) countries – the role it continues to play today. Nonetheless, the design for monetary relations, with the IMF at the centre of a system of fixed exchange rates based on the US dollar and its link to gold, did function – arguably quite well – until the early 1970s.

Since the end of the Bretton Woods international monetary system in 1973, financial markets have changed dramatically through a process of liberalization, internationalization and globalization, undergirded by incredible technological changes.

Fifty years after the creation of the Bretton Woods system, the changes in the international financial system and the deficiencies of the existing international institutions and arrangements (the "international financial architecture") to deal with this changed nature came dramatically to light through the Mexican financial crisis and the east Asian and other crises which followed. Since that time, the IMF, World Bank and WTO gradually have been forced to come to grips with the increasingly globalized nature of financial markets. Discussions both in these institutions and elsewhere have focused on whether there is a need to reform the existing international institutional arrangements – whether there is a need for a "new international financial architecture".

### 2.1.1. *Bretton Woods as Designed*

The Bretton Woods system as designed was largely the result of the work of two economists and civil servants, one British, one American: John Maynard Keynes and Harry Dexter White. Both devised systems which they viewed as coherent, effective designs in the context of then-existing circumstances for a framework to support the future development of the international economy following the end of World War II. Incidentally, both were designed also to some extent to reinforce the economic positions of their respective countries. Both of their respective governments largely adopted their positions (and Keynes and White played central roles in the negotiation process). Representatives of the US, British and allied governments met in Bretton Woods, New Hampshire, and Havana, Cuba, in 1944 to finalize plans for the future design and structure of the post-war international economic architecture.

Largely as a result of the much stronger bargaining position of the United States, White's ideas were adopted to a greater extent than those of Keynes. As noted earlier, the final structure was based on three formal international institutions: the IMF, IBRD and ITO. The three institutions would be governed by a single committee, to ensure coordination among their activities. In addition, all three institutions would be located in Washington, DC.

The essential underlying theory of both designs and the final structure adopted was based, first, on a system of stable exchange rates. All involved felt that, while it was impossible to return to the Gold Standard as it existed prior to World War I, it was important to return to a parallel system, with money circulating on the basis of a fixed relationship to gold, rather than on the basis of purely paper currencies ("fiat money"). This design was intended to provide a stable base for finance, investment and trade – the other central pillars of the structure – and to avoid the sorts of monetary instabilities seen during the period from 1914–44. Under the Bretton Woods international monetary system, the US dollar was fixed to gold at US$32 per ounce. All other currencies were then fixed in value to the US dollar. Capital movements would be largely controlled through domestic restrictions, with the IMF supporting the system through monitoring of flows and facilitating orderly readjustments when necessary. The result gave an important economic benefit to the United States: the US dollar became the world's reserve currency (along with gold) and the backbone of international finance and trade, rather rapidly replacing the British pound sterling which fulfilled similar roles in the 1870–1914 period.

Underpinned by this international system of fixed exchange rates and limited capital mobility, both White's and Keynes' designs focused on the need to re-establish international trade linkages as rapidly as possible. By 1944, due to economic nationalism and the needs and results of war, the system of largely free trade which had existed in the 1870–1914 period had been completely destroyed. All the participants at Bretton Woods agreed there was a vital need to begin rebuilding these linkages as quickly as possible. The design was based around the ITO, which was intended to serve a formal role both in reducing trade barriers and in policing the agreements. Unfortunately, largely due to US political concerns, this institution was not established. Rather, trade relationships were addressed through a system of negotiations, formalized as the GATT. Despite not being of the same magnitude as the ITO as designed, the GATT – over the next fifty years – gradually and successfully reduced trade barriers around the world, especially among developed economies. In 1994, the WTO, an institution in many ways paralleling the ITO, was established, though by this time, the system of fixed exchange rates with which it was meant to operate in tandem had long ceased to exist.

The third element of the Bretton Woods system focused on finance, investment and the need for reconstruction of the decimated economies of Europe. As designed, the IBRD would be the primary mechanism for supporting reconstruction (especially of infrastructure) in Europe and other economies. However, other US initiatives (e.g., the Marshall Plan for European reconstruction) quickly largely displaced the role of the Bank in European reconstruction, leaving it to focus on newly independent states and other developing countries around the world.

### 2.1.2. *Bretton Woods in Practice: 1944–94*

As noted earlier, in practice, the Bretton Woods international economic system never came into existence: while both the IMF and the IBRD were duly formed, the ITO was not. Further, the central role of the IBRD in post-war reconstruction was quickly displaced by bilateral efforts such as the Marshall Plan.

**Money and the IMF.** In the event, only the Bretton Woods international monetary system, centred on the IMF, functioned for a period as designed. The system of fixed exchange rates in fact functioned rather well from 1945–73, at which time the United States finally abandoned the fixed link between the US dollar and gold, largely as a result of domestic financial pressures (fiscal and inflationary) resulting from the expenses of the Vietnam War, the Cold War and domestic social spending. Despite the abandonment of the fundamental link to gold, many economies continued to maintain fixed relationships between their currencies and the US dollar (though subject to periodic, often painful adjustments) and capital flows remained largely restricted during this period (with the exception of the development of the Euromarkets – the foundation of today's international financial markets). During this period, the role of the IMF largely centred on the relationship between the developed economies and necessary (sometimes painful) exchange rate adjustments, especially as the economic importance of Germany and Japan increased and that of the United Kingdom decreased.

Following the final abandonment by the United States of the gold standard in 1973, the IMF faced questions about its role: certainly, without the link between the US dollar and gold, the central pillar of the Bretton Woods international monetary system no longer existed, therefore leaving the IMF without its former function. During the 1970s, the IMF sought to replicate the link through the creation of a new synthetic currency, the Special Drawing Right (SDR); however, this never really worked as intended. Nonetheless, the Fund continued to maintain a role in the process of exchange rate adjustment. There were, however, two amendments to the IMF Articles of Agreement to reflect its new role in the international monetary system.[1] During this period, the IMF increasingly focused on lending to support economies dealing with periodic exchange crises, operating with a developing system of conditions for support: IMF "conditionality".

The period from 1973–94 was a period of gradually increasing capital flows and decreasing capital restrictions, with such restrictions largely eliminated in the developed economies by the late 1980s. In fact, by the early 1990s, the IMF was arguing for a further amendment to its Articles to formalize its role in encouraging and supporting capital liberalization, especially in developing, emerging and transition economies. In addition, with the collapse of the Soviet Bloc at the end of the 1980s, the IMF began to focus on its role in monetary aspects of the transition process. By 1994, the fiftieth anniversary of the Bretton Woods conference, the IMF largely felt that it understood its role and the

---

[1] The IMF Articles were adopted at the United Nations Monetary and Financial Conference, Bretton Woods, New Hampshire, on 22 Jul. 1944 and entered into force 27 Dec. 1945. They have subsequently been amended three times: (1) Board of Governors Resolution No. 23-5, adopted 31 May 1968 and effective 28 Jul. 1969; (2) Board of Governors Resolution No. 31-4, adopted 30 Apr. 1976 and effective 1 Apr. 1978; and (3) Board of Governors Resolution No. 45-3, adopted 28 Jun. 1990 and effective 11 Nov. 1992.

mechanisms through which to achieve its goals – centred on the policy-focused ideas of the Washington Consensus.

**Finance and the World Bank.** While the IBRD was duly established in 1944 and immediately set about addressing the financing of post-war reconstruction, its resources and expertise initially were limited. Further, as noted, with the onset of the Cold War, the United States realized the need to build allies, if necessary on the foundations of former enemies, and initiated a number of bilateral programs to support reconstruction, of which the Marshall Plan for Western Europe is the most well known. As a result, in a very short period following its creation, the primary role and mission of the IBRD (increasingly called the World Bank) had been transferred elsewhere.

The World Bank therefore, almost from the beginning, was forced to search for a role and its focus turned increasingly to the needs of developing countries around the world, rather than post-war reconstruction of the developed countries. This role received a significant boost as the former colonial powers lost their empires, whether through emancipation, revolt or abandonment. The World Bank sought to step in and assist these new countries in developing infrastructure and building their economies. During its initial decades, the World Bank focused on loans to governments for both specific projects and increasingly, through the 1970s, for general budgetary support. Lending was supplemented by provision of grants to the least developed countries, generally through the International Development Agency (IDA) created in 1960.

With the onset of the debt crisis in the early 1980s, the World Bank was faced with a challenge to its previous focus on state lending, as it became obvious that in many cases resources lent for general purposes and even for specific projects had often been squandered and in some cases even caused more harm than benefit. As a result, in addition to state lending and grants, the World Bank began to focus to a greater extent on providing and supporting private sector involvement through the International Finance Corporation (IFC) and Multilateral Investment Guarantee Agency (MIGA), established in 1956 and 1988, respectively.

By the end of the 1980s, the World Bank Group included the IBRD, IFC, IDA and MIGA, dealing with (respectively) state lending and technical assistance, private sector projects, grants to developing countries and investment guarantees. In addition, it also serves as host for the International Centre for Settlement of Investment Disputes (ICSID), founded in 1966 (and along with MIGA, serve to support the development of international investment).

With the collapse of the Soviet Bloc, like the IMF, the World Bank also added the transition economies to its development assistance portfolio. Nonetheless, unlike the IMF, the World Bank was facing many questions about its role and future at the time of the fiftieth anniversary of the Bretton Woods conference in 1994.

**Trade, the GATT and the WTO.** As noted earlier, trade relationships were structured through a series of rounds of negotiations, formalized through the GATT (established in 1948; the General Agreement on Trade in Services – GATS – was added in 1995). Although this was not the initial Bretton Woods intention, the GATT was, in fact, quite effective in gradually reducing trade barriers, especially among the developed countries. GATT members agreed to the establishment of the WTO in 1994, reflecting this success and the general consensus supporting freer trade following the collapse of the Soviet Bloc and the success of the export-centred development model of east Asian emerging economies, as well as of the European single market project and experiences of the developed countries. Therefore, by the fiftieth anniversary of the Bretton Woods conference in 1994, the intellectual successor of the ITO finally had been established through the formation of the WTO.

**Coordination and Linkage.** Because the ITO was never formed, the planned coordinating committee likewise never was formed. Perhaps as a result, the IMF and the World Bank often have been accused of failing to coordinate their activities – despite the fact that they sit on opposite sides of the same street in central Washington, DC. Some efforts had been made in this direction following problems arising in the context of the 1980s debt crisis (i.e., the creation of the "Interim" Committee to coordinate activities). However, by the fiftieth anniversary of the Bretton Woods conference in 1994, these concerns were very much in focus.

### 2.1.3. *Responses to the Mexican Financial Crisis*

While the leading role of the United States in efforts to organize the Mexican rescue package was probably *sui generis* due to the importance of Mexico to the United States and due to Mexico's prominent position among emerging economies, following the Mexican financial crisis certain efforts were made to address future liquidity crises and attempt to prevent them from causing long-term negative consequences, especially the threat of international contagion as seen in the tequila effect on other emerging economies around the world immediately following the onset of the crisis in Mexico.[2]

The profile of international organizations such as the IMF and the World Bank makes them the usual starting point in any discussion of problems in the international financial system, and this was, in fact, the approach chosen following the Mexican crisis in 1995. The increasing role of these institutions in development finance and the debt crisis of the 1980s, the fiftieth year anniversary of the Bretton Woods system in 1994, and the US desire not to lead further international rescues made these institutions the focus of debate regarding sovereign liquidity and debt problems. Further, the role of the IMF reflected its desire to find a new leadership role in the period after the deterioration of the Bretton Woods system.[3] Regardless of the underlying motivation, the IMF's role was both significant and unusual (at least at that time) in that its contribution far exceeded the amount that would normally be available to a country such as Mexico under IMF rules.[4]

**The International Response.** Following the Mexican financial crisis, the Group of Seven Industrialized Countries (G-7) at its Halifax summit in 1995 called on the Group of Ten (G-10) and other countries to support the international monetary system to develop financing arrangements to help prevent and

[2]  See US General Accounting Office (GAO), *GAO Report: Mexico's Financial Crisis: Origins, Assistance, and Initial Efforts to Recover*, GAO/GGD-96–56, 23 Feb. 1996, pp. 112–13 tables 4.1–4.2; IMF, *International Capital Markets: Developments, Prospects, and Policy Issues*, Aug. 1995, pp. 64–9.

[3]  Zanny Minton-Beddoes has suggested that IMF overreached its capacity, not because of the US influence on IMF policies, but rather because of its desire for new relevance in a world economy now characterized by instability and private power. See Z. Minton-Beddoes, "Why IMF Needs Reform", For. Affairs 123 (May 1995). See also R. Chote, "Weaknesses in IMF Shown by Mexico", Financial Times, 25 Apr. 1995.

[4]  G. Graham, "US$50bn Mexico Aid Plan 'Averted a Global Crisis': 'Exceptional' Support Was Required, Says IMF Chief", Financial Times, 3 Feb. 1995, p. 16. The IMF's contribution to support Mexico has been estimated at almost one-fifth of the IMF's liquid resources and seven times Mexico's quota. "Perspective on a Panic", Financial Times, 11 Feb. 1995, p. 8.

In this context, the question arose as to whether the Fund could approve a stand-by arrangement for Mexico, at a time in which it was facing a large capital outflow. Part of the answer was that the outflow was partly due to current payments, including interest on debt. Moreover, Mexico financed the outflow with its reserves and bilateral loans, while IMF resources were used essentially to reconstitute Mexico's reserves and not to meet subsequent capital outflows. While this is somewhat circular, the IMF determined that in reality what mattered was the country observed the reserve targets set by the Fund. Because the adjustment mechanisms implemented by Mexico were sufficient, no restrictions on capital movements were viewed as necessary. F. Gianviti, "The IMF and the Liberalization of Capital Markets", 19 Hous. J. Int'l L. 773 (1997), p. 777.

to deal with the onset of international financial crises in emerging economies.[5] Following this invitation by the G-7 to the G-10, the Deputies of the G-10 established a Working Party to consider the issues arising with respect to the orderly resolution of sovereign liquidity crises.[6] On 22 April 1996, the Finance Ministers and Central Bank Governors of the G-10 nations released a communiqué on international financial emergencies such as the Mexican financial crisis based on and endorsing the Working Party Report.[7]

In its communiqué, the G-10 affirmed that, given the need to contain moral hazard and the desirability of equitable burden-sharing, first, that neither the debtor countries nor their private creditors should expect to be insulated from any adverse financial consequences of their financial decisions by the provision of large-scale official financing in the event of a crisis, and second, that there should be no presumption that any type of debt would be exempt from payment suspensions or restructurings in any future sovereign liquidity crisis.[8] Importantly, the G-10 stated that the existing flexible, case-by-case practices and procedures, as developed over the years, were an appropriate starting point for considering how to respond to future sovereign liquidity crises, that improvements should continue to evolve to meet the needs of specific crises, and stressed that improvements should be led by private sector groups in developing any new contractual arrangements.[9] Further, they affirmed that the official community's primary role in the resolution of sovereign liquidity crises should remain centred on "the promotion of strong and effective adjustment by debtor countries in the context of IMF supported programs"[10], thereby indicating the continued importance of IMF conditionality and structural adjustment programs.

The G-10 noted the on-going discussion between the G-10 countries and other countries aimed at developing new financing arrangements which would double the supplementary resources available to the IMF under the General Agreement to Borrow (GAB) for coping with these sorts of international financial emergencies.[11] The G-10 expressed support for the work of international financial organizations such as the Basel Committee on Banking Supervision

---

[5] G-7, *Halifax Communiqué*, 16 Jun. 1995.

[6] See G-10, Group of Ten Working Party, *The Resolution of Sovereign Liquidity Crises*, May 1996, p. 1 ("G-10 Sovereign Crises").

[7] G-10, *Communiqué of Ministers and Governors of the Group of Ten Nations on International Financial Emergencies*, 22 Apr. 1996.

[8] Id., para. 3. This latter statement seems directly aimed at holders of emerging market bond debt.

[9] Id., para. 4.

[10] Id.

[11] Id., para. 1.

and the International Organization of Securities Commissions (IOSCO), welcomed efforts to increase cooperation among authorities responsible for the supervision and stability of financial markets, and concluded that such organizations provide a helpful basis for further work in this area.[12] The G-10 also emphasized the importance of adherence to "credible and consistent economic policies" and endorsed actions to reinforce market discipline through the establishment of data dissemination standards by the IMF, along with the strengthening of surveillance procedures.[13]

This communiqué and report thus established the framework which was applied subsequently in the Asian financial crisis.

**The Initial IMF Response: Liquidity and Disclosure.** Following on this agreed framework, the IMF moved to enhance its ability to provide liquidity in future situations and to enhance the transparency of the international financial system.

LIQUIDITY. In general terms, the IMF's financial resources are intended to assist members seeking to redress balance of payments problems and to help cushion the impact of adjustment, and are provided through both its general resources and its concessional financing facilities, which are administered separately.[14] IMF financing is subject to Executive Board approval and, in most cases, to the member's commitment to take steps to address the causes of its payments imbalance (termed "conditionality").[15] Access is determined primarily

---

[12]  Id., para. 5.

[13]  Id.

[14]  Regular IMF Facilities include Reserve Tranches, Credit Tranches, Stand-By Arrangements and Extended Fund Facilities. Special facilities include the compensatory and contingency financing facility; the buffer stock financing facility, which has not been used since 1984; and the systemic transformation facility, which ceased operations at end-December 1995. In addition, the IMF also has Concessional Facilities, available in certain situations, including the Structural Adjustment Facility; and the Enhanced Structural Adjustment Facility.

[15]  The explicit commitment that members make to implement remedial measures in return for the IMF's support is known as "conditionality", though this term specifically only applies to standby and extended standby arrangements. Conditions for IMF financial support may range from general commitments to cooperate with the IMF in setting policies to the formulation of specific, quantified plans for financial policies. The IMF requires a "letter of intent", which outlines a government's policy intentions during the program period; policy changes to be taken before approval of the arrangement; performance criteria, which are objective indicators for certain policies that must be satisfied on a quarterly, semi-annual, or in some instances a monthly basis for drawings to be made; and periodic reviews that allow the Executive Board to assess the consistency of policies with the objectives of the program.

IMF-supported programs emphasize a number of aggregate economic variables, for example, domestic credit, the public-sector deficit, international reserves, and external debt, and

by a member's balance of payments need, the strength of its adjustment policies, and its capacity to repay the IMF, and is permitted up to limits defined
in relation to the member's quota, although these limits may be exceeded in
exceptional cases. Traditional IMF funding mechanisms, however, were not
seen as adequate to deal with the potentiality of similar international financial
crises and resultant IMF-led rescues in the future.

In 1995 and 1996, the IMF moved to strengthen the financial support it
could make available to member countries. It formalized the procedures used
following the Mexican crisis as an Emergency Financing Mechanism (EFM),
moved to increase the GAB and negotiated the potential creation of New
Arrangements to Borrow (NAB).

In relation to the first, the Board of the IMF approved in October 1995 the
establishment of the EFM to enable the IMF to respond promptly in the event
of serious financial crises, but with the application of strong conditionality.[16]
The EFM is a set of procedures to facilitate rapid Executive Board approval of
IMF financial support while ensuring the conditionality necessary to warrant
such support.[17] These emergency measures are intended to be used only in
circumstances representing, or threatening to give rise to, a crisis in a member's
external accounts that requires an immediate IMF response.

Identification of such an emergency is based on an initial judgement by IMF
management in consultation with the Executive Board. Conditions for activation of emergency procedures include the readiness of the member immediately to begin accelerated negotiations with the IMF, with the prospect of
early implementation of agreed measures sufficiently strong to address the
problem. Use of these emergency procedures was expected to be rare and the
IMF's role intended to remain catalytic.[18]

The EFM was renamed the Supplemental Reserve Facility (SRF) in 1997.

In relation to the second, principally as a reaction to the sudden and overwhelming nature of the Mexican financial crisis, world leaders agreed to double
the emergency funds of the IMF.[19] The GAB, whereby the IMF may draw upon

---

elements of the pricing system, including the exchange rate, interest rates, and, in some
cases, commodity prices, that significantly affect public finances and foreign trade. See M.
Guitian, "Conditionality: Past, Present, Future", 42:4 IMF Staff Papers (Dec. 1995); idem,
"Fund Conditionality: Evolution of Principles and Practices", IMF Pamphlet Series no. 38
(1981); J. Gold, "Conditionality", IMF Pamphlet Series no. 31 (1979).

[16] IMF, "Communiqué of the Interim Committee of the Board of Governors of the International
Monetary Fund", IMF Press Release No. 95/51, 8 Oct. 1995.

[17] IMF, *Financial Facilities and Policies*, www.imf.org.

[18] Id.

[19] R. Choate, G. Graham and J. Gapper, "IMF Set to Get More Crisis Cash", Financial Times,
9 Oct. 1995.

funds of the G-10 governments and Saudi Arabia was increased to US$52 billion with member government approval.[20] Further, on 27 January 1997, the Executive Board of the IMF adopted a decision on the NAB, following the agreement by the twenty-five potential participants in the NAB on the terms and conditions in which they will be prepared to make loans to the IMF when supplementary resources are needed to forestall or cope with an impairment of the international monetary system or to deal with an exceptional situation that poses a threat to the stability of the system.[21] The amount of resources available under the NAB was set at SDR 34 billion (US$48 billion).

The credit arrangement under the NAB may be activated for the benefit of an IMF member that is a participant in the NAB (or whose institution is a participant), or for the benefit of a member that is not a participant, under circumstances similar to those contemplated in the GAB, except that after activation of the GAB for the benefit of a nonparticipant requires the additional condition that, after consultation, the Managing Director considers that the IMF faces an inadequacy of reserves.

The NAB did not replace the GAB, which remained in force; however, it was to be the facility of first and principal recourse in the event of need to provide supplementary resources to the IMF. The amount of the GAB remained unchanged, but the SDR 34 billion available under the NAB also became the combined limit available under the GAB.

INTERNATIONAL TRANSPARENCY. As a second response to the Mexican financial crisis, the IMF placed attention both on the transparency of its operations and policies (which has been increased remarkably, especially through the IMF website) and on availability of information concerning individual economies.

In the aftermath of the Mexican crisis, the IMF's Interim Committee emphasized at its 26 April 1995 meeting that timely publication of comprehensive economic and financial data by members would give greater transparency to members' economic policies and thereby increase investor confidence and decrease the chances of unexpected surprises that might result in the massive capital outflows that characterized the aftermath of the Mexican financial crisis. The IMF approved the creation of the Special Data Dissemination Standard (SDDS) for the provision of economic and financial statistics to the public by member countries, especially those countries that participate in the

---

[20]  Id.

[21]  IMF, "IMF Adopts a Decision on New Arrangements to Borrow", Press Release No. 97/5, 27 Jan. 1997.

international capital markets or aspire to do so, and including both developed and emerging economies.[22] The purpose of the SDDS is to[23]:

> guide IMF members in the provision to the public of comprehensive, timely, accessible, and reliable economic and financial statistics in a world of increasing economic and financial integration.

The SDDS is discussed further in Chapter Four.

While participation is optional, it was hoped that countries seeking international capital would comply in order to meet investor demands for comparable information on competing countries. Prior to the Asian financial crisis, this was not necessarily the case.

## 2.2. DISCUSSIONS OF THE NEW INTERNATIONAL FINANCIAL ARCHITECTURE

As noted in the preceding section, following the Mexican financial crisis, there were a number of international responses focused largely on the IMF and its role in transparency and liquidity. Following the Asian financial crisis, these discussions increased, with a new focus on whether there was a need to reform the existing international financial architecture: whether, in fact, there was a need for a "new international financial architecture".

These discussions first looked to the changed nature of international finance and the implications of these changes. Two specific areas received the greatest attention: crisis prevention and crisis resolution. Both of these issues largely arose due to the changed nature of the international financial system – the process of globalization.

### 2.2.1. *The Changing Nature of Finance: Globalization*

Over the past sixty years, the international financial system has dramatically changed from an essentially fixed relationship between isolated domestic financial systems, to an increasingly global, integrated and volatile financial system. A number of factors underlie the process of financial market globalization (or re-globalization) which has been taking place since 1944. These include liberalization of money, finance and investment, and trade; the process of

---

[22] See IMF, "IMF Executive Board Approves the Special Data Dissemination Standard", IMF Press Rel. No. 96/18, 16 Apr. 1996. At an early stage it was decided that two sets of standards should be created. Id.

[23] Id.

disintermediation (sometimes labeled as securitization); technological innovation; financial innovation; and privatization.

First, there has been a progressive and comprehensive liberalization of capital flows and financial systems from the original closed and fixed structure established under the Bretton Woods system, resulting in an international system today much more similar to that preceding World War I than that which existed at the end of World War II. Second, financial markets both internationally and domestically have undergone a process of disintermediation, as financial flows have moved from traditional banks to capital markets. This process has changed dramatically the risks and parties involved in both international and domestic finance. Third, technological innovation has increased the speed with which information is transferred around the world, reinforcing interlinkages between formerly isolated financial systems and markets. Fourth, financial innovations have developed to meet the challenges of changing financial markets and their participants, with constant development of new intermediaries and products to deal with the increased volatility and flexibility inherent in international finance. Fifth, there has been a reduction in the role of centralized economic decision-making, evidenced by the spread of privatization around the world since the early 1980s, supporting both the development of international markets as funding sources and reducing government influence and control over domestic markets.

By the beginning of the 1990s, these trends had fundamentally altered the financial landscape around the world, both internationally and domestically. As the decade progressed, a clear feature of international finance in the last decade of the twentieth century was the occurrence of a series of financial crises, often with international or global implications, of a sort not seen since the late nineteenth century – exactly the sort of crises that the Bretton Woods system was designed to prevent. In many ways, financial crises were a defining feature of the last decade of the twentieth century. As these crises have occurred, there has been an increasing focus on their causes, resolution and possible future prevention – often as part of discussions of whether there is a need for a "new" international financial architecture – that is, a reassessment of the Bretton Woods system, its constituents and the issues with which it was designed to address.

Today's financial markets exhibit a number of characteristics:

First, the character of the markets is largely global at the wholesale level, but at best international at the retail level (even in the context of the European Union).

Second, the dominant international monetary system is one based on floating rates between major currencies, with many other currencies fixed to the major currencies through various systems.

Third, capital flows are largely unrestricted.

Fourth, the period so far has been characterized by significant financial crises.

Fifth, international financial cooperation can be characterized, first, by the continued development of the existing international financial architecture, and second, by the creation of the WTO.

Sixth, international financial institutional innovations include the European Union, WTO, Financial Stability Forum, European Bank for Reconstruction and Development, and a proliferation of international financial organizations of various characters and forms.

Seventh, major financial innovations and developments include the massive growth of derivatives instruments and markets (especially the OTC – over-the-counter – market); the on-going process of transition from central planning, state ownership and control to regulated market economies; the huge volume of international capital flows; and technological developments, especially in communications and computing.

Eighth, the dominant economic philosophy has been integration, with a continued role of the Washington Consensus modified by a new focus on incentives and institutions.

Ninth, regulatory developments include an increasing focus on risk-based regulation, especially in the context of discussions of the Basel II Capital Accord, continuing liberalization, and a new focus on legal infrastructure.

Tenth, there continues to be fragmentation among more than 200 different national jurisdictions, including different currencies, different supervisory authorities, different tax systems, different laws and regulations, and different courts.

The table on the next page provides a stylized picture of the development of the international financial system over the past 150 years.

What does this mean for the future of both individual countries and the international financial system? According to Michel Camdessus, speaking in 1998, seven areas of the "architecture of the international financial system" needed to be strengthened in the wake of the Asian financial crisis.[24] First, more effective surveillance over countries' economic policies, coupled with fuller disclosure of all relevant economic and financial data, was needed, given that in each situation market responses were aggravated by a significant lack of proper information. In this regard, the IMF developed the SDDS (and General Data Dissemination Standard [GDDS]) – discussed subsequently

---

[24] M. Camdessus, "The Role of the IMF: Past, Present, and Future", IMF Speech 98/4, Remarks at the Annual Meeting of the Bretton Woods Committee, Washington, DC, 13 Feb. 1998.

TABLE 2.1. *Development of the international financial system*

| | Character of financial markets | International monetary system | Capital flows | Crisis | International financial cooperation | International financial organizations | Major instruments/innovations | Dominant economic philosophy | Regulation |
|---|---|---|---|---|---|---|---|---|---|
| 1870–1914 Golden Age | Global (no distinction) | Gold Standard (Fixed; anchor: British pound sterling) | Unrestricted | Frequent: e.g. Argentina 1890 | Bilateral (Great Britain) | None (Bank of England) | Comprehensive Bonds Telegraph Railway Steam | Mercantilism Laissez-faire (classical) | Self-regulation |
| 1914–1944 Interwar | National/fragmented | None | Restricted/Volatile | Constant: WWI, Depression, WWII | UK/US | BIS | None | Protectionism Nationalization | National restrictions: e.g. US |
| 1944–1973 Bretton Woods | National/off-shore | Bretton Woods (Fixed; Anchor: US dollar) | Limited: current account | Infrequent (ex-UK) | Bretton Woods: (Centre: US; Basel Committee) | Bretton Woods Paris Club Marshall Plan | Euromarkets | Capitalism v. Communism State-led v. Market-led Keynes v. Marx | National control |
| 1973–1982 Oil Crises | International/Domestic | Floating | Limited: current account | Oil Shocks Herstatt Franklin National | Group of Ten | EC Basel Committee Regional development banks | Petrodollars Syndicated lending Calculator | State-led development Import substitution Portfolio theory | State intervention International cooperation: Basel Concordat |
| 1982–1993 International Financial Markets | International (wholesale) Domestic (retail) | Managed float: Plaza/Louvre | Limited: capital account – OECD | LDC Debt Crisis Soviet bloc collapse S&L crisis ERM | Group of Five (Plaza 85/Louvre 87) Group of Seven EC | EC IFOs (limited) US extraterritoriality | Securitization Privatization Computer Air travel | Monetarism Export promotion Washington Consensus: Liberalization Privatization Market-led | Prudential reregulation: Basel I Access deregulation |
| 1993–present Global Financial Markets | Global (wholesale) International (retail) | "Impossible Trinity" | Largely unrestricted | Emerging Markets Financial Crises Japan | NIFA WTO | EBRD EU WTO IFOs (proliferation) FS Forum | Derivatives Transition Capital Flows Internet | Integration Washington Consensus + Incentives Institutions | Risk-based regulation Liberalization Legal infrastructure Basel II |

and in Chapter Four) and promoted disclosure through its programs and policy advice. Second, regional surveillance efforts needed to be improved in
order to encourage neighbouring countries to put pressure on one another to
prevent the sorts of contagion experienced following the Mexican and Thai
crises. While little has yet developed in this respect outside of the context of
the European Union (discussed in Part V), discussions continue in regional
fora world-wide. Third, financial sector reform focusing on improved prudential regulation and supervision is necessary around the world. This effort is
based on on-going efforts to develop "best practices" through the efforts of the
various organizations and institutions in order to transfer lessons learned as
broadly and quickly as possible (discussed further subsequently). Fourth, more
effective structures needed to be developed in regard to debt workouts, both on
a national level through bankruptcy laws and at the international level through
on-going efforts such as those of the G-10 (discussed subsequently and in Part V).
Fifth, capital account liberalization should continue but needs to be based on
prudence and proper sequencing to increase the orderliness of and access
to international capital markets (discussed further in Chapter Eight). Sixth,
world-wide efforts must be increased to promote good governance and to fight
against corruption (discussed in Chapter Five). Seventh, multilateral financial
institutions need to be strengthened, both in terms of resources and authority and in terms of equitable representation (discussed subsequently and in
Part V).[25]

These broad ideas can loosely be broken down into domestic and international responses to the east Asian financial crises.

**Domestic Responses.** According to Stanley Fischer, speaking in autumn 1997,
in order to avoid crises, a country needs both sound macroeconomic policies
and a strong financial system.[26] A sound macroeconomic policy framework is
one that promotes growth by keeping inflation low, the budget deficit small,
and the current account sustainable. This has been the traditional focus of the
IMF through the time of the Asian financial crisis.

The focus on the importance of the financial system, however, is a more
recent development, as discussed in the first chapter. The critical role of the
strength of the financial system was becoming clear before the Mexican crisis,

---

[25] M. Camdessus, "Reflections on the Crisis in Asia", IMF Speech 98/3, Address to the Extraordinary Ministerial Meeting of the Group of 24, Caracas, Venezuela, 7 Feb. 1998.

[26] S. Fischer, "How to Avoid International Financial Crises and the Role of the International
Monetary Fund", 15th Annual Cato Institute Monetary Conference, Washington, DC, 14 Oct.
1997.

it was crystal clear in that crisis and its aftermath, and it has been equally clear in the Asian crisis and its aftermath.

**International Responses.** Following the Asian financial crisis, a number of actions were taken to address these issues and to build on the initiatives undertaken following the Mexican financial crisis.

IMF: MORE LIQUIDITY AND MORE DISCLOSURE. Following its commitments in Asia in the second half of 1997, the IMF acted to further enhance its role both in the provision of international liquidity and in encouraging transparency, extending the steps taken following the Mexican crisis. In regard to additional liquidity, the IMF approved the Supplemental Reserve Facility (SRF) and a general capital increase. In addition, the IMF initially continued to attempt to expand its mandate to include capital account liberalization, though this was largely abandoned by the end of 1998.

On 17 December 1997, the IMF approved the SRF, renaming and modifying the EFM.[27] The facility is designed to provide financial assistance to member countries experiencing exceptional balance of payments difficulties due to large short-term financing needs resulting from sudden and disruptive losses of market confidence reflected in pressure on the capital account and reserves. Assistance under the facility is to be available in circumstances where there is a reasonable expectation that the implementation of strong adjustment policies and adequate financing will result within in a short period in an early correction of the balance of payments difficulties.

Second, on 6 February 1998, the IMF Board of Governors adopted a resolution proposing an increase of 45 per cent in total IMF quotas, equivalent to about US$90 billion. This raised the capital base of the institution to approximately SDR 212 billion (about US$288 billion).[28]

Third, as shown by the Mexican and Asian experiences, the fact that a country has had a capital outflow clearly would not preclude access to Fund resources to reconstitute its reserves, although performance criteria are included in the arrangement to avoid any substantial use of these reserves to meet capital outflows.[29] Nonetheless, an explicit recognition of the role

---

[27] "IMF Approves Supplemental Reserve Facility", IMF Press Release No. 97/59, 17 Dec. 1997.

[28] "Board of Governors Approves IMF Quota Increase", IMF Press Release No. 98/2, 6 Feb. 1998. This resolution required an 85 per cent majority vote of the total voting power of the IMF membership and did not officially take effect until members representing 85 per cent of the total quotas consented to the increase of their quotas.

[29] Gianviti, op. cit., n. 4, p. 777.

of the Fund in encouraging liberalization of capital flows not only would strengthen its mandate to act in such situations, but would broaden the sorts of mechanisms available to it under its Articles of Agreement. As a result, the management of the IMF during the 1990s sought an amendment to its Articles of Agreement to include the liberalization of capital flows as one aspect of the IMF's mandate and to broaden the institution's jurisdiction to include capital movements.[30]

One of the many lessons drawn from Mexico was that the extent of the crisis was worsened by the poor quality of information supplied to both the official sector (including the IMF) and the markets. The Asian crisis reinforced the argument for better and more timely provision of information, including information on central bank forward operations. There are two arguments in this regard: first, better informed markets are likely to make better decisions and in both Mexico and in Asia, this would have meant that markets withdrew funds sooner than they did, thereby hastening adjustment; and, second, the obligation to publish information on certain interventions would affect the extent and nature of those interventions, helping to prevent some unwise decisions. In this regard, the IMF focused on improving the SDDS and introducing a related program, the GDDS, discussed further in the next chapter.

THE WORLD BANK AND REGIONAL DEVELOPMENT BANKS. The focus of the World Bank and the regional development banks[31] (collectively "multilateral development banks") is somewhat different from that of the IMF. In general terms, the IMF can be compared to the fire brigade while the World Bank is more of a construction agency.[32] While these institutions are increasingly working together (especially the IMF and World Bank), a number of differences can be discerned. First, the multilateral development banks' focus is structural and sectoral, as compared with the IMF's traditional focus on macroeconomic aggregates. Second, the multilateral development banks' focus is more on long-term restructuring as opposed to short-term adjustment. Third, the

---

[30] M. Camdessus, "Rebuilding Confidence in Asia", Remarks by the Managing Director of the IMF 97/18, ASEAN ("Association of Southeast Asians Nations") Business Forum, Kuala Lumpur, Malaysia, 2 Dec. 1997.

[31] Multilateral regional development banks include the Inter-American Development Bank, African Development Bank, Asian Development Bank, European Bank for Reconstruction and Development, and Islamic Development Bank.

[32] S. Sandström, "The East Asia Crisis and the Role of the World Bank: Statement to the Bretton Woods Committee", Speech by the Managing Director of the World Bank, Washington, DC, 13 Feb. 1998, paras. 5–6.

multilateral development banks focus not solely on economic and financial issues, but often on a broad array of development issues (especially poverty reduction).

Following the Mexican and Asian financial crises, the division of responsibilities among these various international institutions was still somewhat tentative – a situation that continues largely to the present, though with some important developments (discussed further subsequently). Nonetheless, following the Mexican and Asian financial crises, the multilateral development banks increasingly focused on efforts to strengthen the domestic financial systems of their countries of operations, especially given that precipitous macrocrises such as those in Mexico and Asia can quickly impact the quality of their own respective loan portfolios.

**Lingering Problems.** In circumstances such as occurred during the Mexican and Asian financial crises, in which financial markets essentially ceased to function in terms of access, markets cannot be relied on to provide necessary liquidity[33], and for this reason, an international response was probably necessary for the stability of the both international and domestic financial systems during these crises and probably will be required in future crises. Given that crises of these sorts were not uncommon in developing countries during the nineteenth century, further such crises are certainly possible, if not likely, especially given that the underlying lessons of the Mexican crisis were not translated into reforms in other countries until after the Asian financial crisis, despite the clear need to do so.

In addition, the liquidity measures discussed previously are intended to greatly increase the official lending power of the IMF to deal with the sort of liquidity crises experienced by Mexico and in Asia, and enhance the IMF's capacity as a sort of lender of last resort.[34] Such an institution, however, poses the classic risk of "moral hazard" as investors may begin to rely on the international community rather than monitoring country risks themselves.[35] Further,

---

[33] According to Bank of Mexico data, for three successive weekly auctions between 27 Dec. 1994 and 10 Jan. 1995, the Mexican government was simply unable to sell tesobonos. GAO Mexico Report, op. cit., n. 1, p. 137.

[34] The theory of the lender of last resort was first set out by Walter Bagehot. He explained that if there were an institution ready to guarantee liquidity when the lending community doubted the debtor's liquidity, then commercial lenders would have confidence that new loans would be repaid. See W. Bagehot, *Lombard Street: A Description of the Money Market* (1873 [New York: John Wiley, 1999]).

[35] See R. Macmillan, "Towards a Sovereign Debt Work-out System", 16 NW. J. Int'l L. & Bus. 57 (1995), p. 63 (citing Lawrence Summers, "Summers on Mexico, Ten Lessons to Learn," Economist, 23 Dec. 1995, p. 62).

moral hazard poses high potential costs to the public sector because the capital of IMF is supplied by member governments. While the IMF tends to discount these objections[36], they are nonetheless worthy of some consideration, especially given that international financiers seem to have very short memories indeed.

Overall, one can conclude that the initial changes made following the Mexican and Asian financial crises were small steps, focusing on strengthening the financial resources of the IMF and increasing transparency of financial markets. While both were very useful, in fact, as Fischer suggested, more was required.

### 2.2.2. *Crisis Prevention and Financial Stability: Structure and Process*

In addition to liquidity and transparency issues, the second major area of concern focused on preventing financial crises through enhancing the quality of individual financial systems.

Following the Mexican financial crisis of 1994–95 and the US-led international rescue operation that it required, leaders of the developed economies recognized the need to develop mechanisms to deal with the potentially systemic dangers of such financial crises.[37] In response to an initiative at the Lyon summit of the G-7 in June 1996, representatives of the G-10 countries and of emerging and transition economies jointly sought to develop a strategy for fostering financial stability through the analysis of experiences in previous crises and to elucidate basic standards and principles to guide individual economies in the development of stronger financial systems.[38] The primary conclusion to emerge from this study was that a financial system that is robust is less susceptible to the risk of a crisis in the wake of real economic disturbances and is more resilient in the face of crises that do occur.

---

[36] Arguing that (1) no country would willingly put itself in such a position, and (2) that investors have in fact lost significant amounts of money in these crises. See M. Camdessus, "Reflections on the IMF and the International Monetary System", Address by Michel Camdessus, Managing Director of the International Monetary Fund to the Economic Club of Washington, Washington, DC, 98/6, 12 Mar. 1998.

[37] See D. Arner, "The Mexican Peso Crisis of 1994–95: Implications for the Regulation of Financial Markets", 2 NAFTA L. & Bus. Rev. 28 (1996).

[38] G-10, Report of the Group of Ten (G-10) Working Party on Financial Stability in Emerging Markets, *Financial Stability in Emerging Market Economies: A Strategy for the Formulation, Adoption and Implementation of Sound Principles and Practices to Strengthen Financial Systems*, Apr. 1997 ("G-10 Strategy (1997)"). This framework was developed further in Group of 22 Systemically Significant Countries (G-22), *Reports on the International Financial Architecture*, Oct. 1998. G-10 documents are available at the Bank for International Settlements' (BIS) website at http://www.bis.org.

This enterprise was prompted by the recognition that financial crises can have serious repercussions for economies in terms of heightened macroeconomic instability, reduced economic growth and a less efficient allocation of savings and investment.[39] In its report, the G-10 focused on three central elements necessary to the development of a robust financial system: (1) creation of an institutional setting and financial infrastructure necessary for a sound credit culture and effective market functioning; (2) promotion of functioning of markets so that owners, directors, investors, and other actual and potential stakeholders exercise adequate discipline over financial intermediaries; and (3) creation of regulatory and supervisory arrangements that complement and support market discipline.[40] The World Bank and regional development banks are given a leading role in providing technical assistance to countries seeking to build robust financial systems.

**Financial Stability.** The focus since the Mexican financial crisis has therefore come to rest on the concept of "financial stability" as the primary target in preventing financial crises and reducing the severe risks of financial problems which do occur from time to time. Financial stability, however, is not a clearly defined term. In fact, financial stability is usually more clearly defined by what it is not than by what it is: financial stability is often defined as the absence of a major financial crisis.[41] However, it also seems to be more than this: Garry Schinasi has addressed the use of the term in the literature and practice.[42] He suggests that, in general, financial stability may be defined as[43]:

> the joint stability of the key financial institutions operating within financial markets and the stability of those markets. For the financial institutions, this generally means that they are sound, meaning that they have sufficient capital to absorb normal, and at times abnormal, losses and sufficient liquidity to manage operations and volatility in normal periods of time. Market stability ... generally [means] the absence of the kind of volatility that could have severe real economic consequences [i.e., systemic risk].

[39]  Id., p. 1.
[40]  Id., pp. 3–4.
[41]  See U. Das, M. Quintyn and K. Chenard, "Does Regulatory Governance Matter for Financial System Stability? An Empirical Analysis", IMF Working Paper WP/04/89 (May 2004), pp. 5–6. As a result, they use a definition of "financial system soundness" rather than "financial stability".
[42]  See G. Schinasi, "Responsibility of Central Banks for Stability in Financial Markets", IMF Working Paper WP/03/121 (Jun. 2003).
[43]  Id., p. 4.

Financial stability is therefore both the absence of financial crisis and the normal operation of financial intermediaries and markets. Marc Quintyn and Michael Taylor go one step further, suggesting that the financial sector plays a special and unique role in an economy, and that as a result, "the achievement of **financial stability** . . . is now generally considered a **public good**."[44] With financial stability the agreed international objective, a system has been developed to assist countries to achieve this goal.

**Structure and Process.** The emerging international strategy for the development of financial stability in can be described as a system of international financial standards. The system, as it has developed, has the following primary characteristics: (1) development of an international consensus on the key elements of a sound financial and regulatory system by representatives of the relevant economies; (2) formulation of sound principles and practices by international groupings of domestic authorities with relevant expertise and experience, such as the Basel Committee, the International Accounting Standards Board, IOSCO, the International Association of Insurance Supervisors (IAIS) and the Joint Forum on Financial Conglomerates; (3) use of market discipline and market access channels to provide incentives for the adoption of sound supervisory systems, better corporate governance and other key elements of a robust financial system; and (4) promotion by multilateral institutions such as the IMF, World Bank and regional development banks of the adoption and implementation of sound principles and practices.[45] Importantly, however, the ultimate responsibility for policies to strengthen financial systems lies with governments and financial authorities in the economies concerned.

This system of international financial standards developed in response to the financial crises in the 1990s. It can broadly be described as having four levels, incorporating both existing and new international institutions and organizations. At the first level, there is a structure and process which has largely been established at a political level. At the second level, the process focuses on international standard-setting, largely at a technocratic level. At the third level, there is the process of implementation of standards – largely a domestic process but with technical assistance through a variety of international, regional and bilateral sources. At the fourth level, there is a process of monitoring the implementation of standards.

---

[44] M. Quintyn and M. Taylor, "Regulatory and Supervisory Independence and Financial Stability", IMF Working Paper WP/02/46 (Mar. 2002), p. 8 (emphasis in original).
[45] G-10 Strategy (1997), op. cit., n. 38, p. 49.

This essential structure was affirmed by the G-7 Finance Ministers in the Communiqué from their Köln summit in 1999.[46]

### 2.2.3. *Crisis Resolution: An On-Going Debate*

The second major strand of discussion concerning the international financial architecture has focused on the issue of crisis resolution. Unfortunately, while consensus has largely developed in relation to domestic reforms to support financial stability, centred on the system of international standards, similar consensus has not been reached in respect to arrangements to deal with crises which do occur. These issues are discussed in further in Chapter Nine.

### 2.3. INTERNATIONAL FINANCIAL STANDARDS AND STANDARD-SETTING ORGANIZATIONS

International standards and their development are the central element of the second level of the current system of international financial standards – the only truly new element of the international financial architecture to follow the series of financial crises over the past decade. Given that a safe and efficient financial system is absolutely essential for the functioning of any economy, the G-7 at their Lyon Summit in 1996 directed the international financial institutions and international financial organizations – especially the IMF, World Bank and Basel Committee – to develop standards for financial regulation to be implemented in developed, developing, emerging and transition economies, as well as to develop solutions for domestic crises with international implications. As a result, a wide range of institutions and organizations have been producing standards in a number of areas (discussed further subsequently and in Parts II-IV).

The only new institution to emerge from discussions of the international financial architecture is the Financial Stability Forum (FSF). The FSF was established to serve the role of coordinator in the system of international standards. The FSF also acts in some cases to establish standards. At present, the FSF has agreed a list of twelve "key standard areas", which incorporate fifteen "key standards." In addition to coordination and standard-setting through the FSF, the established international financial institutions such as the IMF, World Bank and Bank for International Settlements (BIS), have a role in standard-setting, as well as implementation and monitoring (discussed subsequently).

---

[46] G-7 Finance Ministers, *Report of the G7 Finance Ministers to the Köln Economic Summit*, Cologne, Germany, 18–20 Jun. 1999.

In addition to the international financial institutions, other formal international organizations such as the Organization for Economic Cooperation and Development (OECD) have a role, though the WTO is not formally included in the framework – a potential weakness in the existing framework (discussed further in Part V). Finally, much standard-setting takes place through various international financial organizations of varying levels of formality.

At the political level, the G-7[47] industrialized countries have taken a leading role in establishing the framework for the operation of the process. In addition, the G-10[48] have led efforts to establish the details of the operation of the process. In addition, other groups such as the Group of Twenty (G-20)[49] are also involved in various aspects. Today, the process has largely been formalized.

### 2.3.1. *Coordination*

The FSF and the BIS currently serve the primary role in coordination of the process of standard-setting.

The FSF was established under the auspices of a G-7 mandate in February 1999. Its purpose is threefold: (1) promote international financial stability; (2) improve the functioning of markets; and (3) reduce systemic risk through enhanced information exchange and international cooperation in financial market supervision and surveillance.

The FSF includes five different types of members: national authorities[50], international financial institutions[51], other international organizations[52],

---

[47] The G-7 includes Canada, France, Germany, Italy, Japan, the United Kingdom, and the United States. The Group of Eight (G-8) also includes Russia. The European Union is also included in both the G-7 and the G-8. For the best resource on the G-7/8, see http://www.g7.utoronto.ca/.

[48] The G-10 includes Belgium, Canada, France, Germany, Italy, Japan, Luxembourg, The Netherlands, Spain, Sweden, Switzerland, the United Kingdom, and the United States. Therefore, it actually includes thirteen countries.

[49] The G-20 includes the finance ministers and central bank governors of 19 countries: Argentina, Australia, Brazil, Canada, China, France, Germany, India, Indonesia, Italy, Japan, Mexico, Russia, Saudi Arabia, South Africa, South Korea, Turkey, the United Kingdom, and the United States. It also includes the European Union (Council President) and the European Central Bank (ECB), as well as (on an ex officio basis) the Managing Director of the IMF, the President of the World Bank, and the chairs of the International Monetary and Financial Committee and Development Committee of the IMF and World Bank.

[50] National authorities are the G-7 plus the ECB plus four economies, therefore: Australia, Canada, France, Germany, Hong Kong, Italy, Japan, The Netherlands, Singapore, the United Kingdom, the United States, and the ECB.

[51] BIS, IMF, World Bank.

[52] Organization of Economic Cooperation and Development (OECD).

international financial organizations[53] and committees of central bank experts.[54] In addition, the FSF has created a number of ad hoc working groups to develop recommendations on specific issues. These include: highly leveraged institutions, capital flows, offshore financial centres, implementation of standards, incentives to foster implementation of standards, deposit insurance, and e-finance.

In addition to the FSF, the BIS plays an important role in coordination. It provides the secretariat for the FSF, as well as the Basel Committee, Committee on Payment and Settlement Systems, Committee on the Global Financial System, G-10 and IAIS.

## 2.3.2. *Key Standards for Sound Financial Systems*

According to the FSF[55]:

> The 12 standard areas ... have been designated by the FSF as key for sound financial systems and deserving of priority implementation depending upon country circumstances. While the key standards vary in terms of their degree of international endorsement, they are broadly accepted as representing minimum requirements for good practice. Some of the key standards are relevant for more than one policy area, e.g. sections of the Code of Good Practices on Transparency in Monetary and Financial Policies have relevance for aspects of payment and settlement as well as financial regulation and supervision.

As noted, the FSF has agreed that twelve standards areas comprise the core; the twelve key standard areas in turn include a total of fifteen key standards (if one assumes one key standard in the key standard area of insolvency). These are grouped into three main categories: (1) macroeconomic policy and data transparency, (2) institutional and market infrastructure, and (3) financial regulation and supervision. The intention is that each set of key standards will be supported by a methodology for assessment and implementation and a variety of related principles, practices and guidelines.

The first category, macroeconomic policy and data transparency, includes three key standard areas: (1) monetary and financial policy transparency, (2)

---

[53] Basel Committee on Banking Supervision, the International Association of Insurance Supervisors (IAIS), and the International Organization of Securities Commissions (IOSCO).

[54] Committee on the Global Financial System (CGFS) and the Committee on Payment and Settlement Systems (CPSS).

[55] http://www.fsforum.org/compendium/key_standards_for_sound_financial_system.html

fiscal policy transparency, and (3) data dissemination. The first two key standard areas include one key standard each, while the third includes two key standards.

The second category, institutional and market infrastructure, includes six key standard areas: (1) insolvency, (2) corporate governance, (3) accounting, (4) auditing, (5) payment and settlement, and (6) market integrity. The second, third, and fourth areas include one key standard each. The fifth and sixth contain two key standards each. The first is still under discussion.

The third category, financial regulation and supervision, includes three key standard areas: (1) banking supervision, (2) securities regulation, and (3) insurance supervision. Each area includes one key standard.

### 2.3.3. *Standard-setting and Standard-setting Organizations*

As noted, standard-setting takes place through a range of different bodies. These can largely be grouped into international financial institutions[56], other formal international organizations[57] and international financial organizations. The international finanical organizations include a range of different forms, including regulators[58], central banks[59], professional groups[60], market associations[61], expert groups[62], and legal groups.[63]

To date, the exact processes of selecting standard areas, designating standard areas and standards as "key", selecting appropriate standard-setting organizations, and developing standards themselves are all unclear – despite the emphasis on transparency since the Mexican finanical crisis. It appears that selection and designation has been something of a bottom-up process, with standard setters selecting areas to address and promoting their respective standards to

---

[56] The international financial institutions include the IMF, World Bank and BIS.

[57] At present, the OECD. The WTO is not officially represented.

[58] Basel Committee, IAIS and IOSCO. The Financial Action Taskforce (FATF) can also be included in this category.

[59] CPSS and CGFS.

[60] These include the International Accounting Standards Board (IASB) and the International Federation of Accountants (IFAC).

[61] Market associations include the International Swaps and Derivatives Association (ISDA), the International Capital Markets Association (ICMA) and the Loan Market Association.

[62] Expert groups include the Institute of International Finance, the Group of Thirty, the Institute for International Economics and a plethora of domestic and academic research and policy institutes.

[63] Legal groups include the International Law Association, International Bar Association, the UN Commission on International Trade Law (UNCITRAL), the International Institute for the Unification of Private Law (UNIDROIT), the Hague Conference on Private International Law, and the Council of Europe.

the political groupings such as the G-7 and the international financial institutions for adoption and support. Nonetheless, a sort of standardized process for standard-setting does appear to be developing.

Standard-setting processes now appear to follow a similar pattern, with the basic elements (for both initial development and revision) appearing to be as follows: (1) networking and lobbying by potential standard setters for mandates to develop standards in various areas; (2) support through the G-7, FSF and/or other bodies for a standard development process to proceed; (3) international process of awareness building and discussion of issues; (4) multilateral technocratic cooperation in drafting; (5) support from the governing body of the standard-setting organization; (6) testing the use of standards in monitoring and implementation; (7) finalization of guidance and supporting materials; and (8) approval by the governing body of the standard-setting organization(s) and referral to other bodies such as the G-7 and/or FSF. Revisions (recently completed in some areas and on-going in others) appear to be following a similar path.

While neither formal nor overly transparent, the process of standard-setting does appear to be taking place on a multilateral political and technocratic basis, thereby resulting in standards with wide support. In addition, more recent processes have included an increasing amount of public consultation and input, enhancing the quality of and support for resulting standards.

### 2.3.4. *Compendium of Standards*

In addition to the key standards, the FSF has produced a "Compendium" of standards, which includes the fifteen key standards. The Compendium also includes the various standards which the FSF has designated as significant for financial stability and domestic implementation. The standards included in the FSF Compendium are organized under three broad headings identical to those used in respect to the twelve key standard areas. The three broad headings are, in turn, subdivided into fifteen subject areas. The fifteen subject areas include the twelve key subject areas, plus three additional areas: data compilation (under the heading of macroeconomic policy and data transparency), market functioning (under the heading of institutional and market infrastructure) and financial conglomerate supervision (under the heading of financial regulation and supervision).

As a result, the broad heading of macroeconomic policy and data transparency includes four subject areas: (1) monetary and financial policy transparency, (2) fiscal transparency, (3) data dissemination, and (4) data compilation.

The broad heading of institutional and market infrastructure includes seven subject areas: (1) insolvency, (2) corporate governance, (3) accounting, (4) auditing, (5) payment and settlement, (6) market integrity, and (7) market functioning.

The broad heading of financial regulation and supervision includes four subject areas: (1) banking supervision, (2) securities regulation, (3) insurance regulation, and (4) financial conglomerate supervision

While the FSF Compendium is a useful web-based source, it has not been updated on a regular basis, limiting its usefulness to some extent. In addition, as noted in the previous section, the exact process for inclusion is not transparent. Both of these issues are worthy of further consideration by the FSF if it wishes to increase its effectiveness and legitimacy.

## 2.4. IMPLEMENTATION AND MONITORING

An important element of the process involves monitoring the implementation of international standards around the world. Implementation is primarily a domestic process; however, it is supported by a range of assistance mechanisms. Monitoring mainly takes place at the international level through the international financial institutions, especially the IMF and World Bank. Specifically, the IMF works through its annual Article IV consultations. The Fund and the Bank work together through Reports on the Observance of Standards and Codes (ROSCs) and Financial Sector Assessment Programs (FSAPs). The OECD and FATF also engage in monitoring, with the FATF playing quite an influential role in the context of money laundering and terrorism financing.

In addition, there are a variety of regional, bilateral and market monitoring processes. At a regional level, the regional development banks[64] encourage implementation through their respective projects and reviews. In addition, regional economic associations[65] may have a role – in some cases (e.g., the European Union) a very important one. At the bilateral level, some countries (especially the United States) are keen to support the implementation of certain standards – for example, those of the FATF. Finally, at the market level, the rating agencies have shown some interest in monitoring standards, though not as much as policy makers had initially hoped.

---

[64] Chiefly, the African Development Bank, Asian Development Bank, European Bank for Reconstruction and Development, and Inter-American Development Bank.

[65] Chiefly, the European Union (EU), Association of Southeast Asian Nations (ASEAN), Mercosur, North American Free Trade Agreement (NAFTA), and Southern African Development Community (SADC)

### 2.4.1. *Implementation: A Domestic Process*

Implementation is largely a domestic process, but supported by technical assistance from a variety of sources, including international, regional, bilateral and domestic.

There are a variety of incentives for implementation, including individual state interest, international interests and market interests. Individual state self-interest includes crisis prevention and support for economic growth through improved financial system efficiency and effectiveness. International interests include prevention and reduction of contagion and support for economic growth. Market interests, while potentially the strongest incentive, have yet to become focused.

### 2.4.2. *International Financial Institutions: The Standards and Codes Initiative*

The international financial institutions (IMF, World Bank and regional development banks) have a role in both implementation and monitoring. The most significant developments in respect to both implementation and monitoring have been through the efforts of the IMF and World Bank standards and codes initiative.

The IMF and World Bank standards and codes initiative operates through two interrelated aspects: (1) ROSCs and (2) FSAPs. The IMF and World Bank ROSCs and FSAPs are perhaps one of the most important developments since the series of financial crises in the 1990s.

According to the IMF[66]:

> The standards and codes initiative is part of the international community's wider strategy for strengthening the stability of the international financial system. The initiative is designed to strengthen institutions and promote good governance and transparency thereby enhancing the accountability and credibility of policy and reducing vulnerability to crisis.

The standards and codes initiative does this through[67]:

(1) encouraging the development of internationally recognized standards in areas endorsed by the Executive Boards of the Fund and the Bank;

---

[66] IMF, "IMF Executive Board Reviews International Standards: Strengthening Surveillance, Domestic Institutions, and International Markets", IMF Public Information Notice No. 03/43 (3 Apr. 2003).

[67] IMF and World Bank, *International Standards: Strengthening Surveillance, Domestic Institutions, and International Markets*, 5 Mar. 2003, p. 6.

(2) encouraging members to adopt and implement these standards including through technical assistance; and

(3) assessing members' observance of selected standards, and producing and publishing ROSCs.

To date, the Bank and Fund have endorsed a list of twelve areas of concern, divided into three categories[68]:

(1) transparency standards: data transparency[69], fiscal transparency[70], monetary and financial policy transparency[71];

(2) financial sector standards: banking supervision[72], securities[73], insurance[74], payment and settlement systems[75], anti-money laundering and combating the financing of terrorism[76]; and

(3) standards concerned with market integrity: corporate governance[77], accounting[78], auditing[79], insolvency and creditor rights.[80]

In March 2003, the Bank and Fund reviewed experiences with 343 ROSCs produced for eighty-nine economies as of 31 December 2002 and reached a number of conclusions[81]:

(1) In relation to data and fiscal transparency, one of the most severe weaknesses of members was coverage and consistency of fiscal data, while

---

[68] See id.

[69] IMF, Special Data Dissemination Standard; idem, General Data Dissemination System (discussed in Chapter Four).

[70] IMF, Code of Good Practices on Fiscal Transparency (discussed in Chapter Three).

[71] IMF, Code of Good Practices on Transparency in Monetary and Financial Policies (discussed in Chapters Four and Eight).

[72] Basel Committee, Core Principles of Effective Banking Supervision (discussed in Chapter Six).

[73] IOSCO, Objectives and Principles of Securities Regulation (discussed in Chapter Seven).

[74] IAIS, Insurance Supervisory Principles (discussed in Chapter Seven).

[75] CPSS, Core Principles for Systemically Important Payment Systems; CPSS/IOSCO, Recommendations for Securities Settlement Systems (discussed in Chapter Four).

[76] FATF, 40 + 8 Recommendations (discussed in Chapter Five).

[77] OECD, Principles of Corporate Governance (discussed in Chapter Five).

[78] IASB, International Accounting Standards (IAS) (discussed in Chapter Five).

[79] International Federation of Accountants, International Standards on Auditing (discussed in Chapter Five).

[80] World Bank, *Principles and Guidelines for Insolvency and Creditor Rights System*, Apr. 2001; UNCITRAL, *Legislative Guide on Insolvency Law* (forthcoming). At present, the IMF, World Bank and UNCITRAL are cooperating to produce a single standard but no agreement has yet been reached.

[81] IMF and World Bank, *International Standards*, op. cit., n. 67, pp. 9-11.

another relates to quasi-fiscal and off-budget activities, especially in transition and some emerging economies.

(2) In relation to banking, political influence over banking supervision is an
important weakness in developing countries.

(3) In insurance and securities, weaknesses often reflect inadequate regulatory and supervisory systems and institutional weaknesses.

(4) In accounting and auditing, good financial reporting laws and standards
are not sufficient without robust regulatory frameworks to ensure adequate monitoring and enforcement.

(5) In corporate governance, there is often a discrepancy between laws on
the books and actual practice, with especial weakness in relation to shareholders' rights and ability of the securities regulator to enforce penalties.

(6) In insolvency, weak implementation rather than inadequate law is the
most common weakness.

As a result of the 2003 review, inter alia, the IMF Executive Board requested
that both members and the Board should receive reports that clearly identify staff views on institutional weaknesses and their significance, on progress
achieved and with explicitly prioritized recommendations.[82] This is to enable
both members and the Fund and Bank to more clearly prioritize follow-up
actions and necessary support, as well as to increase the developmental role of
the standards and codes initiative.

In addition, the Financial Sector Reform and Strengthening (FIRST) Initiative was established to provide systematic technical assistance follow-up
of ROSC/FSAP efforts, as well as financial support.[83] Further, in May 2002,
according to the IMF, the IMF and the World Bank launched a coordinated
effort to support implementation and technical assistance follow-up.[84]

**Reports on the Observance of Standards and Codes.** ROSCs review the extent
of observance of specific international standards and codes selected by the
World Bank and IMF. As of January 2007, ROSCs involving 124 economies
had been published with the consent of the relevant member.[85]

---

[82]  IMF PIN 03/43, op. cit., n. 66.
[83]  See www.firstinitiative.org.
[84]  IMF, *International Standards: Background Paper on Strengthening Surveillance, Domestic Institutions, and International Markets*, 5 Mar. 2003, p. 19.
[85]  Albania, Algeria, Antigua and Barbuda, Argentina, Armenia, Australia, Austria, Azerbaijan,
Bahrain, Bangladesh, Barbados, Belarus, Belgium, Benin, Bolivia, Bosnia and Herzegovina, Botswana, Brazil, Bulgaria, Burkina Faso, Cameroon, Canada, Chile, Colombia, Costa
Rica, Croatia, Cyprus, Czech Republic, Denmark, Dominican Republic, Ecuador, Egypt,
El Salvador, Equatorial Guinea, Estonia, Euro Area, Fiji, Finland, France, Gabon, Gambia,

In terms of structure, ROSCs generally take the following form[86]: (1) description of the member's practice, (2) an assessment against all areas of the standard and (3) prioritized recommendations.

**Financial Sector Assessment Program.** The FSAP is a joint IMF and World Bank initiative introduced in May 1999 to promote sound financial systems in member economies. Work is coordinated through the Bank-Fund Financial Sector Liaison Committee (FSLC).[87]

According to the World Bank and the IMF[88]:

> The [FSAP] is widely recognized by participating countries and by the international community as an important instrument for diagnosis of potential vulnerabilities and analysis of development priorities in the financial sectors of member countries of the [IMF] and the World Bank. . . . One objective of the FSAP is to help countries map a transition to a more diversified and competitive financial sector without creating vulnerabilities. A well-functioning financial services sector is essential for sustained economic development and poverty reduction. The existence of a wide and diversified set of sound, well-managed institutions and markets also reduces the likelihood and magnitude of a financial crisis.

The IMF goes further[89]:

> The FSAP was introduced . . . by the IMF and the World Bank to strengthen the monitoring of financial systems in the context of the IMF's bilateral surveillance and the World Bank's financial sector development work. The FSAP,

Georgia, Germany, Ghana, Greece, Guatemala, Honduras, Hong Kong, Hungary, Iceland, India, Indonesia, Iran, Ireland, Israel, Italy, Jamaica, Japan, Jordan, Kazakhstan, Kenya, Korea, Kuwait, Kyrgyzstan, Latvia, Lebannon, Lithuania, Luxembourg, Macedonia, Madagascar, Malawi, Mali, Malta, Mauritania, Mauritius, Mexico, Moldova, Mongolia, Morocco, Mozambique, Namibia, The Netherlands, New Zealand, Nicaragua, Niger, Norway, Oman, Pakistan, Panama, Papua New Guinea, Paraguay, Peru, Philippines, Poland, Portugal, Romania, Russia, Rwanda, Samoa, Saudi Arabia, Senegal, Serbia, Singapore, Slovakia, Slovenia, South Africa, South Korea, Spain, Sri Lanka, St. Vincent and the Grenadines, Sweden, Switzerland, Tajikistan, Tanzania, Thailand, Trinidad and Tobago, Tunisia, Turkey, Uganda, Ukraine, United Arab Emirates, United Kingdom, United States, Uruguay, and Zambia. See www.imf.org/external/np/rosc/rosc.asp. Some ROSCs were also published as part of FSSAs (discussed subsequently).

[86] IMF Background Paper, op. cit., n. 84, p. 6.

[87] IMF and World Bank, *Financial Sector Assessment Program – Review, Lessons, and Issues Going Forward*, 24 Feb. 2003, p. 5.

[88] Id., p. 4.

[89] IMF, "IMF Reviews Experience with the Financial Sector Assessment Program and Reaches Conclusions on Issues Going Forward", IMF Public Information Notice No. 03/46 (4 Apr. 2003).

which was developed in the wake of the financial crises in the late 1990s, is designed to help countries enhance their resilience to crises and cross-border contagion, and to foster growth by promoting financial system soundness and financial sector diversity. . . . Assessments of financial systems undertaken under the FSAP identify the strengths, risks and vulnerabilities in the financial system, and the two-way linkages between financial sector performance and the macroeconomy; ascertain the financial sector's development needs; and help national authorities design appropriate policy responses.

The Executive Boards of the Fund and the Bank reviewed the program in December 2000 and January 2001[90] and agreed on broad guidelines for continuation and further development.[91] Following its March 2003 review, based on completed assessments in forty-five economies with work underway in twenty-five more and twenty-seven additional scheduled for 2004 or later[92], the IMF Executive Board agreed that the FSAP had been generally successful in a number of respects[93]:

(1) identifying financial sector vulnerabilities and strengths,
(2) strengthening analysis of financial stability issues and development needs and priorities,
(3) providing country authorities with appropriate policy recommendations,
(4) enhancing data availability,
(5) improving assessments of financial system strengths and vulnerabilities, including by markets, and
(6) improving analyses of potential impact of financial crises on macroeconomic conditions.

In terms of structure, the FSAP includes several elements[94]: (1) systematic analysis of financial soundness indicators (FSIs) and stress tests[95]; (2) assessments of standards and codes; and (3) assessment of the broader financial

---

[90] See IMF, "IMF Reviews Experience with the Financial Sector Assessment Program (FSAP) and Reaches Conclusions on Issues Going Forward", IMF Public Information Notice no. 01/11 (5 Feb. 2001); IMF and World Bank, *Financial Sector Assessment Program (FSAP) – A Review: Lessons from the Pilot and Issues Going Forward*, 27 Nov. 2000.

[91] IMF and World Bank FSAP, op. cit., n. 87, p. 8.

[92] Id., pp. 11–12.

[93] IMF PIN 03/46, op. cit., n. 89.

[94] IMF and World Bank FSAP, op. cit., n. 87, p. 18. These are discussed in detail in IMF and World Bank, *Analytical Tools of the FSAP*, 24 Feb. 2003.

[95] See IMF, *Financial Soundness Indicators: Policy Paper*, 4 Jun. 2001; O. Evans, A. Leone, M. Gill, P. Hilbers, W. Blaschke, R. Krueger, M. Moretti, J. Nagayasu, M. O'Brien, J. Berge and D. Worrell, "Macroprudential Indicators of Financial System Soundness", IMF Occasional Paper no. 192 (Apr. 2000).

stability framework, including systemic liquidity arrangements, governance and transparency, and financial safety nets and insolvency regimes. FSAPs are usually conducted over two separate missions.[96] Following completion, an FSAP team prepares an FSAP aide-memoire presenting their findings.[97] IMF staff use the FSAP aide-memoire to prepare a Financial Sector Stability Assessment (FSSA); World Bank staff use the FSAP aide-memoire to prepare a Financial Sector Assessment (FSA). FSSAs then may be issued as ROSCs with the permission of the relevant member.

In November 2001, Bank and Fund staff and external assessors from other institutions involved in the FSAP met in Paris to assess progress to date. They reached a number of conclusions respecting areas requiring further effort, including[98]: (1) assuring consistency in assessments, (2) need for more detailed guidance on assessing actual implementation and (3) further work to measure linkages between financial sector standards and financial stability.

**International Monetary Fund.** The FSAP is used to prepare FSSAs which are included in biannual IMF Article IV surveillance activities. As of January 2007, FSSAs for seventy-five economies had been published with the consent of the relevant IMF member.[99]

In addition, while the Fund has historically not been a major provider of technical assistance, the standards and codes initiative has significantly increased the Fund's activities in this area and it is now one of its priority areas for technical assistance.[100]

**World Bank.** As noted earlier, the World Bank uses FSAP aide-memoires to prepare a FSA, which is used to support the Bank's development work

---

[96] IMF and World Bank FSAP, op. cit., n. 87, p. 25.

[97] These are not published. Prior to March 2003, FSAP teams prepared more lengthy FSAP reports.

[98] IMF and World Bank FSAP Tools, op. cit., n. 87, pp. 23–25.

[99] Albania, Algeria, Australia, Austria, Bahrain, Barbados, Belarus, Belgium, Bosnia and Herzegovina, Bulgaria, Chile, Colombia, Costa Rica, Croatia, Czech Republic, Denmark, Finland, France, Gabon, Georgia, Germany, Ghana, Greece, Hong Kong, Hungary, Iceland, Ireland, Israel, Italy, Jamaica, Japan, Kazakhstan, Kuwait, Kyrgyzstan, Latvia, Lithuania, Luxembourg, Macedonia, Madagascar, Malta, Mauritius, Mexico, Moldova, Morocco, Mozambique, The Netherlands, New Zealand, Norway, Pakistan, Philippines, Poland, Portugal, Romania, Russia, Rwanda, Saudi Arabia, Senegal, Serbia, Singapore, Slovakia, Slovenia, South Korea, Spain, Sweden, Switzerland, Tanzania, Trinidad and Tobago, Tunisia, Uganda, Ukraine, United Arab Emirates, United Kingdom, and Uruguay, plus Central African Economic and Monetary Community and Eastern Caribbean Currency Union. See www.imf.org/external/np/fsap/fsap.asp.

[100] IMF Background Paper, op. cit., n. 84, p. 17.

(especially technical assistance), including in the context of its Country Assistance Strategies.

According to the Bank, there are three reasons for its participation in the standards and codes initiative[101]:

(1) The structural and institutional underpinnings of a market economy are an important complement to sound macroeconomic policies for both successful integration with the world economy and sound development.

(2) Implementation of standards can help countries establish these foundations, in turn contributing to domestic and international financial stability.

(3) Partnership with the IMF provides the basis for a comprehensive approach and broad-based effort for the implementation of standards.

Increasingly, the Bank is attempting to integrate ROSCs, FSAPs and FSAs into its development work; however, given the decentralized nature of the institution, this has not been as easy to achieve as in the context of the more centralized IMF structure.

### 2.4.3. *Other Initiatives*

At present, other initiatives have been more limited that those of the IMF and World Bank. Regional initiatives supporting implementation and monitoring have involved the international financial institutions, regional development banks, regional financial organizations; and regional economic arrangements. These have, to date, been more limited than those of the IMF and World Bank. Bilateral initiatives addressing implementation and monitoring at present have come via two paths: (1) the bilateral aid agencies (such as the US Agency for International Development [USAID]) and (2) bilateral monitoring by individual countries, such as the United States in the context of money laundering. It has been hoped that market initiatives would provide a key incentive for economies to implement international standards and also an additional form of monitoring. While the take-up has not been as significant as had been hoped, there have been some important developments in this respect from rating agencies and investors. In addition, research is beginning to support the effectiveness of the implementation of standards in reducing financial costs.

---

[101] IMF and World Bank, *Assessing the Implementation of Standards: A Review of Experience and Next Steps*, 11 Jan. 2001, p. 26.

## 2.5. CONCLUSION

This chapter has reviewed the development and role of the international financial architecture, focusing on the impact of changes in the global financial system and the responses to the series of financial crises which have underlined these changes, emphasizing the development of international financial standards. Cally Jordan and Giovanni Majnoni[102] discuss the on-going process of financial regulatory convergence and the role of international financial standards and codes. They suggest three issues inherent in the current process: complementarity, coordination and fair representation.[103]

Problems of complementarity arise from inconsistency of implementation and interpretation across jurisdictions and the voluntary nature of compliance.[104] The latter, to some extent, is being addressed by development of the IMF and World Bank international standards initiatives (FSAP/ROSC). The former, while also being addressed by the FSAP and ROSC process, requires further research and analysis to develop appropriate approaches for individual countries with wide differences. This is an area in which regional financial arrangements may have an important role to play (discussed further in Part V).

Coordination problems arise from the proliferation of standards and standard setters.[105] While these have been addressed to some extent through the creation of the FSF, a significant issue that remains is the existence of a relationship between compliance and financial stability – an issue only just beginning to be addressed empirically. A second issue relates to problems of reaching consensus – for example, in relation to accounting standards. These issues are likely to remain, unless the architecture of the international financial system is addressed in a more coherent manner (discussed further in Part V).

Issues of fair representation arise from both the limited nature of the membership of many standard setters and from the focused nature of their membership – that is, lack of consideration of issues outside of the groups' immediate competence.[106] As a result, the standards to date are not coherent in any overall fashion – lacking a true "macro-prudential" approach to financial regulation.[107]

---

[102] C. Jordan and G. Majnoni, "Financial Regulatory Harmonization and the Globalization of Finance", World Bank Policy Research Working Paper 2919 (Oct. 2002).
[103] Id., pp. 15–16.
[104] Id., pp. 15–17.
[105] Id., pp. 20–2.
[106] Id., pp. 22–4.
[107] Id., pp. 23–4.

This has been raised especially in relation to the role of the G-7, with various recommendations for reform. Like issues of coordination, these issues should be addressed in a more coherent manner.

With these provisos, the following chapters turn to matters of detail in addressing the legal and institutional framework for financial stability and development.

# PART TWO

# FOUNDATIONS OF FINANCE

# 3

# Preconditions for and Institutional Underpinnings of Finance

Following the discussions of the role of law in economic growth, and financial stability and development in Chapter One and the role of the international financial architecture in Chapter Two, Parts III and IV of this volume discuss the elements of law and institutional infrastructure necessary for financial stability and development in the context of international financial standards and related research. In this context, Part III first looks toward preconditions for financial sector development.

In order for a financial system or, for that matter, a market economy to function, a number of preconditions must exist. Preconditions for financial sector development and economic growth rest on three pillars: the first institutional and legal; the second, largely legal; and the third, largely related to policy and implementing institutions. First, a market economy and a market-based financial system cannot exist if certain legal and institutional supports are not in place, namely a system of governance which establishes property rights and enforcement of contracts. It is also important to provide for the development of human capital; this has special connotations for the financial sector. On the basis of these institutional foundations, for a modern market-based financial system to function, a number of legal underpinnings must be available, including the means to use property rights for finance (such as collateral and leasing), law supporting companies or corporations ("company law"), and a supportive fiscal system. To support effectiveness, in addition to enforcement of contracts, the governance system should also provide a wider system of the rule of law. Third, a financial sector functions best in the context of an appropriate institutional framework for financial and macroeconomic policy directed towards financial and macroeconomic stability (Chapter Four). Policy choices, while largely outside legal and institutional concern, operate best in the context of an appropriately designed and transparent institutional framework.

At present, the system of international standards covers only the transparency aspects of the third area (macroeconomic policy), categorized (by the Financial Stability Forum [FSF], the International Monetary Fund [IMF] and the World Bank) as "macroeconomic policy and data transparency". This is despite the fact that over the past fifty years an immense literature has developed on the policy aspects of macroeconomic management[1], which is beyond the scope of this volume. However, as noted earlier, the institutional framework in and through which policy decisions are taken and implemented is important to the effectiveness of policy. In this context of the institutional environment for macroeconomic policy, the FSF includes four areas: (1) monetary and financial policy transparency, (2) fiscal policy transparency, (3) data dissemination and (4) data compilation. The first, second and third headings include "key standards for financial sector development".

In addition to these, appropriate mechanisms for payment and settlement and government securities markets are essential for both financial stability and development as well as implementation of macroeconomic policy. Payment and settlement are addressed by two FSF key standards. In addition, the FSF compendium includes "market functioning" (essentially, government securities markets) as a major area (though not a "key" area).

Prudential regulation and market transparency are central to a viable financial system; these are discussed further in Part IV. However, supervision and regulation are only important if participants actually engage in financial transactions. Accordingly, laws promoting prudential regulation and market transparency must be supported by the development of effective legal and institutional infrastructures that foster, in practical terms, financial and other transactions. In addition to a sound public law regulatory framework, private law must provide a means for participating in financial transactions and for enforcing rights with respect to transactions.

These sorts of issues have not been addressed in any coherent fashion until very recently. The result has been that these issues were not given significant attention in emerging, transition and developing economies until the mid-1990s, largely because they existed already in the developed economies and hence were often ignored or assumed in the context of financial research looking to the developed country context. In practical terms, however, the underlying legal and institutional infrastructure should have been addressed at an early stage; the reality, however, has been a general emphasis on larger macroeconomic issues until the mid-1990s rather than institutional and supporting (microstructural) issues.

---

[1]  See e.g., G. Mankiw, *Macroeconomics*, 5th ed. (New York: Worth, 2003).

Without these, a sophisticated market economy cannot exist; likewise, a market-based financial system will not exist. As a result, without these key underlying elements, macroeconomic policy, data transparency and the supporting institutional framework are largely meaningless, at least if the goal is a functioning market-based financial system.

This part looks at each of these preconditions. Chapter Three first discusses foundation issues, including governance, property rights and enforcement of contracts, as well as human capital formation. It then addresses the core legal supports: use of property rights, company law, taxation and the rule of law. Chapter Four discusses the institutional framework for macroeconomic and fiscal policy and the role of central banks, including in relation to payment systems and government securities markets. Chapter Five in turn addresses additional aspects of financial infrastructure such as insolvency and market integrity.

### 3.1. PRECONDITIONS FOR FINANCIAL SECTOR DEVELOPMENT AND ECONOMIC GROWTH

Based on the experiences of law reform efforts, lessons gained from recent international financial crises and the extensive literature on the topic, core areas of the legal infrastructure necessary for the development of functioning decentralized financial markets and the creation of a sound business environment can be identified. No overall international consensus has evolved in respect of these preconditions, though there have been some important developments, both in the literature and in the development of standards in some areas. While it is also a priority for emerging, transition and developing economies to develop appropriate institutional frameworks for financial and macroeconomic policy (discussed in Chapter Four), these policies must be strengthened and supported by the development of an environment of effective laws and institutions. Indeed, experiences in countries around the world have shown that in the context of potentially very lucrative investments (e.g., in the energy sector), the legal and institutional environment can, in fact, be as, if not more, important than the existence of a stable macroeconomic framework.

While the following list is by no means exhaustive, these core areas are of great importance and, when combined with an appropriate "second level" of financial regulation and supervision discussed in Part III, create the necessary environment for the development of viable (basic and functional) financial markets. Part IV in turn addresses the various legal and institutional areas which are necessary for developed and sophisticated financial markets to function properly.

First, a system of governance must be established which provides for basic public order and security, property rights and their protection, and enforcement of contracts, as well as supporting the development of human capital. Without basic public order and security, economic growth and financial development are extremely challenging, to say the least. In addition, clear and defined property rights must be established as a fundamental precondition to economic growth and financial development. The creation of property rights is, of course, a cornerstone of the transition process; it is also fundamental to the development of any market-based financial and economic system. In many ways, without the creation of property rights, market-based economic development or transition is not possible. A system which protects property rights and supports binding and enforceable contracts is necessary in order for financial activity to develop beyond close networks and instantaneous transactions. Investment is predicated on property rights and binding and enforceable contracts, without which parties cannot effectively structure their transactions.

In addition to property rights, their protection and contract enforcement, a governance system also needs to support development of human capital. Human capital development, however, without public order, property rights, their protection and enforcement of contracts, is not sufficient for economic development. One needs to go no further than the example of the Soviet Union for a clear illustration of human capital development without property rights and enforcement of contracts. The detioration of Zimbabwe over the past ten years also shows how quickly deteriorations in the institutional and macroeconomic environment can prevent decades of human capital formation from functioning to support economic development.

In addition to a sound public law regulatory framework, private law must provide individual investors with a means for participating in financial transactions and for enforcing their rights with respect to their investments. The basic functions of the legal/judicial framework in supporting the financial system are: first, to establish clearly the rights, responsibilities and liabilities of the parties to transactions; second, to establish codes to support market forces in maintaining appropriate incentives and adequate information; and third, to provide means to protect rights and enforce legal obligations and claims efficiently. All of these have the effect of reducing transaction costs and market failures. These features may be referred to as institutional infrastructure for the provision of finance.

### 3.1.1. *Governance*

Issues of governance and appropriate political structure have been of central concern to writers probably since the development of the first stationary, agricultural civilizations more than ten thousand years ago and the consequent development of writing systems necessary to support their administrative and governance structures. Building the perfect society and the necessary governance system to achieve this has been a central focus of Plato, Confucius, Thomas Aquinas, John Locke and Karl Marx, among others. While not always considered by the major political theorists, the political system and the economic system work closely together. Certainly, the relationship between politics or governance and the economy has been a key interest of Adam Smith, as well as Marx, and more recently, John Maynard Keynes, Friedrich Hayek and Milton Friedman. In fact, Smith and Marx certainly viewed themselves as "political economists", rather than solely as economists. While politics and economics became quite separate disciplines across the twentieth century, by the end of the twentieth century, the interactions between governance and economics were once again being addressed, at least partially as a result of the lessons learned through the process of transition from centrally planned to market economies, as well as failures of development models focusing largely on economic policy.

The transition process itself, of course, is the result of the end of the competition between two models of political economic structure over much of the twentieth century: capitalism and communism. As described by Daniel Yergin and Joseph Stanislaw[2], the twentieth century was a battle of ideas, specifically a battle between two different models of the role of the government in the economy, with the capitalist models focusing on the fundamental role of markets with limited government involvement and the communist models focusing on central planning combined with state ownership and control. The reality was that, following Hegel, to some extent the dichotomy resulted in a new synthesis – the regulatory state (or as described by Jeffry Frieden, "organized capitalism"[3]). Even though the capitalist model had clearly proven superior to the communist model by the end of the 1980s, the state has assumed a much larger role in the economy than a century ago. Even in market-based systems, the state obtained an increasing role until the end of the 1970s, with another conflict of ideas between those based on Keynes on the one hand and Hayek and Friedman on the other. Today, the regulatory state takes a wide role in the economy, with a range of different systems around the world, though there

[2]  D. Yergin and J. Stanislaw, *The Commanding Heights: The Battle Between Government and the Marketplace that Is Remaking the Modern World* (New York: Simon & Schuster, 1998).

[3]  See J. Frieden, *Global Capitalism: Its Fall and Rise in the Twentieth Century* (New York: W.W. Norton, 2006), esp. 276–77 (arguing that World War II was a conflict between fascist and capitalist democracy models and that the period following World War II was a conflict between communism and social democracy, resulting in the synthesis of "organized capitalism" by the early 1990s).

has been an increasing realization, likewise by the end of the 1980s, that the role of the state should limited in many contexts. All the various models of the regulated market economy, however, are somewhere between the rather idealistic models of laissez-faire and central control.

By the beginning of the 1990s, central planning, state ownership and control on one hand, and laissez-faire on the other, had merged into general consensus on the superiority of a market economy operating in the context of an appropriate regulatory system to address the interests of the society as a whole through the provision of public goods. Nonetheless, as Andre Shleifer and others have recognized, there are many differences among the various economic and governance models around the world.[4] The question naturally arises as to what are the best choices among the options available. This question has become more important as economies have re-opened and reintegrated in the past twenty to thirty years (the process of economic and financial globalization), which has raised questions of competitiveness of different models. The impact of globalization will be discussed in more detail in Part V.

For new institutional economists such as North and many law and economics writers, regardless of its ideological basis and consequent form, the governance system needs to provide for two fundamental features in order to support a market economy. First, the governance system needs to provide for clear and useable property rights. Second, the governance system needs to provide for a system to protect property rights and enforce contracts. Both sets of literature agree that these are necessary in the context of imperfect markets where transaction costs exist. In addition to these, the governance structure must provide a minimum level of public security and order – clearly, the most difficult environment for economic growth and development to occur is in the midst of internal conflict and civil strife. While these basic points appear to be agreed, the type of governance structure which best provides these three foundations for a market economy is not.

Many have argued (often because it was what they wanted to prove) that democratic models of governance are also the best at providing and protecting property rights and enforcement of contracts. However, Mancur Olson has presented a convincing argument that a variety of governance structures can provide both of these necessary features.[5] Specifically, he argued that an autocrat with a sufficiently long-term time horizon has strong incentives to

---

4   See S. Djankov, E. Glaeser, R. La Porta, F. Lopez-de-Silanes & A. Shleifer, "The New Comparative Economics", J. Comp. Econ. (Dec. 2003).

5   M. Olson, *Power and Prosperity: Outgrowing Communist and Capitalist Dictatorships* (New York: Basic Books, 2000).

support both property rights and enforcement of contracts out of economic self-interest – maximizing income through taxation. Likewise, he argued a democracy, while also potentially providing for property rights, their protection and enforcement of contracts, has the potential to result in less efficient outcomes due to the operation of interest groups within the society. As a result, neither autocracy nor democracy is necessarily a superior political system from the standpoint of supporting a market economy – what is necessary is a "market-augmenting government".[6] Anecdotal evidence certainly supports Olson's theory.[7] Further, recent empirical research has begun to test his ideas and appears to be supportive as well.[8]

North sums up the interaction between the political system and property rights[9]:

> Broadly speaking, political rules in place lead to economic rules, though the causality runs both ways. That is, property rights and hence individual contracts are specified and enforced by political decision-making, but the structure of economic interests will also influence the political structure. In equilibrium, a given structure of property rights (and their enforcement) will be consistent with a particular set of political rules (and their enforcement). Changes in one will induce changes in the other.

The result is that the governance structure is important in that it must provide for property rights, their protection and enforcement of contracts, as well as public order and human capital development. However, while some governance structures are clearly not conducive to such ends (e.g., short-term autocrats who behave essentially as stationary bandits), there is no clearly preferable model at present from the standpoint of economic growth. Both autocratic and democratic governance systems can support a market economy. Likewise, both can also provide for institutional choices which do not result in efficient, wealth-maximizing outcomes for a given economy.[10]

---

[6] C. Cadwell, "Foreword", in Olson, op. cit., n. 5, p. x.

[7] Cf. China, Singapore.

[8] See E. Glaeser, R. La Porta, F. Lopez-de-Silanes & A. Shiefer, "Do Institutions Cause Growth?", NBER Working Paper no. 10568 (Jun. 2004). The authors argue that policies are more important than democratic institutions, specifically: (1) human capital is a more basic source of growth than democratic political institutions; (2) poor countries get out of poverty through good policies, often pursued by dictators; and (3) democratic institutions are developed after economic take-off.

[9] D. North, *Institutions, Institutional Change and Economic Performance* (Cambridge: Cambridge University Press, 1990), p. 48.

[10] For the best discussion to date, see D. Acemoglu & J. Robinson, *Economic Origins of Dictatorship and Democracy* (New York: Cambridge University Press, 2006).

is, property that cannot be used as capital.[15] Second, capital itself is difficult to define.[16] Third, governments around the world have missed the importance of (1) and (2)[17]; this is now changing and needs to change faster.[18] Fourth, the process which is taking place in emerging, transition and developing economies around the world has, in fact, taken place in the developed countries, but has been poorly understood and documented.[19] Fifth, laws have to reflect

[15] According to de Soto, most developing countries are filled with "dead" capital:

> It is a world where ownership of assets is difficult to trace and validate and is governed by no legally recognizable set of rules; where the assets' potentially useful economic attributes have not been described or organized; where they cannot be used to obtain surplus value through multiple transactions because their unfixed nature and uncertainty leave too much room for misunderstanding, faulty recollection, and reversal of agreement – where most assets, in short, are dead capital.

Id., p. 32.
Such

> [d]ead capital exists because we have forgotten (or perhaps never realized) that converting a physical asset to generate capital – using your house to borrow money to finance an enterprise, for example – requires a very complex process. . . . [C]apital is the result of discovering and unleashing potential energy from the trillions of bricks that the poor have accumulated in their buildings. . . . [W]e seem to have forgotten the process that allows us to obtain capital from assets. The result is that 80 per cent of the world is undercapitalized; people cannot draw economic life from their buildings (or any other asset) to generate capital.

Id., p. 40.
[16] "What creates capital in the West . . . is an implicit process buried in the intricacies of its formal property systems." Id., p. 46. De Soto proceeds:

> In the West, this formal property system begins to process assets into capital by describing and organizing the most economically and socially useful aspects about assets, preserving this information in a recording system – as insertions in a written ledger or a blip on a computer disk – and then embodying them in a title. A set of detailed and precise legal rules governs this entire process. Formal property records and titles thus represent our shared concept of what is economically meaningful about any asset.

Id., pp. 46–7.
[17] Id., p. 83.
[18] De Soto states this best:

> The substantial increase of capital in the West over the past two centuries is the consequence of gradually improving property systems, which allowed economic agents to discover and realize the potential in their assets, and thus to be in a position to produce the noninflationary money with which to finance and generate additional production.

Id., p. 65.
[19] Once again, de Soto's words make the point:

> A modern government and a market economy are unviable without an integrated formal property system. Many of the problems of non-Western markets today are due mainly to the fragmentation of their property arrangements and the unavailability of standard norms that allow assets and economic agents to interact and governments to rule by law

Id., p. 72.

existing circumstances in order to function effectively to transform assets into capital.[20]

According to de Soto[21]:

> A well-integrated legal property system in essence does two things: First, it tremendously reduces the costs of knowing the economic qualities of assets by representing them in a way that our senses can pick up quickly; and second, it facilitates the capacity to agree on how to use assets to create further production and increase the division of labor.

De Soto argues that formal property systems should produce six effects allowing their citizens to generate capital[22]:

(1) fixing the economic potential of assets[23],
(2) integrating dispersed information into one system[24],
(3) making people accountable[25],
(4) making assets fungible[26],
(5) networking people[27], and
(6) protecting transactions.[28]

Property rights and their identification and protection therefore are clearly essential to a market economy. Unfortunately, as de Soto suggests, property rights have evolved in the developed economies over a significant period, and it is difficult to discern how they are established and function. As a result, it is not simple to transport these experiences and systems to emerging, transition and developing economies.

---

[20] Id., p. 157.
[21] Id., p. 63.
[22] Id., pp. 49–62.
[23] Id., pp. 49–51 (emphasis in original).
[24] Id., p. 52.
[25] Id., p. 55.
[26] "By providing standards, Western formal property systems have significantly reduced transaction costs of mobilizing and using assets." Id., p. 58.
[27] "Property's real breakthrough is that it radically improved the flow of communications about assets and their potential. It also enhanced the status of their owners, who became economic agents able to transform assets within a broader network." Id., p. 59.
[28] "Although they are established to protect both the security of ownership and that of transactions, it is obvious that Western systems emphasize the latter. Security is principally focused on producing trust in transactions so that people can more easily make their assets lead a parallel life as capital." Id., p. 62.

To do these things, de Soto suggests a process he calls the "capitalization process". This capitalization process is divided into two main strategies[29]: (1) discovery and (2) political[30] and legal.[31]

While de Soto's analysis primarily focuses on identification and allocation of property rights to real property (land and buildings), property rights should also extend to other forms of property such as moveable, personal and intellectual property – an area receiving increasing attention around the world.[32]

Property rights, while essential, are not the end of the story: those property rights must be protected from abuse and must also be usable other than in instantaneous transactions. This is the subject of the following part of this sub-section and the following section.

### 3.1.3. *Enforcement of Contracts, Protection of Property Rights and Resolution of Commercial Disputes*

Ronald Coase laid the foundation for the importance of enforcement of contracts.[33] In an environment of imperfect markets where transaction costs exist, parties will seek to reach efficient results through contracting.[34] Unfortunately, transaction costs extend to costs of enforcement and if enforcement does not exist, then contracting cannot produce solutions to imperfections nor lead to

---

[29] See id., pp. 160–1, fig. 6.1. See also www.ild.org.pe.
[30] In de Soto's words:

> Nobody planned the evolution from feudal and patrimonial systems to the modern property systems that exist in the West today. However, on the long evolutionary path to modernity, in those stretches of the journey when reformers embarked on deliberate programs to make property more accessible to a wider range of citizens, these programs were successful because they were supported by well-thought-out political strategies.

De Soto, op. cit., n. 12, p. 188.
[31] Id., p. 187.
[32] L. Klapper, L. Laeven and R. Rajan, "Business Environment and Firm Entry: Evidence from International Data", World Bank Policy Research Working Paper 3232 (Mar. 2004), pp. 27–8.
[33] R. Coase, "The Problem of Social Cost", 17 J. L. & Econ. 53 (1960); idem, "The Nature of the Firm", 4 Economica 386 (1937).
[34] According to North:

> The costliness of information is the key to the costs of transacting, which consist of the costs of measuring the valuable attributes of what is being exchanged and the costs of protecting rights and policing and enforcing agreements. These measurement and enforcement costs are the sources of social, political, and economic institutions.

North (1990), op. cit., n. 9, p. 27.

longer-term outcomes. Rather, transactions will be limited to instantaneous transactions, as in, for example, a souk or bazaar.[35]

In addition to enforcement of contracts, property rights also must be protected from abuse to provide meaning to their existence. Further, there must be effective means for resolving commercial disputes in a fair and transparent manner.

Protection of property rights, enforcement of contracts and resolution of commercial disputes require a governance system which is capable of producing, applying and policing results. As noted earlier, a range of governance systems should be capable of producing this economic function and, in fact, history has shown many different examples.

Mere protection of property rights, enforcement of contracts and commercial dispute resolution mechanisms, however, are not equivalent to the existence of the rule of law; rather, they represent one component of an entire system which can be described by that term. The rule of law, while significant for economic development and more so for financial development, is not strictly necessary for a market economy to exist. Rather, only a governance system which protects property rights, enforces contracts and provides an effective means of commercial dispute resolution is absolutely required for a basic market economy and simple finance to develop beyond single instantaneous transactions.

Clearly, this is a major area of concern for many developing, transition and emerging economies around the world, and also one of great difficulty to address in many cases. Ideally, an economy should have a rule of law system including an effective, noncorrupt and independent judiciary to provide protection of property rights, enforcement of contracts and resolution of commercial disputes. However, this is much easier to say than to deliver. While a system of the rule of law should be an objective in any market economy, the reality is that other alternatives may have to be pursued as interim solutions in order to support economic growth and financial development. Three main examples of alternative arrangements for protection of property rights, enforcement of contracts and commercial dispute resolution include self-enforcing mechanisms, commercial arbitration and specialized commercial courts.

Self-enforcement is frequently viewed as an alternative to be avoided: examples include such mechanisms as intimidation, organized criminal behaviour and violence. At the same time, however, self-enforcement mechanisms have a long history in developed economies and are being tried increasingly in weaker institutional environments. Examples include provisions in laws allowing for

[35] De Soto, op. cit., n. 12, p. 71.

seizure of collateral without prior recourse to the legal system as well as strict legal rules not subject to court interpretation or action.[36] Such mechanisms require careful thought and implementation through appropriately designed laws and rules or other systems, but can be effective in weak institutional environments where judicial action is inconsistent or worse.

Another mechanism is commercial arbitration. Commercial arbitration can provide a means through which property rights can be protected, contracts enforced and commercial disputes resolved outside of the judicial system but within a framework of clear, transparent rules by independent arbitrators. The value of commercial arbitration can be seen from its success in developed economies (where it is often viewed as a more efficient system than judicial dispute resolution). Likewise, an appropriately designed commercial arbitration system may provide an alternative to the formal judicial system in weaker institutional environments present in many developing, transition and emerging economies. In this context, while there is no identified FSF standard, useful guidance is available in the form of the United Nations Commission on International Trade Law (UNCITRAL) Model Law on International Commercial Conciliation with Guide to Enactment and Use.[37] The UNCITRAL Model Law has become the international standard for jurisdictions seeking to develop commercial arbitration. At the same time, for such a system to be effective, it must be tailored to the circumstances of the individual economy and also supported by the existence of qualified arbitrators.

Finally, in more developed institutional environments which nonetheless suffer from concerns about the overall quality and effectiveness of judicial arrangements, an option may be to develop a commercial court system. Essentially, where it is not immediately possible to ensure effective judicial protection of property rights, enforcement of contracts and resolution of commercial disputes via the general court system, an alternative may be to develop a separate, specialized commercial court system to deal with commercial issues. This is an approach that has been adopted in a number of developed economies in order to ensure that appropriate expertise is available to address complex commercial issues as they arise. In some cases, there may be a variety of different specialized courts, for instance courts dealing only with insolvency or taxation matters. Specialized commercial courts are often an alternative explored in developing, transition and emerging economies as well. In such cases, an

---

[36] For the genesis of the latter, see B. Black and R. Kraakman, "A Self-Enforcing Model of Corporate Law", 109 Harv. L. Rev. 1911 (1996).

[37] (2002). Available at the UNCITRAL (United Nations Commission on International Trade Law) website at www.uncitral.org.

initial issue may arise as to whether or not such a system is, in fact, in line with the existing legal system (for instance, there may be constitutional or other concerns, especially in civil law jurisdictions). At the same time, developing an effective commercial court system requires that such system be designed to operate on rule of law principles (discussed further subsequently) and is adequately resourced and supported.

### 3.1.4. *Human Capital Development*

In financial sector development, adequate human resources play a fundamental role. In this context, three main aspects can be identified: (1) individual savers and investors, (2) financial sector professionals and (3) government/regulatory personnel.

Individuals need to have an understanding of finance and especially the risks involved: this is necessary not only to encourage participation in the formal financial system but also to minimize risks of fraud and financial abuse. In respect to participation, greater understanding of the role of finance and its potential benefits serves to increase confidence of individuals and firms in the financial system, thereby increasing supply of financial resources and also demand for formal finance (as opposed to reliance on often expensive informal financing mechanisms, such as moneylenders). At the same time, the financial system and unsophisticated participants run a much higher risk of abuse from predatory participants, for instance from fraudulent investment schemes. The risks of large-scale abuse of unsophisticated participants in the financial system may cause not only the loss of savings but also, in some cases, social and political unrest. An example of the latter was seen in the mid-1990s in Albania, when a series of pyramid schemes defrauded a large percentage of the population of their savings, leading to complete loss of confidence in the financial system, economy and government, and resulting in economic, financial and political turmoil.

In relation to financial sector professionals, development of finance and financial intermediaries requires skilled professionals, especially accountants (to support financial information) and lawyers and judges (to support protection of property rights, contract enforcement and commercial dispute resolution). Such professionals require not only appropriate academic training – for example, through secondary and tertiary education systems – but also appropriate professional training and monitoring, usually as part of an organized self-regulatory professional association. Further, as finance becomes more sophisticated, there is a continual need for more skilled financial professionals. Beyond specialized professionals, finance develops best in an environment where there exist active and independent media coverage and analysis (i.e., a free commercial and financial press).

In relation to government and regulatory personnel, as this volume demonstrates, financial regulation is an increasingly complex subject, both to minimize risks and to maximize benefits to any economy. As a result, government and regulatory personnel, especially those dealing directly with financial sector issues such as staff of the ministry of finance, central bank and regulatory agencies, require understanding of both the policy environment for finance and the practical context in which transactions and risks develop. Such capacity requires secondary and tertiary education and often international exposure as well.

In looking at the needs for human capital development in the financial sector, three significant levels stand out: (1) secondary education, (2) professional and tertiary education and (3) public awareness efforts. Secondary education should lay a foundational understanding of finance, necessary for the general public. Tertiary and professional education must provide additional specialized knowledge for finance professionals and government personnel, as well as ensure an adequate number of quality accounting and legal professionals necessary to support market functioning. In addition, public awareness efforts are necessary to develop an understanding of the financial system and its benefits and risks among the public and also to highlight important changes and developments over time.

## 3.2. INSTITUTIONAL UNDERPINNINGS OF FINANCE

Once the foundations of a governance structure supporting property rights, enforcement of contracts and human resource development are in place, one can expect basic financial transactions and markets to develop, even in a problematic macroeconomic environment. In order to develop functioning financial markets, an economy must provide a number of fundamental institutional tools to underpin financial sector development, including mechanisms supporting use of property rights for finance, company law and an appropriate system of taxation.

In addition, recent research supports the view that excessive regulation of business hampers economic growth. For example, Leora Klapper, Luc Laeven and Raghuram Rajan have supported this view[38] and this is now an important focus for the World Bank through its World Business Environment Survey.[39] Nonetheless, as discussed earlier and in the remainder of this volume, some

---

[38] Klapper, Laeven and Rajan, op. cit., n. 32.
[39] See http://www.ifc.org/ifcext/economics.nsf/Content/ic-wbes.

regulations are important – especially those that enhance property rights, including intellectual property – and lead to a better developed and more stable financial sector.[40]

First, adequate lending infrastructure, including secured transactions law, is necessary to the development of banks and banking.[41] The role of an adequate lending infrastructure was at the heart of financial problems in east Asia and Mexico in the 1990s. A proper legal framework for lending encourages extended loan duration, improves currency matches and enhances the development of domestic finance. In addition to basic use of property rights to provide collateral, other mechanisms such as leasing can also mobilize property-based finance.

Second, law supporting companies or corporations is essential for the development of a modern market-based financial system[42] and arguably fundamental to aggregation of capital necessary for economic growth and development.

Third, an effective fiscal system to support government provision of public goods (such as those discussed in the previous section), including fair and reasonably predictable tax laws, is essential to supplement other legal infrastructure and to clarify the role of the government in any economy.[43] A sustainable fiscal system including fair and reasonably predictable tax laws is an absolute necessity both for the adequate functioning of domestic governments and for the encouragement of investment and growth. The negative impact of Russia's unclear and ineffective tax system on financial development was generally recognized; likewise, the effectiveness of its reform and simplification (although many issues remain) has been significant. While taxation issues are largely beyond the scope of this volume, governments must have in place an appropriate system of taxation and fiscal management (of which markets for government debt have a particular importance, discussed further in Chapters Four and Seven). The systems should be designed to be understandable, even in application, and not provide significant disincentives to private economic activity, including finance.

Finally, in order to support broader and sophisticated financial development, the rule of law is important. The rule of law is a broader issue than merely enforcing contracts and goes to the process by which governance and the legal system operate in a given jurisdiction. The issues addressed in the transparency

[40]  See id.
[41]  See EBRD, *Model Law on Secured Transactions*, 1994; see also J. Norton and M. Andenas (eds), *Emerging Financial Markets and Secured Transactions* (London: Kluwer, 1998).
[42]  See OECD, *General Principles of Company Law in Transition Economies*, 1997.
[43]  See IMF, *Code of Good Practices on Fiscal Transparency*, Apr. 1998.

codes discussed in Chapter Four, as well as the rules of the WTO (discussed in Chapter Eight), reflect many of these ideas.

With these elements in place, one can expect the development of a functional financial system, with finance receiving significant support from the existence of an appropriate financial and macroeconomic policy framework (discussed in the following chapter). Developed and sophisticated financial systems require greater attention to the issues discussed in Parts III and IV, as well as to an appropriate macroeconomic policy environment.

### 3.2.1. *Use of Property Rights*

Adequate lending infrastructure is based on the problem of mismatches between lending and borrowing ("duration") and information costs ("asymmetric information" and "moral hazard"). Adequate lending infrastructure essentially enables lenders to extend the time horizon of their loans and reduce costs of capital through providing greater confidence in regard to security of repayment ("credit risk"). In this regard, two aspects of lending infrastructure are especially important for risk management: an effective system for taking security; and the development of improved sources of information through accounting, auditing, credit rating systems and/or agencies, and credit information systems (all discussed in Chapter Five). In addition, financial intermediaries need to have systems to manage risks appropriately, typically imposed through capital and other prudential regulatory systems (discussed in Part IV).

As the basic level of risk management, an effective system for the taking of security allows lenders to use collateral to reduce credit risk and, further, to be more confident that they will be able to realize different forms of collateral taken to support loans. Providing a system of registering and taking security therefore provides two functions for lenders: first, it allows them to reduce monitoring costs because their investment is protected; and second, it provides greater certainty in making lending decisions, thereby increasing the number of such decisions that will be made.

In order to be able to transform property rights into capital, one must be able to use those property rights to support finance. At its simplest level, one needs to be able to use property as collateral or security for lending. Collateral or security is the simplest form of risk management in lending: one loans money on the basis of being provided with property of equivalent or greater value. If the loan is not repaid, then the lender retains the property and thereby protects against the credit risk of the borrower. Collateral therefore encourages lending. However, for this simple secured transaction to take place, the lender needs to know that if the borrower defaults, it can retain the property. In order for this to be certain, the borrower must actually own the property; the legal system must also allow for transfer of ownership. In addition, the lender must have some way to value the security provided. This is not as simple as it sounds and has been problematic in developed economies, as well as emerging, transition and developing economies, usually in the context of lending secured by real property.

More advanced collateral-based lending or secured transactions involve increasingly sophisticated distinctions concerning property rights and security of contract enforcement, which derive from the legal and institutional framework available. For example, in the transaction described earlier, the borrower provided actual physical collateral to secure his indebtedness to the lender – for example, gold or a piece of machinery. This is collateral at its simplest. Use of collateral in securing transactions advances only to the level supported by the legal and institutional framework for the reasons presented earlier. If the legal system supports it, one can use not only physical collateral placed in the actual possession of the lender, but also physical collateral which remains in the possession of the borrower. In this way, a borrower could use real property (perhaps his house) while retaining use thereof. Clearly, this is an advantage to the borrower, in that he can borrow money, while at the same time retaining possession and use of his physical assets, such as his house and/or productive machinery. At the next level, the loan could be used to purchase a piece of real property or productive machinery, with the loan actually secured by the asset purchased, of which the borrower could retain use, perhaps to generate income to repay the loan. Each additional level of complexity, however, requires an additional level of legal sophistication in order to function.

Beyond physical property (which could be real or moveable – moveable property typically requires an additional level of legal development beyond real property) which, in fact, underlies the largest portion of lending in most emerging and developed economies, one may also be able to use intangible property – for instance, intellectual property or receivables – as collateral. In addition, one can merely use certain property rights, for instance all property rights – the English floating charge – or the right to receive income rather than the income itself, once again, if the legal system provides sufficient legal support.

Basic finance is greatly enhanced as the availability of collateral increases. Functional financial systems certainly require at a minimum use of real property left in the possession of the borrower. Developed financial systems typically operate with a wide range of collateral. Likewise, sophisticated financial systems require sophisticated security – for instance, in the context of securitization. Nonetheless, issues continue to exist even in sophisticated financial systems.[44]

De Soto recognizes that for property to support development, it must be allowed to work as collateral. However, he fails to distinguish between the separate legal and institutional issues concerning property (which he addresses in his "capitalization process") and the use of property as collateral (which he does not, except to the extent that the way in which property rights are recorded, for instance through a registry system, support the use of property as collateral). In fact, it is the combination of property and a framework supporting use of property and property rights as collateral (i.e., secured transactions) that results in the creation of capital.[45] As a result, building on de Soto's work, property rights need to exist, but property rights also have to be usable to support finance if finance is to develop beyond the basic level.

Unfortunately, despite the importance of collateral and secured transactions, this is an area where there are many differences between legal systems and which is highly technical in a developed system. Perhaps as a result, secured transactions have received some international attention, but typically only the advanced levels, which would concern emerging economies which already have systems supporting more basic secured transactions. For transition and developing economies, as property rights are developed, especially in real property, there is a directly related need to support the use of those property rights in basic secured transactions. Once such transactions are supported by a legal and institutional system (e.g., in an emerging economy), then it is very useful to work to develop the legal and institutional support for more advanced secured transactions.

---

[44] One that has been receiving considerable attention recently is the issue of using securities held in accounts with intermediary institutions. See Hague Conference on Private International Law, Convention on the Law Applicable to Certain Rights in respect of Securities held with an Intermediary (20 Aug. 2004). See also J. Benjamin and M. Yates, *The Law of Global Custody*, 2nd ed. (London: Butterworths, 2002).

[45] Bagehot hints at the distinction but likewise does not quite make the connection:

The 'credit' of a person – that is, the reliance which may be placed on his pecuniary fidelity – is a different thing from his property. No doubt, other things being equal, a rich man is more likely to pay than a poor man. But on the other hand, there are many men not of much wealth who are trusted in the market, 'as a matter of business,' for sums much exceeding the wealth of those who are many times richer. A firm or person who have [sic.] been long known to 'meet their engagements,' inspire a degree of confidence not dependent on the quality of his or their property.

W. Bagehot, *Lombard Street: A Description of the Money Market* (1873 [New York: John Wiley, 1999]), p. 283.

**Real Property.** Recent research supports the view that such a system of finance based upon real estate is, in fact, fundamental to financial and economic development.[46] Specifically, in a 1999 World Bank study, Frank Byamugisha develops a theoretical and conceptual framework to guide the empirical analysis of the effects of real estate finance on the economy as a whole.[47] He argues that the conceptual framework linking real estate finance to financial development and economic growth has five key linkages: (1) the land tenure security and investment incentives linkage; (2) the land title, collateral and credit linkage; (3) the land liquidity, deposit mobilization and investment linkage; (4) the land markets, transactions and efficiency linkage; and (5) the labour mobility and efficiency linkage.[48] All five linkages are necessary to support effective real estate-based finance, and all five are, in fact, based upon the existence of appropriate legal infrastructure.[49]

Given the significance of real estate finance for economic development, the next issue focuses on the development of markets in which secondary mortgage markets can have an important role. In a 1997 World Bank study, Dwight Jaffee and Bertrand Renaud analysed factors that hinder the development of mortgage markets in the transition economies of central and eastern Europe and proposed a strategy to expedite development.[50] They show that banks in transition economies are reluctant to make mortgage loans because of the risks in mortgage lending (i.e., credit, interest rate and liquidity risks) and suggest that, together with necessary improvements in the primary market, a secondary

---

[46] See generally de Soto, op. cit., n. 12 (proposing that the reform of legal systems in developing countries can help activate idle capital); D. North and R. Thomas, *The Rise of the Western World* (Cambridge: Cambridge University Press, 1973) (arguing that efficient economic organization is the key to growth); N. Rosenberg and L. Birdzell, *How the West Grew Rich: The Economic Transformation of the Western World* (New York: Basic Books, 1986) (arguing that Western economic development hinged on factors promoting experimentation); A. Goldsmith, "Democracy, Property Rights and Economic Growth", 32 J. Dev. Stud. 157 (1995) (providing empirical evidence that the growth of democratic freedoms and property rights in poor countries may lead to increased local prosperity); J. Torstensson, "Property Rights and Economic Growth – An Empirical Study", 47 Kyklos 231 (1994) (applying empirical analyses of property rights and economic growth to substantiate the earlier findings of Rosenberg and Birdzell as well as North and Thomas).

[47] F. Byamugisha, "The Effects of Land Registration on Financial Development and Economic Growth: A Theoretical and Conceptual Framework", World Bank Policy Research Working Paper 2240 (1999), p. 12.

[48] Id., pp. 6–10.

[49] Byamugisha graphically presents the connections between the five factors and their role in creating a conceptual framework of land registration, financial development and economic growth. Id., p. 7 fig. 2.

[50] D. Jaffe and B. Renaud, "Strategies to Develop Mortgage Markets in Transition Economies", World Bank Policy Research Working Paper 1697 (1996), p. 4.

mortgage market is likely to assist in solving these problems. In this respect, they conclude[51]:

> A housing finance system, however, is unlikely to spring up without government support, whatever one's faith in the dexterity of Adam Smith's *invisible hand*. Government support was required in the developed economies, and it is required now in the transition economies. In fact, the transition economies face the additional major hurdle that they must first create an economic and legal infrastructure that can support the long-term and complex market relationships and contracts that constitute a housing financial system.

In another World Bank study, Ahmed Galal and Omar Razzaz argue that land and real estate reforms, to be successful, must be "comprehensive in design, even if implementation is phased in over time."[52] They contend that such reforms must include three elements[53]: (1) institutional reforms that better define property rights[54], reduce information asymmetry and improve contract performance (property rights, information, contracting and enforcement)[55]; (2) capital market reforms that make mortgage finance available at reasonable rates, especially for the poor (finance and risk management)[56]; and (3) market reforms that reduce or eliminate the main distortions in the prices of goods and services produced by land and real estate assets (market regulation and fiscal policy).[57] Their conclusions clearly link mortgage market development to broader efforts to develop real estate finance to serve as a driving factor in financial and economic development.

In respect to mortgage market development, Jaffee and Renaud suggest that secondary mortgage markets confer two main benefits: (1) the ability of

---

[51] Id., p. 27 (emphasis in original).

[52] A. Galal and O. Razzaz, "Reforming Land and Real Estate Markets", World Bank Policy Research Working Paper 2616 (2001), p. 31.

[53] Id., pp. 31, 10–18 and table 2.

[54] Property rights regimes include constitutional protection of property, laws and regulations defining rights and obligations to property, means of assignment of rights to property, and institutional arrangements that register and enforce such rights. Id., p. 17.

[55] Issues include well-defined property rights, protected through formal, informal or traditional institutions; permissibility of evolution and transformation of property rights; exercisability and related transactions costs; and ability of the poor to access real estate and related finance. Id., p. 38.

[56] Issues include a conducive macro environment; competitive mortgage finance markets; adequate banking regulation and supervision; developed capital markets, including secondary mortgage markets and institutional investors; and well-developed and reliable foreclosure and repossession laws, and procedures and appropriately designed subsidy systems. Id.

[57] Issues include appropriate land use regulations and appropriate incentive systems for real estate, finance, services, and investment. Id., pp. 38–9.

banks to shed risks associated with holding mortgages and (2) the creation of standards for credit evaluation and collateral procedures that directly increase the efficiency of the primary markets for new mortgage originations.[58] In order to secure these benefits, the authors suggest an important and often catalytic role for governments in developing secondary mortgage market systems and institutions. This role is based on similar experiences in developed countries.

At present, despite its clearly fundamental role in financial development and economic growth, no work has been done on developing international standards in relation to legal frameworks for use of real property as collateral. At the same time, however, most economies have developed legal frameworks for such transactions, based on structures from developed common law or civil law jurisdictions.

**Secured Transactions.** In the area of secured transactions, it is generally agreed that there exists wide disparity in the law relating to secured transactions in developed economies – this is often an important element of discussion and disagreement between common law and civil law traditions.[59] Further (and largely as a result of the disparity in systems across developed jurisdictions), even today, no internationally agreed standards or principles in the area of secured transactions exist.[60] To create an effective legal system for secured transactions, it is necessary to have a good grasp of many details of the legal system (in the laws of property, obligations, insolvency, civil procedure, etc.) and the administrative practices and procedures (e.g., registration and enforcement). Nonetheless, research shows that the development of legal infrastructure supporting secured transactions underlies the development of functioning collateral-based credit provision and that weaknesses in such infrastructure hinder financial and economic development.[61]

In relation to international standards, the most developed international guidance is the Model Law on Secured Transactions of the European Bank for Reconstruction and Development (EBRD). At the same time, UNCITRAL has been working for some years now to develop a Legislative Guide on Secured

---

[58] Jaffee and Renaud, op. cit., n. 50, p. 5.

[59] For an excellent discussion, see F. Dahan, "Secured Transactions Law in Western Advanced Economies: Exposing Myths", Law in Transition 37 (Aut. 2000) and sources cited therein.

[60] See A. Goswami and H. Sharif, "Preface", in N. de la Pena, H. Fleisig and P. Wellons, "Secured Transactions Law Reform in Asia: Unleashing the Potential of Collateral", *Law and Policy Reform at the Asian Development Bank 2000*, vol. 2 (ADB, 2000), pp. v–xii.

[61] See generally N. de la Pena, H. Fleisig and P. Wellons, "Secured Transactions Law Reform in Asia: Unleashing the Potential of Collateral", *Law and Policy Reform at the Asian Development Bank 2000*, vol. 2 (ADB, 2000).

Transactions. The latter, once agreed, is likely to become the most important international guidance in this area.

In addition to the Model Law on Secured Transactions, the EBRD has also developed Core Principles and a Glossary to support its efforts. Further, the EBRD has developed a process for approaching collateral law reform projects.[62] In response to a specific request from the country, EBRD lawyers who specialize in secured transactions laws have given advice and support to governments during the legislative process, including, in particular, those involved in drafting new laws or amending existing legislation that deals with pledges or mortgages. Specifically, the process includes the following stages (and admitting to some overlap)[63] (1) consensus building, (2) commitment and division of responsibilities, (3) drafting of the law, (4) adoption, (5) practical operation, (6) acceptance, (7) court application and (8) monitoring. In a related Asian Development Bank (ADB) report, the authors suggest a similar sequence for secured transactions law reform.[64]

The EBRD, to put its expertise into a readily accessible format, has developed a Regional Survey[65] of the secured transactions laws in all of its twenty-six countries of operations and has made this information available on the Bank's website.[66] This Survey can be used as a more detailed "framework analysis" to permit a standard methodology for reviewing the state of the secured transactions law in any country and for diagnosing the weaknesses that may prevent it from operating efficiently in the context of a market economy. This Survey is useful to show the specific strengths and weaknesses in collateral law reform. It also shows a strong correlation between the perceptions of collateral law held by respondents in the EBRD's Legal Indicator Survey.[67]

In addition to the work of the EBRD, the ADB is also providing assistance in the area of secured transactions.[68] The World Bank has also addressed some

---

[62] See J. Simpson and J. Menze, "Ten Years of Secured Transactions Reform", Law in Transition 20 (Aut. 2000).

[63] Id., pp. 22–5.

[64] de la Pena, Fleisig and Wellons, op. cit., n. 60, pp. 133–4, specifically: (1) prepare diagnostic study; (2) fix the sequence of reform; (3) prepare draft law; (4) pass the draft law; (5) write regulations and choose operation of a registry filing system; and (6) hold training and public awareness campaign.

[65] D. Fairgrieve and M. Andenas, "Securing Progress in Collateral Law Reform: The EBRD's Regional Survey of Secured Transactions Laws", Law in Transition 28 (Aut. 2000).

[66] www.ebrd.com.

[67] See J. Taylor and F. April, "Fostering Investment Law in Transitional Economies: A Case for Refocusing Institutional Reform", 4 Parker Sch. J. E. Eur. L. 1 (1997).

[68] ADB Regional Technical Assistance Program for Secured Transactions Law Reform (TA No. 5773-REG) (cited in World Bank, *Principles and Guidelines for Effective Insolvency and Creditor Rights Systems*, Apr. 2001, p. 83 n. 40).

of these issues as they relate to insolvency.[69] In addition, UNCITRAL's Legislative Guide on Secured Transactions is due for completion in 2007.[70] Other significant efforts at the international level have been undertaken by UNCITRAL[71] and the International Institute for the Unification of Private Law (UNIDROIT).[72] A number of regional efforts are also currently under way in North America[73], Asia[74] and the European Union. In addition, important harmonization efforts took place in the context of the US Uniform Commercial Code (UCC) Article 9 and the Canadian Personal Property Security Acts.

**Leasing and Licensing.** Beyond mechanisms supporting the use of property rights as collateral, especially for real and moveable property, other mechanisms also serve to mobilize property rights for finance. One of the best examples is leasing and related structures such as licensing (which usually refers to intellectual property). In a leasing or licensing transaction, the right to use property (of whatever sort) is contracted by the owner to another party. The party contracting to use the property concerned (which could be of any sort, including intellectual property) pays the owner of the property for the right to use the property. In many cases, the user of the property will use the property itself to generate income to compensate the owner of the property for its use: examples include commercial vehicles or franchising rights. At the end of the contract, ownership and possession may pass to the user of the property right or revert to the original owner. Such mechanisms therefore mobilize property for finance.

In relation to international guidance, UNIDROIT has been most active, with its UNIDROIT Convention on International Financial Leasing[75], Convention on International Interests in Mobile Equipment[76], and Model Franchise

---

[69] See World Bank, *Principles and Guidelines for Effective Insolvency and Creditor Rights Systems* (Apr. 2001), esp. pp. 3, 13–15.

[70] See www.uncitral.org.

[71] See UNCITRAL Working Group on Int'l Contract Principles, *Draft Convention on Assignment in Receivables Financing* (available at www.uncitral.org); UNCITRAL, Report of the Secretary-General: Study on Security Interests, VIII Y. B. Comm'n Int'l Trade L. 171 (1977), U.N. Doc. A/CN.9/SER.A/1977 ("Drobnig Report").

[72] See UNIDROIT, *Draft UNIDROIT Convention on International Interests in Mobile Equipment*; idem., *UNIDROIT Convention on International Factoring* (1988) (both available at www.unidroit.org).

[73] See American Law Institute, International Secured Transactions Project (www.ali.org).

[74] See de la Pena, Fleisig and Wellons, op. cit., n. 60.

[75] (1998) (available at www.unidroit.org).

[76] UNIDROIT (2001) (available at www.unidroit.org).

Disclosure Law[77] the most relevant. In addition, UNIDROIT is currently working to develop a Model Law on Leasing.

### 3.2.2. *Company Law*

Adequate company law is essential for the development of a modern, decentralized financial system. While company or corporate law is a massive area of legal practice and related writing, the development of company law was not really considered in detail until the requirements of privatization and transition of the late 1980s and 1990s. Nonetheless, it was a subject of much debate in today's developed economies in the eighteenth and nineteenth centuries.[78] Arguably, company law is fundamental to aggregation of capital necessary for exploitation of capital-intensive industries and projects.

Significantly, over the past fifteen years, the role of corporate or company law and its importance for economic development have come under increasing scrutiny, especially as previously centrally planned economies move towards market-based systems and as countries have focused more on the role of law and legal and institutional infrastructure in supporting financial development and economic growth.[79] Private business corporations are a vital aspect of a market economy, and analysis of the law's role in their development aids others attempting to develop functioning corporations and financial markets.

Despite the usefulness of comparative historical analysis for contemporary economic development and transition, little study has been devoted to early development of corporate law in the United States and Britain, despite the fact that the Anglo-American model of corporate structure and governance has become the paradigm to which other countries aspire. Much of early US corporate law (which began as state law, and today remains state law, albeit with a very influential overlay of federal regulation of corporations issuing securities)

---

[77] UNIDROIT (2002) (available at www.unidroit.org).

[78] See D. Arner, "Development of the American Law of Corporations to 1832", 55 SMU L. Rev. 23 (2002).

[79] See e.g., R. La Porta, F. Lopez-de-Silanes, A. Shleifer and R. Vishny, "Investor Protection and Corporate Valuation", 57 J. Fin. 1147 (2002); J. Coffee, Jr., "The Rise of Dispersed Ownership: The Roles of Law and the State in the Separation of Ownership and Control", 111 Yale L. J. 1 (2001); B. Black, "The Legal and Institutional Preconditions for Strong Securities Markets", 48 UCLA L. Rev. 781 (2001); B. Cheffins, "Does Law Matter? The Separation of Ownership and Control in the United Kingdom", 30 J. Legal Stud. 459 (2001); J. Norton and D. Arner, "Development of Capital Markets, Stock Exchanges and Securities Regulation in Transition Economies", in Y. Kalyuzhnova & M. Taylor (eds), *Transitional Economies: Banking, Finance, Institutions* (London: St. Martin's Press, 2001).

is derived from English sources; however, formal recognition of the legal foundations of business corporations developed earlier in the United States than in England.[80] Moreover, the law governing the behaviour of corporations issuing securities to the public has remained more developed until very recently in the United States than in Britain. The combination of early recognition of the fundamental legal supports to business corporations and the development of separate and comprehensive regulation of those companies issuing securities to the public may underlie the earlier development of the Berle and Means corporation[81] (characterized by dispersed ownership and separation of ownership and control) in the United States than in Britain or any other jurisdiction.

Overall, the development of the law of private corporations in the United States was not planned, immediate or even uncontroversial, but rather (in the tradition of the common law) a gradual building up of the various supports necessary for the commercial and financial effectiveness of the form. For those today seeking to advance corporate (and thereby economic) development in individual economies, the lesson to draw should be to focus on the economic goals, needs and issues (e.g., corporate governance) and seek to put in place the legal structures necessary to meet those needs and goals, while minimizing inherent difficulties.

Empirical research supports the role of the company: Asli Demirguc-Kunt, Inessa Love and Vojislav Maksimovic have found that[82]:

> corporations are better adapted than unincorporated businesses for facilitating access to financial markets and for formal contracting with customers and investors.... Unincorporated businesses have a comparative advantage in operating in informal environments where businesses are self-financing

---

[80] See generally R. Harris, *Industrializing English Law: Entrepreneurship and Business Organization, 1720–1844* (Cambridge: Cambridge University Press, 2000); S. Bowman, *The Modern Corporation and American Political Thought: Law, Power, and Ideology* (Pittsburgh: Pennsylvania State University Press, 1996); J. Hurst, *The Legitimacy of the Business Corporation in the Law of the United States 1780–1970* (Charlottesville: University Press of Virginia, 1970); L. Gower, "Some Contrasts Between British and American Corporation Law", 69 Harv. L. Rev. 1369 (1956). Note that in the English practice, private business corporations as known in the US practice are called "companies", and are organized under specific company statutes governing their various aspects. See also C. Cooke, *Corporation, Trust and Company: An Essay in Legal History* (Manchester: Manchester University Press, 1950), pp. 127–90; A. DuBois, *The English Business Company after the Bubble Act, 1720–1800* (New York: Commonwealth Fund, 1938).

[81] See A. Berle and G. Means, *The Modern Corporation and Private Property* (New York: Macmillan, 1933).

[82] A. Demirguc-Kunt, I. Love and V. Maksimovic, "Business Environment and the Incorporation Decision", World Bank Policy Research Working Paper 3317 (May 2004), pp. 4–5.

and rely on their reputations rather than on legally enforceable contractual obligations.

John Micklethwait and Adrian Wooldridge sum up the value of the company[83]:

> The central good of the joint-stock company is that it is the key to productivity growth in the private sector: the best and easiest structure for individuals to pool capital, to refine skills, and to pass them on.

In order to do so, company law must provide, at a minimum, limited liability of shareholders, free transferability of shares and accountable structures of corporate governance (the last of which is discussed in greater detail in Chapter Five).[84]

At present, there are no international standards for company law, although there has been considerable related work in the specific aspect of corporate governance (discussed in Chapter Five). At the same time, an annex to the Objectives and Principles of Securities Regulation[85] of the International Organization of Securities Commissions provides the following useful outline of major issues which should be addressed by the company law framework, namely:

(1) company formation,
(2) duties of directors and officers,
(3) regulation of takeover bids and other transactions intended to effect a change in control,
(4) laws governing the issue and offer for sale of securities,
(5) disclosure of information to security holders to enable informed voting decisions, and
(6) disclosure of material shareholdings.

Of these, duties of directors and officers are dealt with in greater detail in the context of corporate governance[86], while the latter four are dealt with in greater detail in the context of securities and derivatives.[87] In relation to company formation, the law should provide for a simple, clear and transparent mechanism for company formation, with graduated standards for small private companies, larger private companies and public or listed companies, including

---

[83] J. Micklethwait and A. Wooldridge, *The Company: A Short History of a Revolutionary Idea* (New York: Modern Library, 2003), p. 190.
[84] See C. Cooke, op. cit., n. 83.
[85] (2003).
[86] See Chapter Five.
[87] See Chapter Seven.

filing and registration requirements and financial disclosure and reporting requirements. At the same time, many company laws also address insolvency, though other systems address insolvency issues through separate legislation.[88]

### 3.2.3. *Sustainable Fiscal and Taxation System*

An effective, transparent and sustainable fiscal system, including taxation, is necessary for a government to be able to provide necessary public goods (including enforcement of contracts, commercial dispute resolution and protection of property rights, as well as maintaining public order and stability). Such a system is also important in addressing issues of corruption.[89]

The IMF Code of Good Practices on Fiscal Transparency Code ("FT Code"), identified by the FSF as the key standard for the area of fiscal policy transparency, provides the leading set of international standards in this area.[90] The IMF FT Code was approved by the Fund's then–Interim Committee (now International Monetary and Finanical Committee [IMFC]) on 16 April 1998; a revised version was approved by the Fund's Executive Board on 23 March 2001[91] and subsequently acknowledged by the IMFC. As in several other areas, the FSF Compendium includes the original version, but provides a link to the revised version; the Fund uses the revised version. Guidance for review and implementation is provided in a separate Manual (not included in the FSF Compendium), initially released in November 1998 and revised and released in March 2001 to coincide with the revised FT Code.[92]

The FT Code is designed to provide assurances to the public and markets that a clear picture of the structure and finances of government is available and that the soundness of fiscal policy can be reliably assessed. The FT Code only addresses fiscal policy transparency and not the efficiency of fiscal policy or the soundness of public finances.[93] Fiscal transparency is defined on the basis of openness to the public regarding the structure and functions of government, fiscal policy intentions, public sector accounts and fiscal projects.[94] The FT Code is based on four key objectives: (1) clarity of roles and responsibilities of government; (2) public availability of information on government

---

[88] See Chapter Five.
[89] See Chapter Five.
[90] IMF, *Code of Good Practices on Fiscal Transparency*, Apr. 1998.
[91] IMF, *Revised Code of Good Practices on Fiscal Transparency*, Feb. 2001 updated.
[92] IMF, *Manual on Fiscal Transparency*, Mar. 2001 ("FT Manual").
[93] Id., p. 3.
[94] Id., p. 2. According to the FT Manual, this definition was derived from G. Kopits and J. Craig, "Transparency in Government Operations", IMF Occasional Paper No. 158 (1998).

activities; (3) open government budget preparation, execution and reporting; and (4) integrity through accepted standards of data quality and independent assurance.

The first part of the FT Code deals with clarity of roles and responsibilities. It is concerned with specifying the structure and functions of government, responsibilities within government and relations between government and the rest of the economy.[95] As recognized by the Fund, this section is very concerned with the details of governance structure – a topic discussed more generally earlier.[96] Specifically, it requires that the government sector should be distinguished from the rest of the public sector and policy and management roles with the public sector should be clear and publicly disclosed (s. 1.1). This includes structure and function of government (s. 1.1.1), definition of responsibilities of the constituent parts of government (s. 1.1.2), clear description of relations between government and other public sector institutions (s. 1.1.4), and open and public description of government involvement in the private sector on the basis of clear rules and procedures applied in a nondiscriminatory manner (s. 1.1.5). In addition, there should be a clear legal and administrative framework for fiscal management (s. 1.2), including clear and public ethics standards for public servants (s. 1.2.3).

The second part of the FT Code deals with public availability of information. Specifically, it addresses publication of comprehensive fiscal information at clearly specified times.[97] Information on past, current and projected government fiscal activity should be public (s. 2.1) and publication of fiscal information should be a legal obligation of government (s. 2.2.1).

The third part of the FT Code deals with open budget preparation, execution and reporting and covers the type of information made available regarding the budget process.[98] Specifically, the government budget should specify fiscal policy objectives, the macroeconomic framework, the policy basis for the budget and identifiable major fiscal risks (s. 3.1), with information presented in a manner which facilitates policy analysis and promotes accountability (s. 3.2). Procedures for execution and monitoring of expenditure and revenue collection should be clearly specified (s. 3.3), including audit (s. 3.3.3, 3.3.4) and public reporting (s. 3.4).

---

[95] FT Manual, op. cit., n. 92, p. 2.

[96] See IMF, *Assessing and Promoting Fiscal Transparency: A Report on Progress*, Mar. 2003, Supp. 2 of SM/03/86 *International Standards: Strengthening Surveillance, Domestic Institutions, and International Markets*, pp. 3, 9–10 ("Assessing FT").

[97] FT Manual, op. cit., n. 92, p. 2.

[98] Id., p. 2.

The fourth part of the FT Code deals with assurances of integrity and addresses the quality of fiscal data and the need for independent scrutiny of fiscal information.[99] Specifically, fiscal data should meet accepted data quality standards (s. 4.1) and be subjected to independent scrutiny (s. 4.3).

In March 2003, the IMF released an assessment of experiences with the FT Code.[100] As of 24 February 2003, the Fund had completed fifty-four fiscal ROSCs, with forty-eight of these published on the IMF website, encompassing four different groups of countries (using the Fund's categories of advanced, emerging market, transition and developing).[101] The report identified four significant aspects[102]:

(1) Most countries participating in the ROSCs had undertaken or were in the process of undertaking significant fiscal reforms.
(2) A high proportion of countries seeking access to financing has chosen or plan to undertake a fiscal ROSC.
(3) ROSCs provide an indication of a number of common problems that occur across a wide range of countries (developing, emerging market, transition); in particular, problems of fiscal data quality, use of off-budget mechanisms, lack of clarity in tax policy and administration, and poor definition of intergovernmental relations.
(4) Many of these issues are associated with a set of underlying institutional problems, also observed in the ROSCs, and these need to be addressed on a sustained basis.

As of January 2007, the IMF and World Bank had published fiscal transparency FSAP/ROSCs for eighty countries.[103]

In addition to the FT Code and supporting Manual, the IMF has developed a series of guidance notes and draft tax laws which provide standard guidance in this respect. Beyond taxation, developing government securities markets

---

[99] Id.
[100] Assessing FT, op. cit., n. 96.
[101] Id., p. 3.
[102] Id.; see pp. 7–12.
[103] Albania, Algeria, Argentina, Armenia, Australia, Azerbaijan, Bangladesh, Belarus, Benin, Brazil, Bulgaria, Burkina Faso, Cameroon, Canada, Chile, Colombia, Croatia, Cyprus, Czech Republic, El Salvador, Equatorial Guinea, Estonia, Fiji, France, Georgia, Germany, Ghana, Greece, Guatemala, Honduras, Hong Kong, Hungary, India, Indonesia, Iran, Israel, Italy, Japan, Jordan, Kazakhstan, Kyrgyzstan, Latvia, Lebannon, Lithuania, Macedonia, Malawi, Mali, Mauritania, Mexico, Moldova, Mongolia, Morocco, Mozambique, The Netherlands, Nicaragua, Pakistan, Papua New Guinea, Paraguay, Peru, Philippines, Poland, Portugal, Romania, Russia, Rwanda, Samoa, Slovakia, Slovenia, South Korea, Spain, Sri Lanka, Sweden, Tanzania, Tunisia, Turkey, Uganda, Ukraine, United Kingdom, United States, Uruguay.

(discussed in Chapter Four) may assist in supporting fiscal sustainability, though they also bring about the opposite risk: of borrowing too much.

### 3.2.4. *Rule of Law*

Law plays a variety of roles in societal organization and in governance, with governance systems dating back at least to Assyria relying on legal systems to structure and institutionalize governance and economic organization. Specifically, law has typically played a number of different roles in governance, from rule by force to rule of law. Under the typical governance model relying on a system of rule by force, an autocrat imposes his (or their, in the case of an oligarchy) will through force, typically implemented by a series of underlings or retainers (a feudal structure is a prime example) which may or may not eventually develop into an aristocracy or bureaucracy. Often, rule by force will evolve into a system of rule by law, if the autocrat is successful in becoming entrenched beyond a short period. The autocrat establishes formal laws and rules by which governance and the economic system operate, in Olson's analysis, in order to secure the maximum economic gain for himself. Rule by law systems are capable of persisting for long periods; likewise, Olson suggests that they can result in economically efficient governance and economic structures under the right circumstances. In other models, religion (theocracy), custom (typically tribal societies, though custom has a role in every society) or ethics (Confucian or libertarian anarchy models) may provide the central form of organization and/or control. Finally, a system may also be based on the rule of law. While rule of law is typically associated with democratic models, democratic models can certainly include other models (rule by force and by law of the noncitizen populations of Athens and the Americas, in addition to various roles for religion, custom and ethics). Likewise, a rule of law system may develop in nondemocratic polities, though it tends to do so over a gradual period and not always completely successfully.

While the importance of the rule of law is increasingly emphasized in discussions of the requirements for transition and development, it is still not well understood or defined in practice.[104] This is especially the case in relation to

---

[104] For discussion of the role of the rule of law in economic development, see T. Carothers, "The Rule of Law Revival", For. Affairs 95 (1998); C. Clague, P. Keefer, S. Knack and M. Olson, "Property and Contract Rights in Autocracies and Democracies", 1 J. Econ. Growth 243 (1996); D. North, "Economic Performance Through Time", 84 Amer. Econ. Rev. 359 (1994); M. Olson, "Dictatorship, Democracy, and Development", 87 Amer. Pol. Sci. Rev. 567 (1993); idem, "Big Bills Left on the Sidewalk: Why Some Nations Are Rich, and Others Poor", 10 J. Econ. Persp. 3 (1996).

the role of the rule of law in financial development and transition. The rule of law as applied in the context of financial activities involves issues such as the enforcement of financial contracts, the creation of efficient insolvency and collateral laws and the existence of clear standards of corporate governance. Another significant aspect of the development of the rule of law is the effort to combat corruption and enhance integrity, which is of great significance in the financial sector (and discussed further in Chapter Five).

In the context of transition economies, as noted earlier, the rule of law was unnecessary and nonexistent. However, when questions of transition were first being analysed in the late 1980s, law was not seen as significant to financial development; rather, emphasis was placed on various models of mass privatization and "big bang" transformation, with the theory being that appropriate structures would develop naturally as part of the transition process. In the event, this has not been the case; rather, drastic transitions undertaken without attention to the institutional fabric, including law, have not generally proceeded as successfully as more gradual transition processes integrating development of supporting institutions.[105] As a result, increasing attention is devoted to supporting institutions and the development of the rule of law in transition economies, as well as emerging and developing economies; unfortunately, until recently, there has been no general consensus on what factors are significant, especially in respect to financial sector development.

For many, the rule of law is the foundation upon which democratic societies and market economies are built. As such, the concept of the rule of law is being identified as the solution to a variety of political and economic ills plaguing transition, emerging and developing economies, from the problems of transforming statist economies into capitalist market economies to helping stem the spread of financial crises.[106]

At its core, the rule of law includes a mix of technical or procedural components, as well as in many cases substantive moral content. It can be defined to encompass:

(1) a system of government where institutions and officials are guided by and constrained by the law – that is, government accountable to, not above, the law;
(2) a body of laws that are transparent, reasonably predictable, validly derived, and fairly and equitably applied;

---

[105] The best examples here are those of Hungary and China; the contra example has been Poland.
[106] See generally T. Carothers, op. cit., n. 104, p. 95.

(3) laws, principles and procedures that protect those civil, political and economic rights that have become enshrined as universal human rights; and

(4) a fair and effective legal system led by an independent and professionally competent judiciary that acts as the final arbiter of the law.

Many of these ideas are now encapsulated in the term the "rule of law". Generally speaking, this is a term not subject to a simple definition. Rather, it includes an array of ideas. One can say that the term largely relates to process rather than substance and includes:

(1) creation by a legitimate authority, certain, clear, publicly accessible, mutually consistent, prospective, and able to be obeyed;

(2) application through transparent processes, principled reasoning and subject to organized appeal;

(3) interpretation and monitoring by an independent judiciary free of political control; and

(4) congruence with the behaviour of administering officials.

From this definition, it becomes apparent that the rule of law is a critical component of democratic governance. It is required to hold leaders and government institutions accountable to the public; encompasses free speech and political thought; supports free and fair elections; and provides breathing space for civil society, that is, opening the channels for the free flow of information that makes civil society effective.

The rule of law reaches beyond the realm of democratic governance to foster sustainable economic development. The primary economic role for governments, according to the currently prevailing view, is to create the environment necessary to attract private investment and support economic growth. The rule of law is a central component of this environment and its establishment is a necessary precondition for sustainable, long-term economic growth. Alan Greenspan has described the rule of law, consisting of property rights protected by the state, laws of contract and bankruptcy, and judicial review and enforcement, as the "essential infrastructure of a market economy".[107] To Greenspan's list of components should be added criminal law enforcement that can ensure a level of personal security and effectively combat corruption.

Empirical research increasingly supports the value of the rule of law in economic and financial development. Studies have shown that the difference

---

[107] A. Greenspan, Remarks at the Woodrow Wilson Award Dinner, Woodrow Wilson International Centre for Scholars, 10 Jun. 1997.

in the rates of growth and investment across countries can be explained to some extent by the existence and quality of a country's institutions, in particular the legal institutions that support property and contract rights and the third-party enforcement of these rights.[108] These studies conclude that the best way to achieve sustainable economic growth is to develop a "market-augmenting state" – one that creates and is supported by the rule of law.[109] In the context of the operations of firms, Luc Laeven and Christopher Woodruff suggest[110]:

> [T]he legal system affects the growth prospects of firms. Where courts are more efficient, capital is shifted from entrepreneurs with less entrepreneurial ability to those with more entrepreneurial ability. These results suggest that policies that improve the administration of courts and the enforcement of verdicts would be expected to result in the growth of firms, an increase in the demand for workers, and a reduction in the rate of self employment.

The rule of law provides an essential framework for economic activity. Without a predictable, enforceable set of rules, uncertainty reins in an economy. Without transparent legal rules enforced by a competent judiciary, the cost of business rises: raising capital becomes more expensive, entrepreneurs require higher risk premia, debtors do not repay debts because they know that laws and contracts are not consistently enforced, and lenders do not make loans because they have no certainty of repayment.[111] Lack of confidence in law enforcement and fair, effective dispute resolution supervised by the courts may lead to the creation of undesirable alternative institutions, criminalization of the economy and corruption.

It is true that foreign investment seeking high returns may flow into economies lacking the rule of law. However, as recent financial crises have shown, instability, economic mismanagement and corruption that may exist in the absence of the rule of law will ultimately lead to the outflow of foreign and even domestic funds. The rule of law serves as an effective counter to volatile capital outflows. In addition, the existence of the rule of law is crucial in those economies that have implemented the first level of economic reforms – freeing the market, rewriting constitutions, laws and regulations – but still must tackle the more difficult tasks of reforming and restructuring institutions,

---

[108] M. Olson (1996), op. cit., n. 104; see generally Clague et al., op. cit., n. 104.

[109] M. Olson (1993), op. cit., n. 104.

[110] L. Laeven and C. Woodruff, "The Quality of the Legal System, Firm Ownership, and Firm Size", World Bank Policy Research Working Paper 3246 (Mar. 2004), p. 37.

[111] OECD, News Release: "OECD Symposium on the Rule of Law and the Development of a Market Economy in the Russian Federation, Remarks by Kumiharu Shigehara, Deputy Secretary-General of the OECD", 25 Mar. 1998.

privatizing state industries and retraining administrative and judicial personnel. This link between the rule of law and stable economic development was stated most clearly by North: "While economic growth can occur in the short run in autocratic regimes, long-run economic growth entails the development of the rule of law."[112]

## 3.3. CONCLUSION

This chapter has provided an overview of the essential preconditions for and institutional underpinnings of financial sector development and economic growth, focusing on available international standards and research. Overall, in many ways, these aspects are of the most fundamental importance for financial systems to develop. At the same time, appropriate financial and macroeconomic policy frameworks are also significant for economic growth. These issues are the subject of the following chapter.

[112] D. North (1994), op. cit., n. 104.

# 4

# Central Banking and Financial Policy

At the same time as one considers the institutional foundations of financial sector development and economic growth, it is also necessary to consider issues relating to macroeconomic policy. In this context, an economy's central bank plays a leading role.

Unlike institutional underpinnings of financial sector development, macroeconomic policy issues have long received significant attention. As a result, this area includes a number of international standards. However, the Financial Stability Forum (FSF) framework addresses only institutional arrangements for and transparency of macroeconomic policy – it does not address policies themselves, reflecting the largely legal and institutional focus of the system of standards and codes, as well as the focus of this volume. Specifically, the FSF includes "macroeconomic policy and data transparency" as one of its major subject areas, subdivided in turn into four standard areas, the first three of which are identified as key standard areas: (1) monetary and financial policy transparency, (2) fiscal policy transparency, (3) data dissemination and (4) data compilation. Fiscal policy transparency was addressed in the previous chapter in the context of sustainable fiscal and taxation systems; the remainder are dealt with below.

## 4.1. CENTRAL BANKING

Central banks historically have incorporated a number of different functions, including currency issuance, monetary policy, banking supervision and/or regulation, financial stability and lender of last resort, the government's bank, management of gold and foreign exchange reserves, debt management, responsibility for exchange controls, and various developmental and promotional tasks.[1]

---

[1] See R. Lastra, *Central Banking and Banking Regulation* (London School of Economics, 1996), Appendix.

Typically, a central bank is defined as such. Today, it is generally agreed that the primary function of a central bank is monetary stability.[2] In addition, central banks are also frequently responsible for financial stability and also certain aspects of financial and economic development.

While actual economic policy choices are beyond the scope of this volume, there is now general consensus on the appropriate institutional designs through which such policies should be pursued (namely, an institutional framework for transparency, independence and accountability). Regardless of the specific objectives chosen for the central bank by lawmakers (in most cases one or more of monetary stability, financial stability and/or financial/economic development), the central bank and its supporting legal and institutional framework should have: first, one or more clear objectives; second, independence to pursue those objectives in a transparent manner; and third, a framework of accountability to government for achieving the objective(s) in a transparent manner.

In this regard, the FSF identifies the Monetary and Financial Policy (MFP) Transparency Code of the International Monetary Fund (IMF) as the key international standard.[3] The MFP Transparency Code was approved by the Interim Committee of the Board of Governors of the IMF (renamed the International Monetary and Financial Committee [IMFC] in September 1999).[4] It is supported and explained by a subsequent Supporting Document[5], approved by the Fund's Executive Board on 24 July 2000. It also is intended to interact with other standards in related areas, for example, banking, securities, insurance, payment and settlement.

The rationale of the document rests on two premises relating to transparency[6]: (1) effectiveness of monetary and financial policies is strengthened

---

[2] See R. Lastra, *Legal Foundations of International Monetary Stability* (Oxford University Press, 2006), pp. 34–41.

[3] IMF, *Code of Good Practices on Transparency in Monetary and Financial Policies*, Jul. 1999 ("MFP Transparency Code").

[4] See IMF, *Communiqué of the Interim Committee of the Board of Governors of the International Monetary Fund*, 26 Sep. 1999, para. 9.

[5] IMF, *Supporting Document to the Code of Good Practices on Transparency in Monetary and Financial Policies*, Jul. 2000. The Supporting Document has a very useful structure, which could serve as a model for other guidance/methodology documents. It is divided into three parts: Part I includes background and reference materials, Part II deals with central banks and Part III covers "financial agencies" (i.e., financial regulatory authorities). For each section of the Code, the Supporting Document includes an explanation and rationale, application in various countries, and (for some standards) implementation considerations dealing with certain practical considerations. As a result, the document is a very useful reference for both monitoring and implementation. It also includes (in Part I) a very useful bibliography of references on transparency and accountability of central banks and financial agencies.

[6] MFP Transparency Code, op. cit., n. 3, p. 5.

if the goals and instruments of policy are known to the public and if the authorities can make a credible commitment to meeting them; and (2) good governance calls for central banks and financial agencies to be accountable, particularly where the monetary and financial authorities are granted a high degree of autonomy.

For the purposes of the MFP Transparency Code, "transparency" is defined as[7]:

> an environment in which the objectives of policy, its legal, institutional, and economic framework, policy decisions and their rationale, data and information related to monetary and financial policies, and the terms of agencies accountability, are provided to the public on an understandable, accessible and timely basis.

In addressing transparency, the MFP Transparency Code covers four main areas[8]: (1) clarity of roles, responsibilities and objectives of central banks and financial agencies; (2) the processes for formulating and reporting of monetary policy decisions by the central bank and of financial policies by financial agencies; (3) public availability of information on monetary and financial policies; and (4) accountability and assurances of integrity by the central bank and financial agencies.

Interestingly, despite the general international consensus on the value of independence for central banks and regulatory authorities (combined with clear objectives and proper accountability)[9], independence is not specifically addressed in the context of the MFP Transparency Code. This is an issue that probably should be revisited when the Code is revised. It is also an area which has received attention in several recent papers by IMF staff.[10]

As monetary and financial policy responsibilities are typically distributed between a central bank and one or more other financial agencies, the MFP Transparency Code is divided into two main sections: the first addressing transparency and monetary policy for central banks, and the second addressing transparency of financial policies for what the Code calls "financial agencies" – which could be more clearly termed "regulatory and supervisory authorities" which vary depending on the allocation of objectives and which may

---

7   Id., p. 4.
8   Id., pp. 4–5.
9   See M. Quintyn and M. Taylor, "Regulatory and Supervisory Independence and Financial Stability", IMF Working Paper WP/02/46 (Mar. 2002); R. Lastra (1996) op. cit., n. 1.
10  See e.g. Quintyn and Taylor, op. cit., n. 9.

include the central bank. Reflecting this division, the following sections address monetary stability (a primary role of the central bank) and financial stability (increasingly the second role of the central bank, but also shared in a variety of ways with other financial regulatory and supervisory agencies, such as securities regulators).

## 4.2. MONETARY STABILITY

Rosa Lastra defines monetary stability as[11]:

> the maintenance of the internal value of money (i.e., price stability) as well as the external value of the currency (i.e., the stability of the currency vis-à-vis other currencies, which is, in turn, influenced by the choice of exchange rate regime).

This definition highlights two central aspects: price stability and foreign exchange regime. Both of these, in many ways, result from the adoption of paper currencies by most countries by some point in the nineteenth century. In relation to price stability, the consensus in recent years has been to focus on control of inflation through a variety of mechanisms.

In relation to foreign exchange, two trends have been noteworthy, relating to capital liberalization and exchange rate regimes. Prior to the Bretton Woods system, countries (once having adopted paper currency), in general, operated fixed exchange rate regimes, typically based on a fixed relationship to gold (the "Gold Standard") or other precious metals (most commonly silver). Under the Bretton Woods system, countries operated fixed exchange rate regimes in the context of largely closed capital accounts, with exchange rates fixed to the US dollar which was, in turn, fixed to gold. As noted in Chapter Two, this arrangement functioned on the whole quite well for the maintenance of both monetary and financial stability. However, as the Bretton Woods international monetary system gradually broke down and finally ended with the US decision to sever the tie between the US dollar and gold, capital flows gradually became more liberalized, though they still remained largely restricted even among developed countries until the 1980s. With the end of any link between most currencies and gold during the 1970s, countries were faced with the challenge of devising new exchange rate systems to deal with the realities of fiat currencies (not backed by metals and instead only by the credibility of the issuing authority/government) and increasing capital flows.

---

[11] Lastra (2006), op. cit., n. 2, p. 35.

As a general matter, most countries adopted either freely floating exchange regimes or fixed exchange rate regimes (with exchange rates fixed at various levels of formality to other currencies, most commonly, by the end of the 1980s, the US dollar). Fixed exchange rate regimes included managed mechanisms whereby central banks sought to maintain the value of the currency through various means as well as more formally fixed arrangements such as currency boards.

In addition to highlighting institutional and financial sector weaknesses, the series of financial crises over the past fifteen years has also brought increasing focus on the twin aspects of capital liberalization and exchange regime. Essentially, many countries came to grief as a result of opening to capital flows without appropriately strengthening their financial sector while at the same time seeking to maintain fixed exchange rate regimes. Berry Eichengreen has defined this problem as the "impossible trinity"[12]: a country cannot have (1) full capital liberalization, (2) a fixed exchange rate and (3) independent control over monetary policy. At most, an economy can only have any two of these.

Following the series of financial crises discussed in Chapter One, the trend has been towards (1) a sequenced financial reform process prior to capital liberalization (the primary subject of Chapters Eight and Ten) and (2) floating exchange rate regimes with independent monetary policy (though often managed to some extent). This trend is exemplified in the twin objectives for central banks of monetary stability and financial stability.

### 4.2.1. *Monetary and Financial Policy Transparency Code*

In looking to the institutional framework for monetary stability, the key international guidance is provided by the IMF's MFP Transparency Code with primary responsibility allocated to the central bank. In fact, for purposes of the MFP Transparency Code, a central bank is defined as the "institution responsible for conducing monetary policy".[13]

In respect to good transparency practices for monetary policy by central banks, the MFP Transparency Code includes four general areas of guidance: (1) clarity of roles, responsibilities and objectives (Part I); (2) open process for monetary policy decisions (Part II); (3) public availability of information on

---

[12] B. Eichengreen, *Financial Crises and What to Do about Them* (New York: Oxford University Press, 2002); idem, *Globalizing Capital: A History of the International Monetary System* (Princeton, NJ: Princeton University Press, 1996). Frieden attributes the idea of the "unholy trinity" to Robert Mundell. J. Frieden, *Global Capitalism: Its Fall and Rise in the Twentieth Century* (New York: W.W. Norton, 2006), p. 461.

[13] MFP Transparency Code, op. cit., n. 3, p. 18.

monetary policy (Part III); and (4) accountability and assurances of integrity by the central bank (Part IV).

In respect to clarity of roles, responsibilities and objectives, these should be clearly defined in legislation or regulation such as a central bank law (section 1.1). In addition, the institutional relationship between monetary and fiscal operations should be clearly defined and disclosed and be consistent with the Fiscal Policy Transparency Code (discussed in Chapter Three) (section 1.2). Further, responsibilities of the central bank on behalf of the government should be clearly defined and disclosed (section 1.3).

In respect to an open process for formulating and reporting monetary policy decisions, the framework, instruments and targets (if any) used to pursue the objectives of monetary policy need to be publicly disclosed and explained (section 2.1), changes should be publicly announced and explained (section 2.3), and public progress reports in relation to achieving the objective(s) should be made (section 2.4). Where there is a permanent monetary policy-making body, information on its composition, structure and function should be publicly disclosed (section 2.2). In addition, reflecting the relationship between transparency and the process inherent in the rule of law, regulations on data reporting by financial intermediaries for monetary policy purposes should be publicly disclosed (section 2.6) and any substantive changes to monetary regulations should be subject to public consultation (section 2.5).

In respect to public availability of information on monetary policy, the central bank should make periodic reports, consistent with IMF data dissemination standards (Part III) (discussed subsequently).

Finally, in respect to accountability and integrity, central bank officials should periodically report to a designated public authority (section 4.1), in addition to publicly disclosing audited financial statements (sections 4.2 and 4.3). There should also be public rules addressing integrity and legal protections for central bank officials and staff (section 4.4).

Oddly, the IMF has not published a review of its experiences with monetary and financial policy transparency under the Financial Sector Assessment Program (FSAP)/Reports on the Observance of Standards and Codes (ROSC) process, despite having conducted a large number of such reviews. As of January 2007, the IMF and World Bank, however, had published FSAP/ROSCs in this area for fifty-five economies.[14]

---

[14] Algeria, Argentina, Australia, Barbados, Bulgaria, Cameroon, Canada, Chile, Costa Rica, Croatia, Czech Republic, Estonia, Euro Area, France, Gabon, Georgia, Germany, Hong Kong, Hungary, Iceland, Ireland, Israel, Italy, Jamaica, Japan, Kyrgyzstan, Latvia, Lithuania, Luxembourg, Macedonia, Malta, Mauritius, Mexico, Moldova, Morocco, Namibia, New Zealand, Pakistan, Poland, Romania, Russia, Rwanda, Saudi Arabia, Senegal, Serbia, Singapore, Slovakia, South Korea, Sweden, Switzerland, Tunisia, Uganda, Ukraine, United Arab Emirates, United Kingdom.

As noted earlier, although there is now general consensus in regard to the importance of central bank independence in relation to achievement of the monetary stability objective, this is an area that is not specifically included in the MFP Transparency Code.[15] Lastra, however, identifies the major elements which need to be addressed[16]: (1) statement of independence; (2) functional and/or operational guarantees of independence; (3) economic independence, especially in relation to government pressures to finance government deficits and financial intermediary bailouts (discussed further subsequently in the context of financial stability); and (4) regulatory powers. As Lastra notes, independence needs to be balanced by appropriate accountability and transparency mechanisms, as detailed in the MFP Transparency Code and data standards discussed in the following section.

### 4.2.2. *Transparency of Macroeconomic Data*

Public availability and comparability of macroeconomic information play an important role in both monetary and financial stability. In addition, they also play a significant role in maintaining confidence in an economy's currency, government and financial system: this was a major conclusion to emerge in the wake of the Mexican and east Asian financial crises. In this regard, the FSF has identified standards in relation to data dissemination and compilation.

The key standard area of data dissemination includes two standards – both identified as key: the Special Data Dissemination Standard (SDDS)[17] and the General Data Dissemination System (GDDS).[18] The SDDS and the GDDS, along with the Data Quality Reference Sites (DQRS), make up the IMF Dissemination Standards Board (DSBB).[19]

**Special Data Dissemination Standard.** As a response to the Mexican financial crisis in 1994–95, the IMF approved the SDDS for the provision of economic and financial statistics to the public by member countries, especially those countries that participate in the international capital markets or aspire to do so, and including both developed and emerging economies.[20]

---

[15]  See Lastra (2006), op. cit., n. 2, pp. 44–6.
[16]  Id., pp. 46–50.
[17]  IMF, *Special Data Dissemination Standard*, Mar. 1996.
[18]  IMF, *General Data Dissemination System*, Dec. 1997.
[19]  See http://dsbb.imf.org.
[20]  See IMF, "IMF Executive Board Approves the Special Data Dissemination Standard", IMF Press Release No. 96/18, 16 Apr. 1996. At an early stage, it was decided that two sets of standards should be created. Id.

In the aftermath of the Mexican crisis in 1995, the IMF's Interim Committee (now IMFC) emphasized at its 26 April 1995 meeting that timely publication by members of comprehensive economic and financial data would give greater transparency to members' economic policies and thereby increase investor confidence and decrease the chances of unexpected surprises that might result in the massive capital outflows that characterized the aftermath of the Mexican crisis. The SDDS was established in March 1996. The purpose of the SDDS is to[21]:

> guide IMF members in the provision to the public of comprehensive, timely, accessible, and reliable economic and financial statistics in a world of increasing economic and financial integration.

While participation is optional, countries seeking international capital were hoped to comply in order to meet investor demands for comparable information on competing countries. Prior to the Asian financial crises, this was not necessarily the case.

**General Data Dissemination System.** The GDDS is designed to complement the SDDS and to be a sort of stepping stone to eventual SDDS participation; it was established in December 1997.

According to the IMF, the purpose of the GDDS is threefold[22]:

(1) to encourage member countries to improve data quality;
(2) to provide a framework for evaluating needs for data improvement and setting priorities in this respect; and
(3) to guide member countries in the provision to the public of comprehensive, timely, accessible and reliable economic, financial and socio-demographic statistics.

Like the SDDS, guidance comprises four dimensions, with data covering the real, fiscal, financial and external sectors of an economy.[23] In addition, it covers a range of socio-demographic data reflecting the indicators included in the United Nations Millennium Development Goals (MDG).[24]

---

[21] Id. The SDDS comprises four elements: (1) coverage, periodicity, and timeliness of data; (2) access by the public; (3) integrity of the disseminated data; and (4) quality of the disseminated data. See id. As part of the IMF's efforts at dissemination and timeliness, data for participating countries are available on the DSBB.

[22] IMF, *The General Data Dissemination System*, Nov. 2003, p. 1.

[23] Namely: (1) coverage, periodicity and timeliness of data; (2) access by the public; (3) integrity of the disseminated data; and (4) quality of the disseminated data. Id.

[24] See UN Statistical Division, Millennium Indicators Database, http://millenniumindicators.un.org.

**Data Compilation.** In addition to the key standards and standard areas just described, the FSF Compendium also includes one additional standard area: data compilation. The data compilation standard area includes four standards, dealing with monetary and financial statistics[25], government finance statistics[26], balance of payments data[27] and national accounts data.[28] Together, these create a framework supporting the data included in the SDDS and GDDS and ensuring the comparability of data produced on the basis of this framework across economies.

**Implementation.** The Fund has undertaken a number of reviews of its data dissemination initiatives. Following the Asian financial crisis, criteria addressing international reserves and foreign currency liquidity were added.[29] Following the Third Review[30], the Fund developed the DQRS and an assessment framework (the Data Quality Assessment Framework (DQAF)). The DQAF was integrated into the ROSC data module following the Fourth Review.[31]

The IMF Executive Board considered the Fifth Review of the Fund's Data Dissemination Initiatives on 9 July 2003. In summary, the Fund's Directors supported the initiatives and on-going refinements.[32] The review reaches a number of important conclusions regarding, and recommendations for, the Funds Data Standards Initiatives, including[33]:

(1) The standards have led to significant improvements in data dissemination for SDDS members and to significant progress in statistical improvement for GDDS members.

(2) There is an increasing body of evidence that SDDS membership ("subscription") has a positive impact on a member's ("subscriber's") access to international capital markets.[34]

(3) The GDDS should give explicit recognition to the MDG indicators.

---

[25]  IMF, *IMF Manual of Monetary and Financial Statistics*, 5th ed., Oct. 2000.
[26]  IMF, *IMF Manual on Government Finance Statistics*, Nov. 2002 updated.
[27]  IMF, *IMF Balance of Payments Manual*, 1993.
[28]  IMF, *System of National Accounts*, 1993.
[29]  IMF, *Fifth Review of the Fund's Data Standards Initiatives*, 18 Jun. 2003, p. 8. See IMF, *Second Review of the Fund's Data Standards Initiatives*, 2 Dec. 1998.
[30]  IMF, *Third Review of the Fund's Data Standards Initiatives*, 15 Mar. 2000.
[31]  IMF, *Fourth Review of the Fund's Data Standards Initiatives*, 10 Jul. 2001.
[32]  IMF, *Public Information Notice: IMF Executive Board Reviews Data Standards Initiatives* [undated].
[33]  IMF, *Fifth Review of the Fund's Data Standards Initiatives*, 18 Jun. 2003, pp. 3–4.
[34]  Id., p. 18.

(4) A Compendium of Good Statistical practices should be developed to provide guidance to countries seeking to improve their statistical systems.

The main findings from a review of the ROSC data modules as of 3 June 2003 included[35]: (1) countries with robust legal and institutional frameworks for statistical production performed generally better in terms of overall data quality and (2) production of comprehensive source data was a major challenge in most countries.

As of January 2007, the IMF and World Bank had published data dissemination FSAP/ROSC modules for eighty-one countries.[36]

### 4.3. FINANCIAL STABILITY

One of the major themes of this volume is that financial stability should be a priority for both individual economies and the international financial architecture (as well as regional financial architecture, where relevant). As noted in Chapter Two, financial stability is often defined in a negative manner: as the absence of financial crisis (domestic, regional and/or international). At the same time, this is not sufficient guidance.

Garry Schinasi has defined financial stability in a positive and comprehensive manner[37]:

> Financial stability is a situation in which the financial system is capable of satisfactorily performing its three key functions simultaneously. First, the financial system is efficiently and smoothly facilitating the intertemporal allocation of resources from savers to investors and the allocation of economic resources generally. Second, forward-looking financial risks are being assessed and priced reasonably accurately and are being relatively well managed. Third, the financial system is in such condition that it can comfortably if not smoothly absorb financial and real economic surprises and shocks.

---

[35] Id., p. 31 (citing IMF, *The Fund's Experience with Data Module ROSCs*, SM/03/86 Supp.3).

[36] Albania, Argentina, Armenia, Australia, Azerbaijan, Bangladesh, Belarus, Botswana, Bulgaria, Burkina Faso, Cameroon, Canada, Chile, Colombia, Costa Rica, Czech Republic, Dominican Republic, Ecuador, Egypt, El Salvador, Estonia, Finland, France, Gambia, Georgia, Germany, Greece, Guatemala, Honduras, Hong Kong, Hungary, Iceland, India, Indonesia, Israel, Italy, Japan, Jordan, Kazakhstan, Kenya, Kyrgyzstan, Latvia, Lithuania, Macedonia, Malawi, Malta, Mauritius, Mexico, Moldova, Mongolia, Morocco, Mozambique, Namibia, Nicaragua, Niger, Norway, Oman, Pakistan, Panama, Paraguay, Peru, Philippines, Poland, Romania, Russia, Senegal, Slovakia, South Africa, South Korea, Sri Lanka, Sweden, Tajikistan, Tanzania, Thailand, Tunisia, Turkey, Uganda, Ukraine, United Kingdom, Uruguay, Zambia.

[37] G. Schinasi, *Safeguarding Financial Stability: Theory and Practice* (Washington, DC: International Monetary Fund, 2006), p. 82.

This definition implies that the objective is[38]:

> Maintaining the smooth functioning of the financial system and maintaining the system's ability to facilitate and support the efficient functioning and performance of the economy; and having in place the mechanisms to prevent financial problems from becoming systemic or from threatening the stability of the financial and economic system, but without undermining the economy's ability to sustain growth and perform its other important functions.

As noted at the outset of this chapter, financial stability is being given as an objective to central banks with increasing frequency, and this author would suggest that financial stability should be seen as one of the main objectives of any central bank (along with monetary stability). Schinasi's definition also extends beyond crisis prevention to support for financial development (and thereby, directly or indirectly, economic growth), therefore, to some extent, encompassing the development objective frequently given to central banks and discussed further subsequently and in Chapter Ten. At the same time, the central bank is not the only domestic financial agency responsible for financial stability, but the central bank should have the primary responsibility for macro level financial stability in any financial system.

At the outset, the overriding concern should be the overall design of the financial safety net.

Financial safety nets are, in general terms, a set of institutions, laws and procedures that strengthen the ability of the financial system to withstand bank runs and other systemic disturbances, as well as support appropriate financial system functioning. The primary concern of the financial safety net is financial stability, and the objectives of the establishment of a financial safety net include increasing financial efficiency, controlling systemic risk and protecting consumers in order to increase confidence in the financial system. Systemic risk is defined as[39]:

> the risk that an event will trigger a loss of economic value or confidence in, and attendant increases in uncertainty about, a substantial portion of the financial system that is serious enough to quite probably have significant adverse effects on the economy. Systemic risk events can be sudden and unexpected, or the likelihood of their occurrence can build up through time in the absence of appropriate policy responses. The adverse real economic effects from systemic

---

[38] Id., p. 100.

[39] G-10, *Consolidation in the Financial Sector* (Basel: Bank for International Settlements, 2001), pp. 126–7.

problems are generally seen as arising from disruptions to the payment system, to credit flows, and from the destruction of asset values.

At the same time, however, safety nets have significant potential costs.[40] Good corporate governance and sound risk management of individual financial intermediaries, effective market discipline, and frameworks for strong prudential regulation, supervision and laws can mitigate moral hazard; and these elements are most effective when used in concert.[41]

A well-designed financial safety has four major advantages[42]:

(1) Such procedures help to ensure that the incentives facing market participants are not unduly distorted – for example, by a widespread expectation that all bank liabilities ultimately have state underpinning.

(2) Credible plans with clear guidelines for the type of action to be taken in the event of a particular contingency help to limit forbearance.

(3) Such procedures should reduce the need for ad hoc, ex post actions which, even if effective in dealing with an immediate crisis, may, through moral hazard, significantly distort incentives for the future.

(4) A clear ex ante procedure reduces uncertainty and can thus have the additional advantage of limiting depositors' loss of confidence.

As a general rule, a number of principles should guide the design and on-going operations of a safety net: First, safety nets should strengthen rather than supplant private capital, monitoring and closure mechanisms.[43] Second, safety nets must take into account both aggregate risk and idiosyncratic risk.[44] Third, the design of the net should tie securely into the characteristics of the particular financial system and economy in which it is embedded.[45] Fourth, each component of the safety net should be designed to impose a margin of loss on financial claimants.[46] Fifth, in order to reduce the risk of an indiscriminate extension of public guarantees, authorities should be explicit in describing the nature and extent of the safety net and should implement appropriate supervisory and

---

[40] F. Mishkin, "Prudential Supevision: Why is it important and what are the issues?", NBER Working Paper 7926 (Sep. 2000), p. 7.

[41] FSF, *Guidance for Developing Effective Deposit Insurance Systems*, Sep. 2001, Principle 2a.

[42] G-22, *Report of the Working Group on Strengthening Financial Systems* (Basel: BIS, Oct. 1998), p. 21.

[43] P. Brock, "Financial Safety Nets and Incentive Structures in Latin America" (Aug. 1998, mimeographed), p. 28.

[44] Id.

[45] E. Kane, "Financial Safety Nets: Reconstructing and Modelling a Policymaking Metaphor", NBER Working Paper 8224 (Apr. 2001), pp. 4–5.

[46] A. Demirguc-Kunt, "Designing a Bank Safety Net – A Long-term Perspective", Website Policy Note (World Bank, 1999), p. 2.

regulatory policies.[47] Sixth, a complete standard would require authorities to develop and regularly review strategic plans for managing financial crises and to train their staff in the use of crisis-management protocols.[48]

### 4.3.1. *Design of the Financial Safety Net*

In essence, the financial safety net is the overall system for supporting financial stability in the financial system. As such, a complete description includes a number of elements[49]: (1) contingency planning, (2) lender of last resort, (3) financial regulation and supervision, (4) systems for addressing problem financial intermediary resolution and insolvency, and (5) depositor and consumer protection mechanisms. The first and second elements are addressed subsequently. In relation to the third, fourth and fifth elements (financial regulation and supervision, systems for problem financial intermediary resolution and insolvency, and depositor and customer protection), general principles are presented subsequently, with detailed discussion the subject of Chapters Five through Eight.

In terms of central bank responsibilities, due to the central bank's essential role in acting as lender of last resort, it also must have a major role in overall financial safety net design and contingency planning. Central banks may or may not be involved in financial regulation and/or financial intermediary resolution and/or liquidation. These issues are discussed in greater detail in Chapter Eight.

### 4.3.2. *Contingency Planning*

Neither the financial safety net nor financial supervision can, nor should, provide an assurance that financial intermediaries will not fail or that financial system participants will not take losses. As a general principle, supervisors should develop contingency plans for dealing with financial insolvencies in the context of their individual financial systems, as well as consideration of any cross-border situations that could arise.

Contingency planning should involve both the agency responsible for macro financial stability (i.e., the central bank) as well as any agencies responsible for aspects of financial regulation and supervision and financial intermediary resolution and insolvency, as well as the ministry of finance. Such planning

---

[47]  G-22, op. cit., n. 42, p. 20.
[48]  Kane, op. cit., n. 45, pp. 4–5.
[49]  Cf. G-22, op. cit., n. 42, p. 20.

requires a comprehensive analysis and understanding of the risks present in the financial system and the sorts of problems which may emerge. With possible problems identified, appropriate mechanisms and systems can be developed in order to deal with eventualities which may arise.

The distribution of powers and responsibilities among the financial safety net participants is a matter of public policy choice and individual country circumstances, with issues discussed in greater detail in Chapters Eight and Ten.[50]

### 4.3.3. *Lender of Last Resort*

The second element, the lender of last resort function, is designed to provide emergency liquidity to otherwise solvent financial intermediaries. Financial agencies (especially the central bank) should develop appropriate systems of liquidity support for financial intermediaries and the financial system generally. The most common mechanism to ensure the provision of liquidity in conditions of stress is the lender of last resort function.

Under the current formulation, provision of lender of last resort support should follow the following rules[51]:

(1) Support should only be provided to temporarily illiquid but solvent financial intermediaries.
(2) Support should be provided freely but at penalty interest.
(3) Support should be provided to anyone with good collateral who meets both rules (1) and (2).
(4) The lender of last resort should make its readiness to lend clear ex ante.
(5) Nonetheless, the decision to provide support should remain discretionary.
(6) This discretion should be based upon the test of the existence of potential systemic risk.

While the lender of last resort is typically not thought of in terms of legal issues, in fact, the formulation is clearly based upon the presupposition of a functioning legal system supporting financial transactions, as well as upon an effective regulatory and supervisory process.[52]

"Temporarily illiquid but solvent" requires two sets of preconditions: (1) supervisory information in order to determine the respective condition;

---

[50] FSF, op. cit., n. 41, p. 7.
[51] See R. Lastra, "Lender of Last Resort: An International Perspective", 48 ICLQ 339 (1999).
[52] In fact, this is the basis of international efforts to support financial stability.

and (2) a definition of insolvency, which is generally a public policy choice enshrined in insolvency legislation. "Freely but at penalty interest", fortunately, is relatively self-sufficient, except that the lender of last resort must have the ability, in fact, to provide potentially unlimited support, which will often only be available through control over the monetary supply (which most central banks control, except those with currency board arrangements) and consequent possible inflationary implications. "Anyone with good collateral" clearly requires both a legal judgement and a qualitative judgement. The legal judgement is based upon the ability to take collateral – different legal systems vary greatly on this point[53] – and also the issue of where the lender of last resort ranks in the context of insolvency – a significant issue when dealing with a potentially insolvent intermediary. "Readiness to lend clear ex ante" requires a legal system that supports lending, which is very much determined by the respective system of private law. The remaining two criteria "simply" require an effective system of information gathering on the part of the lender of last resort in order to make the respective determination – and if that system were perfect, of course, there would be no need for the support in the first place.

This brief discussion is simply intended to show how seemingly fundamental formulations in relation to financial crisis management are based on the underlying legal system. If the requisite elements are not in place, the system cannot meet its goals of preventing systemic risk, while at the same time controlling moral hazard. Around the world, there are a mixture of implicit and explicit structures for the lender of last resort, though in most cases it is the central bank, but in some cases it is the deposit insurance authority (usually in conjunction with the central bank).

Such support should not be provided to otherwise insolvent financial intermediaries, especially those which do not raise systemic concerns. Any such support is actually a form of subsidy or government bailout and should only be undertaken with government approval.

### 4.3.4. *Financial intermediary Resolution and Insolvency*

Effective and timely resolution of insolvencies is probably one of the most important elements of a well-designed safety net.[54] The existence of weak

---

[53] See e.g., "Focus on secured transactions", Law in Transition (Aut. 2000); N. de la Pena, H. Fleisig and P. Wellons, "Secured Transactions Law Reform in Asia: Unleashing the Potential of Collateral", in *Law and Policy Reform at the Asian Development Bank 2000*, vol. 2 (ADB, 2000); J. Norton and M. Andenas (eds), *Emerging Financial Markets and Secured Transactions* (London: Kluwer, 1998).

[54] Demirguc-Kunt, op. cit., n. 46, p. 5.

financial intermediaries – especially banks – can undermine the entire financial system. Therefore, weak financial intermediaries should either be on a path that will restore their financial health or, if that is not deemed to be feasible, closed in timely fashion.[55]

A coherent system for the restructuring and resolution of weak financial intermediaries, that is properly implemented, is crucial in reducing the risk of contagion within the financial system and to the economy at large. An effective resolution system also reduces the overall costs to the government of dealing with failing intermediaries, as well as other costs (ranging from the loss of asset values to the social costs of having a smaller financial system). Finally, it greatly facilitates the alternative of taking action at the right time. For these reasons, methods for restructuring and resolution of financial intermediaries are important for maintaining financial stability.[56]

## 4.4. PAYMENT AND SETTLEMENT

In pursuing monetary and financial stability, central banks usually also acquire certain responsibilities in relation to payment and settlement systems and government securities markets, and these responsibilities may be highlighted if a central bank also has an objective relating to financial and/or economic development.

According to the central banks in the European Union[57]:

> . . . a payment system consists of a defined group of institutions and of a set of instruments and procedures, used to ensure the circulation of money within a geographic area, usually a country. Any country's economy can be shown as a series of layers in an inverted pyramid, in which each layer is supported by all layers beneath it. The broadest layer of the pyramid represents the real economy and the financial markets – the buying and selling of goods and services throughout the nation. It is supported by the country's banking system – the next level of the pyramid – which provides payment services. The third level consists of a limited number of interbank fund-transfer systems

---

55 G-22, op. cit., n. 42, p. 23. It should be recognized that because of the key role of banks in the economy (e.g., in the payments system), and because of the loss of value which typically occurs if a bank is closed and illiquid loan-book assets are sold, the approach of bank regulators to resolution and insolvency is quite different from that of corporate insolvency practitioners. The main concern of securities regulators also differs in that they seek to ensure an orderly wind-down to protect the interests of the customers and counterparties of the troubled securities firm.

56 Id.

57 Ad Hoc Working Group on EC Payment Systems, *Issues of Common Concern to EC Central Banks in the Field of Payment Systems*, Sep. 1992, p. 8.

through which payment transactions are processed. The final settlement of payment transfers takes place across the accounts which banks hold with the central bank, whose pivotal role is vital for the functioning of the economy as a whole.

Clearing, netting and settlement are three distinct processes pertaining to the payment system environment, each with its own, very specific, purpose. Netting, as a means to minimize liquidity required for settlement, can be applied either as a post-clearing operation or a pre-settlement operation.

A payment system defines the procedures, rules, standards and instruments used to exchange financial value between two parties discharging an obligation. Payment transactions have two parts: the flow of payment instructions and the flow of funds. These two flows are always related, but may follow different paths and have different timings.

Payment methods are the instruments, procedures, and institutions which enable users to meet payment obligations. Traditionally, payment methods have been classified as credit or debit transfers depending on whether the payor's payment instructions are given directly to its financial intermediary (credit transfer) – usually a bank – or pass via the payee (a debit transfer). Payment methods are paper based, electronic or a combination of both. An additional classification divides payment systems into small- and large-value systems.

Humphrey, Sato, Tsurami and Vesala have concluded that five attributes determine an economy's payment structure and illustrate the critical areas that will affect developing, transition and emerging economies as they seek to modernize their own payment systems[58]:

(1) the geographical size of a country and its population density (making the communication of payment information easy or difficult);
(2) the concentration of the banking system and its interconnectedness (permitting greater movement of funds internally within a single entity rather than externally between separate entities);
(3) the legal structure concerning rights and liabilities of payment participants (reducing risk for certain payment instruments but not others) and antitrust laws (affecting cooperation and competition among suppliers of payment services);
(4) the influence of cultural factors such as crime rates (affecting the need for cash substitutes); and

[58] D. Humphrey, S. Sato, M. Tsurumi and J. Vesala, "The Evolution of Payments in Europe, Japan, and the United States", World Bank Policy Research Working Paper 1676 (Oct. 1996).

(5) the role of economic factors that affect the trade-off between risk and efficiency by type of transaction and payment instrument (reflected in relative payment costs, user convenience, payment timeliness, and the availability of payment alternatives).

Ineffective payment, settlement and custody arrangements undermine the proper functioning of financial systems. As early as 1994, a World Bank report[59] concluded that effective, efficient payment systems are vital for the economic development of emerging economies. Efficient payment systems help promote the development of commerce, enhance economic policy oversight, control the risk inherent in moving large values, and reduce the financial, capital and human resources devoted to the transfer of payments. The authors recommended that a new payment system should be kept simple because many such countries lack the infrastructure and banking sophistication to leapfrog from basic to state-of-the-art payment systems. The first task is therefore to fix the most serious problems. The second is to upgrade the current systems incrementally, to meet basic standards of timeliness, security and reliability. Development of the system should follow a disciplined plan for defining the needs of users and for organizing the project team and project goals.

### 4.4.1. International Efforts

In the area of payments and settlements, two organizations have been active. The first, the Committee on Payment and Settlement Systems (CPSS), which operates under the aegis of the Group of Ten (G-10) central bank governors at the Bank for International Settlements (BIS), addresses issues related to the development of practices fostering efficient and viable payment and settlement systems and has established a set of Core Principles for payment systems.[60] The second, the Emerging Markets Committee of the International Organization of Securities Commissions (IOSCO), in which regulators from sixty-four emerging economies participate, has released a report proposing the basis for the development of a legal framework for clearance and settlement in emerging economies.[61] The report highlights the main legal concerns which must be

---

[59] R. Listfield and F. Montes-Negret, "Modernizing Payment Systems in Emerging Market Economies", World Bank Policy Research Working Paper 1336 (Aug. 1994).

[60] See Committee on Payment and Settlement Systems ("CPSS"), *Core Principles for Systemically Important Payment Systems*, Dec. 1999 revised Jan. 2001.

[61] IOSCO, *Report of the Emerging Markets Committee, Towards a Legal Framework for Clearing and Settlement in Emerging Markets*, Nov. 1997.

addressed in order to achieve an efficient clearance and settlement system for securities in emerging markets.

### 4.4.2. *International Standards*

The FSF key area of payment and settlement includes two key standards: (1) the CPSS Core Principles and (2) a set of IOSCO Recommendations.

**General: Core Principles for Systemically Important Payment Systems.** The CPSS established a Task Force on Payment System Principles and Practices in May 1998 to consider what principles should govern the design and operation of payment systems in all countries.[62] It comprised the representatives from the G-10 central banks, the European Central Bank, eleven other national central banks, the IMF and World Bank, and consulted with groups of central banks in Africa, the Americas, Asia-Pacific, and Europe.[63]

Released in January 2001, the CPSS *Core Principles for Systemically Important Payment and Settlement Systems* is the key FSF standard in the area of payment and settlement. According to the FSF, the document sets out core principles for the design and operation of systemically important payment systems.[64]

The Core Principles are expressed deliberately in a general way to help ensure that they can be useful in all countries and that they will be durable. They do not represent a blueprint for the design or operation of any single system, but suggest the main characteristics that all systemically important payment systems should satisfy. The second part of the Report discusses in more depth the interpretation of the Core Principles, as well as implementation in a number of specific contexts, including paper-based instruments (e.g., cheques) and cross-border issues.[65]

The Core Principles delineate ten principles to achieve the policy objective of safety and efficiency in systemically important payment systems. The

---

[62] CPSS, *Core Principles for Systemically Important Payment Systems*, Jan. 2001, Forward.

[63] Id. Members of the task force included individuals from the central banks of Belgium, Brazil, Canada, the ECB, France, Germany, Hong Kong, Hungary, Italy, Japan, Malaysia, Mexico, The Netherlands, Russia, Saudi Arabia, Singapore, South Africa, Sweden, Switzerland, the United Kingdom, the United States, the Central Bank of the West African States (BCEAO), the IMF, the World Bank, the BIS, with additional contributions from the central bank of Australia. Id., Annex, pp. 91–2.

[64] CPSS, op. cit., n. 62.

[65] Id., p. 2.

system should have a well-founded legal basis under all relevant jurisdictions (Principle I). The system's rules and procedures should enable participants to have a clear understanding of the system's impact on each of the financial risks they incur through participation in it (Principle II). The system should have clearly defined procedures for the management of credit risks and liquidity risks, which specify the respective responsibilities of the system operator and the participants and which provide appropriate incentives to manage and contain those risks (Principle III). The system should provide prompt final settlement on the day of value, preferably during the day and at a minimum at the end of the day (Principle IV). A system in which multilateral netting takes place should, at a minimum, be capable of ensuring the timely completion of daily settlements in the event of an inability to settle by the participant with the largest single settlement obligation (Principle V). Assets used for settlement should preferably be a claim on the central bank; where other assets are used, they should carry little or no credit risk and little or no liquidity risk (Principle VI). The system should ensure a high degree of security and operational reliability and should have contingency arrangements for timely completion of daily processing (Principle VII). The system should provide a means of making payments which is practical for its users and efficient for the economy (Principle VIII). The system should have objective and publicly disclosed criteria for participation, which permit fair and open access (Principle IX). The system's governance arrangements should be effective, accountable and transparent (Principle X).

Systems should seek to exceed the minima included in Principles IV and V.

The Core Principles also establish four responsibilities of the central bank in applying the Core Principles. The central bank should define clearly its payment system objectives and should disclose publicly its role and major policies with respect to systemically important payment systems (Responsibility A). The central bank should ensure that the systems it operates comply with the Core Principles (Responsibility B). The central bank should oversee compliance with the Core Principles by systems it does not operate and it should have the ability to carry out this oversight (Responsibility C). The central bank, in promoting payment system safety and efficiency through the Core Principles, should cooperate with other central banks and with any other relevant domestic or foreign authorities (Responsibility D).

In addition, the CPSS has released specific guidance on the central bank's role in supervising payment and settlement systems.[66] Although not

---

[66] CPSS, *Central Bank Oversight of Payment and Settlement Systems*, May 2005.

incorporated into the FSF framework, it provides very useful guidance to central banks in this regard.

In relation to central bank oversight of payment and settlement systems, the CPSS outlines five general oversight principles similar to those in the CPSS Core Principles but providing additional detail. Principle A (transparency) requires central banks to set out publicly their oversight policies, including the policy requirements or standards for systems and the criteria for determining to which systems these apply. Principle B (international standards) requires central banks to adopt (where relevant) internationally recognized standards for payment and settlement systems, such as the CPSS Core Principles and the CPSS-IOSCO Recommendations (discussed subsequently). Principle C (effective powers and capacity) requires central banks to have powers and capacity to carry out their oversight responsibilities effectively. Principle D (consistency) requires that oversight standards be applied consistently to comparable payment and settlement systems, including systems operated by the central bank. Principle E (cooperation with other authorities) requires central banks, in promoting the safety and efficiency of payment and settlement systems, to cooperate with other relevant central banks and authorities.

Further, the CPSS presents five "cooperative oversight principles" to address issues relating to cross-border and multicurrency systems.[67] Cooperative oversight Principle 1 (notification) requires each central bank that has identified the actual or proposed operation of a cross-border or multicurrency payment or settlement system to inform other central banks that may have an interest in the prudent design and management of the system. Principle 2 (primary responsibility) requires that cross-border and multicurrency payment and settlement systems should be subject to oversight by a central bank which accepts primary responsibility for such oversight, with the presumption that the central bank where the system is located will have such primary responsibility. Principle 3 (assessment of the system as a whole) requires the authority with primary responsibility in its oversight of a system to periodically assess the design and operation of the system as a whole, including consultation with other relevant authorities. Under Principle 4 (settlement arrangements), the determination of the adequacy of a system's settlement and failure-to-settle procedures in a currency is the joint responsibility of the central bank of issue and the authority with primary responsibility for oversight of the system. Under Principle 5 (unsound systems), central banks should in the absence of confidence in the soundness

---

[67] These principles are derived from a review of the CPSS, *Report of the Committee on Interbank Netting Schemes of the Central Banks of the Group of Ten Countries*, Nov. 1990 (the "Lamfalussy Report").

of the design or management of any cross-border or multicurrency system, if necessary, discourage use of the system or the provision of services to the system, for example, by identifying such activities as unsafe and unsound practices.

**Securities: Recommendations for Securities Settlement Systems.** Released in 2001, the joint CPSS/IOSCO document identifies minimum requirements that securities settlement systems should meet and the best practices for which systems should strive.[68] These encompass the legal framework for securities settlement, risk management, access, governance, efficiency, transparency, and regulation and oversight. The recommendations are designed to cover all systems for securities, including equities, corporate and government bonds and money market instruments, and securities issued in developed, developing, transition and emerging economies. They also aim to cover settlement of both domestic and cross-border trades.

The document includes nineteen recommendations under six headings: (1) legal risk (Recommendation 1), (2) presettlement risk (Recommendations 2 to 5), (3) settlement risk (Recommendations 6 to 10), (4) operational risk (Recommendation 11), (5) custody risk (Recommendation 12), (6) other issues (Recommendations 13 to 19). In addition, the document provides guidance on implementation and assessment.

In relation to legal risk, securities settlement systems should have a well-founded, clear and transparent legal basis (Recommendation 1). In relation to presettlement risk, trade confirmation should occur no later than the trade date (Recommendation 2), with rolling settlement occurring no later than three days after trading (Recommendation 3). Central counterparties (CCPs) should be considered (Recommendation 4) and securities lending and borrowing should be encouraged (Recommendation 5). In relation to settlement risk, central securities depositories (CSDs) are encouraged (Recommendation 6) and should implement appropriate risk controls (Recommendation 9), along with delivery versus payment settlement (Recommendation 7). Final settlement should occur not later than the end of the settlement day with real-time settlement preferred (Recommendation 8) and should be secure (Recommendation 10). Appropriate systems and contingency plans should be developed to reduce operational risk (Recommendation 11) and custodians should employ appropriate procedures to protect customer assets to reduce custody risk, including protection from claims by custodian creditors (Recommendation 12).

[68] CPSS and IOSCO Technical Committee, *Recommendations for Securities Settlement Systems*, Nov. 2001.

In addition, CCPs and CSDs should have appropriate objectives and governance structures (Recommendation 13), along with objective and transparent criteria for participation permitting fair and open access (Recommendation 14) as well as transparency in their operations (Recommendation 17). Further, securities settlement systems, in addition to safety and soundness, should also be cost-effective and efficient (Recommendation 15), use appropriate communication procedures (Recommendation 16), and be subject to effective regulation, with central banks and securities regulators working together (Recommendation 18). Finally, CSDs with cross-border links should design and operate such systems so as to reduce cross-border settlement risks (Recommendation 19).

**Other Financial Stability Forum Standards.** In addition to the two key standards, the FSF Compendium also includes a number of other standards under the subheadings of banking and securities. Payment and settlement standards for banking address real-time gross settlement (RTGS) systems[69], foreign exchange settlement risks[70] and interbank netting.[71] Payment and settlement standards relating to securities address over-the-counter (OTC) derivatives settlement[72], clearing of exchange-traded derivatives[73] and delivery versus payment systems.[74]

**Implementation.** At the end of 2002, the IMF and World Bank conducted a review of FSAP/ROSC experiences to date.[75] In the area of payment systems[76], FSAP/ROSC assessments began in 1999; by December 2002, fifty-seven assessments had been undertaken in forty-two economies. According to the Bank and Fund, the assessments revealed a number of weaknesses, with many systems failing to meet a number of standards, especially in relation to legal basis. As a result of these identified issues, the Bank and Fund, with the CPSS, developed additional guidance in the area.[77]

---

[69] CPSS, *Real Time Gross Settlement Systems*, Mar. 1997.
[70] CPSS, *Settlement Risk in Foreign Exchange Transactions*, Mar. 1996.
[71] CPSS, Lamfalussy Report, op. cit., n. 67.
[72] CPSS, *OTC Derivatives: Settlement Procedures and Counterparty Risk Management*, Sep. 1998.
[73] CPSS, *Clearing Arrangements for Exchange-Traded Derivatives*, Mar. 1997.
[74] CPSS, *Delivery Versus Payment in Securities Settlement Systems*, Sep. 1992.
[75] IMF and World Bank, *Analytical Tools of the FSAP*, Feb. 2003.
[76] Id., pp. 29–30; IMF and World Bank, *Financial Sector Assessment Program – Experience with the Assessment of Systemically Important Payment Systems*, Apr. 2002.
[77] IMF, World Bank and CPSS, *Guidance Note for Assessing Observance of Core Principles for Systemically Important Payment Systems* [undated].

As of January 2007, the IMF and World Bank had published FSAP/ROSC payment systems modules for fifty-five economies.[78]

### 4.4.3. *Developing Payment and Settlement Systems*

In developing payment and settlement systems, the CPSS has provided certain useful guidance.[79] The CPSS guidance, while not included in the FSF compendium, could also be seen as a model for incorporating developmental aspects into other areas of international financial standards.

The document includes fourteen guidelines for developing national payment systems grouped under four main headings. According to the CPSS, the main elements of a national payment system include[80]:

(1) payment instruments used to initiate and direct the transfer of funds between the accounts of payers and payees at financial intermediaries (such as cheques);
(2) payment infrastructures for transacting and clearing payment instruments, processing and communicating payment information, and transferring funds between the paying and receiving intermediaries;
(3) financial intermediaries that provide payment accounts, instruments and services to consumers, and businesses and organizations that operate payment transactions, clearing and settlement service networks for those financial intermediaries;
(4) market arrangements such as conventions, regulations and contracts for producing, pricing, delivering and acquiring the various payment instruments and services; and
(5) laws, standards, rules and procedures set by legislators, courts and regulators that define and govern the mechanics of the payment transfer process and the conduct of payment service markets.

At the outset, the central bank should be kept at the centre due to its overall responsibility for a sound currency, including the development of the use of

---

[78] Albania, Australia, Barbados, Bulgaria, Cameroon, Canada, Colombia, Costa Rica, Croatia, Czech Republic, Denmark, Estonia, Euro area, Finland, France, Georgia, Germany, Hong Kong, Hungary, Iceland, Ireland, Israel, Italy, Jamaica, Japan, Kyrgyzstan, Latvia, Lithuania, Luxembourg, Macedonia, Malta, Mauritius, Mexico, Morocco, Mozambique, The Netherlands, Norway, Philippines, Poland, Russia, Saudi Arabia, Serbia, Singapore, Slovakia, Slovenia, South Korea, Spain, Sweden, Switzerland, Trinidad and Tobago, Uganda, Ukraine, United Arab Emirates, United Kingdom, Uruguay.

[79] CPSS, *General Guidance for National Payment System Development*, Jan. 2006.

[80] Id., p. 2.

money as an effective means of payment (Guideline 1). Second, because payment accounts, instruments and services available to end users are provided by banks and other similar financial intermediaries through cooperative systems, the role of a sound banking system should be promoted (Guideline 2).

In relation to planning, complexity needs to be recognized and planning should be based on a comprehensive understanding of all the core elements of the national payment system and the principal factors influencing its development (Guideline 3). On this basis, the focus should be on identifying and being guided by the payment needs of all users in the national payment system and by the capabilities of the economy (Guideline 4). Clear priorities need to be set to plan and prioritize development of the national payment system strategically (Guideline 5). Overall, ensuring effective implementation of the strategic plan is the goal (Guideline 6).

In relation to the institutional framework, because the expansion and strengthening of market arrangements for payment services are important aspects of the evolution of the national payment system, market development needs to be promoted (Guideline 7). Effective consultation among relevant stakeholders in the national payment system supports development (Guideline 8). In addition, effective payment system oversight by the central bank often requires collaborative arrangements with other authorities (Guideline 9). To promote legal certainty, it is necessary to develop a transparent, comprehensive and sound legal framework for the national payment system (Guideline 10).

In relation to infrastructure, it is desirable to expand the availability and choice of efficient and secure non-cash payment instruments and services available to consumers, businesses and government by expanding and improving retail payment infrastructures (Guideline 11). For the large-value payment system, development should be based primarily on the needs of financial markets and the growth in time-critical interbank payments (Guideline 12). Payment and securities systems should be aligned between securities and large-value systems for financial system safety and efficiency (Guideline 13). Finally, settlement processes for the core processes of retail, large-value and securities systems should be operationally coordinated to efficiently manage interrelated liquidity needs and settlement risks (Guideline 14).

The CPPS also provides a checklist of elements of a stocktaking exercise to support Guidelines 3 and 4.[81] Further, the CPSS provides an overview of central elements of the legal framework for payment systems, including for: (1) payment instruments, (2) settlement of payment obligations, (3) collateral and credit, (4) payment network organization and participation, (5) securities

---

[81] Id., Annex 3.

settlement systems, (6) conflict of laws, (7) central bank oversight, and (8) relevant international legal standards.[82]

The legal framework for payment instruments includes laws relating to (1) currency, (2) cheques and negotiable instrument, (3) credit transfers, (4) card instruments, (5) electronic payments and commerce, and (6) evidence. The legal framework for settlement of payment obligations includes laws relating to (1) netting and novation and (2) settlement. The legal framework for collateral and credit includes laws relating to (1) credit and (2) pledging and collateral.

### 4.5. MARKET FUNCTIONING: GOVERNMENT SECURITIES MARKETS

According to the BIS Committee on the Global Financial System (CGFS) of the G-10 central banks, following financial crises over the past fifteen years[83],

> there seems to be a growing consensus that deep and liquid financial markets, especially government securities markets, are needed to ensure a robust and efficient financial system as a whole.

Certainly, there has been an increasing amount of attention paid to debt securities markets around the world in the past several years.

Once a government has developed a sustainable fiscal and taxation system, it may consider developing government securities markets. Government securities markets, in addition to assisting with government liquidity management (through regular offerings of short-term government securities), support the functioning of the payment and settlement systems (by providing means to secure payment exposures prior to final settlement), and macroeconomic and monetary policy. They also provide useful information to financial sector participants through the development of a yield curve. Further, once short-term government securities markets are functioning and providing an effective yield curve, a government may be able to extend the tenor of its borrowing, thereby providing a means of longer-term financing as well as support for investment opportunities.

While consensus has yet to fully develop, the CGFS has formulated recommendations related to one central aspect: government securities markets. The guidance contains five guiding principles which, in turn, are used to draw more specific policy recommendations[84]: (1) competitive market structure should be

---

[82] Id., Annex 4.

[83] Committee on the Global Financial System (CGFS), *How Should We Design Deep and Liquid Markets? The Case of Government Securities*, 1999, p. 1.

[84] Id., pp. 2–4.

maintained; (2) markets should have low levels of fragmentation; (3) transaction costs should be minimized to the extent consistent with market stability; (4) sound, robust, and safe market infrastructure should be ensured[85]; and (5) heterogeneity of market participants should be encouraged.[86] Based on these guiding principles, the CGFS has established five recommendations for the creation of deep and liquid government securities markets: (1) desirability of coherent debt management strategies (i.e., ensuring an appropriate distribution of maturities and issue frequency as a means of establishing benchmark issues at key maturities); (2) taxation (i.e., minimization of liquidity-impairing effects of taxes); (3) transparency of sovereign issuers and issue schedules should be ensured and transparency of trading information encouraged, with due attention being paid to the anonymity of market participants[87]; (4) safety and standardization of trading and settlement practices should be addressed through appropriate trading rules and infrastructure[88]; and (5) related markets, including repurchase ("repo"), futures, and options markets should be developed.[89] Further, according to the CGFS, central banks have a clear role in market development and financial stability.[90]

## 4.6. FINANCIAL DEVELOPMENT

As noted earlier and in the preceding section, central banks frequently are also given financial and/or economic development objectives. Even in the limited formulation of the monetary stability and financial stability objectives, however, certain development roles may be necessary, for example in relation to government securities markets to support monetary policy implementation, collateral development to support financial stability or payment systems development to support both monetary stability and financial stability. We return to these issues in Chapter Ten.

## 4.7. CONCLUSION

The preceding two chapters have analysed the preconditions for financial stability and financial sector development. Some of these preconditions have

---

[85] The CGFS defines this as comprising "payment and settlement systems, the regulatory and supervisory framework as well as market monitoring / surveillance". Id., p. 4.

[86] This includes allowing foreign participation. However, the CGFS notes that "due attention should be paid to the sequential development of domestic markets, as highlighted by the recent episodes of financial market turbulence in emerging markets." Id.

[87] The CGFS notes the importance of transparency in three contexts: issuers, issue schedule and market information. Id., p. 6.

[88] This includes the availability of short sales. Id., p. 7.

[89] Id., pp. 4–8.

[90] Id., p. 8.

been addressed by the international financial standards initiatives (namely, those dealing with macroeconomic issues), but many of the most significant areas have not been addressed to a significant or sufficient extent.

Niall Ferguson has emphasized the importance of four institutions as the "bases of financial strength", which he calls the "square of power"[91]: (1) a tax-collecting bureaucracy, (2) a representative parliament, (3) a national debt and (4) a central bank. He suggests that these developed from the imperatives of war, first in the United Kingdom, and were later exported to the United States and adopted by competitors of both, until today – though usually unrecognized – they are the essence of financial and hence economic and political power. Ferguson's points in many ways sum up the lessons of the previous discussion: in order to support a functioning market economy and a market-based financial system, a variety of legal and institutional supports are necessary.

As noted earlier, with these supports in place, a basic market-based financial sector can develop. However, to support both financial stability and economic growth, it is necessary to move beyond this basic level of financial developments, to address issues of financial infrastructure and financial regulation necessary to support functioning and developed finance.

---

[91] N. Ferguson, The *Cash Nexus: Money and Power in the Modern World*, 1700–2000 (New York: Basic Books, 2001), p. 420.

# 5

## Financial Infrastructure

This chapter builds on the foundations established in the previous two chapters and looks to the elements of legal, institutional and market infrastructure necessary for developed and sophisticated financial systems to function properly – what could be called essential financial infrastructure. Aspects include insolvency regimes, corporate governance, and financial information frameworks such as accounting and auditing systems. These are supported by appropriate measures to protect market integrity and thus confidence in the financial system. It is only when both the foundations and the supporting infrastructure are in place that financial regulation and supervision, in conjunction with appropriately sequenced financial liberalization (discussed in Chapter Eight and Part V) can function properly to support developed and sophisticated financial systems.

While the following list is by no means exhaustive, these core areas are of great importance and, when combined with an appropriate "third level" of financial regulation and supervision discussed in the next part, create the necessary environment for the development of an effective financial system.

First, adequate company law and securities regulation incorporating principles of good corporate governance are essential for corporatization[1], privatization and the development of a modern decentralized financial system.[2] Prospective investors need to be assured that the legislative and contractual frameworks within which corporate entities operate provide adequate protection of their legitimate interests and expectations. The importance of effective corporate governance has been underlined by the Group of Seven (G-7), Organization of Economic Cooperation and Development (OECD) and recent

---

[1] Corporatization is the process of creating corporations or companies.
[2] See OECD, *General Principles of Company Law in Transition Economies*, 1997.

international financial crises. In addition, its impact can be seen directly in the context of investors' decisions not to invest in companies (and sometimes even countries, of which the clearest recent example is Russia) which are viewed as problematic in this respect.

Second, effective insolvency provisions, including for financial intermediaries (discussed in the following part), are required to enable the redirection of capital and the closure of inefficient enterprises, hence improving governance and performance.[3] Once again, experiences in east Asia have underlined the significance of functioning insolvency procedures, not only for economic renewal, but also for adequate protection of investor rights in the context of business failures.

Third, financial markets require information. Accounting and auditing standards are central to the provision of information to markets. Accounting and auditing are also supported by other information infrastructure, including credit information systems, credit rating agencies and a free commercial and financial press.

Fourth, as has been emphasised throughout this volume, financial markets are based on confidence. A central aspect of confidence relates to preventing, to the greatest extent possible, use of the financial system by criminal elements. Focus areas include corruption, money laundering and terrorist financing, and financial market fraud and misconduct.

These elements – all to some extent addressed by international standards – build upon the underpinnings discussed in Chapters Three and Four and are necessary for the financial regulatory systems discussed in Part Three to function properly in a market economy.

## 5.1. INSOLVENCY

A functioning legal framework for insolvency management is crucial for the operation of a modern market-based economy and is linked with most of the major areas of concern in such an economy. There can be no well-functioning corporate sector as a whole without effective mechanisms which govern the exit of insolvent market participants from trading. Likewise, the financial sector will not engage in lending activities on a large scale if lenders do not have certainty regarding their position as secured creditors in the context the liquidation of their borrowers and that sufficient means for the enforcement of

---

[3] See Asian Development Bank, *Law and Development at the Asian Development Bank*, Apr. 1999, pp. 7–36.

security will be available. According to the Group of Ten (G-10), the general objectives of a system of corporate insolvency are reduction of uncertainty, promotion of efficiency, and fair and equitable treatment.[4] A functioning insolvency regime thus helps reduce the risk of lending and the cost of debt service and, thereby, increases the availability of credit and the making of investments generally.[5]

Further, a properly administered insolvency system operates as a valuable instrument for the promotion of market discipline. An effective insolvency regime provides the means for the ultimate identification of noncompetitive market participants and their controlled exit. It provides, in other words, for an effective "penalty" for the least competitive or otherwise unsuccessful. While these considerations stress the retroactive character of insolvency law, it also has a considerable preventive element in that it creates a strong incentive for the owners to strive for efficient and cost-effective performance so as to avoid administration by a third party on behalf of their creditors in the context of insolvency. Overall, an insolvency system serves as a means to ensure "the allocation of risk among participants in a market economy in a predictable, equitable, and transparent manner."[6]

A functioning insolvency system, therefore, is at the core of the legal and institutional environment for finance in any market-based economy.

While the existence of transparent, enforceable and therefore reliable insolvency rules is a necessary element of the legal environment in a market economy, the specific circumstances in an economy may well demand modifications. It is unlikely that insolvency provisions in themselves can actually drive industrial redevelopment since, for reasons indicated earlier, their efficient implementation in turn depends on other factors, such as an intact set of rules concerning collateral, corporate governance, rules ensuring transparency (e.g., by way of a company registry) and, not least, an independent and competent system of insolvency administration in charge of the enforcement of the legal framework and the supervision of the administration or liquidation of the insolvent company's estate.

The traditional Western concept of insolvency law is directed first and foremost to the liquidation of insolvent market participants in the interest of their creditors. Consequently, reorganization of insolvent companies, though often

---

[4] G-10, *Report of the Contact Group on the Legal and Institutional Underpinnings of the International Financial System*, Dec. 2002.

[5] IMF Legal Department, *Orderly and Effective Insolvency Procedures: Key Issues*, 1999, s. 2; C. Averch, "Bankruptcy Laws: What Is Fair?", Law in Transition 26 (Spr. 2000), pp. 26–7.

[6] IMF Legal Department, op. cit., n. 5.

expressly promoted by legislation[7], is normally conceived only where it is in the advantage of the (majority of) the creditors – that is, where it appears "economically reasonable" in the sense that a reorganization of the insolvent company as a going concern will enhance the overall value of the business and thus the assets available to the creditors.[8] While this principle may be fully legitimate, appropriate and functional in a developed market economy, its application in other environments may well face severe problems, and has done so in the past. In an economic environment dominated by nontransparent corporate conglomerates which account for a considerable percentage of a particular economy, public policy considerations may prevent the liquidation of a firm whose failure would, at the expense of the public, render thousands of workers unemployed. While a developed market economy may well remain passive as to the decision between liquidation and reorganization, an economy may feel a legitimate bias in favour of the latter, and may indeed demand insolvency rules that facilitate reorganization even against the will of the majority of creditors if public policy so requires. In fact, as the so-called "London approach" indicates, even fully liberalized economies such as the United Kingdom have in the past favoured the restructuring of businesses and avoided outright liquidation in cases where the public interest was at stake.[9] It has been noted, in this context, that the liquidation of insolvent companies appears "neither desirable nor practical" in economies where there is no market in which to liquidate certain types of assets and where, on the other hand, the liquidation of insolvent enterprises would result in the "virtual disappearance of the economy altogether".[10]

The implementation of a modern, predictable insolvency regime is therefore highly desirable. As described earlier, proper insolvency legislation is crucial for the operation of any market economy. It also helps encourage international investment and thus efforts to integrate an economy into the international economic and financial system.

### 5.1.1. *International Efforts*

A number of international organizations and associations have become involved with the development of standards for modern insolvency law and

---

[7] For example, by the introduction of the administration procedure in the United Kingdom.

[8] IMF Legal Department, op. cit., n. 5.

[9] See, e.g., id., s. 2.

[10] H. Kryshtalowych and S. Craig, "Ukraine's New Bankruptcy Law: The Demise of the Dinosaurs", Law in Transition 56 (Spr. 2000), pp. 57–8 (with reference to scholarly analysis of the situation in eastern Europe generally).

related systems. Many of these activities have focused on the development of standards for cross-border insolvency cases in particular, such as the United Nations Commission on International Trade Law (UNCITRAL) Model Law on Cross-Border Insolvency[11] and, in the European Union, the Insolvency Regulation of 2000.[12] More recently, a working group chaired by the Legal Department of the International Monetary Fund (IMF) presented a document containing very detailed principles for the development of workable, modern insolvency legislation.[13]

**Financial Stability Forum Key Standard: Principles and Guidelines for Effective Insolvency and Creditor Rights Systems.** At present, there is no internationally agreed key standard in the area of insolvency. However, the World Bank is coordinating an effort to develop an agreed standard and is working with UNCITRAL to develop a framework for implementation.

In April 2001, the Board of the World Bank approved a first set of *Principles and Guidelines for Effective Insolvency and Creditor Rights Systems*.[14] A revised set of the Principles, taking into account further feedback and lessons from insolvency assessments conducted under the Reports on the Observance of Standards and Codes (ROSC) initiative, is under development. The Bank is also working on a technical paper containing more detailed implementation guidelines to complement the Principles. In addition, building upon the work done by other international institutions (including the World Bank, IMF and Asian Development Bank (ADB)), UNCITRAL is currently finalizing a legislative guide for insolvency – a combination of model provisions, recommendations and explanatory notes, which is currently set for release, along with a revised version of the World Bank Principles, in 2007.[15]

---

[11] See IMF Legal Department, op. cit., n. 5. Cf. G. Johnson, "Towards International Standards on Insolvency: The Catalytic Role of the World Bank", Law in Transition 69 (Spr. 2000).

[12] Council Regulation (EC) No. 1346/2000 of 29 May 2000 on Insolvency Proceedings, OJ L 160, 30/06/2000, pp. 1–13.

[13] IMF Legal Department, op. cit., n. 5.

[14] World Bank, *Principles and Guidelines for Effective Insolvency and Creditor Rights Systems*, Apr. 2001. The Principles (ICRPs) were prepared by World Bank staff in collaboration with the African Development Bank, Asian Development Bank, European Bank for Reconstruction and Development (EBRD), Inter-American Development Bank, International Finance Corporation, IMF, OECD, UNCITRAL, INSOL International and International Bar Association. Id., p. 2 n. 2.

[15] See UNCITRAL, "Report of Working Group V (Insolvency Law) on the Work of its Thirtieth Session" (New York, 29 Mar.–2 Apr. 2004), A/CN.9/551 (United Nations, 30 Apr. 2004), pp. 3–7.

According to the World Bank, effective corporate insolvency principles should aim to[16]:

(1) integrate with a country's broader legal and commercial systems;

(2) maximize the value of a firm's assets by providing an option to reorganize;

(3) strike a careful balance between liquidation and reorganization;

(4) provide for equitable treatment of similarly situated creditors, including similarly situated foreign and domestic creditors;

(5) provide for timely, efficient and impartial resolution of insolvencies;

(6) prevent the premature dismemberment of a debtor's assets by individual creditors seeking quick judgements;

(7) provide a transparent procedure that contains incentives for gathering and dispensing information;

(8) reorganize existing creditor rights and respect the priority of claims with a predictable and established process; and

(9) establish a framework for cross-border insolvencies, with recognition of foreign proceedings.

In supporting these objectives, the thirty-five insolvency principles outlined by the World Bank cover five main areas: (1) the legal framework for creditor rights (Principles 1 to 5)[17], (2) the legal framework for corporate insolvency (Principles 6 to 16), (3) corporate rehabilitation (Principles 17 to 24), (4) informal workouts and restructuring (Principles 25 and 26) and (5) institutional and regulatory frameworks for implementation of the insolvency system (Principles 27 to 35).

To date, the IMF and World Bank have published two experimental ROSCs (for Colombia and the Slovak Republic) undertaken on the basis of these standards and conducted in the context of a comprehensive Financial Sector Assessment Program (FSAP).

The most recent version of the UNCITRAL Guide[18] is divided into two parts: Part I deals with the design of the main objectives and structure of an insolvency law, while Part II includes core insolvency law provisions.

Unfortunately, until the revised World Bank Principles and the final UNCITRAL Guide are integrated, approved and released, it is impossible to identify exactly the international consensus in this area.

---

[16] World Bank ICRP 6, p. 24. According to the World Bank, these elements were identified by the G-22. Id., p. 24 n. 10, citing G-22, *Report of the Working Group on International Financial Crises* (1998), pp. 16, 44–5.

[17] This section, while at first glance appearing to address collateral and secured transactions, only addresses these in the context of insolvency. See Chapter Four for further discussion.

[18] UNCITRAL, *Draft Legislative Guide on Insolvency Law*, A/CN.9/WB.V/WP.70 (parts I and II) (United Nations, 30 Sep. 2003).

## 5.2. CORPORATE GOVERNANCE

Over the past decade, an immense amount has been written and said about corporate governance. While corporate governance is an important issue for the functioning of any market economy or financial system, it is certainly not a new issue: Adam Smith wrote of these issues in 1776; Walter Bagehot provided a timely description of the typical problems, albeit in the context of banking, in 1873[19]; and Adolf Berle, Jr and Gardiner Means analysed the issues in some detail in 1932. Attention once again began to crystallize around these issues in the early 1990s, with major attention arising following high profile corporate collapses such as Enron in the United States and Parmalat in Europe.

Corporate governance has been defined as the set of relationships among shareholders, board, management and other constituencies of a company.[20] In recent years, various organizations and interest groups have been promoting corporate governance standards. For example, institutional investors have been promoting a corporate governance model focused on the interests of shareholders. These efforts are mainly focused on improving access to influence and control of management action. Other constituencies have stressed the broader responsibilities of enterprises towards their various stakeholders in addition to shareholders, including employees, suppliers and the community in which they operate as well as local and national governments.

As a starting point, improving corporate governance seeks to improve the efficiency and attractiveness of the markets for capital, following from the successful development of dispersed ownership of public corporations in the United States (the "Berle and Means corporation"), which underpins the efficiency and attractiveness of the markets for equity securities there.

The essential problem is well known: Companies suffer from the classic agent-principal conflict of interest between shareholders and management described by Berle and Means.[21] This conflict is most obvious in situations involving widely dispersed share-ownership and the potential conflict between the interests of management (those in control) and owners (the shareholders), most typical of markets in the United States and the United Kingdom (the Anglo-American model of corporate ownership, control and governance). The focus typically is on the rights of minority shareholders. The problems in a family-controlled or state-controlled context, while at first glance appearing

[19] W. Bagehot, *Lombard Street: A Description of the Money Market* (1873 [New York: John Wiley, 1999]), pp. 257–65.

[20] EBRD, *Sound Business Standards and Corporate Practices: A Set of Guidelines*, Sep. 1997.

[21] A. Berle and G. Means, *The Modern Corporation and Private Property* (New York: Macmillan 1933).

different from those in the traditional Berle and Means corporation, are, in reality, more pronounced, in that ownership and control are both combined to a large extent, thereby reducing the capacity of noncontrolling shareholders to influence management. The end result is a potential conflict of interest between controlling shareholders and noncontrolling shareholders. So long as the interests of the controller (whether family or state) are identical to those of the corporation, these models can both be quite effective under many circumstances. Problems occur in situations in which the interests of the controllers diverge from those of the corporation, and the controller is able to use the corporation for personal benefit and to the detriment of the interests of the company as a whole. To the extent that noncontrolling shareholders feel that their interests are not being served by the controllers, they will feel less inclination to invest in such companies. The end result is a potential governance problem, which feeds into lower share prices, higher costs of capital and decreased confidence, thereby reducing the potential scope and efficiency of the financial system and reducing the rate of economic growth.

The basic significance of good corporate governance is premised on corporate performance. Investors are willing to pay increased prices for shares in companies with good governance (a corporate governance premium) because well-governed companies perform better than poorly governend companies. Increased share prices reduce companies' cost of capital and therefore increase competitiveness of companies across a given market. Higher share prices also increase the attractiveness of a given market to investors (both domestic and international). Further, investors will be more likely to invest in companies and markets with good governance (good governance increases confidence in the market), enhancing the transfer of funds through the financial system, thereby increasing its scale and efficiency, in turn enhancing economic growth.

The result has been an increased focus over the past decade on a rather nebulous idea, namely corporate governance.

### 5.2.1. Recent Empirical Evidence

McKinsey & Company has stated the situation well[22]:

> Increased shareholder activism in the US and elsewhere stems from the conviction that better corporate governance will deliver higher shareholder returns. Yet repeated attempts by academics to show an irrefutable link between the two have failed, such is the complexity of the relationship.

---

[22] McKinsey & Co., *Investor Opinion Survey on Corporate Governance* (Jun. 2000), p. 1.

In order to investigate the actual value that investors place on corporate governance, McKinsey, in cooperation with the World Bank and the periodical *Institutional Investor*, conducted a series of surveys to discover how shareholders perceive and value corporate governance in both developed and emerging economies. The surveys gathered responses about investment intentions from more than 200 institutional investors responsible for approximately US$3.25 trillion in assets; 40 per cent of the respondents were based in the United States, with the remainder drawn world-wide.

Among the main findings from the surveys are the following[23]:

(1) Three-quarters of investors said board practices are at least as important to them as financial performance when evaluating companies for investment.[24]

(2) More than 80 per cent of investors indicated they would pay more for the shares of a well-governed company than for those of a poorly governed company with comparable financial performance. (For the purposes of the surveys, a well-governed company was defined as: (1) having a majority of outside directors on the board with no management ties, (2) holding formal evaluations of directors and (3) being responsive to investor requests for information on governance issues. In addition, directors hold significant stockholdings in the company, and a large proportion of directors' pay is in the form of stock/options.)

(3) The actual premium investors say they would be willing to pay for a well-governed company differs by country.[25] Figures varied from 17.9 per cent (United Kingdom) to 27.6 per cent (Venezuela).[26] Local investors were willing to pay on average a premium of 20.2 per cent; foreign investors were, on average, willing to pay a premium of 26.3 per cent.[27]

(4) Based on the evidence, the size of the premium that institutional investors said they were willing to pay for good governance seems to reflect the extent to which they believe there is room for improvement.[28] In Asia and Latin America, McKinsey concluded that the higher premia on offer reflected the need for more fundamental disclosure of information and stronger shareholder rights.[29]

---

[23] Id.
[24] Id.
[25] Id.
[26] Id., p. 10.
[27] Id., p. 11.
[28] Id., p. 2.
[29] Id.

Based upon the survey, McKinsey concludes[30]:

Although it remains difficult to measure the impact on market prices of the premiums investors say they are willing to pay for well-governed companies, the amounts they are prepared to pay leave little doubt that good governance does feed through. Precise measurement apart, the fact that a majority of investors say they already take corporate governance into account when making investment decisions is a powerful argument in favor of corporate governance reform.

As a result of this conclusion, McKinsey recommends that policy makers wishing to attract more foreign investors should also play their part, as companies alone cannot produce the magnitude of change that is necessary, particularly in emerging economies. At the regulatory level, the corporate governance framework should encourage governance reforms or, at the very least, not hinder them.[31] Specifically, two areas were singled out as the most significant target areas: (1) improved disclosure of information, and (2) stronger shareholder rights.[32]

In targeting these areas, good corporate governance depends on the broader legal and regulatory environment prevailing in the country of origin of a given company[33]:

Strong legal regimes are positively related to the quality of individual firm governance, implying that strengthening regulation will help invigorate economies by improving investor confidence and encouraging corporate investments.

The relationship between firm valuation and corporate governance is stronger in countries with less investor-friendly legal regimes.[34] Research also suggests that firms with better investment opportunities, higher concentration of ownership and more reliance on external financing have better corporate governance, and that these relations are stronger in legal regimes that are less investor-friendly.[35]

---

[30] Id., p. 3.

[31] Id.

[32] Id.

[33] A. Durnev and E. Han Kim, "To Steal or Not to Steal? The Interplay of Firm-specific Factors and Legal Regimes in Corporate Governance and Firm Valuation" (2002, mimeographed), p. 43.

[34] See id.; L. Klapper and I. Love, "Corporate Governance, Investor Protection, and Performance in Emerging Markets", World Bank Working Paper 2818 (2002).

[35] Durnev and Han Kim, op. cit., n. 33, p. 3.

Corporate governance has been a significant on-going issue in many developing, emerging and transition economies and can be considered perhaps the most significant issue to be faced following the initial challenges of monetization and stabilization.[36] The foundation of good institutional governance – the oversight and control by directors, managers and staff – is a sound business strategy and a competent and responsible senior management. Obviously, management ability and business acumen have developed and will continue to develop in emerging, developing and transition economies only with time, experience and education.

In addition, good governance requires comprehensive internal control procedures and policies, including means to ensure that staff act in the interest of the firm and do not engage in insider dealing, disclose proprietary information, or provide credit on grounds other than objective assessments of potential returns and risks. Maintenance of good institutional governance also requires that owners, directors and senior management have adequate incentives and are subject to appropriate legal sanctions in the event that they behave improperly. These sorts of requirements, unlike development of quality management, can be influenced by the legal framework, most clearly through property, contract and company law and accounting standards.

In relation to financial intermediaries, special problems arise. Around the world, government ownership of financial intermediaries has frequently been the basis of management failures because political pressure may place prudential and commercial considerations second to other objectives.[37] With many financial intermediaries still in state hands in developing, transition and emerging economies around the world, these problems are likely to continue. Another major cause of management failure, often at the root of banking problems, is insider lending or lending to related enterprises, when lending decisions are not based solely on the borrower's creditworthiness. This is an issue that has plagued financial intermediaries in emerging, developing and transition economies, as well as developed economies, and is one of the most difficult to address. Good institutional governance is more likely to be sustained if there exist outside shareholders (i.e., depositors, creditors, investors and other actors with a sufficient direct stake in a firm) to bear some of the cost and effort of exercising diligent corporate oversight. These sorts of relationships, however, clearly require a developed legal and judicial framework in order to be effective. How

[36] See generally EBRD, Law in Transition (Aut. 1999) (focusing on corporate governance).
[37] See P. Honohan, "Banking System Failures in Developing and Transition Countries: Diagnosis and Predictions", BIS Working Paper No. 39 (Jan. 1997).

can this be achieved? One of the most direct methods is liability for management and owners of financial intermediaries in certain clear cases on insolvency. Of course, this means also that there must be an effective system of insolvency, as discussed in the previous section.

Efficient markets for subordinated debt also encourage large holders to exercise oversight in much the same way as private shareholders. In addition, good interbank markets in which bank creditors have effective systems for counterparty appraisal and exposure control, and the ability to reduce credit lines or increase risk charges to poorly managed banks help to promote oversight.

### 5.2.2. *International Efforts*

While the debate about corporate governance has been going on for some years, it has recently become an issue of considerable concern following financial crises over the past decade. As a result of this concern, the G-7 mandated the OECD[38] to develop a comprehensive set of corporate governance principles to serve as the primary guidance in this area.[39]

### 5.2.3. *Financial Stability Forum Key Standard: Principles of Corporate Governance*

The OECD has been active in the area of corporate governance for a number of years, beginning in 1996 with the commissioning of a study of corporate governance. The study, intended to review and analyse international corporate governance issues and suggest an agenda and priorities for further OECD initiatives, led to the establishment of the Business Sector Advisory Group on Corporate Governance which produced a report in April 1998.[40]

As a result of the G-7 mandate, the OECD Council, meeting at Ministerial level on 27–28 April 1998, called upon the OECD to develop, in conjunction

---

[38] Australia (1971); Austria (1961); Belgium (1961); Canada (1961); Czech Republic (1995); Denmark (1961); Finland (1969); France (1961); Germany (1961); Greece (1961); Hungary (1996); Iceland (1961); Ireland (1961); Italy (1961); Japan (1964); Korea (1996); Luxembourg (1961); Mexico (1994); The Netherlands (1961); New Zealand (1973); Norway (1961); Poland (1996); Portugal (1961); Slovak Republic (2000); Spain (1961); Sweden (1961); Switzerland (1961); Turkey (1961); United Kingdom (1961); United States (1961). The EU Commission also participates.

[39] OECD documents are available at www.oecd.org.

[40] OECD Business Sector Advisory Group on Corporate Governance, *Corporate Governance: Improving Competitiveness and Access to Capital in Global Markets, A Report to the OECD by the Business Sector Advisory Group on Corporate Governance*, 1998.

with national governments, other relevant international organizations and the private sector, a set of corporate governance standards and guidelines. In order to fulfill the Council's objective, the OECD established the Ad-Hoc Task Force on Corporate Governance to develop a set of nonbinding principles embodying the views of member countries on this issue.

The Principles contained in the resulting document[41] are built upon the experiences gained from national initiatives in OECD member countries and previous work carried out within the OECD, including that of the OECD Business Sector Advisory Group on Corporate Governance. During their preparation, a number of OECD committees also were involved, as well as non-OECD countries, the World Bank, the IMF, the business sector, investors, trade unions and other interested parties.

The Principles were adopted by the OECD Council in May 1999. Further, on 21 June 1999, the OECD and the World Bank entered into a Memorandum of Understanding envisaging cooperation between the two organizations to lead the development of international norms of corporate governance.[42] In 2002, the OECD Council Meeting at Ministerial Level supported the assessment and revision of the Principles, which, after extensive international and public consultation, were approved and published by the OECD in 2004.[43]

The document is divided into two parts. The Principles are presented in the first part of the document and cover six areas: (1) ensuring the basis of an effective corporate governance framework, (2) the rights of shareholders and key ownership functions, (3) the equitable treatment of shareholders, (4) the role of stakeholders, (5) disclosure and transparency and (6) the responsibilities of the board. Each of the sections is headed by a single Principle that is followed by a number of sub-principles. The second part of the document contains annotations and commentary on the Principles and their rationale, with analysis of trends and alternative models.[44] Unusually for these sorts of documents, the OECD Principles thus incorporate their own methodology or guidelines.

The first Principle addresses the underlying basis for corporate governance, including incentive structures, legal and regulatory requirements

---

[41] OECD Directorate for Financial, Fiscal and Enterprise Affairs, Ad Hoc Task Force on Corporate Governance, OECD *Principles of Corporate Governance*, SG/CG(99)5, Apr. 1999.

[42] World Bank and OECD, Memorandum of Understanding between the World Bank and the OECD, *A Framework for Cooperation between the Organization for Economic Cooperation and Development and the World Bank* (Paris, 21 Jun. 1999).

[43] OECD, *OECD Principles of Corporate Governance* (2004).

[44] Id., p. 4.

consistent with the rule of law, transparency and enforceability, clear articulation of regulatory responsibilities, and related transparency, independence and accountability.

The second Principle concerns the protection of shareholder rights and the ability of shareholders to influence the behaviour of the corporation. Basic rights are listed, including those to secure ownership and registration, convey and transfer shares, obtain relevant information, share in residual profits, participate in basic decisions and at general shareholder meetings, and fair and transparent transfers of control.

The third Principle on the equitable treatment of shareholders emphasises that all shareholders, including foreign shareholders, should be treated equitably by controlling shareholders, boards and management. Insider dealing and abusive self-dealing are to be prohibited. The Principle calls for disclosure of material interests that board members and management might have in transactions that affect the corporation.

The stakeholder principle (Principle 4) states that the competitiveness and success of a company is the result of teamwork that embodies contributions from a range of different resource providers, including employees. The Principle recognizes the rights of stakeholders that are established by law. It encourages active cooperation between corporations and stakeholders in creating wealth, jobs and the sustainability of financially sound enterprises.

The disclosure and transparency principle (Principle 5) calls for timely and accurate disclosure on all material matters regarding the corporation including its financial situation, performance, ownership and governance. A list of basic disclosures is included. High quality standards of accounting, disclosure, and audit should be followed and there is support for the development of high quality, internationally recognized accounting and audit standards. They indicate that an annual independent audit is required. Channels for disseminating information should provide for fair, timely and cost-efficient access to information by users.

The final principle (Principle 6) calls for the effective monitoring of management by the board and the board's accountability to the company and the shareholders. Accordingly, board members should act on a fully informed basis, in good faith, with due diligence and care, and in the best interests of the company and shareholders. The Principle states that they should also take into account the interests of other stakeholders. Other responsibilities of board members include reviewing strategy and planning, managing potential conflicts of interest, ensuring compliance with the law, and assuring the integrity of the company's accounting, reporting and communications. The Board should be able to exercise objective judgement independent of management, and requires access to accurate, relevant and timely information to fulfill its responsibilities.

In addition to the OECD, the European Bank for Reconstruction and Development (EBRD) published *Sound Business Standards and Corporate Practices* on 15 October 1997 to help companies in the region understand some of the broader concerns that lenders and investors have when considering a potential loan or investment opportunity in the region.[45] These Standards delineate guidelines for businesses to consider in their dealings with customers, shareholders, lenders, employees, suppliers, communities in which they operate, and government and local authorities. Such relationships build upon the basic requirements for success of a company having a sound strategy, competent management, valuable assets and a viable market.

### 5.2.4. *Implementation*

The OECD has established a Steering Group on Corporate Governance, which includes delegates from all OECD member countries, to guide and coordinate its work on corporate governance. An important part of its work is to oversee global outreach activities. These activities are carried out in cooperation with the World Bank, and also aim to encourage the use and implementation of the OECD Principles in nonmember countries. Significantly, the OECD Principles serve as the basis for IMF/World Bank corporate governance ROSCs and related aspects of FSAPs. As of January 2007, six coporate governance ROSCs had been completed and published on the IMF website (each as part of a comprehensive FSAP).[46] Given the importance of corporate governance for financial development and economic growth, this is an area that should receive more attention from especially the World Bank and regional development banks.

### 5.3. FINANCIAL INFORMATION

A precondition to efficient financial markets is perfect information. In the real world, perfect information does not exist; however, the better the information available, the better financial markets are able to function. As a result, information problems are among the most significant imperfections in the financial

---

[45]  EBRD Guidelines, op. cit., n. 20.
[46]  Bosnia and Herzegovina, Czech Republic, Georgia, Hong Kong, South Korea and Slovak
       Republic.

system; likewise, information costs are among the greatest transaction costs in finance. The legal and institutional framework can play a very important role in improving the quality of information available in economies, whether developed, emerging, transition or developing and regardless of the level of financial development.

Effective financial regulation and supervision and the legal infrastructure supporting financial transactions depend on the timely provision of understandable and reliable financial information. The development of both financial intermediaries and financial transactions is impossible without financial information based on reliable accounting and auditing standards. There are significant differences in accounting practices among nations and regions, particularly developing and transition economies, and these differences can obscure the relative financial positions among nations, sectors and companies in the same industries. Such systems did not exist in any meaningful fashion is many state-owned companies in developing and transition countries, and the development of adequate systems of valuation and accounting is one of the primary difficulties faced in the process of financial sector development.[47]

In order for financial transactions to move beyond basic collateralized or relationship-based lending, appropriate systems for financial information must be developed, especially those relating to accounting and auditing. In addition, credit information systems for lending and credit rating agencies are also useful. Reflecting the importance accorded to financial information, as of January 2007, the IMF and World Bank have published ROSCs covering both accounting and auditing for forty-five economies.[48]

### 5.3.1. *Accounting*

Accounting standards provide the essential means of communication for valuation of companies necessary to any sort of investor choice. An important lesson to emerge from the financial crises of the past fifteen years is the significance of transparency of information, especially financial information, for the stability and proper functioning of any financial system, whether domestic or

---

[47] See D. Cairns, "Improving Financial Reporting in Transition Economies", Law in Transition 8 (Spr. 1999).

[48] Azerbaijan, Bangladesh, Bosnia and Herzegovina, Botswana, Bulgaria, Chile, Colombia, Croatia, Czech Republic, Dominican Republic, Ecuador, El Salvador, Egypt, Estonia, Ghana, Hungary, India, Indonesia, Jamaica, Jordan, Kenya, Latvia, Lebanon, Lithuania, Macedonia, Mauritius, Mexico, Moldova, Morocco, Nigeria, Pakistan, Peru, Philippines, Poland, Romania, Senegal, Serbia, Slovakia, Slovenia, South Korea, Sri Lanka, South Africa, Tanzania, Uganda, Ukraine.

international. Accounting standards provide the fundamental means of communicating financial information and are therefore crucial to transparency of finance. Historically, accounting standards have been primarily nationally determined, so in effect, preparers and users of financial statements from different countries essentially used different languages for the preparation, communication and interpretation of financial information.[49] As a result, the international comparability of financial statements prepared on the basis of varying accounting standards is limited because it is difficult to understand and translate what the information means and burdensome to determine if all material financial and nonfinancial information has been disclosed.[50] Further, from the standpoint of accountants preparing financial statements and the companies involved, disharmony of national accounting standards is an impediment to international securities offerings, exchange listings and cross-border mergers and acquisitions.[51] The disharmony in national accounting standards that exists today creates difficulties for both users and preparers of financial statements[52], and presents obstacles to the process of internationalization of financial markets, especially capital markets.[53]

The Office of the Chief Accountant of the US Securities and Exchange Commission (SEC) surveyed international accounting and auditing standards in 1987 and found significant disparities in a number of respects.[54] In general terms, systems of accounting rules in different countries at the time could be

---

[49] See Cheney, "Western Accounting Arrives in Eastern Europe", 170 J. Accountancy 40 (Sep. 1990) (describing accounting as the "language of production and transaction" and discussing difficulties in integrating eastern European and Western countries due to differences in accounting).

[50] The case of Daimler-Benz is illustrative in this context: In 1994, its reported profit under German accounting rules was DM 895 million, whereas its profit under US accounting rules was DM 1,052 million. In 1993, however, accounting under German rules showed a profit of DM 615 million, but US rules led to a loss of DM 1,839 million. B. Carlsberg, "Harmonizing Accounts Worldwide", Financial Times, 12 Jan. 1996, p. xii.

[51] A survey of multinational corporations indicated that the greatest potential benefit of harmonization would be the acceptance by securities exchanges around the world of "one set of accounts" complying with international accounting standards, instead of requiring different financial information prepared in accordance with local accounting standards. "Support for International Standards", 169 J. Accountancy 15 (Apr. 1990).

[52] T. Evans, M. Taylor and O. Holzmann, *International Accounting and Reporting* (New York: Macmillan, 1985), pp. 85–6.

[53] See US SEC, *Staff Report: Internationalization of the Securities Markets*, 1987, s. IV-8. A study of international accounting problems has confirmed that the lack of international accounting standards greatly diminishes the utility of financial statements in world markets. See Scott and Torberg, Eighty-Eight International Accounting Problems in Rank Order of Importance – a DELPHI Evaluation (1980).

[54] SEC Staff Report, op. cit., n. 53.

grouped into two categories[55]: (1) countries "where business finance is provided more by loans than by equity capital, where accounting rules are dominated by taxation considerations and where legal systems customarily incorporate codes with detailed rules for matters such as accounting"[56]; and (2) countries "in which equity sources of finance are more important, accounting measurements are not dominated by taxation considerations because tax breaks can be enjoyed independently of [the mechanism of reporting], and common law systems prevail."[57] Overall, however, at the time of the SEC study, no one system seemed to have such clear merit as to deserve adoption by the entire world.

The task of harmonization is especially important for financial markets and most especially in the area of securities regulation because of the critical link between information and stability in the world's securities markets.[58] Overall, the usefulness of financial statements prepared on the basis of varying accounting standards is limited because it is difficult and time consuming to understand what the information means.

The significance of this subject has been emphasised in international efforts to address deficiencies in the architecture of the international financial system.[59] Partially as a result, major initiatives are on-going to establish internationally agreed accounting standards, involving the International Organization of Securities Commission (IOSCO) and the International Accounting Standards Board (IASB).

Globalization of stock markets and other trading markets is driving the movement toward international harmonization of accounting standards. Further, businesses and capital markets desire both uniformity and higher quality, thereby stemming fears of regulatory arbitrage and a race for the bottom. Interestingly, the debate surrounding the collapses of Enron, WorldCom and Parmalat also appears to be focusing on certain philosophical questions such as rules-based systems (e.g., US standards) versus more judgement-based systems (e.g., UK standard and International Financial Reporting Standards [IFRS]).

---

[55] Carsberg, Harmonizing Accounts Worldwide, op. cit., n. 50.

[56] SEC Staff Report, op. cit., n. 53. Reporting under these systems often leads to a "lack of full transparency" for investors due to their basis on the tax systems. Major countries in this category include France, Germany and Japan. Id.

[57] "These countries generally have some private sector system for setting accounting standards, often within a general statutory framework," and "capital market pressures [lead to the increased] quality of available information to investors. Major countries in this category include the US, UK, Australia and The Netherlands." Id.

[58] United Nations, UN Centre on Transnational Corporations, International Accounting and Reporting Issues: 1989 Review III, 1990. See also B. Thomas, "International Accounting and Reporting – Developments Leading to the Harmonization of Standards", 15 N.Y.U. J. Int'l L. & Pol'y 517 (1983).

[59] See generally G-22 Reports, op. cit., n. 16.

These needs have been highlighted with the publication and approval of various principles for financial regulation by the Basel Committee and IOSCO. As an example, the IOSCO Objectives and Principles[60] recommend high standards of accounting and disclosure in order to achieve their objectives.[61] Specifically, in order to provide adequate market information, issuers of securities must meet requirements for "full, timely and accurate disclosure of financial results and other information material to investor decisions."[62] In addition, legal safeguards should exist to ensure that holders of securities in a company are treated in a fair and equitable manner.[63] Such accounting and auditing standards need to be of a "high and internationally acceptable quality".[64]

Credible accounting systems are central to the provision of information needed by investors and others with an actual or potential stake in an enterprise to evaluate its past performance, to help predict future performance and to determine the financial strength of the enterprise. Effective accounting standards should serve four basic needs: accuracy, relevance and transparency, comprehensiveness, and provision in a timely and regular manner.[65] The best assurance that financial statements contain understandable information is if they are prepared and presented in accordance with accounting standards and principles that are generally acceptable internationally. The work of the IASB in publishing IFRS has been instrumental both in forming the content of optimal national standards and in providing standards with which individual financial intermediaries and other enterprises may prepare their accounts.[66] The best assurance that such financial statements are reliable is if they have been audited to standards that are broadly acceptable internationally. Auditing mechanisms are essential to ensure that accounting norms are effectively

---

[60] IOSCO, *Objectives and Principles of Securities Regulation*, 1998 updated 2003.

[61] Work by the Basel Committee has also highlighted the importance of accounting standards for the regulation and supervision of credit institutions. See Basel Committee, *Core Principles for Effective Banking Supervision*, Sep. 1997 (Principle 21: banks must maintain and publish fair and accurate financial statements in accordance with consistent accounting policies, "preferably of an internationally accepted standard"); idem., *Consultative Paper: Sound Practices for Loan Accounting, Credit Risk Disclosure and Related Matters*, Oct. 1998 (presenting twenty-five principles for bank accounting).

[62] IOSCO, *Objectives and Principles of Securities Regulation*, 2003, Principle 14.

[63] Id., Principle 15.

[64] Id., Principle 16.

[65] See G-10, "A Strategy for the Formulation, Adoption and Implementation of Sound Principles and Practices to Strengthen Financial Systems", *Report of the Group of Ten (G-10) Working Party on Financial Stability in Emerging Markets, Financial Stability in Emerging Market Economies*, Apr. 1997.

[66] For details, see the IASB website at www.iasb.org. See also M. Steinberg, D. Arner and C. Olive, "The Development of Internationally Acceptable Accounting Standards: A Universal Language for Finance in the 21st Century?", 27 Securities Regulation Law Journal 324 (1999).

applied and maintained and to monitor the quality of internal control procedures, with both internal and external audits being necessary.

Empirical research supports the value of effective accounting standards: Klapper, Laeven and Rajan have found that regulations that protect investors, such as accounting standards, "tend to improve access to credit".[67]

As described earlier, effective systems for providing information are also essential to stakeholder monitoring, with accounting standards based on principles and rules that command wide international acceptance being crucial in this regard as they facilitate the comparison of performance across countries. Rigorous accounting and auditing standards also help prevent money laundering and other financial crime, thereby supporting market integrity, an important function given the potentially disastrous impact such problems can have on both individual financial intermediaries and confidence in the financial system as a whole. In this area, the Financial Action Task Force on Money Laundering (FATF) has made recommendations and established principles and guidelines that serve as the starting point.[68]

**International Efforts.** The leading actors in the development of internationally acceptable accounting standards are the IASB and IOSCO.

Formed initially in 1973 by agreement among the accounting bodies of ten industrialized countries[69], by 1989, the International Accounting Standards Committee (IASC) had grown to include approximately 100 accountancy bodies from eighty countries.[70] The IASC was renamed the IASB in 2001 and is engaged in an effort to harmonize and improve accounting principles. This task is especially difficult for two reasons: first, the IASB seeks harmonization on a worldwide basis[71], and second, since the IASB has no official status, its standards are essentially recommendations.[72] Further, the IASB standards are generally broad and allow alternative practices; hence, they do not necessarily achieve uniformity across different implementing jurisdictions.[73]

---

[67] L. Klapper, L. Laeven and R. Rajan, "Business Environment and Firm Entry: Evidence from International Data", World Bank Policy Research Working Paper 3232 (Mar. 2004), p. 5.

[68] Financial Action Task Force on Money Laundering (FATF), "The Forty Recommendations" (OECD, 1996 revised Jun. 2003). FATF documents are available at www.oecd.org/fatf.

[69] The founding members were Australia, Canada, France, Germany, Ireland, Japan, Mexico, The Netherlands, the United Kingdom and the United States.

[70] S. Collins, "The Move to Globalization", J. Acct. 83 (1989). Note that the membership of the IASB consists of accountancy bodies rather than nations.

[71] See "IASC Moves to United Worldwide Standards", 165 J. Acct. 22 (1988), p. 26.

[72] See L. Herbert, "Developments in the Harmonization of Accounting Standards", 3 J. Comp. Corp. L. & Sec. Reg. 175 (1981), p. 177.

[73] Note, however, that the IASB in recent years has been making efforts to eliminate alternatives, thereby increasing the possibility of real harmonization. See Carsberg, op. cit., n. 50.

The IASB's overall objectives are to formulate and publish accounting standards to be observed in the presentation of financial statements and to promote their worldwide acceptance, and to work generally for the improvement and harmonization of regulations, accounting standards, and procedures relating to the presentation of financial statements through development of and support for IFRS. (Prior to 2001, IFRS were named "International Accounting Standardes" or IAS.) These standards are not binding on nations or the IASB members themselves, and the IASB has no enforcement authority.

In the area of international accounting standards for financial reporting connected with securities exchange listings, the barriers created by the lack of a single financial language are especially significant to the process of international capital formation. Prior to 1993, IOSCO had always withheld any endorsement of the various IAS, feeling that a core set of standards that dealt comprehensively with all the main financial reporting issues should be completed first.[74] In 1993, IOSCO agreed on[75]

> the necessary components of a reasonably complete set of accounting standards (core standards) that would comprise a comprehensive body of principles for enterprises undertaking cross-border offerings and listings.

IOSCO's list identified forty core standards.

The IASB (then IASC), however, was unwilling to undertake such a process, until July 1995, at which time the IASB and IOSCO published a joint agreement to complete a comprehensive set of core standards by 1999.[76] Under the agreement, IASB and IOSCO agreed to collaborate to produce a comprehensive set of core standards for the global listing of securities, which then would be submitted to IOSCO for endorsement by its membership.[77] Overall, "the two groups' goal is the development of financial statements, prepared in accordance with such international rules, that can be read world-wide in cross-border securities listings as an alternative to the use of national accounting standards", thereby resulting in an increase in market efficiencies.[78]

---

[74] Id.

[75] P. Pacter, "International Accounting Standards: The World's Standards by 2002", CPA J. Online (1998).

[76] The IASB concluded that completion of this core set was a desirable objective for IASB in any event, and acceptance of this goal made an agreement possible under which both IOSCO and the IASB would cooperate in order to fulfill an objective that was in the best interest of both organizations. Id. The completion date for this agreement was later advanced to March 1998. See S. Burkholder, "International Accounting Standards Panel Accelerates Release of Rules", 28 Sec. Reg. & L. Rep. 540 (1996).

[77] Id.

[78] Id. (citing joint IOSCO/IASC statement of Jul. 1995).

**Financial Stability Forum Key Standard: International Accounting Standards.** The Core Standards as set forth in IOSCO's 1993 list are grouped into five major categories: general, income statement, balance sheet, cash flow statement and other. General standards deal with the following areas: (1) disclosure of accounting policies[79], (2) changes in accounting policies[80] and (3) information disclosed in financial statements.[81] Core standards related to the income statement are addressed to: (1) revenue recognition[82], (2) construction contracts[83], (3) production and purchase costs[84], (4) depreciation[85], (5) impairment[86], (6) taxes[87], (7) extraordinary items[88], (8) government grants[89], (9) retirement benefits[90], (10) other employee benefits[91], (11) research and development[92], (12) interest[93] and (13) hedging.[94]

Standards governing the balance sheet address: (1) property, plant and equipment[95]; (2) leases[96]; (3) inventories[97]; (4) deferred taxes[98]; (5) foreign currency[99]; (6) investments[100]; (7) financial instruments/off balance sheet

---

79 IAS 1, Presentation of Financial Statements (1 Jul 1998) (replacing IAS 1, Disclosure of Accounting Policies, which remained in effect until 7 Jan. 1998).

80 IAS 8, Profit or Loss for the Period, Fundamental Errors and Changes in Accounting Policies (1 Jan. 1979).

81 IAS 1, op. cit., n. 79.

82 IAS 18, Revenue (1 Jan. 1984).

83 IAS 11, Construction Contracts (1 Jan. 1980).

84 IAS 2, Inventories (1 Jan. 1976; revised 1993).

85 IAS 4, Depreciation (1 Jan. 1977) and IAS 16, Property, Plant and Equipment (1 Jan. 1983; revised 1993) (currently being revised).

86 IAS 36, Impairment of Assets (1 Jul. 1999) (issued June 1998, effective for financial reporting periods beginning 1 Jul. 1999).

87 IAS 12, Income Taxes (1 Jan. 1998) (replacing IAS 12, Accounting for Taxes on Income, which remained in effect until 1 Jan. 1998) (revised 1996 and effective for financial reporting periods beginning on or after 1 Jan. 1998).

88 IAS 8, op. cit., n. 80.

89 IAS 20, Accounting for Government Grants and Disclosure of Government Assistance (1 Jan. 1984).

90 IAS 19, Employee Benefits (1 Jan. 1985) (revised Jan. 1998 and effective for reporting periods beginning 1 Jan. 1999).

91 Id.

92 IAS 38, Intangible Assets (1 Jul. 1999) (issued Sep. 1998 and effective for annual financial statements covering periods beginning on or after 1 Jul. 1999).

93 IAS 23, Borrowing Costs (1 Jan. 1986; revised 1993).

94 Financial Instruments: Recognition and Measurement; IAS 39.

95 IAS 16, Property, Plant and Equipment (1 Jan. 1983; revised 1998).

96 IAS 17, Accounting for Leases (1 Jan. 1984) (to be superseded by IAS 17 [revised 1997], Leases, effective 1 Jan. 1999).

97 IAS 2, op. cit., n. 84.

98 IAS 12, op. cit., n. 87.

99 IAS 21, The Effects of Changes in Foreign Exchange Rates (1 Jan. 1985; revised 1993).

100 IAS 39, op. cit., n. 94.

items[101]; (8) joint ventures[102]; (9) contingencies[103]; (10) events occurring after the balance sheet date[104]; (11) current assets and current liabilities[105]; (12) business combinations (including goodwill)[106]; and (13) intangibles other than research and development and goodwill.[107]

A single standard details cash flow statement contents.[108] Other relevant core standards cover: (1) consolidated financial statements[109], (2) subsidiaries in hyperinflationary economies[110], (3) associates and equity accounting[111], (4) segment reporting[112], (5) interim reporting[113], (6) earnings per share[114], (7) related party disclosures[115], (8) discontinuing operations[116], (9) fundamental errors[117] and (10) changes in estimates.[118]

The IASB proposal was submitted and approved by the membership of IOSCO[119] and has also been reviewed both by domestic authorities and other international institutions and organizations, such as the Basel Committee.[120] Although IOSCO endorsement of comprehensive IAS was not guaranteed, IOSCO did commit to undertake a review of the completed project, and upon completion of the IASB core standards working program, IOSCO evaluated the resulting standards.[121] The IOSCO evaluation commenced after the final

---

[101] Id.

[102] IAS 31, Financial Reporting of Interests in Joint Ventures (1 Jan. 1992).

[103] IAS 37, Provisions, Contingent Liabilities and Contingent Assets (7 Jan. 1999) (issued Sep. 1998 and effective for annual financial statements covering periods beginning on or after 1 Jul. 1999).

[104] IAS 10, Contingencies and Events Occurring after the Balance Sheet Date (1 Jan. 1980).

[105] IAS 1, op. cit., n. 79.

[106] IAS 22.

[107] IAS 38, op. cit., n. 92.

[108] IAS 7, Cash Flow Statements (1 Jan. 1979; revised 1992).

[109] IAS 27, Consolidated Financial Statements and Accounting for Investments in Subsidiaries (1 Jan. 1990).

[110] IAS 21, op. cit., n. 99; IAS 29, Financial Reporting in Hyperinflationary Economies (1 Jan. 1990).

[111] IAS 28, Accounting for Investments in Associates (1 Jan. 1990).

[112] IAS 14, Segment Reporting (1 Jul. 1998).

[113] IAS 34, Interim Financial Reporting (1 Jan. 1999).

[114] IAS 33, Earnings Per Share (1 Jan. 1998).

[115] IAS 24, Related Party Disclosures (1 Jan. 1986).

[116] IAS 35, Discontinuing Operations (1 Jan. 1999).

[117] IAS 8, op. cit., n. 80.

[118] Id.

[119] IOSCO Technical Committee, *IASC Standards – Assessment Report*, May 2000; see IOSCO, *Final Communiqué of the 25th Annual Conference of the International Organization of Securities Commissions*, 2000.

[120] Basel Committee, *Report to G7 Finance Ministers and Central Bank Governors on International Accounting Standards*, 2000.

[121] IOSCO IAS Assessment, op. cit., n. 119.

draft standards were completed and resulted in substantial approval. The standards were subsequently approved by the full membership of IOSCO (including the US SEC), with a recommendation for implementation in member jurisdictions.[122] As a result, there exists the clear possibility for the eventual employment of core standards developed by the IASB and approved by IOSCO being thereafter accepted by the SEC for acceptance in the US capital markets.

As noted, the IASB core program has been approved by IOSCO, reviewed and largely recommended by the Basel Committee, and included as one of the key standards for sound financial systems by the FSF.[123] In addition, they have been accepted for international offerings and listings by a wide range of securities exchanges around the world.[124] Among the largest capital markets in the world, the European Union determined to use IFRS as the basis for reporting by all EU listed companies by 2005, while the US is currently discussing future usage of IFRS in its markets. Significantly, with the on-going debate over Enron, WorldCom, Parmalat and others (such as Shell and AIG), pressure for adoption of a set of accounting standards agreed between the United States and the European Union may increase. At the moment, though, both jurisdictions are focusing on their internal markets (including standards applicable to foreign issuers) and are unprepared to agree to any deviation from their respective positions.

The fundamental issue facing the IASB is whether it should, in the future, be responsible for the development of international accounting standards or for harmonizing currently existing national accounting standards (thereby leaving the individual jurisdictions responsible for developing accounting standards). At the very least, the IASB provides a sophisticated forum for debate. Issuing IFRS serves to limit the range of potential options for bodies developing national accounting standards. The role of the IASB and its core standards is likely to increase, especially given the support of the G-7 and its allocation of international responsibility in this area to the IASB, with responsibility for review lying with international regulatory standard-setting organizations such as the Basel Committee, IOSCO and the International Association of Insurance Supervisors (IAIS).[125] This increasing importance of the IASB and

---

[122] IOSCO, *Resolution and List of IASC 2000 Standards*, May 2000.

[123] FSF, *International Standards and Codes to Strengthen Financial Systems* (Jun. 2001). See also FSF, *Compendium of Standards*, available at www.fsforum.org.

[124] For a current summary, see the IASB website at www.iasb.org.

[125] According to the G-7:

> We call upon: . . . the IASC to finalize by early 1999 a proposal for a full range of internationally agreed accounting standards. IOSCO, IAIS, and the Basle Committee should complete a

IFRS is highlighted by the EU's decision to adopt these standards for financial reporting by EU listed companies and the current US discussion respecting greater acceptance of the use of IFRS by foreign issuers.

The reaction of jurisdictions to IFRS has been divided into three categories: (1) for some economies that do not have a developed national system of accounting, IFRS have been given essentially the same status given domestic standards[126]; (2) a number of economies have accounting systems that are for the most part compatible with IFRS[127]; and (3) some economies have well-developed accounting standards that in large part are incompatible with IFRS.[128] Given the general reception and the overall necessity of harmonization, increasing use of IFRS appears likely.[129]

### 5.3.2. *Auditing*

The best assurance that financial statements are reliable is if they have been audited to standards that are broadly acceptable internationally. Auditing mechanisms are essential to ensure that accounting norms are effectively applied and maintained and to monitor the quality of internal control procedures, with both internal and external audits being necessary.[130]

**International Efforts.** As with accounting standards, the most significant international initiatives have been those of the European Union and of international financial organizations, in this case the International Federation of Accountants International Auditing Practices Committee (IFAC).

The IFAC, organized in 1977, is an international organization of national accountancy organizations representing accountants.[131] The IFAC organization includes, inter alia, the International Auditing Practices Committee (IAPC), which is charged with the responsibility of developing and issuing

---

timely review of these standards. . . . We commit ourselves to Endeavour to ensure that private sector institutions in our countries comply with these principles, standards and codes of best practice.

G-7, *Declaration of G7 Finance Ministers and Central Bank Governors*, 30 Oct. 1998.

[126] Evans et al., op. cit., n. 52, p. 94. Cf. Cheney, op. cit., n. 49.
[127] Evans et al., op. cit., n. 52, p. 95 (e.g., Canada, United Kingdom and United States).
[128] Id. (e.g. Japan, although this may be changing somewhat).
[129] Note that the London Stock Exchange began accepting IAS soon after the foundation of the IASC. See Carsberg, op. cit., n. 50. Canada, Japan and the United States, however, still refuse to permit the use of IAS for securities exchange purposes. Id.
[130] See EBRD Guidelines, op. cit., n. 20.
[131] See the IFAC website at www.ifac.org for details.

guidelines on generally accepted auditing practices and the content of audit reports.[132] Overall, the problems facing the IAPC are quite similar to those facing IASB; however, the focus of the IAPC is on auditing rather than on accounting standards.

The IFAC is charged with the responsibility of developing and issuing guidelines on generally accepted auditing practices and the content of audit reports.[133]

**Financial Stability Forum Key Standard: International Standards on Auditing (ISA).** Unlike the IASB, the IAPC has compiled and codified a complete set of International Standards on Auditing.[134] The Standards are comprehensive and seem to be gaining greater acceptance.[135] In addition, the IAPC released, in late 1997, a draft set of standards on credibility of reporting[136], addressing many of the concerns raised by the EU task force on auditing. In 2005, the Public Interest Oversight Board (PIOB) was established to oversee the international standard setting activities of the IFAC in the areas of audit performance standards, independence and other ethical standards for auditors; audit quality control and assurance standards; and education standards, and to oversee the IFAC's Member Body Compliance Program. The establishment of the PIOB was the result of a collaborative effort by the international financial regulatory community, working with IFAC, to ensure that auditing standards set by IFAC and its committees are set in the public interest.

ISAs are broken down into nine categories: (1) general, (2) responsibilities, (3) planning, (4) internal control, (5) audit evidence, (6) using work of others, (7) audit conclusions and reporting, (8) specialized areas and (9) International Auditing Practice Statements.

According to the FSF, the ISAs to date are[137]:

(1) General standards include an introductory preface[138], glossary of terms[139] and framework.[140]

---

[132] See IFAC, Preface to International Auditing Guidelines of the International Federation of Accountants, *AICPA Professional Standards*, § 8000.01–02 (1 Jul. 1979).

[133] See id.

[134] IFAC, *Bound Volume: International Standards on Auditing – Codified*, 1998.

[135] See Oliverio and Newman, "Accounting in the Global Business Environment", 12 CPA J. 52 (Dec. 1997).

[136] IFAC/IAPC, *Exposure Draft: Reporting on the Credibility of Information*, 1998.

[137] FSF website, http://www.fsforum.org/Standards/Standard60.html (checked 25 Jun. 2004).

[138] ISA 100, Preface to ISAs and RSs.

[139] ISA 110, Glossary of Terms.

[140] ISA 120, Framework of ISAs.

(2) Standards addressing responsibilities include objectives[141], terms of audit[142], quality control[143], fraud and error[144], and consideration of laws and regulations.[145]

(3) Standards respecting planning address planning generally[146], knowledge of the business[147] and materiality.[148]

(4) Standards on internal control cover risk assessments[149], computer information systems[150] and service organizations.[151]

(5) Standards cover a variety of issues respecting audit evidence.[152]

(6) Standards address use of the work of others, including work of other auditors[153], internal audit[154] and experts.[155]

(7) Standards on audit conclusions and reporting cover the auditor's report[156], comparatives[157] and other information.[158]

(8) Specific standards have been developed to address specialized areas, such as special purpose engagements[159], engagement for agreed procedures[160] and engagements to compile information.[161]

Finally, the IFAC has a number of "International Auditing Practice Statements", addressing a variety of issues such as interbank confirmations[162],

---

[141] ISA 200, Objective.

[142] ISA 210, Terms of Audit.

[143] ISA 220, Quality Control for Audit Work.

[144] ISA 240, Fraud and Error.

[145] ISA 250, Consideration of Laws and Regulations in an Audit of Financial Statements.

[146] ISA 300, Planning.

[147] ISA 310, Knowledge of the Business.

[148] ISA 320, Audit Materiality.

[149] ISA 400, Risk Assessments and Internal Control.

[150] ISA 401, Auditing in a Computer Information Systems Environment.

[151] ISA 402, Audit Considerations Relating to Entities Using Service Organizations.

[152] ISA 500, Audit Evidence; ISA 501, Audit Evidence-Additional Considerations for Specific Items; ISA 510, Initial Engagements – Opening Balances; ISA 520, Analytical Procedures; ISA 530, Audit Sampling and other Selective Testing Procedures; ISA 540, Audit of Accounting Estimates; ISA 550, Related Parties; IAS 560, Subsequent Events; ISA 570, Going Concern; ISA 580, Management Representations.

[153] ISA 600, Using the Work of Another Auditor.

[154] ISA 610, Considering the Work of Internal Auditing.

[155] ISA 620, Using the Work of an Expert.

[156] ISA 700, The Auditor's Report on Financial Statements.

[157] ISA 710, Comparatives.

[158] ISA 720, Other Information in Documents Containing Audited Financial Statements.

[159] ISA 800, The Auditor's Report on Special Purpose Audit Engagements.

[160] ISA 920, Engagements to Perform Agreed-Upon Procedures Regarding Financial Information.

[161] ISA 930, Engagements to Compile Financial Information.

[162] ISA 1000, Inter-Bank Confirmation Procedures.

microcomputers[163], databases[164], the relationship with bank supervisors[165], audit of small entities[166], audit of international commercial banks[167], communications with management[168], risk assessment and internal control in computer information systems[169], computer-assisted audit techniques[170] and environmental matters.[171]

### 5.3.3. *Other Issues: Credit Ratings and Credit Information Systems*

Credit rating systems and agencies serve similar functions in that they decrease the need for initial research and subsequent monitoring, thereby reducing the cost of credit and increasing lending and loan maturities.

Inessa Love and Natalyia Mylenko have analysed this issue and found that[172]: (1) the existence of private credit registries is associated with lower financing constraints and a higher share of bank financing, with special impact on small and medium-sized enterprises; (2) a stronger rule of law is associated with more effective private credit registries; and (3) public credit registries (usually maintained by central banks for financial stability purposes) do not have the same sort of effects, though they may benefit younger firms as well as have other benefits in terms of financial stability.

This is thus an issue deserving further attention.

### 5.4. MARKET INTEGRITY: CORRUPTION, MONEY LAUNDERING AND FINANCIAL CRIME

Twenty years ago, there was very limited focus outside of North America on issues relating to financial market integrity, with frequent debates regarding whether or not it was of significance, especially in relation to legal enforcement. Today, the debate is essentially settled, with general consensus that issues relating to integrity are central to economic development. In this area, three

---

[163] ISA 1001, CIS Environments-Stand-Alone Microcomputers.
[164] ISA 1002, CIS Environments-Database Systems; and ISA 1003, CIS Environments-Database Systems.
[165] ISA 1004, The Relationship Between Bank Supervisors and External Auditors.
[166] ISA 1005, The Special Considerations in the Audit of Small Entities.
[167] ISA 1006, The Audit of International Commercial Banks.
[168] ISA 1007, Communications with Management.
[169] ISA 1008, Risk Assessments and Internal Control-CIS Characteristics and Considerations.
[170] ISA 1009, Computer-Assisted Audit Techniques.
[171] ISA 1010, The Consideration of Environmental Matters in the Audit of Financial Statements.
[172] I. Love and N. Mylenko, "Credit Reporting and Financing Constraints", World Bank Policy Research Working Paper 3142 (Oct. 2003).

aspects are of note: (1) corruption (especially relating to governments), (2) money laundering and terrorist financing and (3) financial crime.

Overall, financial development occurs best in an environment of confidence, and concerns regarding government and market integrity impact directly thereon.

### 5.4.1. *Corruption*

As discussed in Chapter Three, governance is an important theme in both finance and development today. Governance is defined as the manner of governing and is not something that can be measured easily; nonetheless, it is fundamental to economic growth and development, to development of democracy and the rule of law, and to the process of development and transition.[173] Corruption can be seen as one aspect of governance.

Corruption is generally regarded as widespread throughout emerging, transition and developing economies and, indeed, the developed world; however, the problem is often regarded as particularly pervasive and severe among the transition and developing economies.[174] Surveys of foreign investors and local entrepreneurs, as well as private risk rating agencies and the assessments of regional analysts, all tend to rate the extensiveness of corruption as an important element in determining overall country risk to foreign investors, especially those involved in direct investment. It therefore is a factor taken into consideration by several of the commercial risk rating agencies.[175]

According to commentators, rampant corruption undermines popular support for market reform in emerging, transition and developing economies.[176] This conclusion was supported with by a World Bank review of studies and experiences in regard to the impact of corruption on development.[177] Based on a review of the relevant economic and sector work addressing the topic and its own internal experiences, the World Bank concluded that corruption imposed costs on their borrowers in five ways: (1) macroeconomic stability may be undermined by loss of government revenue and excessive spending; (2) foreign

---

[173] EBRD, *Transition Report 1997*, Oct. 1997, p. 3.

[174] Id., p. 37.

[175] Id.

[176] See C. Gray and W. Jarosz, "Law and the Regulation of Foreign Direct Investment", Colum. J. Transnat'l L. 1 (1995), p. 27 ("Charges of bribery and corruption can easily erode popular support for economic reform in general, and foreign investment in particular."); K. Meesen, "Essay: Fighting Corruption Across the Border", 18 Fordham Int'l L. J. 1647 (1995) ("Corruption both in government and private business has no little role in discrediting freshly installed democratic procedures and freshly installed free market systems.")

[177] World Bank, *Poverty Reduction and Economic Management*, Sep. 1997, ch. 2 (reviewing research and experience in this area).

direct investment may be reduced, especially if bribery is not affordable and the results are not predictable; (3) the growth of small entrepreneurs may be affected disproportionately; (4) the environment may be endangered by the use of corruption to avoid controls; and (5) the poor suffer because of their inability to pay necessary bribes.[178]

Experience has shown that arbitrary, self-interested or corrupt bureaucratic interference can stifle investment and growth in emerging, developing and transition economies: "[c]orruption is not only pernicious in itself; it also undermines free competition and therefore endangers one of the fundamentals of transition."[179] Moreover, financial intermediaries and businesses, as they become increasingly active both internationally and directly in emerging, transition and developing economies, must deal directly not only with the practical costs and problems of corruption, but also with international, domestic and extra-territorial efforts to deal with corruption and their attendant risks, responsibilities and costs.

Interestingly, of all the multifarious aspects of corruption which could be (and in many cases have been) addressed, the FSF only highlights two key standards in this area: (1) anti-money laundering (AML) and (2) countering terrorist financing (CFT). This may be one reason why the IMF/World Bank FSAP/ROSC framework includes AML/CFT under financial standards rather than the broader FSF heading of market integrity.

Easterly states the situation as of 2001 succinctly[180]:

[T]he international financial institutions like the World Bank and [IMF] paid virtually no attention to corruption for decades. Only recently has corruption become a hot issue for these institutions. Even then we are often reluctant to utter the word *corruption*; *problems with governance* is the bureaucratic jargon we use instead. (italics in original)

**International Efforts.** International efforts regarding corruption have been slow to develop. According to Karl Meessen writing in 1995[181]:

The need for international action against corruption may never have been more acute than today. This is not to say that such need has not been felt before, not that international action has never before been advocated.... There may be more organizations that have advocated doing something about

---

[178] Id., pp. 17–19.

[179] EBRD *Transition Report 1997*, op. cit., n. 173, p. 4.

[180] W. Easterly, *The Elusive Quest for Growth: Economists' Adventures and Misadventures in the Tropics* (Cambridge, MA: MIT Press, 2001), p. 241.

[181] K. Meessen, op. cit., n. 176, pp. 1650–51 (arguing for the necessity of an enforceable international convention on combating corruption).

the problem. So far, however, efforts have nowhere passed beyond the stage of mutual encouragement or, technically speaking, of soft law recommendations. In the case of fighting corruption across borders, unlike other cases, this is not enough. Mere recommendations are bound to be abortive. The reason is simple: states that follow a recommendation can never be certain that others will do so as well.

Importantly, today international efforts are increasingly formalized. This is a significant development in that these efforts have, until recently, been more of a voluntary rather than a formal nature[182]:

> To a large degree, the international action to date represents the evolution of "soft" rather than "hard" law. Only recently have the first incremental steps in the transition from "soft" law to substantive law and business practices begun to emerge.

Early efforts in the field of corruption included a 1976 United Nations General Assembly resolution condemning all corrupt practices in business, including bribery.[183] An ad hoc Intergovernmental Working Group on Corrupt Practices of the UN Economic and Social Council was formed[184] and issued a draft agreement in 1979, condemning illicit payments and requiring all signatories to prohibit bribes to foreign officials, including "grease" payments.[185] These attempts went nowhere.[186]

The United Nations, under the auspices of the UN Centre on Transnational Corporations of the Economic and Social Council (ECOSOC), finalized a Code of Conduct for Transnational Organizations in 1990.[187] Negotiations

---

[182] S. Deming, "Foreign Corrupt Practices", Int'l Law. 695 (1997), p. 698.

[183] UN General Assembly, Thirteenth Session, G.A. Res. 3514, U.N. G.A.O.R., Supp. No. 34, p. 69, UN Doc. A/10034, reprinted in 15 I.L.M. 180 (1976). The Resolution was adopted without a vote on 15 Dec. 1975, and "condemn[ed] all corrupt practices, including bribery, by transnational and other corporations" and called upon nations to investigate and prosecute those involved in corrupt practices.

[184] See UN Economic & Social Council, *Economic and Social Council Resolution 2041 (LXI)* of 5 Aug., 1976, reprinted in 15 I.L.M. 1222 (1976).

[185] UN Economic and Social Council, *International Agreement in Illicit Payments*, UN Doc. E/104/1979 (25 May 1979), reprinted in 18 I.L.M. 1025 (1979).

[186] See "ABA Section of International Law and Practice Reports to the House of Delegates, Corrupt Practices in the Conduct of International Business", 30 Int'l Law. 193 (1996), pp. 194–5 (summarizing UN efforts).

[187] UN Economic and Social Council, Second Session, *Development and International Economic Cooperation: Transnational Corporations*, UN Doc. E/1990/94 (1990). After producing this Code, the Centre closed. See ABA Section Reports, op. cit., n. 186, p. 195; L. Compa and T. Hinchliffe-Darricarrere, "Enforcing International Labor Rights Through Corporate Codes of Conduct", 33 Colum. J. Transnat'l L. 663 (1995), p. 669.

on the Code halted in 1992. Further efforts were moved to the UN Conference on Trade and Development (UNCTAD), under the auspices of the renamed Commission on International Investment and Transnational Corporations.[188]

During 1996, the United States introduced a proposal for a "United Nations Declaration on Corruption and Bribery in Transnational Commercial Activities", calling on member states to criminalize both domestic and international bribery and to prohibit the tax deductibility of bribes. The proposal was adopted by ECOSOC on 23 July 1996 and adopted by the UN General Assembly on 16 December 1996 as the "United Nations Declaration Against Corruption and Bribery in International Commercial Transactions".[189] The Declaration provides that member states must "pledge" to deny tax deductibility and to criminalize bribery of foreign public officials in "an effective and coordinated manner".[190] Although not legally binding, according to the World Bank, the Declaration's wording on criminalizing foreign bribery and ending its tax deductibility "signifies broad political agreement in the international community on this matter."[191] Further, in February 1996, the UN General Assembly recommended that the ECOSOC take steps to prevent illicit payments.[192]

In many ways, the OECD has been more successful than the United Nations. The OECD issued guidelines in 1976, calling for member nations to voluntarily shun illicit payments.[193] Also in 1976, the OECD established Guidelines for Multinational Enterprises.[194] Further, on 27 May 1994, the twenty-six then-member governments of the OECD agreed to take collective action in the area of bribery in international business transactions, calling on member countries to take effective measures to deter, prevent and combat bribery of foreign public officials.[195] The OECD Recommendation on Bribery in International Business

---

[188] UN General Assembly, Forty-ninth Session, G.A. Res. 49/130, Supp. No. 49, p. 152, UN Doc. A/49/130 (1994).

[189] UN, "General Assembly Endorses Outcome of UNCTAD IX, Adopts Anti-Corruption Declaration, Stresses Challenges of Global Financial Integration", GA/9206 Press Release, 16 Dec. 1996.

[190] Id.

[191] World Bank (1997), op. cit., n. 177, p. 61.

[192] Id.

[193] OECD, *Regulation of Foreign Investment*, OECD/GD(92)16 (1976).

[194] OECD, *Declaration on International Investment and Multinational Enterprises*, 1976 revised 1979.

[195] OECD 829th Session, *Recommendation of the Council on Bribery in International Business Transactions*, 27 May 1994 ("1994 OECD Recommendation"). Acts of the OECD are generally divided into Decisions, binding on member countries, and Recommendations, which member countries may, "if they consider it opportune", provide for implementation thereof. Convention on the Organization for Economic Cooperation and Development, 14 Dec. 1960, 12 U.S.T. 1728, 888 U.N.T.S. 179, Arts V(a)i), V(b).

Transactions was the first multilateral agreement among governments to combat the bribery of foreign officials.[196] Measures called for included reviewing criminal, civil and administrative laws and regulations and taking "concrete and meaningful steps to meet this goal".[197] Strengthening of international cooperation was also called for, and the Recommendation appealed to non-member countries to join with OECD members in their efforts to eliminate bribery in international business transactions. A follow-up mechanism was also provided.

In autumn 1995, the Committee on Fiscal Affairs of the OECD approved a report calling on member countries to discontinue the practice of providing tax deductions for bribes made by their companies overseas. This action led to the adoption of the Recommendation on Tax Deductibility of Bribes to Foreign Public Officials at the May 1996 Ministerial Conference.[198] The Recommendation called on OECD member countries to "re-examine such treatment with the intention of denying this deductibility".[199] In addition, the OECD Committee on International Investment and Multinational Enterprises has followed the progress of each member country's implementation of the 1994 Recommendation, and, as a consequence, reported in 1996 that "it is necessary to criminalize the bribery of foreign public officials in an effective and coordinated manner."[200] At the time, more than half of the OECD member countries considered bribery to be deductible as a business expense for tax purposes.[201]

Also at the May 1996 Conference, the OECD Ministers made a political commitment to criminalize bribery "in an effective and coordinated manner", and to examine the "modalities and appropriate international instruments to facilitate criminalization and consider proposals in 1997." Member countries agreed to report to working groups the action that each has taken in implementing these recommendations. In 1996, the OECD Council adopted a recommendation on ending tax deductibility of foreign bribery, and member states, within the framework of their laws, are now amending legislation to

---

[196] S. Deming, op. cit., n. 182, p. 695.

[197] 1994 OECD Recommendation, op. cit., n. 195, Arts III–IV.

[198] OECD, *Recommendation of the Council on the Tax Deductibility of Bribes to Foreign Public Officials*, C(96)27/Final (17 Apr. 1996).

[199] Id., Art. I.

[200] OECD Committee on International Investment and Multinational Enterprises, *Implementation of the Recommendation on Bribery in International Business Transactions*, OECD/GD(96)(83), para. 13:1.

[201] US Senate, *Hearings of the Senate Caucus on International Narcotics Control and the Senate Finance Committee Subcommittee on International Crime*, 104th Cong., 1996.

reflect this recommendation.[202] At the May 1996 High Level Meeting of the OECD Development Assistance Committee, the committee recommended that members "introduce or require anti-corruption provisions governing bilateral aid-funded procurement."[203]

At its 1996 summit in Lyon, France, the G-7 resolved "to combat corruption in international business transactions".[204] Such corruption was seen as "detrimental to transparency and fairness" and as imposing heavy economic and political costs. At its 1997 summit in Denver, Colorado, the G-7 developed this theme further[205]:

> We urge the IMF and the multilateral development banks to strengthen their activities to help countries to fight corruption, including measures to ensure the rule of law, improve the efficiency and accountability of the public sector, and increase institutional capacity and efficiency, all of which help remove economic and financial incentives and opportunities for corrupt practices. We support and encourage the [international financial institutions] in their efforts to promote good governance in their respective areas of competence and responsibility.

Importantly, this political agreement has led to important practical developments internationally.[206]

At its ministerial meeting in May 1997, the OECD Council endorsed the Revised Recommendation on Combating Bribery in International Business Transactions, prepared by the OECD Working Group on Corruption, reaffirming its commitment to criminalizing bribery of foreign public officials in an effective and coordinated manner, and urged prompt implementation of the 1996 Recommendation on ending tax deductibility for foreign

---

[202] World Bank (1997), op. cit., n. 177, p. 60.

[203] Id.

[204] G-7, *Lyon Economic Summit Communiqué*, 28 Jun. 1996.

[205] G-7, *Denver Summit Statement by Seven: Confronting Global Economic and Financial Challenges*, 22 Jun. 1997.

[206] See *Statement of G7 Finance Ministers and Central Bank Governors*, Washington DC, 26 Apr. 1999, para. 15 under the subheading Anti-corruption:

> We noted with satisfaction the increased attention being given in key international organizations to governance and corruption issues. We agree that the corruption is a serious impediment to effective macroeconomic policy and economic development and growth. We will strengthen our efforts both through our domestic policies and through the International Financial Institutions, OECD, World Customs Organization and the WTO to combat corruption including the financial channels of bribery and improve governance.

bribery.[207] The Council recommended that member countries submit criminalization proposals to their legislative bodies by 1 April 1998 and seek their enactment by the end of 1998. It also decided to open negotiations on a convention to be completed by the end of 1997, with a view to its entry in force as soon as possible in 1998.

On 21 November 1997, the Convention on Combating Bribery of Foreign Public Officials in International Business Transactions was adopted by all twenty-nine member countries of the OECD and five nonmember countries (Argentina, Brazil, Bulgaria, Chile, Slovak Republic).[208] The Convention was signed in Paris on 17 December 1997 and provided the framework under which all the signatory countries undertook to prohibit and act against the bribery of foreign public officials. The OECD convention came into force on 15 February 1999.

Outside of formal international intergovernmental organizations, a number of international nongovernmental organizations (NGOs) have taken important steps in monitoring and combating corruption. The highest profile has been Transparency International, formed in May 1993. Transparency International, an international nonprofit NGO, was established to curb corruption in international and national business transactions.[209] It is headquartered in Berlin, has national chapters in more than seventy countries and has taken a prominent role in pressing governments and international organizations to adopt measures to deter corruption in the conduct of international business.[210] It aims to curb corruption through international and national coalitions encouraging governments to establish and implement effective laws, policies and anti-corruption programs; build public support for anti-corruption programs and enhance public transparency and accountability in international business transactions and public procurement; and encourage all parties to international business transactions to operate at the highest levels of integrity, guided by its Standards of Conduct.[211]

Tranparency International publishes an annual Corruption Perception Index (CPI). The CPI draws on a broad base of international surveys and data gathered from the internet. The index is not an absolute rating of a country's

---

[207] World Bank (1997), op. cit., n. 177, p. 60.

[208] OECD, "Convention on Combating Bribery of Foreign Public Officials in International Business Transactions", 1997. This Convention was negotiated in the framework of the OECD but is not an official OECD document.

[209] See www.transparency.de.

[210] S. Deming, op. cit., n. 182, p. 698.

[211] World Bank (1997), op. cit., n. 177, p. 62.

"corruptness"; rather, it reports how business people, political analysts and the general public around the world perceive global levels of corruption. The organization also has produced a number of publications with respect to various aspects of corruption. Among these is the *TI Source Book*, which is a compilation of many different efforts from governments and organizations around the world to deal with the issue.[212]

In addition, the international financial institutions, including the World Bank group and its constitutents, the IMF, regional organizations, states and private companies have been active, as have the various international financial organizations. In respect to money laundering and terrorist financing (discussed below), all these efforts increasingly centre on the FATF, based at the OECD.

**Lessons from Experience.** Corruption is difficult to address. However, based on experiences around the world and especially in Asia, a number of major steps can be identified:

(1) High-level political commitment to reduce corruption is an essential first step.

(2) Fiscal improvement and sustainability. Corruption can be the result of low public pay levels. Before a government can improve public sector pay levels, it must be able to generate sufficient and sustainable revenue through a sustainable, simple taxation and fiscal regime. These issues have been highlighted earlier. In this context, a tax regime that can be obeyed and that requires reasonable levels of payment also encourages respect for the government and the law.

(3) Increase government salaries (especially those of the judiciary) to a reasonable level once fiscal sustainability has been achieved in order to reduce incentives for official corruption.

(4) Tough laws on corruption combined with an amnesty for pre-existing offences. At the same time public sector pay levels are increased, tough laws on corruption also need to be enacted. In this respect, guidance is available from the OECD's Convention on Bribery of Public Officials and from the public procurement code of the World Trade Organization (WTO). Such laws should be enacted in tandem with an amnesty for pre-existing offences.

---

[212] J. Pope (ed.), *The TI Source Book* (London: Transparency International, Sep. 1996).

(5) An independent corruption enforcement authority should be established. At the same time anti-corruption laws are enacted and the amnesty period is triggered, an independent corruption investigation and enforcement authority needs to be established in order to implement the new system.

### 5.4.2. *Money Laundering and Terrorist Financing*

In relation to money laundering and terrorist financing, the primary international guidance is that from the FATF.

**Money Laundering: The Forty Recommendations of the Financial Action Task Force.** Issued in 1990, revised in 1996 and again in 2003, the Forty Recommendations set out the basic framework for anti-money laundering efforts and they are designed to be of universal application.[213] The Forty Recommendations address four main areas: (1) the legal system (Recommendations 1 to 3), (2) financial intermediaries and related businesses and professions (Recommendations 4 to 25), (3) institutional aspects (Recommendations 26 to 34) and (4) international cooperation (Recommendations 35 to 40).

Legal systems need to include a criminal offence of money laundering (Recommendations 1 and 2) and measures for confiscation and related matters (Recommendation 3).

In respect to market participants, secrecy laws should not prevent implementation (Recommendation 4). Further, intermediaries should undertake appropriate customer due diligence (know-your-customer or KYC procedures) and record-keeping (Recommendations 5 to 12), as well as reporting of suspicious transactions (Recommendations 13 to 16). In addition, there should be appropriate sanctions and other legal precautions (Recommendations 17 to 20). Further, special measures should be taken in respect to transactions involving noncooperative jurisdictions (Recommendations 21 and 22). These various measures should also be supported through the financial regulatory system (Recommendations 23 to 25).

Institutional requirements address competent authorities, their powers and resources (Recommendations 26 to 32) and transparency of legal persons and arrangements (Recommendations 33 and 34).

International cooperation includes signature and implementation of a number of international conventions (Recommendation 35), as well as putting in place appropriate arrangements for mutual legal assistance and extradition

---

[213] FATF, *The Forty Recommendations*, Jun. 2003.

(Recommendations 36 to 39), with clear and effective gateways for informal as well as formal cooperation (Recommendation 40).

**Terrorist Financing: Eight Special Recommendations against Terrorist Financing.** In addition, the FATF has addressed the issue of terrorist financing and moved immediately after the 11 September 2001 terrorist attacks in the United States to address the issue. Released on 31 October 2001, the recommendations address eight areas[214]: (1) ratification and implementation of related UN instruments; (2) criminalization of financing of terrorism and associated money laundering; (3) implementation of measures to freeze and confiscate terrorist assets; (4) expansion of reporting of suspicious transactions to include transactions related to terrorism; (5) international cooperation; (6) requirements for licensing of financial transmission services and application of AML/CFT rules thereto; (7) requirements to record and monitor funds transfers; and (8) regulation of entities, especially nonprofit organizations, so that they cannot be misused.

In addition to the 40+8 Recommendations, the FATF has also produced a methodology for assessment, which is being used by the FATF, related regional bodies and the IMF and World Bank.[215] As of January 2007, 36 AML/CFT ROSCs had been published by the IMF and World Bank (including for the United States), demonstrating a significant level of commitment to this area on the part of both institutions and their leading shareholders.[216]

### 5.4.3. *Financial Crime*

As a general matter, issues relating to financial crime are addressed in the FSF framework either in the context of financial regulation (discussed in the following part) or specifically in relation to money laundering and terrorist financing. In addition to these aspects, the FSF has also highlighted one high-level principle relating to international cooperation. Released in May 1999, the "Ten Key Principles for the Improvement of International Cooperation Regarding Financial Crimes and Regulatory Abuse" sets out principles for improving

---

[214] FATF, *Special Recommendations on Terrorist Financing*, Oct. 2001.

[215] FATF, *Methodology for Assessing Compliance with the FATF 40 Recommendations and the FATF 8 Special Recommendations*, Feb. 2004.

[216] Australia, Austria, Bahrain, Belgium, Bolivia, Brazil, Chile, Czech Republic, France, Germany, Greece, Hong Kong, Hungary, Israel, Italy, Japan, Kazakhstan, Kuwait, Luxembourg, Macedonia, Madagascar, Mauritius, Mexico, Mozambique, The Netherlands, New Zealand, Norway, Romania, Rwanda, Serbia, Singapore, Slovak Republic, South Africa, United Kingdom, United States, Uruguay.

international cooperation between law enforcement authorities and financial regulators on cases involving financial crime and regulatory abuse.

## 5.5. CONCLUSION

This chapter has reviewed the complex matrix of legal and institutional infrastructure necessary to support a functioning, developed or sophisticated financial system. As noted, these elements interact with aspects addressed in Chapters Three and Four. While no economy or financial system is perfect, attention to these details will improve financial stability and development, both serving to enhance economic growth and development. From these foundations, we can now turn to financial regulation and supervision.

# PART THREE

# FINANCIAL REGULATION AND SUPERVISION

# 6

# Banking: Regulation, Supervision and Development

Weak financial intermediaries and problems with financial regulation and supervision have been significant factors in many financial crises, including the problems surrounding the developing country debt crisis and the US savings and loan crisis in the 1980s, the collapses of Bank of Credit and Commerce International (BCCI) and Barings, and the Mexican and Asian financial crises in the 1990s. As discussed in the Part I, these various problems have led to a wide range of international efforts directed towards supporting financial stability.

This part discusses a central focus of recent international efforts: financial markets, their regulation and supervision. Specifically, it addresses the main areas covered by international financial standards: banking, securities, insurance, pensions, microfinance and financial conglomerates. In general, however, standards only address stability and not the role of development. This part attempts to take both into account.

Effective prudential regulation and supervision of financial markets and intermediaries (including banks, insurance companies, securities intermediaries and pension funds) are essential to the financial stability and efficient functioning of any economy because of the central role of the financial system in collecting and allocating savings and investment. Financial intermediaries, by their nature, raise dangers very familiar indeed to any market economy (e.g., financial intermediation and consequent systemic risk). Regulation and supervision are therefore necessary, however, the implications of this for legal and institutional development were largely ignored outside of developed countries prior to the 1990s. This changed with the advent of significant financial crises in a number of countries from the mid-1990s.[1]

---

[1]  See M. Goldstein and P. Turner, "Banking Crises in Emerging Economies: Origins and Policy Options", BIS Economic Paper No. 46 (Oct. 1996).

Official oversight of the financial system encompasses financial regulation, including the formulation and enforcement of rules and standards governing financial behaviour as well as the on-going supervision of individual intermediaries. Regulation and supervision play an essential role in fostering stable and effective financial systems, and should seek to support and enhance market functioning, rather than to displace it, by establishing basic "rules of the game" and seeing that they are observed.[2] As individual countries experienced significant financial crises, attention began to focus not just on macroeconomic factors, but also on the importance of financial regulation and supervision.

At the most basic level, prudential regulation and supervision serve to promote the public confidence on which decentralized financial systems are based. Further, supervision and regulation are essential complements to effective management and market discipline. Different segments of the financial system, however, have varying motivations and requirements. The task of such regulation and supervision is to ensure that financial intermediaries operate in a prudent manner and that they hold capital and reserves sufficient to support the risks that arise in their business. In addition, regulations can be, themselves, a source of vulnerability to the extent that they are too lax, too intrusive, poorly designed, outdated or inadequately implemented. Strong and effective financial regulation and supervision therefore provide a necessary public good. However, in emerging, transition and developing economies, the needs are greater even than those in developed economies: financial regulation and supervision are needed to support the development of finance and the financial system. Unfortunately, this was only seen clearly through the negative effects of financial crises, which opened most eyes to the very real dangers of ineffective financial regulation and supervision, not only to economic transition and development, but to political stability and public order.

A fundamental guiding principle in the design of all regulatory/supervisory arrangements is that they should seek to support and enhance market functioning, rather than to displace markets. Bureaucracies in emerging, developing and transition economies have not always found it easy to understand their role and that of the intermediaries and markets with which they deal. Luckily, this is much less so today than in the early 1990s, but must be the focus of continued training and educational initiatives.

In the broadest sense, regulatory/supervisory authorities collectively need to pursue three broad objectives: (1) define clearly the types of intermediaries subject to regulation and oversight along with the jurisdiction of each regulatory/

---

[2] See C. Goodhart, P. Hartmann, D. Llewellyn, L. Rojas-Suarez and S. Weisbrod, *Financial Regulation: Why, How and Where Now?* (London: Routledge 1998).

supervisory agency for those intermediaries; (2) promote the reliability, effectiveness and integrity of market infrastructure; and (3) foster efficient operation and competition in the financial system. In a broad sense, these objectives can serve as a road-map for reform: the first stage must be to establish the regulator and its areas of authority, typically through a central bank law, banking law or law establishing an individual regulatory authority. The second step must be for those regulators to have an understanding of what a financial market is and what it does; otherwise, they will not be able to support its needs and protect the public from risks. Third, in order to foster the operation of and competition in the financial system, rules need to be in place for participants in that system and their relationships with one another, with the regulator and with the general public (viz. a banking law, a securities law, an insurance law etc.).

In the context of this broad framework, core aspects of regulation and supervision should be highlighted. First, supervisory and regulatory authorities need to be both independent and accountable.[3] This applies also to central banks, whether or not they have supervisory responsibilities.[4] Ideally, this should be delineated in the law establishing the regulator and/or central bank and its relationship to the government. Second, authorities need to have powers of licensing, prudential regulation, consolidated supervision and access to accurate and timely information as well as the ability to engage in remedial action. As a general matter, these should be enumerated in the law establishing the regulator or in the legislation governing specific financial markets (e.g., the banking law); while regulations will be important in this regard, the general principles should be clearly placed in legislation. Finally, authorities must have adequate powers and resources to cooperate and exchange information, both with other authorities in their own jurisdiction and with those from outside, concerning the status of financial intermediaries or activities. This is a factor that is often underemphasized. Ideally, financial sector legislation should be viewed as an opportunity to design the overall plan of the financial system – for example, what sort of intermediaries will be allowed, what they will be allowed to do, who will monitor them and how those responsible authorities will relate to one another and the government – a topic discussed in more detail in Chapters Eight and Ten. Unfortunately, this has rarely been done. It is worth mentioning the example of China in this context, as it shows one

---

[3] See E. Hüpkes, M. Quintyn and M. Taylor, "The Accountability of Financial Sector Supervisors", IMF Working Paper WP/05/51 (Mar. 2005); M. Quintyn and M. Taylor, "Regulatory and Supervisory Independence and Financial Stability", IMF Working Paper WP/02/46 (Mar. 2002).

[4] See id. See also R. Lastra, *Central Banking and Banking Regulation* (London School of Economics, 1996).

example of attempts at a coherent (and planned) approach to financial sector development.[5]

In order to achieve these general goals, from a pragmatic point of view, financial regulation generally seeks to promote financial market efficiency, protect consumers and prevent instability in the financial system through institutions and systems designed to address market failures. It is increasingly agreed that, from an economic standpoint, financial regulation seeks to address a variety of problems that occur when finance is left solely to market forces ("market failures"). On the basis of this analytical framework, financial regulation should seek to address four specific issues: (1) anticompetitive behavior (competition regulation), (2) market misconduct (market integrity regulation), (3) information asymmetries (usually referred to as "prudential concerns" – prudential regulation; also used to support consumer protection/market integrity regulation) and (4) systemic instability (financial stability regulation).

As noted throughout this volume, financial sector weaknesses have played a significant role in many financial crises, especially over the past fifteen years. As a result, much work has been undertaken to address especially financial regulation and supervision to support financial stability and also financial development and economic growth. Clearly, given the significance of financial regulatory weaknesses in financial crises, these are significant issues. However, as noted in Part II, financial intermediaries and markets function best when supported by an appropriate legal and institutional environment designed to underpin a market economy and market-based financial system. In order to support financial development beyond a basic level, both types of legal and institutional frameworks must be addressed to achieve the goals of financial stability and development, namely those discussed in Chapters Three and Four. For developed or sophisticated financial systems, a complex matrix of legal and institutional issues must be addressed in order to achieve, to the greatest extent, the twin goals of financial stability and development necessary to support economic growth and development. These issues were addressed in Chapter Five.

### 6.1. BANKING DEVELOPMENT

Approaches to effective regulation and supervision differ significantly between banking and non-bank activities, reflecting fundamental differences between the natures and risks – including risks to the public exchequer, for example,

---

[5] For discussion, see J. Barth, Z. Zhou, D. Arner, B. Hsu and W. Wang (eds), *Financial Restructuring and Reform in Post-WTO China* (London: Kluwer, 2006); J. Norton, C. Li and Y. Huang (eds), *Financial Regulation in Greater China* (London: Kluwer, 2000).

the cost of depositor bailouts – of these activities. For that reason, economies must carefully consider their approach to banks and banking. Under the traditional view, banking basically transforms the liquid deposits of many small and dispersed savers into largely illiquid loans to borrowers. These loans are extended on the basis of bank-client relationships and private information (thereby alleviating asymmetric information problems). This combination of liquid deposits and illiquid loans, however, is potentially unstable because of the risk that depositors may commence a run on a bank if its liquidity or solvency becomes doubtful, a risk that is increased further because of the limited information depositors have about banks.[6] Prudential oversight in banking provides a measured alternative to the disruptive discipline of bank runs and is often accompanied by government provision of deposit guarantees.

In market economies, banking crises have tended to occur when financial markets were recently liberalized but when supervision and regulation were not upgraded to cope with expanded activity.[7] In emerging, developing and transition economies, the challenge has been to build institutions for sound finance in step with the expansion of financial activity. Such synchronization is undoubtedly difficult to achieve; and not surprisingly, there have been many banking crises in developing, emerging and transition economies. Not only have severe economic upheavals rendered many enterprises and banks insolvent, but also banking crises have persisted even as development and transition advance, as highlighted by the series of emerging and developed economy financial crises in the 1980s and 1990s. Pervasive connected lending by banks has been a common factor; new (or recently privatized) financial intermediaries rapidly expanding their activities has been another. Financial intermediary borrowing in foreign currency combined with unhedged on-lending in local currency, especially for property and infrastructure development (or speculation), has been another common factor. In each episode, there were serious gaps in the prudential regulation and supervision of banks that allowed imprudent exposures or fraud to go unchecked.

In most emerging, developing and transition economies, banks, more so than securities markets, are the major suppliers of funds to new and existing enterprises. Further, banks also have a major role to play as the predominant savings outlet in such economies. Therefore, it is important to create a legal and regulatory framework that allows banks to channel savings to enterprises in an efficient manner while also minimizing the system's exposure to corruption and instability.

---

[6] This is also a coordination problem, in that banks can honour some withdrawals at any time, but not all depositors demanding repayment at any one time (a bank run).

[7] See Goldstein and Turner, op. cit., n. 1.

Despite significant problems with the banking systems in many economies around the world, in the long-run, the development of these countries' financial systems will probably depend on the emergence of stable and efficient banking systems, consistent with the historical experience of the development of the world's leading economies.[8] At the same time, however, financial stability will be enhanced with the development of a diversified financial structure, including securities markets and insurance functions. It is arguable that this is a characteristic of more developed and sophisticated market-based financial systems (discussed further in Chapter Seven). In general, banking intermediaries in a market economy provide basic payment, clearing and settlement services; serve as the main conduit for the mobilization of private savings and other capital resources and for their employment in productive uses, in the form of loans to commercial and industrial enterprises; and have a vital function in the creation of the money supply upon which the growth of an economy depends.[9] For these reasons, banks and securities markets are not only complementary in that both serve to mobilize savings and allocate investment, thereby increasing the size of the financial system[10], but also competitors in that both seek to attract the same resources (namely scarce savings) and direct such resources to their most efficient uses, earning their profits from the provision of their respective financial intermediation mechanisms.

Prudential and related standards that apply to banks commonly cover the following areas: (1) entry requirements; (2) ownership and control structures, including the position of banks in groups of corporations; (3) bank governance requirements; (4) prudential standards, including capital adequacy and liquidity requirements, risk management and control systems, and various credit limits; (5) prevention of crime such as money laundering and the financing of terrorism; (6) accounting and reporting requirements; (7) special criteria for the licensing, prudential supervision and liquidation of branch and representative offices of foreign banks in cooperation with foreign bank regulators;

---

[8]  C. Hadjiemmanuil, "Central Bankers' 'Club' Law and Transitional Economies: Banking Reform and the Reception of the Basel Standards of Prudential Supervision in Eastern Europe and the Former Soviet Union", in J. Norton and M. Andenas (eds), *Emerging Financial Markets and the Role of International Financial Organizations* (London: Kluwer, 1996), p. 180. See id., pp. 180–1, 202 ("[T]he development of policies aiming at the construction of a functioning financial system from scratch has never been pursued by either the Basel Committee or the EC, since all the participating countries have already firmly in place developed payment, banking and financial structures.").

[9]  Id., p. 179. See generally G. Kaufman, *The US Financial Systems: Money, Markets and Institutions* (Engelwood Cliffs, NJ: Prentice Hall, 1995).

[10]  See Kaufman, op. cit., n. 9, pp. 37–57 (discussing the function of financial intermediaries in the expansion of the money supply).

(8) systems for closure and exit; and (9) customer support schemes (such as deposit insurance and industry guarantee funds).

Prudential regulation also relates closely with regulation addressing systemic stability, which traditionally includes: (1) sustainable macroeconomic environment (monetary stability), (2) prudentially sound system of financial intermediaries (financial stability), (3) lender of last resort facility (financial stability) and (4) direct regulation of the payments system (monetary stability and financial stability). While certain of these are outside the scope of this chapter, recognition and analysis of their interrelationship is essential in order to achieve the overall goals of financial development and stability.

Overall, the objective is to develop a competitive, integrated and efficient banking system that is properly regulated and supervised and effectively mobilizes savings to provide financing to support economic growth. Such a banking sector will support economic growth while at the same time minimizing risks of financial crisis.

This overall objective contains two central elements: (1) financial stability and (2) financial development to support economic growth and poverty reduction.

The importance of financial stability (usually seen as the absence of financial crisis) has been emphasised by the string of financial crises over the past twenty years, especially those in Asia in 1997–98. In supporting financial stability, two main methodologies exist: (1) financial regulation and supervision and (2) improving financial intermediary operations.

In relation to financial stability, while some causes of instability are beyond the control of individual financial intermediaries (such as currency or economic crises, which are best addressed through appropriate macroeconomic policies and related institutional framework) if individual financial intermediaries manage their own businesses in a prudentially safe and sound manner, then crises triggered by problems within individual financial intermediariess will be minimized, thereby increasing financial stability. As such, financial intermediaries should be provided with appropriate incentives (both economic and regulatory/supervisory) as well as support for capacity development to enable them to improve their own operations over time. Improvement in operations will not only decrease risks of financial crisis but also enhance the role of financial intermediaries in financial intermediation and resource allocation, thereby supporting economic growth.

Financial regulation and supervision are therefore essential to protecting against financial crisis not only through the protection provided by the regulator but also through the incentives and guidance to financial intermediaries provided through regulation and supervision to enhance their own operations.

In relation to financial development to support economic growth, three central elements are: (1) an effective means of payment and settlement for transactions, (2) savings mobilization and (3) resource allocation/ intermediation. Underlying all three of these is confidence: (1) confidence of savers and borrowers in the financial system and financial intermediaries so that they place their savings in the formal financial system and utilize it for financing, and (2) confidence of financial intermediaries in one another. In many ways, this confidence of savers, borrowers and financial intermediaries results from confidence in the regulatory and supervisory system, which, in turn, depends on its effectiveness.

## 6.2. INTERNATIONAL STANDARDS

In looking at financial stability and banking development, the starting point is the key international standard and related guidance identified by the Financial Stability Forum (FSF).

### 6.2.1. *Financial Stability Forum Key Standard: Core Principles for Effective Banking Supervision*

In the area of banking regulation and supervision, the Basel Committee on Banking Supervision, comprising the central bank governors of the Group of Ten (G-10), has been most active, especially with its *Core Principles for Effective Banking Supervision*.[11] Released in September 1997 and revised in 2006, this document, prepared in close cooperation with non–G-10 supervisory authorities, is intended to serve as a basic reference for supervisory and other public authorities in all countries and internationally.

Prior to the development of its Core Principles, the Basel Committee historically was most active in establishing internationally agreed minimum standards for adequate capitalization for financial institutions, as well as in regard to supervision of foreign banks.[12] In this regard, capital standards should constitute a minimum floor: capitalization standards applied in practice need to be higher if the risks are higher because of vulnerabilities to external disturbances, a history of weak macroeconomic performance, or an undeveloped financial system.

---

[11] Basel Committee on Banking Supervision (Basel Committee), *Core Principles for Effective Banking Supervision*, Sep. 1997 revised 2006. Basel Committee documents are available at the BIS Web site at http://www.bis.org.

[12] See J. Norton, *Developing International Bank Supervisory Standards* (Dordrecht: Martinus Nijhoff, 1995).

In the 1997 Core Principles, summarized briefly subsequently, the Basel Committee, in conjunction with regulators from sixteen other jurisdictions, including transitioning and emerging economies, produced twenty-five basic principles that should underlie banking supervisory policies and structures, outline fundamental guidance for effective banking supervision and serve as a basic reference for supervisory and other public authorities in all countries and internationally. These principles are then enumerated in a *Compendium* of existing Basel Committee documents which are cross-referenced in the Core Principles and are intended to expand upon them and explain their application. These are to be periodically updated, as additional documents are released.[13] In addition, a methodology for implementation has been produced.[14] Detailed guidance in the implementation of the Core Principles is, in turn, provided through the Basel Committee's compilation of its on-going pronouncements over the years.[15]

The twenty-five Core Principles themselves are divided into seven sections: (1) preconditions for effective banking supervision (Principle 1), (2) licensing and structure (Principles 2 to 5), (3) prudential regulations and requirements (Principles 6 to 15), (4) methods of on-going banking supervision (Principles 16 to 20), (5) information requirements (Principle 21), (6) formal powers of supervisors (Principle 22) and (7) cross-border banking (Principles 23 to 25). While these Principles are very instructive in terms of coverage and issues, they nonetheless must be implemented by domestic authorities.

As a precondition, an effective system of banking supervision requires the delineation of clear objectives and responsibilities for those involved, along with operational independence and adequate resources. This precondition should be established as part of the legal framework for banking supervision, which should also provide for authorization and on-going supervision of banking organizations, adequate regulatory powers, and legal arrangements for confidentiality and information sharing between supervisors. The legal framework must clearly define permissible activities of banks and restrict the use of the term to regulated entities, with clear requirements for licensing and changes in ownership, whether through merger or transfer.

Powers and responsibilities for prudential regulation must include appropriate minimum capital requirements and appropriate evaluation of banks' lending, investment, asset quality and loan provisioning policies. In addition, supervisors must ensure the existence of adequate management information systems and compliance with limits on exposures to single or groups of related

---

[13] Basel Committee, *Compendium of Documents Produced by the Basle Committee on Banking Supervision*, Apr. 1997 as updated.

[14] Basel Committee, *Core Principles Methodology*, Oct. 1999.

[15] Basel Committee, *Compendium*, op. cit., n. 13.

borrowers. Such supervision must extend to requirements to prevent connected lending and other non-arm's length transactions. Beyond credit risk monitoring, supervisors must monitor banks' market risk systems as one aspect of banks' overall risk management systems – an especially difficult task in volatile markets with thin banking experience. Adequate internal controls also must be ensured, including appropriate "know-your-customer" mechanisms and ethical standards to prevent money laundering and financial crime.

Beyond initial systems, on-going supervision requires both on-site and off-site monitoring, including regular contact with bank management to provide a thorough understanding of each institution's operations. This must include both solo and consolidated information collection and analysis, along with independent validation of information supplied by supervised intermediaries. Consolidated supervision of banking groups is essential. In order for such on-going supervision to be effective, each bank must maintain adequate records drawn up in accordance with consistent accounting standards and practices, preferably employing an international standard.

In order to be effective in their supervisory efforts, supervisors must have adequate powers to bring about timely corrective action in circumstances where banks fail to meet prudential requirements outlined earlier. This should include the ability to revoke banking licenses in extreme cases.

Finally, because of the increasingly cross-border nature of banking activities and the greater risks that such activities lead to in the international financial system, banking supervisors must practice global consolidated supervision over their authorized internationally active banking organizations. An important component of this is contact and information sharing with other supervisors, especially host country supervisors. Host country supervisors in turn must require local operations of foreign banks to conduct business at the same high standards as required for domestic banks.

### 6.2.2. *Other Financial Stability Forum Standards*

In addition to the Basel Core Principles, the FSF has included a number of other documents of the Basel Committee in its *Compendium*. These are divided into five categories: (1) general, (2) capital adequacy, (3) cross-border supervision, (4) disclosure and transparency and (5) risk management. The general category includes, in addition to the Core Principles, standards for customer due diligence for banks[16] and the Core Principles methodology[17] to be used for assisting in implementation of and assessing compliance with the

---

[16] Basel Committee, *Customer Due Diligence for Banks*, Oct. 2001.
[17] Basel Committee, *Core Principles Methodology*, op. cit., n. 14.

Core Principles. In regard to capital adequacy, the FSF includes the 1988 Basel Accord[18] and its various amendments and modifications with respect to market risks.[19] In all likelihood, this eventually will be supplemented as an alternative by the Basel II Capital Accord, which is intended to apply to all internationally active banks and may be appropriate for application to all banks.[20] (In contrast, the 1988 Basel Accord was only intended to apply to internationally active banks from G-10 countries.) In regard to cross-border supervision, the FSF includes the Basel Concordat[21] and its subsequent development.[22] In regard to disclosure and transparency, the FSF includes guidance with respect to bank transparency[23] and accounting.[24] Finally, regarding risk management, the FSF includes guidance on management of credit risk[25], interaction with highly leveraged institutions such as hedge funds[26], operational risk[27], internal control systems[28], electronic banking and electronic money[29], interest rate risk[30], and derivatives.[31]

### 6.2.3. Implementation

At the end of 2002, the International Monetary Fund (IMF) and the World Bank conducted a review of Financial Sector Assessment Program/Reports on the Observance of Standards and Codes (FSAP/ROSC) experiences with the 1997 standards to date.[32] In the area of banking

---

[18] Basel Committee, *International Convergence of Capital Measurement and Capital Standards*, Jul. 1988 ("1988 Basel Accord").

[19] Basel Committee, *Amendment to the Capital Accord to Incorporate Market Risks*, Apr. 1998 as updated; idem., *Overview of the Amendment to the Capital Accord to Incorporate Market Risks*, Jan. 1996; idem., *Supervisory Framework for the use of "Backtesting" in Conjunction with the Internal Models Approach to Market Risk Capital Requirements*, Jan. 1996.

[20] Basel Committee, *International Convergence of Capital Measurements and Capital Standards: A Revised Framework*, Jun. 2004 ("Basel II").

[21] Basel Committee, *Principles for the Supervision of Banks' Foreign Establishments*, May 1983.

[22] Basel Committee, *Minimum Standards for the Supervision of International Banking Groups and their Cross-border Establishments*, Jul. 1992; Basel Committee and Offshore Group of Banking Supervisors, *The Supervision of Cross-border Banking*, Oct. 1996.

[23] Basel Committee, *Enhancing Bank Transparency*, Sep. 1998.

[24] Basel Committee, *Sound Practices for Loan Accounting, Credit Risk Disclosure and Related Matters*, Jul. 1999.

[25] Basel Committee, *Principles for the Management of Credit Risk*, Sep. 2000.

[26] Basel Committee, *Sound Practices for Banks' Interactions with Highly Leveraged Institutions*, Jan. 1999.

[27] Basel Committee, *Operational Risk Management*, Sep. 1998.

[28] Basel Committee, *Framework for Internal Control Systems in Banking Organizations*, Sep. 1998.

[29] Basel Committee, *Risk Management for Electronic Banking and Electronic Money Activities*, Mar. 1998.

[30] Basel Committee, *Principles on the Management of Interest Rate Risk*, Sep. 1997.

[31] Basel Committee, *Risk Management Guidelines for Derivatives*, Jul. 1994.

[32] IMF and World Bank, *Analytical Tools of the FSAP*, Feb. 2003.

supervision[33], assessments began in 1997; by December 2002, sixty-three assessments had been undertaken under the FSAP. A number of conclusions emerged from the reviews, including:

(1) effective supervision and full compliance are not possible unless the preconditions for effective supervision are met, namely (a) stable macroeconomic policies, (b) well-developed legal and judicial infrastructure, (c) effective market discipline, (d) procedures for effective resolution (exit) of banks, and (e) effective safety nets. Unfortunately, these are not actually included in the Basel Core Principles. They are, however, dealt with in detail in this volume, in Chapters Three through Six.
(2) Independence of the supervisory authority (Principle 1) is especially important.
(3) Improvement in compliance is especially needed in relation to credit policies and connected lending.
(4) Loan evaluation and provisioning practices tend to be weaker than the rules, placing doubt on capital adequacy issues; consolidation is also often weak.

Signifying the significance of banking and the Basel Core Principles, as of January 2007, the IMF/World Bank had published FSAP/ROSCs dealing with banking for seventy-seven countries – all under the original 1997 framework.[34]

## 6.3. BASEL CORE PRINCIPLES (2006)

After several years of work, the Basel Committee in 2006 released a revised version of the Basel Core Principles for public consultation.[35] In addition, the Basel Committee released a revised consultation Core Principles methodology to support the revised Core Principles.[36]

---

[33] Id., pp. 25–6; IMF and World Bank, *Implementation of the Basel Core Principles for Effective Banking Supervision, Experiences, Influences, and Perspectives*, Sep. 2002.

[34] Albania, Algeria, Antigua and Barbuda, Argentina, Australia, Austria, Bahrain, Barbados, Belgium, Bosnia and Herzegovina, Bulgaria, Cameroon, Canada, Chile, Costa Rica, Croatia, Cyprus, Czech Republic, Denmark, Estonia, Finland, France, Gabon, Georgia, Germany, Ghana, Greece, Hong Kong, Hungary, Iceland, Ireland, Israel, Italy, Jamaica, Japan, Kazakhstan, Kuwait, Kyrgyzstan, Latvia, Lithuania, Luxembourg, Macedonia, Madagascar, Malta, Mauritius, Mexico, Moldova, Morocco, Mozambique, The Netherlands, New Zealand, Norway, Pakistan, Philippines, Poland, Portugal, Romania, Russia, Rwanda, Saudi Arabia, Serbia, Singapore, Slovakia, Slovenia, South Korea, Spain, St. Vincent and the Grenadines, Sweden, Switzerland, Tanzania, Trinidad and Tobago, Tunisia, Uganda, Ukraine, United Arab Emirates, United Kingdom, Uruguay.

[35] Basel Committee, Consultative Document: *Core Principles for Effective Banking Supervision*, Apr. 2006.

[36] Basel Committee, *Consultative Document: Core Principles Methodology*, Apr. 2006.

As with the 1997 Basel Core Principles, the 2006 Basel Core Principles essentially formalize the international experience in the area of banking supervision, and can be expected to become the benchmark by which banking stability and development around the world are tested. The 2006 Basel Core Principles are based first upon a series of "preconditions" which highlight fundamental elements that must be in place for banks and banking to function in a market economy and that are the essential basis for regulation and supervision. In relation to regulation and supervision, there are twenty-five Principles, addressing: (1) objectives, independence, powers, transparency and cooperation (Principle 1); (2) regulation of banking activities (Principles 2 through 18 and 22); and (3) the role of banking supervisors (Principles 19 through 21 and Principles 23 through 25).

These Preconditions and Principles therefore provide the most up-to-date benchmark for supporting banking development, especially when read in conjunction with the 2006 Methodology and related work.

### 6.3.1. *Preconditions for Banking*

As noted earlier, for banking regulation and supervision to be effective in supporting financial stability and financial development, a number of preconditions must be in place. As outlined in the 2006 Basel Core Principles, these preconditions are: (1) sound and sustainable macroeconomic policies, (2) well-developed public infrastructure, (3) effective market discipline and (4) mechanisms for providing an appropriate level of systemic protection (public safety net).

In many ways, when looking at banking development (as opposed to stability) concerns, these are the fundamental issues for consideration. The first (sound and sustainable macroeconomic policies) is addressed in the context of Chapter Four; the remainder are discussed in further in this chapter.

**Well-developed Public Infrastructure.** The 2006 Basel Core Principles define "well developed public infrastructure" as:

(1) A system of business laws (corporate, insolvency, contract, consumer protection, private property), consistently enforced and providing fair resolution of disputes. These issues were addressed in the context of Chapters Three and Five.

(2) Accounting and auditing standards of international standard. These issues were addressed in the context of Chapter Five.

(3) An efficient and independent judiciary, accounting, auditing and legal professions. These issues were addressed in the context of Chapters Three and Five.

(4) Regulation and supervision of other financial sectors. These issues are discussed further in the context of Chapters Seven and Eight.
(5) Secure and efficient payment and clearing system. This issue was highlighted in the context of Chapter Four.

These issues are central not only to banking but to economic growth generally, and underlie the approach of this volume.

**Effective Market Discipline.** According to the 2006 Basel Core Principles, effective market discipline requires:

(1) availability of quality financial information,
(2) effective incentives for both public and private sector actors,
(3) an appropriate framework for markets to function,
(4) mechanisms to support effective corporate governance and appropriate behaviour, and
(5) lack of government interference in commercial decisions.

Likewise, these issues are central to the functioning of a market economy, and highlight the role of institutional and legal infrastructure in finance and economic growth.

### 6.3.2. *Objectives, Independence, Powers, Transparency and Cooperation (Principle 1)*

Basel Core Principle 1 (BCP 1) addresses the requirements in relation to objectives, independence, powers, transparency and cooperation of the banking supervisor. According to the 2006 Methodology, BCP 1 comprises six component parts[37]:

(1) responsibilities and objectives;
(2) independence, accountability and transparency;
(3) legal framework;
(4) legal powers (amplified in BCP 23);
(5) legal protection; and
(6) cooperation (developed further in BCP 18, BCP 24 and BCP 25).

### 6.3.3. *Banking Activities (Principles 2 through 18 and 22)*

Basel Core Principles 2 through 18 and 22 provide the framework for banking regulation. They require the following elements to be addressed: permissible

---

[37] Id., pp. 6–10.

activities of banks (Principle 2); licensing criteria (Principle 3); transfers of significant ownership (Principle 4)[38]; major acquisitions (Principle 5); capital adequacy (Principle 6)[39]; risk management processes (Principle 7)[40]; credit risk (Principle 8)[41]; problem assets, provisions and reserves (Principle 9)[42]; large exposure limits (Principle 10)[43]; exposures to related parties (Principle 11)[44]; country and transfer risks (Principle 12)[45]; market risks (Principle 13)[46]; liquidity risk (Principle 14)[47]; operational risk (Principle 15)[48]; interest rate risk (Principle 16)[49]; internal controls and audit (Principle 17)[50];

---

[38] According to the 2006 Methodology (Id., p. 12), the two main reference documents in this respect are: idem., *Parallel-owned Banking Structures*, Jan. 2003, and *Shell Banks and Booking Offices*, Jan. 2003.

[39] According to the 2006 Methodology (op. cit., n. 36, p. 14), the two main reference documents in this respect are: *International Convergence of Capital Measurement and Capital Standards*, Jul. 1998 ("1988 Basel Accord"); and *International Convergence of Capital Measurement and Capital Standards: A Revised Framework*, Jun. 2004 ("Basel II").

[40] According to the 2006 Methodology (op. cit., n. 36, p. 15), the main reference document in this respect is *Enhancing Corporate Governance for Banking Organizations*, Feb. 2006.

[41] According to the 2006 Methodology (op. cit., n. 36, p. 17), the main reference document in this respect is *Principles for the Management of Credit Risk*, Sep. 2000.

[42] According to the 2006 Methodology (op. cit., n. 36, p. 18), the main reference documents in this respect are: *Sound Practices for Loan Accounting and Disclosure*, Jul. 1999; and *Principles for the Management of Credit Risk*, Sep. 2000.

[43] According to the 2006 Methodology (op. cit., n. 36, p. 20), the main reference documents in this respect are: *Measuring and Controlling Large Credit Exposures*, Jan. 1991; and *Principles for the Management of Credit Risk*, Sep. 2000.

[44] According to the 2006 Methodology (op. cit., n. 36, p. 21), the main reference document in this respect is *Principles for the Management of Credit Risk*, Sep. 2000.

[45] According to the 2006 Methodology (op. cit., n. 36, p. 22), the main reference document in this respect is *Management of Banks' International Lending*, Mar. 1982.

[46] According to the 2006 Methodology (op. cit., n. 36, p. 23), the main reference document in this respect is *Amendment to the Capital Accord to Incorporate Market Risks*, Jan. 1996.

[47] According to the 2006 Methodology (op. cit., n. 36, p. 23), the main reference document in this respect is *Sound Practices for Managing Liquidity in Banking Organizations*, Feb. 2000.

[48] According to the 2006 Methodology (op. cit., n. 36, p. 25), the main reference documents in this respect are: *Sound Practices for the Management and Supervision of Operational Risk*, Feb. 2003; and Joint Forum on Financial Conglomerates, *Outsourcing in Financial Services*, Feb. 2005.

[49] According to the 2006 Methodology (op. cit., n. 36, p. 26), the main reference document in this respect is *Principles for the Management and Supervision of Interest Rate Risk*, Jul. 2004.

[50] According to the 2006 Methodology (op. cit., n. 36, p. 27), the main reference documents in this respect are: *Framework for Internal Control Systems in Banking Organizations*, Sep. 1998; *Internal Audit in Banks and the Supervisor's Relationship with Auditors*, Aug. 2001; and *Compliance and the Compliance Function in Banks*, Apr. 2005.

abuse of financial services (Principle 18)[51]; and accounting and disclosure (Principle 22).[52]

In addition, the 2006 Methodology provides significant additional information in respect to other work by the Basel Committee in relation to the majority of these aspects. At the same time, due to the significance of capital, it bears spending a bit of time on this subject here.

**1988 Basel Capital Accord: The 8 Per Cent Standard.** In 1988, the Basel Committee reached a secret agreement (subsequently published) regarding an agreed approach among the G-10 regarding regulation of bank capital of internationally active banks.[53] Although only intended to apply to internationally active G-10 banks, the 1988 Basel Accord in the following decade and a half became the international standard for bank capital regulation around the world[54] and has been implemented through formal domestic legal arrangements in more than 100 countries. At its simplest, the 1988 Accord was intended to (1) reduce systemic risk through requiring banks to hold a minimum amount of capital against risks, and (2) limit regulatory competition and arbitrage, thereby providing a level playing field for internationally active banks. In essence, the first goal was a response to the problems which resulted from the 1980s debt crisis, wherein large international banks made significant loans to developing countries, which subsequently defaulted. The subsequent default raised a very real risk of an international systemic banking crisis. Failure of the majority of the world's ten largest banks was only averted through careful regulatory forbearance and financial restructuring efforts (for both the international banks and their developing country borrowers) across the second half of the 1980s.

The 1988 Basel Accord is a fairly simple framework, focusing on one aspect: capital in relation to credit risk in banks. At its heart is an equation: total capital divided by total risk-adjusted assets must equal at least 8 per cent. The simple definition therefore has two major components: capital and risk-adjusted assets.

---

[51] According to the 2006 Methodology (op. cit., n. 36, p. 29), the main reference documents in this respect are: *Prevention of Criminal Use of the Banking System for the Purpose of Money Laundering*, Dec. 1988; *Customer Due Diligence for Banks*, Oct. 2001; *Shell Banks and Booking Offices*, Jan. 2003; *Consolidated KYC Risk Management*, Oct. 2004; *FATF, 40 + 8*, 2003; and *FATF AML/CFT Methodology*, 2004 as updated.

[52] According to the 2006 Methodology (op. cit., n. 36, p. 35), the main reference document in this respect is *Enhancing Bank Transparency*, Sep. 1998.

[53] Basel Committee, *International Convergence of Capital Measurement and Capital Standards*, Jul. 1998 ("1988 Basel Accord").

[54] See Norton, op. cit., n. 12.

Under the 1988 framework, capital is divided into two forms: Tier 1 and Tier 2, of which Tier 1 capital must make up at least 50 per cent of total capital. Tier 1 capital is essentially shareholder equity, while Tier 2 capital includes a variety of forms of subordinated debt.

Total-risk adjusted assets are primarily composed of a bank's loan portfolio. Loans (and related debt instruments) are grouped into four "baskets": Category 1, Category 2, Category 3 and Category 4. Each category groups different forms of obligations together very loosely on the basis of simple risk classifications and assigns a weighting to those assets:

| | |
|---|---|
| Category 1: | Primarily Organization of Economic Cooperation and Development (OECD) country and local government securities – 0 per cent, |
| Category 2: | Primarily interbank claims – 20 per cent, |
| Category 3: | Primarily debt secured by real property – 50 per cent, |
| Category 4: | All other obligations, including, most importantly, private sector corporate debt – 100 per cent. |

In addition to primary assets (e.g., loans), the 1988 Accord also provides mechanisms for drawing certain otherwise off-balance sheet obligations into total risk-adjusted assets for purposes of capital. Once again, off-balance sheet obligations are grouped into four baskets, each with a different conversion factor: 100 per cent, 50 per cent, 20 per cent and 0 per cent.

Overall, this simple framework, while not very precise in term of risk calculation, provides for the majority of economies around the world a central element of bank regulation.

Over time and in reaction to various international banking crises, the 1988 Accord has been modified in certain significant ways through a variety of "amendments", the most significant of which can be summarized as:

(1) amendment of the Basel Capital Accord with respect to the inclusion of general provisions/general loan-loss reserves in capital (November 1991), which defines general provisions/loan-loss reserves with greater precision;

(2) amendment to the Capital Accord of July 1988 (July 1994), which redefines countries which can qualify for OECD weighting, disqualifying countries which have rescheduled external debt within the previous five years;

(3) treatment of potential exposure for off-balance sheet items (April 1995), which amends the treatment of off-balance sheet items in order to (a)

recognize netting in the calculation of "add-ons" and (b) enlarge the matrix of add-ons;

(4) amendment to the Capital Accord to incorporate market risks (January 1996, modified September 1997), which adopts two alternative approaches to market risk (a standardized approach and an internal models-based approach); and

(5) amendment to the Basel Capital Accord of July 1988 (April 1998), which reduces risk weight for claims on regulated securities firms, subject to certain conditions, and substitutes "loans" for "claims" in parts of the text.

In addition, recognizing that the 1988 Accord suffered from numerous problems (especially relating to the way in which it deals with risk classification) and also as a result of the Asian financial crisis, the Basel Committee began work on developing a new capital accord in 1999.

**Basel II: The Three Pillars.** After approximately five years of discussion, consultation and market testing, in 2004, the Basel Committee released the final agreed framework.[55] In 2005, the Committee released a slightly revised and updated version to address certain aspects of trading activities[56] and, in 2006, released a comprehensive document incorporating unchanged elements of the 1988 Accord and subsequent amendments into a single framework.[57]

Basel II is intended to provide an overall system of risk-based supervision and risk management (internal and market) for banks. It focuses on five major categories of risk: (1) credit, (2) market, (3) operational, (4) liquidity and (5) legal.

This framework involves four levels: (1) identification of risk, (2) risk measurement, (3) risk disclosure and (4) internal risk management.

Following this framework, Basel II implements a number of changes through elements based upon three "pillars": Pillar I addresses minimum capital requirements; Pillar II addresses supervisory review; and Pillar III addresses market discipline through disclosure requirements. The system is intended to be an evolutionary system which can develop over time.

---

[55] Basel Committee, *International Convergence of Capital Measurement and Capital Standards: A Revised Framework*, Jun. 2004.

[56] Basel Committee, *International Convergence of Capital Measurement and Capital Standards: A Revised Framework*, Nov. 2005.

[57] Basel Committee, *International Convergence of Capital Measurement and Capital Standards: A Revised Framework – Comprehensive Version*, Jun. 2006 ("Basel II").

The three pillars are intended to support the fundamental objectives of (1) "strengthening the soundness and stability of the international banking system" while (2) "maintaining sufficient consistency that capital adequacy regulation will not be a significant source of competitive inequality among internationally active banks" through "promoting the adoption of stronger risk management practices by the banking industry."[58] As with the 1988 Accord, Basel II is intended to apply to the consolidated activities of internationally active banks, initially G-10 but gradually incorporated into other systems.[59]

In attempting to achieve these objectives, Basel II incorporates a number of significant elements, including a menu-based approach to capital charges, greater use of both credit assessments by rating agencies and through banks' own internal models, increased recognition of a variety of risk mitigation techniques, a new charge for operational risk, and new requirements relating to supervisory review and new market disclosure obligations imposed on banks.

In relation to Pillar I (revised minimum capital requirements), the essential equation, required minimum ratio and definition of capital remain largely unchanged. The main changes relate to the denominator, which is now the sum of risk-weighted assets, market risk and operational risk charges.

Market risk essentially remains as under the 1996 Amendment, with a standardized approach and an internal models based (IRB) option. For the new operational risk charge, there are three options: Basic Indicator, Standardized and Advanced Measurement Approaches (essentially, IRB).

In relation to capital, there is now a standardized approach and two IRB approaches (foundation and advanced). The standardized approach includes much greater specificity in relation to risk weightings (often based on ratings by external agencies) as well as new operational requirements. In addition, it allows much greater use of credit risk mitigation techniques such as collateral, guarantees and credit derivatives, and on-balance sheet netting. The two IRB approaches are based on banks' internal risk models and include rules relating to use of IRB models ("qualification"), data requirements and minimum charges. In terms of asset classes, separate requirements address: (1) corporate, sovereign and bank exposures; (2) retail exposures; (3) equity exposures; (4) purchased receivables; and (5) securitization.

Pillar II includes four central principles.[60] First, banks should have a process for assessing their overall capital adequacy in relation to their risk profile and a strategy for maintaining their capital levels (Principle 1). Second, supervisors

[58] Id., p. 2.
[59] Id., p. 7.
[60] Id., pp. 205–12.

should review and evaluate banks' internal capital adequacy assessments and strategies, as well as their ability to monitor and ensure their compliance with regulatory capital ratios. Supervisors should take appropriate supervisory action if they are not satisfied with the result of this process (Principle 2). Third, supervisors should expect banks to operate above the minimum regulatory capital ratios and should have the ability to require banks to hold capital in excess of the minimum (Principle 3). Fourth, supervisors should seek to intervene at an early stage to prevent capital from falling below the minimum levels required to support the risk characteristics of a particular bank and should require rapid remedial action if capital is not maintained or restored (Principle 4).

Pillar III deals with the supervisory review process through which supervisors should monitor the activities of banks. In many ways, Pillar III relates directly to the framework summarized in the 2006 Basel Core Principles and associated Methodology.

### 6.3.4. *Supervisors (Principles 19 through 21 and 23 through 25)*

Basel Core Principles 19 through 21 and 23 through 25 deal with the role of the banking supervisor and address the following: supervisory approach (Principle 19), supervisory techniques (Principle 20), supervisory reporting (Principle 21), corrective and remedial powers (Principle 23), consolidated supervision (Principle 24)[61], and home-host relationships (Principle 25).[62]

Beyond the primary international standards of the Basel Committee relating to banking regulation and supervision, additional standards and guidance have been developed in relation to banking problems and the framework supporting their resolution.

### 6.4. FRAMEWORK FOR ADDRESSING BANKING PROBLEMS

Another area of necessary focus for banking regulation – and one not currently dealt with adequately by the 1997 or 2006 Basel Core Principles, perhaps under

---

[61] According to the 2006 Methodology (op. cit., n. 36, p. 38), the main reference documents in this respect are: *Consolidated Supervision of Banks' International Activities*, Mar. 1979; *Principles for the Supervision of Banks' Foreign Establishments*, May 1983; *Minimum Standards for the Supervision of International Banking Groups and Their Cross-Border Establishments*, Jul. 1992; and *The Supervision of Cross-Border Banking*, Oct. 1996.

[62] According to the 2006 Methodology (op. cit., n. 36, p. 40), the main reference documents in this respect are: *Principles for the Supervision of Banks' Foreign Establishments*, May 1983; *Report on Cross-Border Banking Supervision*, Jun. 1996; *Shell Banks and Booking Offices*, Jan. 2003; and *The High-Level Principles for the Cross-Border Implementation of the New Accord*, Aug. 2003.

the view that these are not strictly covered by "supervision" – is the provision of appropriate safety net and exit arrangements.[63] The high cost to society of a collapse of the banking system is a principal reason why authorities in virtually all developed countries provide some sort of a safety net for depositors, usually in the form of deposit insurance. This involves the potential outlay of public funds in the event that the stability of the banking system is threatened. While the intention is usually to minimize potential losses of public funds, the reality is that in the context of apparent or actual systemic instability, more often than not, governments around the world have supported not only healthy individual banks in the context of circumstances of potential or actual systemic risk but also often unhealthy banks, whether systemically significant or not. Such arrangements (or the general belief in de facto government guarantees) inevitably create moral hazards because they hold open the prospect that stakeholders will be at least partially indemnified from losses from failing intermediaries. These problems were most clearly illustrated during the US savings and loan crisis of the 1980s and have been (and in many cases continue to be) a feature of banking weaknesses over the past fifteen years.

At the outset, depositor protection schemes, and specifically deposit insurance systems, do not exist in a vacuum, but rather are components of an overall financial safety net. At its heart, the purpose of a financial safety net in any given economy is to minimize systemic risk, while at the same time promoting financial stability and (hopefully) financial and hence economic development. Of central significance is that all parts of the financial safety net are interrelated and must be designed to work together in an integrated manner. According to Mario Giovanoli[64]:

> the topics of prudential supervision, liquidation, the potential liability of financial authorities and deposit guarantee schemes are linked and form a vast cluster of interrelated topics which need to be addressed globally.

Further, it is generally agreed that law and legal infrastructure have a fundamental role not only in building an effective financial safety net, but also in financial stability generally and moreover in financial and economic development.[65] In a 2001 paper, Asli Demirgüç-Kunt and Edward Kane analysed

---

[63] Thanks to Michael Taylor for this explanation.

[64] M. Giovanoli, "Preface", in M. Giovanoli and G. Heinrich (eds), *International Bank Insolvencies: A Central Bank Perspective* (London: Kluwer, 1999), p. xv.

[65] See A. Demirgüç-Kunt and R. Levine (eds), *Financial Structure and Economic Growth: A Cross-Country Comparison of Banks, Markets, and Development* (Cambridge, MA: MIT Press, 2001).

the relationship between deposit insurance and financial stability.[66] They conclude[67]:

> [c]ross-country empirical research on deposit insurance strongly supports the hypothesis that in institutionally weak environments, poorly designed deposit-insurance arrangements tend to increase the probability of future banking crises.

While the methodology and the result may be criticized, based on this conclusion, they recommend that governments should address weaknesses in transparency, deterrency and accountability before adopting explicit deposit insurance schemes, with specific focus on banking regulation and supervision, protection of property rights, enforceability of contracts, and quality of accounting and disclosure.[68] Similarly, James Barth, Gerald Caprio and Ross Levine stress that[69]:

> ... regulations and supervisory practices that force accurate information disclosure and limit the moral hazard incentives of poorly designed deposit insurance critically boost bank performance and stability.

This section does not analyse the specific policy and design features of deposit insurance, as this has been done elsewhere.[70] Rather, the author, to present an analogy, focuses on structural issues, much as would a structural engineer when faced with implementation of an architect's overall design.

In analysing depositor protection schemes, it is first necessary to place them in the appropriate context, namely, as one aspect of an overall financial safety net designed to prevent systemic risk and maintain financial stability. In general terms, the financial safety net has developed out of specific regulatory objectives (broadly speaking, to include general objectives of addressing and preventing systemic risk) to form the traditional regulatory and supervisory process. In this process, the main authorities and their functions can be categorized as: (1) monetary policy authorities, (2) supervisory authorities, (3) lender of last resort, (4) deposit insurance authorities, (5) insolvency authorities, (6) criminal authorities, (7) the legislature and government (policy), (8) the judicial system

---

[66] A. Demirgüç-Kunt and E. Kane, *Deposit Insurance around the Globe: Where does it work?* (World Bank, Jul. 2001, mimeographed).

[67] Id., p. 24.

[68] Id., p. 25.

[69] J. Barth, G. Caprio and R. Levine, *Bank Regulation and Supervision: What Works Best?* (World Bank, Aug. 2001, mimeographed), p. 41.

[70] See FSF, *Guidance for Developing Effective Deposit Insurance Systems*, Sep. 2001; Demirgüç-Kunt and Levine, op. cit., n. 65; Demirgüç-Kunt and Kane, op. cit., n. 66; and Barth, Caprio and Levine, op. cit., n. 69.

(dispute resolution, contract enforcement and judicial review) and (9) international commitments (e.g., World Trade Organization/General Agreement on Trade in Services).

Historically, banking regulation developed as a response to crises resulting from the nature of banking business as a fractional reserve system based upon the management of credit and duration risks – a system that works wonderfully so long as depositors remain confident in the safety of their money with individual banks. The risk, of course, is that the collapse of one bank could lead to contagious loss of confidence, resulting in bank runs, potentially causing the collapse not only of individual banks, but also of the banking system as a whole (systemic risk) and the consequent collapse of economic activity generally.[71]

The response to this classic, and very real, problem was the development of the theory of the need for a "lender of last resort" by Henry Thornton in 1802 and Walter Bagehot in 1873.[72] The lender of last resort would provide liquidity support in order to allow banks to meet depositors' demands and avoid closure, thereby supporting confidence and stemming potential systemic collapse.

The problem, of course, is the equally classic theory of "moral hazard". Specifically, in this context, moral hazard has two components: first, potential incentives to management to take additional (perhaps excessive) risks due to the promise of a government bailout; and second, the consequent risk to the public purse due to the potential expense. Ideally, the second should not exist, but as noted earlier, more often than not, authorities become overactive in their support measures, shifting from pure liquidity support (which should not entail public expense) to more general solvency support (which can entail very high public expense).

The response to this problem has been the development of what may be termed the traditional process of bank regulation and supervision. Under this formulation, the goal of the traditional regulatory and supervisory process is simple on its face: the prevention and resolution of financial intermediary crises. Unfortunately, while the goal is simple, its achievement is anything but. Nonetheless, it is worth reviewing the contents of the traditional formulation for preventing and resolving bank crises. At its most basic, the formulation involves two sets of processes: one ex ante, the other ex post crisis.

The ex ante measures focus on two related goals: first, supporting sound management and internal controls (a well-managed bank is less likely to be

---

[71] See R. Lastra (1996), op. cit., n. 4.
[72] H. Thornton, *An Enquiry into the Nature and Effects of the Paper Credit of Great Britain* (London: J. Hatchard, 1802); W. Bagehot, *Lombard Street: A Description of the Money Market* (1873 [New York: John Wiley, 1999]).

the subject either of a crisis or of contagion); and second, regulation and supervision (bank management, and arguably public authorities, have short memories and need to be given rules to follow; bank management also needs to be monitored to make sure that it, in fact, follows the rules). Stylistic issues, of course, relate to the administrative process and rule versus discretion-based approaches (e.g., prompt corrective action). Of course, once again, while both appear relatively simple on their face, only recently have we begun to arrive at agreed formulations of their content.[73]

The ex post measures focus on bolstering confidence, stemming contagion and resolving problem intermediaries. Immediate measures focus on suspension of deposit redemption (never popular), the provision of support through the lender of last resort mechanism (to deal with illiquidity) and various mechanisms for depositor protection, of which deposit insurance is the most significant (to address insolvency). In addition to the immediate measures, other ex post measures are required to deal with the insolvency of individual intermediaries. In respect to individual intermediary insolvencies, four main mechanisms exist: (1) organization of a rescue package, (2) provision of open financial assistance, (3) merger or acquisition (public or private) and (4) liquidation and pay-off. Finally, in some cases, measures will be required to address systemic insolvency (which is a very different sort of problem from "ordinary" bank failures), but these are rarely (if ever) organized in advance of such an actuality.[74]

In considering the role of law, it is worth looking in greater depth at issues that arise in the traditional crisis management process. Typically, suspension of redemption rights is not provided for ex ante (although it may be and has been, e.g., in Sweden); related issues are not discussed further.

### 6.4.1. *Depositor Protection Schemes*

Turning now to the next mechanism of immediate crisis resolution: the idea is that some sort of depositor protection scheme can be put in place to support confidence in times of crisis and also to assist in the resolution of normal bank failures. In recent years, increasing numbers of economies have been turning to these sorts of systems, especially deposit insurance.[75] There are three interconnected legal and policy issues that are fundamental for the

---

[73] See generally J. Norton (1995), op. cit., n. 12 and the ever-growing body of work emanating from the Basel Committee.

[74] For discussion, see D. Hoelscher and M. Quintyn, et al., "Managing Systemic Banking Crises", IMF Occasional Paper 224 (Aug. 1993).

[75] See Demirgüç-Kunt and Kane, op. cit., n. 66; Barth, Caprio and Levine, op. cit., n. 69.

understanding – from a legal point of view – of deposit insurance, before turning to explicit and implicit systems, respectively. The first issue is the mandatory nature of deposit insurance, as opposed to the contingent nature of the lender of last resort role of the central bank. The second issue is the difference between explicit and implicit deposit insurance. The third issue is the status of preferred creditors that insured depositors have under an explicit deposit guarantee scheme.

Deposit insurance provides a guarantee on certain deposits that is noncontingent. Lender of last resort support, on the other hand, is contingent. The injection of liquidity in times of crises is not mandatory, but discretionary, that is, subject to the discretion of the central bank authority. Thus, explicit deposit insurance provides legal certainty regarding the coverage of insured depositors. There is always a degree of uncertainty (some economists refer to it as "constructive ambiguity") regarding the provision of emergency liquidity assistance by the central bank.[76]

It should also be pointed out that while explicit deposit insurance protects mainly depositors, the lender of last resort function protects mainly the financial system (systemic considerations).[77]

To minimize the risk of moral hazard, it is important to demarcate what each institutional arrangement can do and what it cannot or should not do. Explicit deposit insurance can protect insured depositors, but it cannot – and should not – protect other depositors or creditors, shareholders or managers. Explicit deposit insurance cannot protect banks, because it can only be activated once a bank is closed. The lender of last resort[78]:

> ...can provide emergency liquidity – quick cash up front – over a short period of time, when no other sources of funding are readily available. What the central bank should not do is lend over an extended period of time nor commit funds without the explicit approval of the fiscal authority.

As the starting point, any form of depositor protection can either be implicit or explicit. In addition, it is clearly possible for any jurisdiction to have no such system in place at all; while some suggest that no system is, in fact, an implicit government guarantee, it is possible (though certainly not politically easy) not to provide government support at all and on occasion governments have managed to stand aside. In most cases, however, no deposit insurance system

---

[76] It is also sometimes suggested that this is an argument for implicit deposit insurance.

[77] This point also underlines that deposit insurance should only be triggered when a bank is declared insolvent.

[78] See R Lastra, *Legal Foundations of International Monetary Stability* (Oxford: Oxford University Press, 2006), p. 344.

does, in fact, imply an implicit government guarantee, at least for depositors of the largest financial intermediaries. While an implicit guarantee certainly raises many issues, these are typically political rather than legal.

Explicit systems typically take one of two forms: (1) an explicit blanket guarantee of all deposits or (2) an explicit, limited-coverage system of deposit insurance. Each raises a variety of legal issues.

Explicit deposit insurance, that is, the creation of a deposit guarantee scheme by law, with rules with regard to the extent of the "insurance" or protection, the rules of the scheme and the type of deposits/depositors protected can be a useful instrument of protective bank regulation. Indeed, explicit deposit insurance has traditionally served two purposes: consumer protection and the prevention of bank runs. This author suggests that a third rationale of explicit deposit insurance is that it allows the public authorities to close banks more easily, as it becomes politically acceptable to liquidate insolvent intermediaries, in the knowledge that unsophisticated depositors are protected.

Under an explicit deposit guarantee scheme, depositors are only paid once the bank is closed and, in many cases, liquidated (though there is, in fact, a strong argument that payment should be made as soon as possible after closure rather than held for liquidation, resolution, etc.). Thus, there can be no deposit insurance if the bank remains open. Therefore, explicit deposit insurance presupposes that a bank has failed and, hence, it is not compatible with the "too big to fail" doctrine (i.e., certain intermediaries, because of their significance within a financial system, inevitably pose risks of a systemic nature and therefore must be treated with special care).

Implicit deposit insurance, as opposed to explicit deposit insurance, is potentially a "blanket guarantee" for all sorts of depositors (insured and uninsured), other creditors, shareholders and even managers – as it is implicit, the exact meaning can only be inferred from previous behaviour. Implicit deposit insurance often presupposes that the bank remains in business (either because it is "too big to fail" or because it is politically difficult to close the bank), thus creating pervasive moral hazard incentives. While explicit deposit insurance is applied ex post (following the closure of a bank), implicit deposit insurance is often applied while a bank is still in operation.

Explicit deposit insurance is intended to inflict only very limited damage upon taxpayers, and, depending on the funding of the scheme, there may be no damage at all, though this is certainly not always achieved in practice. However, implicit deposit insurance has the potential of shifting the burden onto taxpayers, since rescue packages tend to be financed by the government. The use of rescue packages not only results in moral hazard considerations, but may also affect competition, especially if a "too big to fail" doctrine is applied.

An explicit blanket guarantee can take either a formal legal form (Japan, Mexico, Taiwan, Turkey) or simply be a government pronouncement or policy (South Korea, Malaysia, Sweden, Thailand). Either will likely be sufficiently clear and robust for purposes of confidence; the difficulty arises if the government decides to eliminate the guarantee and move to an explicit, limited-coverage system of deposit insurance. The central issue is the credibility of the guarantee: Is the government able to mobilize sufficient fiscal resources and political commitment to make good the guarantee? A number of countries (including Japan, South Korea, Sweden and Turkey) appear to have made successful transitions from blanket guarantees to limited, explicit systems.

Explicit deposit insurance is a guarantee limited to one type of "preferred creditor", that is, insured depositors. Under explicit deposit insurance, uninsured depositors, other creditors, shareholders and managers are not protected. Therefore, explicit deposit insurance is more compatible with market discipline, as uninsured depositors and other creditors have an interest in monitoring the solvency of the bank while still in operation.

Explicit deposit insurance, by limiting the protection of "insured depositors", exposes uninsured depositors, general creditors, subordinated debt holders, shareholders and management to increased risk exposure, thereby encouraging them to monitor and limit the riskiness of the bank.[79] These incentives are very important, particularly in the case of shareholders, whose limited liability renders them more prone to lend on a high risk/high return basis, while restricting their own exposure through high leverage.[80] In the absence of open bank assistance, management will also be inclined to operate the bank in a prudent manner, or risk being removed from office. Explicit deposit insurance must be set at a level that enables national authorities to accept the political consequences of bank liquidations.

In September 2001, the FSF endorsed the report of its Working Group on Deposit Insurance as international guidance for jurisdictions considering the adoption of an explicit, limited-coverage deposit insurance system.[81] According to Andrew Crockett, the report is built on three general findings[82]: (1) explicit and limited deposit insurance is preferable to implicit coverage if it clarifies obligations to depositors and creditors and limits the scope for discretionary decisions that may result in arbitrary actions; (2) deposit insurance systems

---

[79] See Lastra (1996), op. cit., n. 4, p. 130.

[80] See generally R. Dale, "Deposit Insurance, Policy Clash over EC and US Reforms", in F. C. Schadrack and L. Korobow (eds), *The Basic Elements of Bank Supervision* (New York: Federal Reserve Bank of New York, 1993).

[81] FSF Deposit Insurance Guidance, op. cit., n. 70, preface.

[82] Id.

must be properly designed, well implemented and understood by the public to be credible and to avoid moral hazard; and (3) to be effective, the deposit insurance system needs to be part of a well-designed financial safety net, and be supported by strong prudential regulation and supervision, effective laws that are enforced, and sound accounting and disclosure regimes.

According to the FSF report, the principal objectives of a deposit insurance system are[83]: (1) to contribute to the stability of a country's financial system and (2) to protect less financially sophisticated depositors from the loss of their deposits when banks fail.

The Working Group developed twenty "key points of guidance" for countries considering the adoption or reform of an explicit, limited-coverage deposit insurance system.[84] The key points are grouped under four main headings[85]:

(I)   Contextual issues for deposit insurance systems, specifically: (1) contextual background and (2) moral hazard.
(II)  Processes for adopting and maintaining a deposit insurance system, specifically: (3) public policy objectives, (4) situational analysis, (5) transition: blanket guarantee to deposit insurance and (6) self-assessment methodology.
(III) structure and design features, specifically: (7) mandate and powers, (8) structure, (9) governance, (10) human resources and statutory indemnification, (11) interrelationships among safety net participants, (12) membership, (13) coverage, (14) funding, (15) public awareness and (16) cross-border issues.
(IV)  Resolutions, reimbursements, claims and recoveries, specifically: (17) failure resolution, (18) reimbursing depositors, (19) claims and recoveries, and (20) depositor ranking, collateralization and rights of set-off.

The FSF thus provides the essential guidance in this regard, though it is not included in either the FSF list of standards or the framework of the IMF and World Bank.

### 6.4.2. Bank Insolvency

Beyond immediate measures to deal with banking crises (such as the lender of last resort function), some system needs to be in place to deal with individual situations of bank insolvency. Clearly, however, no system is necessary

---

[83]  Id., p. 3.
[84]  Id., p. 41.
[85]  Id., pp. 41–51. See generally FSF, Working Group on Deposit Insurance, *Guidance for Developing Effective Deposit Insurance Systems: Background Documents*, Sep. 2001.

in jurisdictions which do not intend to allow any banks to become insolvent. (Historically, this has been the case in Japan and the People's Republic of China, but appears to be changing in both cases.)

Generally speaking, the goals of bank insolvency are threefold: (1) fair treatment of all creditors, (2) maximization of the value of the estate and (3) reduction of systemic risk – with all three goals potentially in conflict.[86] Typically, however, the various functions concerned are often embedded in different institutions.[87] The primary authorities and their functions can be categorized as: (1) insolvency authorities, (2) supervisory authorities, (3) lender of last resort, (4) monetary policy authorities, (5) deposit insurance authorities and (6) criminal authorities.[88] Most of these have been reviewed earlier; criminal issues are beyond the present scope.

As noted earlier, the availability of the traditional methods very much depends upon the individual legal system. The organization of a rescue package typically will not require specific authorization. On the other hand, the ability to provide open assistance may be clearly constrained by law. The availability of merger or acquisition, whether public or private, likewise varies, with some jurisdictions having specific legislation addressing financial intermediary mergers/acquisitions, while in others (especially common law jurisdictions) such issues are primarily dealt with through the relevant company law. In most cases, however, issues will arise under banking law/regulation concerning licenses/authorization. Finally, the availability of liquidation and pay-off varies greatly, with some jurisdictions having completely separate stand-alone systems for bank insolvencies (e.g., United States), while in others, bank insolvencies are largely dealt with through the general system of corporate insolvency, although typically modified in some way by banking law/regulation (e.g., United Kingdom). The greater concern is typically in the latter sorts of jurisdictions where insolvency law and systems may not always be overly effective.[89] Significantly, an ineffective system of insolvency may also be a barrier to effective out-of-court workouts.

Beyond individual bank insolvencies, measures to address systemic insolvency are typically only developed in the context of an actual situation. Unfortunately, not only can weakness in the overall design of the financial safety

---

[86] "Bank insolvencies entail systemic risks which are absent in the bankruptcy of most commercial concerns." E. Patrikis, "Role and Functions of Authorities: Supervision, Insolvency Prevention and Liquidation", in Giovanoli and Heinrich, op. cit., n. 64, p. 283.

[87] Id., p. 284.

[88] Cf. id., pp. 284–5.

[89] This problem is well recognized and is the subject of a joint project between the World Bank and UNCITRAL to establish "Principles of Insolvency", discussed in Chapter Five of this volume.

net potentially lead to such problems, but weaknesses in supporting legal infra-structure can also make resolution more difficult.

This section has sought to highlight both the significance of depositor pro-tection schemes and the diversity of their implementation in different juris-dictions around the world. Further, analysis reveals a central role for the legal and institutional design in effective functioning not only of the depositor pro-tection function, but of the financial safety net generally. Certainly, one lesson to emerge from recent experiences with financial crises around the world, not only over the past decade but over the past century and a half, is the vital importance of institutions (especially laws, legal institutions and financial reg-ulatory structures) to financial crisis prevention and resolution, financial sector development and economic growth generally. It is in this context that insti-tutional design of the role of both the architects of those institutions and the structural designers responsible for implementation becomes essential.

## 6.5. CONCLUSION

A safe, efficient and effective banking sector is absolutely essential to support financial development and economic growth. Unsafe banks can lead to sys-temic financial crisis and economic collapse, as in the Asian financial crises in 1997–98. Hence, the key consideration is first to address risks: the goal is main-taining financial stability through developing an effective financial safety net, focusing on (1) financial stability, (2) banking regulation and supervision and (3) depositor protection. Likewise, to the extent that other financial interme-diaries (such as microfinance providers, money lenders and money changers) are conducting banking business and therefore raise risks similar to banks, they should likewise be addressed. As such, this section should be seen to address not only banks and banking but also related intermediaries such as money lenders and microfinance intermediaries (discussed further in Chapter Seven) to the extent they are conducting banking activities.

At the same time, developing banks and banking and related intermediaries is important to support savings and financial resource allocation. The focus here is on providing rules and incentives to support banks and related intermediaries to do banking business in a safe and efficient manner, through (1) foundations of the financial system, (2) preconditions to effective banking supervision (espe-cially a safe and efficient payment system), and (3) effective supervision of banks and similar intermediaries such as microfinance providers, money lenders and money changers, to the extent they are conducting banking business.

In most developing, emerging and transition economies, the banking sector plays the most significant role in financial resource allocation and savings in the economy, highlighting the central role of the banking sector in financial stability and economic growth. At the same time, other "bank-like" intermediaries such as microfinance providers, money lenders and money changers also tend to be very active in developing, emerging and transition financial systems and play a very important role in financial resource accumulation and allocation. As such, it is important to have a comprehensive system to address the risks of banking activities conducted by various differing types of intermediary as well as to support the development of the positive roles of these various forms of intermediary in economic growth and financial development.

Overall, the main challenges and priorities for supporting the development of banking in the context of financial stability may be summarized as:

(1) addressing risks;
(2) improving financial intermediary operations and increasing intermediation through human capital development, education and appropriate regulation and supervision;
(3) increasing confidence through improving financial intermediary and supervisory functioning and education;
(4) formalizing finance through increasing confidence;
(5) linking finance through increasing confidence in regulation, supervision and enforcement and developing appropriate financial infrastructure (especially payment system, money/interbank markets including short-term government securities, and improving financial information quality and transparency); and
(6) treating providers of similar financial services similarly (avoiding regulatory arbitrage) and providing a progressive, developmental system for non-banks conducting banking type activities.

Generally, one finds three major forms of banking: (1) relationship based, (2) collateral based and (3) cash-flow based.

Relationship banking is common in all financial systems around the world and is one means to address information asymmetries present in lending. At the same time, while relationship-based banking can be an extremely effective form of business, it can also bring risks if the lending is not done carefully and on the basis of commercial judgement. After all, it is often said that one of the greatest underlying causes of the Asian financial crisis was "crony capitalism", characterized by lending not on the basis of commercial judgement but rather on the basis of political support and position. In the end, commercial judgement must underlie relationship-based banking for it to support both financial stability and economic growth.

Collateral-based banking is perhaps the most common form of banking business around the world. As discussed in Chapter Three, collateral is a mechanism which can reduce the risks inherent in lending. At the same time, however, collateral-based lending brings its own risks: a great number of banking crises have been brought about by excessive lending collateralized by overvalued commercial real estate. Therefore, once again, collateral-based lending has an important role in encouraging finance through risk mitigation but is a tool that requires careful use and, because of the dangers, is a major focus of banking regulation and supervision.

Cash-flow based banking has perhaps the most potential economic benefits for economic growth of the three major techniques but at the same time requires, by far, the most sophisticated institutional framework to function. Especially important are high-quality financial information and reliable contract enforcement – signatures of a developed institutional environment. Basel II, at the least, may help to support more cash-flow based lending as it is implemented and shows the linkages between financial regulation and financial development.

# 7

# Nonbank Finance: Securities, Insurance, Pensions and Microfinance

As discussed in the previous chapter, the traditional focus of banking regulation and supervision has been systemic risk. As a result, banking until quite recently has received much greater attention than nonbank finance from regulators and researchers. At the same time, in most developing, emerging and transition economies, banking accounts for the majority of finance and is therefore a central focus in terms of financial development to support economic growth. In many ways, this predominance of banking often is due to the fact that banking (and related activities) develops more easily in weaker institutional environments than many forms of nonbank finance.

Most forms of nonbank finance – especially securities, insurance and pensions and with the notable exception of microfinance – tend to require a stronger institutional environment in order to develop and function well. At the same time, in many sophisticated financial systems (including the international financial system), nonbank finance now accounts for the majority of finance, with the share of banking having decreased steadily over the past fifty years and the share of securities, insurance and pensions increasing steadily over the same period. As a result, from the developmental perspective, there has been increased attention to developing securities, insurance and pensions not only in developing, emerging and transition economies but also in developed economies (the best example being continental Europe). Because of the challenges in terms of institutional environment facing many countries, as well as needs to expand access to finance in all economies to the widest range of customers possible in order to support broad-based economic growth, there has also been much attention given to a new area: microfinance.

In addition to interest from the developmental standpoint, attention has focused on securities, insurance and pensions as these areas have shown themselves also to be potential sources of systemic risk and therefore of concern from the standpoint of financial stability. Examples include the near collapse of the hedge fund Long Term Capital Management (LTCM) in 1999 in the wake of the Asian, Brazilian and Russian financial crises (in which a collapse would have had potentially systemic implications for the international financial system) and the collapse of insurance companies in a number of jurisdictions including the United Kingdom and Australia (which impacted severely on their customers and therefore the elected government). In addition, many developed countries (as well as some developing, emerging and transition economies – notably China) are facing rapidly aging populations and related concerns about retirement and pension stability, thereby raising considerable concern about and interest in pensions stability and development.

## 7.1. SECURITIES AND DERIVATIVES

Securities activities, in contrast to banking activities, are market-based and require transparency and public disclosure of information for the markets to function well. This information is necessary not only for the accurate valuation of equities and bonds in securities markets, but also for the holders of these securities to protect their rights and to perform a corporate governance role. However, as clearly demonstrated by the social disruption caused by failures in securities regulation in, inter alia, Albania, there are also considerable risks in regulatory failures. Standards and institutions that promote market transparency generate investor confidence in capital markets. In many countries, individual investors lack confidence in their securities markets and investments. Further, the failure in various countries of large investment funds that were largely unregulated (like LTCM) has caused investors in some cases to lose confidence in the marketplace. Many jurisdictions have not established adequate requirements for information to be provided to investors in connection with public offerings and investment funds. Investors, in turn, are unable to assess the accuracy of the information on which they need to make investment decisions. Failures in the regulatory framework for securities regulation also open the possibility of significant financial fraud and market manipulation in emerging, developing and transition economies, which negatively impact prospects for financial sector development.

In looking at securities development in the context of financial stability, the first consideration is the key standard in this respect identified by the Financial Stability Forum (FSF).

### 7.1.1. *Financial Stability Forum Key Standard: Objectives and Principles of Securities Regulation*

As part of the international financial standards initiative discussed in Chapter Two, the International Organization of Securities Commissions (IOSCO) was instructed to develop internationally acceptable principles and standards for securities regulation, which it did with its publication and adoption of *Objectives and Principles of Securities Regulation*.[1] IOSCO released slightly revised and updated versions in 2002[2] and 2003.[3] IOSCO's Objectives and Principles are recognized by the FSF as the key standard in the area of securities regulation and reflect IOSCO's agreement that there are certain principles that form the basis for an effective system of regulation of securities and derivatives markets. The document represents the joint efforts of IOSCO's Executive, Technical and Emerging Markets Committees and was formally adopted during IOSCO's annual conference in September 1998.[4]

The IOSCO Objectives and Principles set out three main objectives of securities regulation[5]: (1) the protection of investors; (2) ensuring that markets are fair, efficient and transparent; and (3) the reduction of systemic risk. To achieve these objectives, IOSCO has developed principles to be implemented as part of a legal framework for securities and capital markets.[6] The IOSCO Objectives and Principles are divided into three parts. Part I provides an introduction to the paper and a statement of the objectives and the principles of securities regulation. There is a brief discussion of each of the objectives. Part II describes the desirable attributes of a regulator and the potential role of self-regulatory organizations. It also considers the enforcement and market oversight work of the regulator and the need for close cooperation between regulators. Part III considers the practical implications of the objectives in securities regulation with particular reference to issuers of securities, collective investment schemes, market intermediaries, secondary trading, and the clearance and settlement of transactions. Each substantive section in Parts II and III includes a boxed subsection that provides a summary list of the principles to be addressed in giving effect to the objectives.

As a starting point, the responsibilities of the securities regulator should be clear and objectively stated, with the regulator operationally independent and accountable in the exercise of its functions and powers.[7] The regulator must have adequate powers, proper resources and the capacity to perform its functions, including staff required to observe the highest professional standards, including appropriate confidentiality and disclosure of personal

---

[1] IOSCO, *Objectives and Principles of Securities Regulation*, Sep. 1998, updated 2002 and 2003. IOSCO documents are available at the IOSCO website at http://www.iosco.org.

[2] IOSCO, *Objectives and Principles of Securities Regulation*, 2002.

[3] IOSCO, *Objectives and Principles of Securities Regulation*, May 2003.

[4] Id.

[5] Id., pp. 6–8.

[6] Id., p. 9 and Annexure 3 (listing areas of implementation necessary as a precondition).

[7] Principles 1 and 2.

interests.[8] In addition, in the exercise of its functions, the regulator must adopt clear and consistent regulatory processes.[9] In order to support proper enforcement, the regulator must have comprehensive inspection, investigation and surveillance powers as support to comprehensive enforcement powers.[10]

As part of the regulatory regime, appropriate use should be made to the extent appropriate to the size and complexity of the relevant market of self-regulatory organizations (SROs), which might include such institutions as securities exchanges, that would exercise direct oversight responsibility for their respective areas of competence.[11] Any SRO, however, should be subject to the oversight of the regulator to observe standards of fairness and confidentiality when exercising any powers and delegated responsibilities.[12]

Regardless of the division of responsibilities between the regulator and any SRO(s), overall, the regulatory system should ensure an effective and credible use of inspection, investigation, surveillance and enforcement powers and implementation of an effective compliance program.[13] As one aspect, clear and appropriate authority and mechanisms need to be established for information sharing and cooperation with domestic and foreign counterparts.[14]

In regard to market intermediaries, regulation must provide for minimum entry standards, initial and on-going capital requirements and other prudential requirements (such as those dealing with market risk and off-balance sheet activities).[15] Market intermediaries must also be required to comply with standards for internal organization and operational conduct that aim to protect the interests of clients and under which management of the intermediary accepts primary responsibility for these matters.[16] Appropriate areas include risk management and controls and custody arrangements.[17] In addition, procedures for dealing with the failure of a market intermediary need to be created in order to minimize damage and loss to investors and to contain confidence shocks that might pose a systemic risk to the financial system through contagious panic.[18] More specific requirements address the special risks posed by

---

[8]  Principles 3 and 5.
[9]  Principle 4.
[10] Principles 8 and 9.
[11] Principle 6.
[12] Principle 7.
[13] Principle 10.
[14] Principles 11–13.
[15] Principles 21 and 22.
[16] Principle 23.
[17] IOSCO, *Risk Management and Control Guidance for Securities Firms and their Supervisors*, May 1998.
[18] Principle 24.

collective investment schemes (e.g., unit trusts or mutual funds), including the establishment of licensing and regulation of those who wish to market such schemes.[19] Legal rules must exist governing the legal form and structure of such schemes, including the segregation and protection of client assets.[20] Disclosure of risks and asset valuation, pricing and redemption of units must also be delineated.[21]

In order to provide adequate market information, issuers of securities must meet requirements for full, timely and accurate disclosure of financial results and other information material to investor decisions.[22] Legal safeguards should exist to ensure that holders of securities in a company are treated in a fair and equitable manner.[23] In addition, accounting and auditing standards need to be of a high and internationally acceptable quality (discussed previously in Chapter Five).[24] Beyond the primary market, the secondary market also requires attention. Trading systems including securities exchanges must be subject to regulatory authorization and oversight, including on-going supervision to ensure maintenance of trading integrity and transparency through detection and deterrence of manipulation and unfair trading practices.[25] In addition, proper management of large exposures, default risk and market disruption is essential, as is regulatory oversight of the clearing and settlement system.[26]

The objectives of the Principles thus extend beyond the traditional arena of financial regulation and supervision (i.e., protection of investors and reduction of systemic risk) to cover fairness, efficiency and equity of markets. Historically, securities regulation has not been accorded similar prominence to that accorded to banking. However, experience has shown (both in the United States and increasingly in Europe) that requirements for adequate disclosure and transparency in securities markets increase investor confidence in such markets, thereby encouraging development and expansion.[27]

---

[19] Principle 17.
[20] Principle 18.
[21] Principles 19 and 20. Further requirements are discussed in IOSCO, *Principles for the Supervision of Operators of Collective Investment Schemes*, 1997.
[22] Principle 14.
[23] Principle 15.
[24] Principle 16.
[25] Principles 25–8.
[26] Principles 29 and 30.
[27] See B. Steil, *The European Equity Markets: The State of the Union and an Agenda for the Millennium* (London: Royal Institute for International Affairs, 1996) and J. Seligman, *The Transformation of Wall Street: A History of the Securities and Exchange Commission and Modern Corporate Finance*, 3rd ed. (New York: Aspen, 2003).

### 7.1.2. *Other Financial Stability Forum Standards*

Similar to the area of banking, the FSF Compendium also includes a variety of standards relating to securities regulation beyond the key IOSCO Objectives and Principles. The FSF framework for securities regulation includes standards in six areas: (1) general, (2) capital adequacy, (3) cross-border information sharing, (4) disclosure and transparency, (5) risk management and (6) market functioning. The general category includes, in addition to the IOSCO Objectives and Principles and the key standard for securities settlement[28] discussed in Chapter Four, a general commitment to high regulatory standards and mutual cooperation.[29] Capital adequacy is covered by a single standard.[30] In regard to cross-border information sharing, the FSF includes guidance on information sharing[31], cooperation[32] and memoranda of understanding (MoUs).[33] In regard to disclosure and transparency – an issue of especial concern in securities markets – the FSF provides guidance on public disclosure of trading and derivatives activities of banks and securities firms[34] and disclosure for cross-border securities offerings and listings.[35] Risk management standards address internal controls and related supervisory issues[36], client assets[37] and over-the-counter (OTC) derivatives.[38] Market functioning covers a range of issues not addressed in the related infrastructure category (discussed in Chapter Five).

---

[28] IOSCO, *Recommendations for Securities Settlement Systems*, Nov. 2001.

[29] IOSCO, *Report on the Self-Evaluation Conducted by IOSCO Members Pursuant to the 1994 IOSCO Resolution on "Commitment to Basic IOSCO Principles of High Regulatory Standards and Mutual Cooperation and Assistance"*, Nov. 1997.

[30] IOSCO, *Methodologies for Determining Minimum Capital Standards for Internationally Active Securities Firms which Permit the Use of Models Under Prescribed Conditions*, May 1998.

[31] IOSCO, *Guidance on Information Sharing*, Mar. 1998.

[32] IOSCO, *Report on Cooperation Between Market Authorities and Default Procedures*, Mar. 1996.

[33] IOSCO, *Principles of Memoranda of Understanding (MoU)*, Sep. 1991.

[34] Basel Committee and IOSCO Technical Committee, *Recommendations for Public Disclosure of Trading and Derivatives Activities of Banks and Securities Firms*, Oct. 1999. Interestingly, though issued jointly, this paper is not included in the similar FSF category for banking.

[35] IOSCO, *International Disclosure Standards for Crossborder Offerings and Initial Listings by Foreign Issuers*, Sep. 1998. For discussion, see D. Arner, "Globalization of Financial Markets: An International Passport for Securities Offerings?", 35 Int'l L. 1543 (2001).

[36] IOSCO, *Risk Management and Control Guidance for Securities Firms and their Supervisors*, May 1998.

[37] IOSCO, *Client Asset Protection*, Aug. 1996.

[38] IOSCO Technical Committee, *Operational and Financial Risk Management Control Mechanisms for Over-the-counter Derivatives Activities of Regulated Securities Firms*, Jul. 1994.

These include exchange-traded derivatives[39], the internet[40] and collective investment schemes.[41]

### 7.1.3. *Implementation*

At the end of 2002, the IMF and the World Bank conducted a review of experiences under the Financial Sector Assessment Program (FSAP) and Reports of Observance of Standards Codes (ROSC) initiative to date.[42] In the area of securities regulation[43], assessments began in 1999; by December 2002, forty-eight assessments had been undertaken under the FSAP. A number of important common weaknesses emerged from the reviews:

(1) institutional weaknesses, particularly limited supervisory resources;
(2) spread of authority over several authorities, often with lack of clarity of roles;
(3) lack of budgetary independence of the regulator;
(4) weaknesses in enforcement powers;
(5) lack of adequate powers to prevent issue of a prospectus if content requirements were not met;
(6) shortcomings in continuous disclosure regimes;
(7) weaknesses in protection of minority shareholders;
(8) weaknesses regarding auditors in ensuring disclosure;
(9) weaknesses in regulation of intermediaries, including risk management, internal organization, capital adequacy and failure resolution;
(10) weaknesses in detection of manipulation and other unfair trading practices; and
(11) weaknesses in oversight of clearing and settlement systems.

In relation to the process itself, the absence of an assessment methodology was also problematic. While the methodology issue has not been properly

---

[39] IOSCO, *The Application of the Tokyo Communiqué to Exchange-Traded Financial Derivatives Contracts*, Sep. 1998; idem, *Coordination between Cash and Derivatives Markets: Contract Design of Derivative Products on Stock Indices and Measures to Minimize Market Disruption*, Oct. 1992.

[40] IOSCO, *Securities Activity on the Internet*, Sep. 1998.

[41] IOSCO, *Principles for the Supervision of Operators of Collective Investment Schemes*, Sep. 1997; idem., *Report on Investment Management Principles for the Regulation of Collective Investment Schemes and Explanatory Memorandum*, Oct. 1994.

[42] IMF and World Bank, *Analytical Tools of the FSAP*, 24 Feb. 2003.

[43] Id., pp. 27–9; IMF and World Bank, *Experience with the Assessments of the IOSCO Objectives and Principles of Securities Regulation under the Financial Sector Assessment Program*, Apr. 2002.

addressed, by January 2007, the IMF and World Bank had published securities regulation FSAP/ROSCs based on the IOSCO Objectives and Principles for forty-nine countries, reflecting the increasing attention being paid to this area.[44]

### 7.1.4. *Developing Securities Markets*

All developed, emerging, transition and developing economies have some form of banking system, albeit operating at very different levels of development and playing roles of differing effectiveness in their respective economic systems. However, until recently, in most economies, securities markets have been much less developed than banking.

This is something that should and is changing: E. Philip Davis has shown that "the existence of active securities markets alongside banks is indeed beneficial to the stability of corporate financing, both during cyclical downturns and during banking and securities market crises", thus supporting the benefits of "multiple avenues of financial intermediation" to an economy.[45]

Governments around the world therefore are continuing to seek to support development of their domestic securities markets. Law and regulation have an important role both in securities market development and in maintaining financial stability. Important work has been done at the international and regional levels in recent years to devise standards to support financial stability and securities market development.[46] Nonetheless, current standards do not focus sufficiently on development. Likewise, insufficient guidance has been developed to support economies' efforts to integrate domestic markets into the international securities markets, while at the same time maintaining domestic stability. While global markets are important for the largest, most successful companies to acquire financing at the most competitive cost of capital, domestic markets remain very important for development of smaller companies.

Much exciting research has been done and is being done in regard to the various institutional arrangements to support securities market development and especially in respect to which sorts of institutional choices are more effective

---

[44] Australia, Austria, Bahrain, Barbados, Belgium, Bulgaria, Canada, Chile, Colombia, Croatia, Cyprus, Czech Republic, Estonia, Finland, France, Germany, Ghana, Greece, Hong Kong, Hungary, Iceland, Israel, Italy, Japan, Kuwait, Latvia, Luxembourg, Malta, Mexico, Morocco, The Netherlands, New Zealand, Pakistan, Poland, Portugal, Romania, Russia, Senegal, Singapore, Slovakia, Slovenia, South Korea, Spain, Sweden, Switzerland, Tunisia, Uganda, United Kingdom.

[45] E. Davis, "Multiple Avenues of Intermediation, Corporate Finance and Financial Stability", IMF Working Paper WP/01/115 (Aug. 2001), p. 22.

[46] See M. Steinberg and D. Arner, *International Securities Law*, 2nd ed. (London: Kluwer, 2007).

than others in supporting market development. At this point, however, the research has not yet advanced to the level of a coherent general understanding of the elements of the best institutional infrastructure to support securities market development. Nonetheless, economies are beginning to look to the research to date for lessons to be applied to the development of their own markets. (This is explicitly being pursued by Mexico, for instance.) It remains to be seen, however, whether this research and its application will represent a real advancement in economic development advice or whether it will turn out to be yet another theory that, when applied in the real world, results in yet another dead end on the difficult road to economic growth and development.

**Developing Equity Securities Markets.** The development of equity capital markets depends on the existence of a body of effective company law covering, at the very least, the regulation of corporate structures, protection of minority shareholders, and sound policies of corporate governance. Beyond formal rules of company law, some form of functioning, reliable and transparent accounting system is critical, not only for the operation of capital markets, but also as a fundamental aspect of any meaningful corporate business structure. These issues were discussed in more detail in Chapters Three and Five. Moreover, well-trained management capable of adequately understanding and fulfilling its responsibilities is essential.

Legal infrastructure is especially important in the context of equity market development, with much emphasis placed on investor protection. Based on country-level data, researchers have found that better legal protection for investors is associated with: (1) higher stock market valuations[47], (2) higher value of listed firms relative to their assets or changes in investments[48], (3) larger listed firms in terms of their sales and assets[49] and (4) greater reliance on external financing by firms for growth.[50] Potentially significant legal aspects of minority shareholder protection include[51]: fair and reliable judicial systems, regulation of voting rights attaching to shares, pre-emptive rights, directors' duty

---

[47] R. La Porta, F. Lopez-de-Silanes, A. Shleifer and R. Vishny, "Legal Determinants of External Finance", 52 J. Fin. 1131 (1997).

[48] R. La Porta, F. Lopez-de-Silanes, A. Shleifer and R. Vishny, "Investor Protection and Corporate Valuation", 57 J. Fin. 1147 (2002).

[49] K. Kumar, R. Rajan and L. Zingales, "What Determines Firm Size?", NBER Working Paper 7208 (1999).

[50] R. Rajan and L. Zingales, "Financial Development and Growth", 88 Am. Econ. Rev. 559 (1998), pp. 559–86; A. Demirguc-Kunt and V. Maksimovic, "Law, Finance, and Firm Growth", 53 J. Finance 2107 (1998), pp. 2107–37.

[51] Summarized in B. Cheffins, "Does Law Matter? The Separation of Ownership and Control in the United Kingdom", 30 J. Legal Stud. 459 (2001), pp. 463–4.

of loyalty, minority shareholders' mechanisms to contest perceived oppression by controllers, laws prohibiting insider dealing and regulation of disclosure.

Of these, disclosure and private enforcement are probably the most important. In a major study, Rafael La Porta, Florencio Lopez-de-Silanes and Andrei Shleifer have found little evidence that public enforcement benefits securities markets; rather, laws mandating disclosure and facilitating private enforcement through liability rules provide the greatest benefit.[52] In support of the importance of disclosure regulation to securities market development, Prentice, through a review of behavioural research, cautions that it is overly optimistic to expect issuers voluntarily to disclose optimal levels of information, to expect securities intermediaries to appropriately consider the interests of investors, or to expect investors to be able to bargain effectively for fraud protection.[53]

INTERNATIONAL DISCLOSURE STANDARDS. In relation to disclosure, IOSCO has released a set of standards. In order to build upon the general principles respecting offering and listings standards in the IOSCO Objectives and Principles, the organization developed a framework for the minimum content of public offer prospectuses. This latter document is intended to set a basic framework for international offering documents acceptable to regulators and securities exchanges around the world. Such a framework could serve as an internationally acceptable basis for the further development of securities exchange listing requirements and prospectus regulations throughout the world. According to IOSCO, "this report presents a set of non-financial statement disclosure standards (financial statements standards are the subject of another project) that will apply to foreign companies seeking to enter a host-country market, facilitating cross-border offerings and initial listings."[54] The intention is that these standards will allow issuers to prepare a single disclosure document that will serve as an "international passport" to capital raising and listing in more than one jurisdiction at a time. If successful, the implementation of these standards will represent an important step forward in reducing the costs of raising capital for companies, enabling them to issue or list securities in multiple jurisdictions without concern for the burdens of complying with a multiplicity of nonfinancial statement disclosure requirements. Following

---

[52] R. La Porta, F. Lopez-de-Silanes and A. Shleifer, "What Works in Securities Law?" (Jun. 2004, mimeographed).

[53] R. Prentice, "Whither Securities Regulation? Some Behavioral Observations regarding Proposals for its Future", 51 Duke L.J. 1397 (2002).

[54] IOSCO, *Press Communiqué*, 1998.

the receipt of comments from the IOSCO Emerging Markets Committee and from the international financial community, the standards were approved by the membership of the entire organization, including the US Securities Exchange Commission (SEC).

Part I sets out International Disclosure Standards (IDS) for use by companies in connection with cross-border public offerings and listings of equity securities. The Standards are to apply to listings, public offers and sales of equity securities for cash, and, unless otherwise indicated, are intended to be used for prospectuses, offering and initial listing documents and registration statements.[55] The Standards relate to nonfinancial statement disclosure requirements and do not address a number of issues, including[56]: (1) appropriate accounting and/or auditing standards; (2) specific disclosure requirements relating to other types of transactions, such as business combinations, tender offers, exchange offers, "going private" transactions or interested party transactions; (3) collective investment schemes or "start up" companies with no history of operations; (4) continuous reporting disclosure requirements; and (5) securities exchange suitability criteria, such as operating history, profitability, market float, share price, and so on.[57]

In addition, companies engaging in certain specialized businesses, such as banking, insurance and natural resources, may be required to provide additional information, with specific requirements set forth in Part II (addressing disclosure issues outside of the Standards).[58] The disclosure requirements for certificates representing shares, such as depository receipts, voting trust certificates, or similar forms of ownership representation, are also referenced in Part II.

The Standards are intended to apply to cross-border offerings and listings. Under the International Disclosure Standards, an offering or listing of securities is considered to be "cross-border" "when it is directed to one or more countries other than the company's home country (whether or not the offering or listing also is being made concurrently in the company's home country)."[59] As a general matter, according to IOSCO, all foreign companies, subject to certain exceptions, can apply the Standards to offerings or listings in a particular host country.[60]

---

[55] IOSCO, *Report of the Technical Committee, International Disclosure Standards for Cross-Border Offerings and Initial Listings by Foreign Issuers*, 1998, p. 3.

[56] Id., pp. 3 4.

[57] Id., p. 4.

[58] Id., p. 3.

[59] Id., p. 4.

[60] Id.

The International Disclosure Standards were issued "with a recommendation that IOSCO members accept in their respective home jurisdictions a
disclosure document containing the information set forth in the Standards."[61]
According to IOSCO, additional actions, however, "may be needed in some
jurisdictions to implement the Standards, and issuers are encouraged to ver-
ify that the Standards are in effect in the host country jurisdiction prior to
their use."[62] While the International Disclosure Standards are not necessarily intended to substitute for or to replace disclosure requirements applicable
to any jurisdiction's domestic issuers, they are intended to provide alternative standards for the preparation of a single disclosure document by foreign
issuers.[63]

In addition to the specific disclosures required in the Standards, according
to IOSCO, "most countries rely on an overriding principle that in connection
with a registration or listing of securities or a public offering of securities, a
company should disclose all information that would be material to an investor's
investment decision and that is necessary for full and fair disclosure."[64] Accordingly, information called for by specific requirements contained in the Standards may need to be expanded under this general principle of disclosure
of material information, where supplemental information is deemed to be
material to investors and necessary to keep the mandated disclosure provided
pursuant to specific requirements from being misleading.[65]

The Standards also address omission of information and supplementary
information.[66] Specifically, "[i]f a disclosure requirement is inapplicable to
an issuer's sphere of activity or legal form, no information need be provided
in response to that requirement, although equivalent information should be
given, if possible."[67] Further, "[a]ny significant change or any inaccuracy in
the contents of the document which may materially affect the company or
its securities, that occurs between the date of publication of the document
and the date of sale or listing also must be adequately disclosed and made
public."[68]

Following an introduction (summarized in the previous section) and a glossary of terms, the Standards, in Part I, outline the contents of an acceptable

---

[61] Id., p. 3.
[62] Id.
[63] See id., p. 3.
[64] Id., p. 5.
[65] Id.
[66] Id.
[67] Id.
[68] Id.

offering/listing document. Part II provides country specific information on areas not covered within the standards, necessary to validate the document in a given jurisdiction, which should be incorporated as a "wrapper" to the prospectus following the International Disclosure Standards. In outline form, the cross-border prospectus is to comprise the following ten information categories: (1) identity of directors, senior management and advisers; (2) offer statistics and expected timetable; (3) key information; (4) information on the company; (5) operating and financial review and prospects; (6) directors and employees; (7) major shareholders and related party transactions; (8) financial information; (9) the offer and listing; and (10) additional information.

IMPLEMENTATION. Recognizing the importance of implementation, in May 2000, IOSCO produced a report on the implementation of International Disclosure Standards[69], surveying the progress of implementation among the seventeen members of the Working Party.[70] Sixteen indicated either that they:

(1) currently accepted documents prepared in accordance with the International Disclosure Standards from foreign companies or
(2) had taken steps to be in a position to do so at some point in 2000.

According to information supplied by those surveyed, progress in implementation fell into five categories: (1) those that had implemented the Standards through changes in laws or rules by May 2000 (four jurisdictions: Spain, United Kingdom, Mexico and Italy); (2) those that were in the process of implementing the Standards through changes in laws or rules by end-2000 (two jurisdictions: France and the United States); (3) those that permitted use of International Disclosure Standards without any need for rule changes, through discretionary authority or other means (eight jurisdictions: Australia, Belgium, Germany, Hong Kong, Japan, Luxembourg, The Netherlands and Switzerland); (4) those that planned to undertake rule changes to implement International Disclosure Standards, but in the interim would permit use through discretionary authority (two jurisdictions – both in Canada: Ontario and Quebec); and (5) those that would not allow use of the Standards (one jurisdiction: Sweden).

Another survey (an informal one) of the implementation of International Disclosure Standards conducted by Samuel Wolff was published in

---

[69] IOSCO, *Report on Implementation of International Disclosure Standards*, May 2000.
[70] The seventeen Working Party members surveyed were: Australia, Belgium, France, Germany, Hong Kong, Italy, Japan, Luxembourg, Mexico, The Netherlands, Ontario, Quebec, Spain, Sweden, Switzerland, the United Kingdom and the United States.

February 2001.[71] Of the respondents to the informal survey, Wolff found four in which International Disclosure Standards had been implemented through rule and/or legislative changes applicable to foreign and domestic issuers[72]: two (Italy and Mexico) required use of the Standards for both foreign and domestic issuers; one (Argentina) required them for foreign issuers and intended to apply the same requirements to domestic issuers by sometime in 2002; and one (Singapore) required use of the Standards with modifications for both foreign and domestic issuers.

Of the respondents, Wolff found five jurisdictions which had implemented International Disclosure Standards for foreign issuers only by rule and/or legislative change[73]: in two (United States and Switzerland), the Standards were optional for foreign issuers, but different standards applied to domestic issuers, although foreign issuers could also comply with the domestic requirements; in one (France), changes were in progress during 2001 to allow use of the Standards by foreign issuers; one (Spain) required their use for foreign issuers; and the listing rules of one (United Kingdom) exempted foreign issuers complying with International Disclosure Standards from certain provisions, but would nonetheless require them to furnish listing particulars in accordance with the remaining provisions of the listing rules.[74] Wolff found that seven of the respondents anticipated no legislative and/or rules changes were necessary, but International Disclosure Standards were acceptable for issuers: in four (Luxembourg, Hong Kong, The Netherlands and Belgium), they would be accepted under discretionary authority; in one (Germany), the Standards were deemed to meet listing requirements; in one (Japan), they would be accepted on a discretionary basis, but only if in proper Japanese format; and in one (Australia), Wolff was not able to confirm the response to the IOSCO survey, indicating that the Standards would be accepted under discretionary authority. In one jurisdiction (South Africa), it was unclear whether International Disclosure Standards would be accepted, and they were not acceptable in four jurisdictions (Israel, Canada, India and Taiwan).

From these surveys, use of International Disclosure Standards by different jurisdictions appears to be falling into four categories: (1) required for all companies, foreign and domestic; (2) optional for all companies, foreign and domestic; (3) inapplicable to domestic companies, but required for foreign

---

[71] S. Wolff, "Implementation of International Disclosure Standards", 22 U. Pa. J. Int'l Econ. L. 91 (2001). Wolff surveyed twenty IOSCO member organizations. Id., p. 94.

[72] See id., pp. 95–104.

[73] See id.

[74] Public offerings without listing are governed by regulations based upon the EU Prospectus Directive, to which no change had been made in respect to IDS.

companies; and (4) inapplicable to domestic companies and optional for foreign companies. Wolff concludes[75]:

> . . . the record so far, two and one-half years after promulgation of the IOSCO Standards, is mixed at best . . . While some progress has been made toward the implementation of International Disclosure Standards, the move toward implementation has probably been slower than IOSCO contemplated. There is still a hodge-podge of prospectus and listing rules which foreign issuers have to sort through as before on a country-by-country basis to determine applicable disclosure standards. More often than not, there is no reference at all to the IOSCO Standards.

While Wolff's conclusion does not appear optimistic, closer analysis of implementation of the Standards and international accounting standards (discussed in Chapter Five) in the two most significant capital markets (the United States and the European Union) actually suggests that significant progress is, in fact, being made, with both jurisdictions now requiring all cross-border offerings to follow International Disclosure Standards.[76]

**Developing Debt Securities Markets.** While equity markets seem to require a certain level of institutional support in order to develop, experience with debt markets seems to indicate that market development requires a greater level of public initiative. In essence, debt markets are based on interest rates; in order to function, domestic debt markets require a benchmark interest rate on which to price variations between risk levels with different issues. This benchmark generally is based upon the yield curve for government debt in a given economy. As such, in order to support debt market development, the government of a jurisdiction must issue sufficient debt of differing maturities to provide a market sufficiently liquid to price interest rates across a variety of durations. In order to develop such a market, in addition to sales of government debt instruments in local currency, a government will also typically need to establish some sort of sales and trading system in order to provide a mechanism to support liquidity.

In fact, the historical experience of most developed economies supports this assertion; for instance, bond markets in England developed on the basis of pricing information provided by the Bank of England in bonds backed by the Crown.

---

[75] Wolff, op. cit., n. 71, p. 105.
[76] For detailed discussion, see Steinberg and Arner, op. cit., n. 46.

Following financial crises around the world over the past fifteen years, international attention has increasingly focused on developing local bond markets. In a study published in 2000, the International Finance Corporation of the World Bank analysed bond market development in Asia and provides some lessons to guide future development efforts.[77] At the most general level, the study found that a number of interactive factors make up the environment necessary for bond market development and need to be considered from the bottom up. These factors include factors around the market, factors across other parts of the financial system, and factors inside the market.[78]

In this context, the study suggests that whether a primary market can be built depends upon the existence of four main factors: (1) market participants (inside), (2) government commitment (inside), (3) macroeconomic stability and credibility (around) and (4) taxation (around).[79] If these are in place, four second-layer success factors in turn become significant (all across)[80]: (1) government securities markets, (2) equity and money markets, (3) the banking system and (4) credit-rating agencies. Secondary markets are even more difficult, and in some cases impossible, to develop.[81] Regardless, markets must be developed in stages, the sequencing and content of which necessarily depend upon the specific domestic context.[82]

Following positive experiences in the area of equity disclosure discussed in the previous section, IOSCO has also recently released debt disclosure standards for public consultation.[83]

**Securitization.** Securitization is certainly not a panacea to underdeveloped domestic debt markets. Nonetheless, it is a useful financing tool that can support both debt market development and also other public policy

---

[77]  A. Harwood (ed.), *Building Local Bond Markets: An Asian Perspective* (Washington, DC: International Finance Corporation, 2000). The study looked at five South Asian countries: India, Pakistan, Sri Lanka, Bangladesh and Nepal. For a more recent analysis of cross-border debt market development in Asia, see D. Arner, J.H. Park, P. Lejot and Q. Liu (eds), *Asia's Debt Markets: Prospects and Strategies for Development* (New York: Springer, 2006).

[78]  A. Harwood, "Building Local Bond Markets: Some Issues and Actions", in A. Harwood (ed.), op. cit., n. 77, pp. 1, 6–7, 8 fig. 1. (fig. 1 depicts the "Bond Market Environment", showing the relationship among various factors inside, around and across the market and the "Capital Market Infrastructure").

[79]  Id., pp. 10–13.

[80]  Id., pp. 13–15.

[81]  Id., pp. 15–16. Nonetheless, even without an effective secondary market, the development of debt capital markets supports diversification of finance and financial stability.

[82]  Id., pp. 25–6.

[83]  IOSCO, *Consultation Report: International Disclosure Principles for Cross-Border Offerings and Listings of Debt Securities by Foreign Issuers*, Oct. 2005.

objectives[84], including financial stability through reduction of maturity mismatches. In fact, today, securitized debt is the single largest segment of both US and European debt markets. Once again, however, markets for securitized debt typically do not develop without a certain level of government support. For instance, in the United States, the establishment of the largest issuers of securitized debt (Freddie Mac, Fannie Mae, etc.) were all government initiatives, albeit not explicitly guaranteed obligations. Experience in many other economies around the world supports the important role that government can have in promoting the development of securitization.

Securitization in its broadest meaning refers to the process of transforming traditional forms of bilateral, illiquid financial relationship (e.g., loans) into freely tradable market instruments (i.e., securities). In this broad meaning, securitization has been an important trend in financial markets over the past thirty years, as finance has moved away from traditional bank lending to the capital markets.[85] More frequently, however, securitization is used to refer to a specific form of financial transaction in which assets (typically loans or other receivables of some sort, but possibly any future stream of revenue) are packaged together and used to collateralize or "back" an issuer or an issue of securities. This process may be effected under varying structures, but most commonly through the issue of bonds by a separate special purpose vehicle (SPV). This type of transaction is more appropriately referred to as asset securitization. In the developed financial markets of the United States, asset securitization serves a number of different purposes: (1) supporting public policy objectives such as broad home ownership and the development of financial markets (especially capital and mortgage markets)[86]; (2) addressing regulatory requirements for financial institutions, especially capital adequacy and lending limit requirements applicable to banks; (3) transferring risk, especially in the context of nonperforming assets and portfolio diversification[87]; and (4) providing finance.[88] The usefulness of these sorts of financial structures in a variety of contexts has prompted countries and market participants from around the

[84] See D. Arner, "Emerging Market Economies and Government Promotion of Securitization", 12 Duke J. Comp. & Int'l L. 505 (2002).

[85] See generally R. Smith and I. Walter, *Global Banking*, 2nd ed. (New York: Oxford University Press, 2003) (describing international capital market structures, operations and trends).

[86] See D. Barbour, J. Norton and T. Slover, "Asset Securitization in Emerging Market Economies: Fundamental Considerations", Essays in Int'l Fin. & Econ. L. no. 13 (1998), pp. 8–11.

[87] Id., pp. 8–11.

[88] Id. See generally S. Schwarcz, "The Alchemy of Asset Securitization", 1 Stan. J. L. Bus. & Fin. 133 (1994)(describing asset securitization and its benefits); C. Hill, "Securitization: A Low cost Sweetener for Lemons", 74 Wash. U. L.Q. 1061 (1996) (expanding on Schwarcz's analysis to examine the underlying basis of securitization benefits).

world to seek to develop similar structures in their own markets.[89] The most successful examples have been in Europe.[90] These efforts, however, need to be placed in the appropriate context: asset securitization is a sophisticated capital market-based financial structure that rests on a complex matrix of supporting elements, all of which have a significant legal element. The lesson: traditional asset securitization structures cannot simply be "parachuted" into individual financial systems (especially those of emerging economies with a civil law tradition) and expected to fulfill the sorts of functions for which they are so useful in the United States and Europe. Nonetheless, undertaking an asset securitization transaction in any given jurisdiction serves as a useful "stress test" of the limits in that specific jurisdiction, especially in respect to legal impediments.

The requisite elements necessary for asset securitization transactions can be derived from analysis of the most common form of asset securitization, the securitization of mortgages.[91] At the most basic level, a mortgage securitization involves a variety of supporting elements: (1) a market for real estate-based finance, such as mortgages; (2) capital markets (e.g., markets for securities); and (3) infrastructure to support securitization, such as the legal support for appropriate SPVs. All three elements are interrelated and encourage financial stability and economic development, but the fundamental premise remains that mortgage securitization (and by extension more complex forms of asset securitization) is not possible without all three elements.

A 1999 Asian Development Bank report surveying securitization in eight Asian countries[92] found the following overall characteristics: (1) shallow domestic bond markets with the greatest liquidity concentrated in short-term securities, (2) weak legal frameworks in support of securitization and (3) large and growing primary mortgage markets despite the Asian financial crisis.[93] On the basis of this prevailing state, the report made thirteen recommendations

---

[89] See e.g., C. Hill, "Latin American Securitization: The Case of the Disappearing Political Risk", 38 Va. J. Int'l L. 293 (1998), pp. 328–9.

[90] See generally L. Jones, "European CMBS: All Talk and No Action", 16 J.I.B.L. 149 (2001) (describing the strengths of Europe's commercial mortgage backed securitization market); G. Thieffry and J. Walsh, "Securitization: The New Opportunities Offered by Economic and Monetary Union", 12 J.I.B.L. 463 (1997) (forecasting that the introduction of a common currency in Europe will have a favourable effect on European securities markets).

[91] Mortgage securitization is chosen because of the important role real estate finance plays in economic development (addressed in Chapter Three). For a discussion in the context of receivables financing, see S. Schwarcz, "Towards a Centralized Perfection System for Cross-border Receivables Financing", 20 U. Pa. J. Int'l Econ. L. (1999).

[92] The surveyed countries include China, India, Indonesia, South Korea, Malaysia, Pakistan, Philippines and Thailand.

[93] S. G. Rhee and Y. Shimomote (eds), Mortgage-Backed Securities Markets (Manila: Asian Development Bank, 1999), p. 54.

to encourage the development of mortgage-backed securities markets in the Asian region:

(1) foster macroeconomic stability[94],

(2) develop legal infrastructure to support primary and secondary mortgage markets[95],

(3) establish secondary mortgage corporations[96],

(4) use special-purpose trusts in economies with a dominant mortgage lender (typically state owned)[97],

(5) improve and standardize the mortgage underwriting process[98],

(6) create competitive domestic bond markets with appropriate taxation[99],

(7) establish a benchmark yield curve[100],

(8) eliminate investment restraints[101],

(9) develop appropriate technology for trading, clearing and settlement[102],

(10) improve disclosure and develop ratings systems[103],

---

[94] Id.

[95] With respect to the domestic mortgage markets, economies must have a legal and regulatory framework conducive to building liquidity in the primary and secondary markets for mortgages and for mortgage-backed securities (MBS). Foreclosure laws must be restructured to facilitate the recovery of properties, clear tax and accounting rules must govern the conveyance/assignment and true sale of mortgages, and transaction costs must be minimized. Id., p. 55.

[96] Experience indicates that a secondary mortgage corporation (SMC), though not a necessary condition for the introduction of MBS, facilitates its development if there are many competitors in the primary mortgage markets. Therefore, while current MBS markets may not justify the development of a SMC, the future growth of MBS markets may entail the establishment of one. Id., p. 56.

[97] In economies where the dominant primary mortgage lender is (still) expected to be a single firm, securitization should (in theory) be easier to develop. This is because a single firm will have all of the relevant information for securitization (loans, borrower histories, portfolio quality, etc.). In this case, it may be advisable to explore securitization through a special-purpose trust arrangement with a bank rather than through SMCs. Id., p. 57.

[98] Economies should also strive to improve overall mortgage underwriting procedures, including the quality of borrower and credit history information, to improve borrower screening and ultimately the overall quality of mortgages. Then, they should introduce practices such as credit scoring to help standardize the underwriting process and facilitate the development of the MBS market. Id.

[99] Id., p. 58.

[100] Id.

[101] "Constraints on eligible instruments by potential investors, such as contractual savings institutions, inhibit the development of domestic bond markets." Id., p. 59.

[102] To reduce transaction risk in MBS, the private sector and the government may consider investing in technology to improve overall clearing and settlement. Establishing formal and organized OTC markets for bonds and MBS, or allowing MBS to be issued and traded in the local securities exchange, will encourage the adoption of modern technology in MBS markets, and will also improve market liquidity. Id.

[103] Id., p. 60.

(11) create legal infrastructure to support credit enhancement[104],

(12) reduce or eliminate interest-rate controls and subsidies[105] and

(13) enhance regulatory capacity.[106]

Significantly, most of these elements relate directly to legal infrastructure, but more importantly, many also require (or at least may be encouraged through) government promotion.

In a short space, this section has attempted to make a number of points: First, the promotion of asset-backed securitization, especially mortgage-backed securitization, can have a significant impact on financial development and stability, in turn supporting economic growth and development. Second, securitization is one aspect of an overall process of financial market development and cannot be separated from the larger process. Third, securitization rests on a complex matrix of legal and institutional structures and must be addressed in this context.

Based upon the previous analysis, a number of steps may be identified to guide any government seeking to promote the development of securitization.[107] At the most basic level, the creation of a functioning system of real estate-based finance involves a number of issues beyond the precondition of macroeconomic stability: (1) clear property rights to real estate, (2) clear rights to transfer property rights (including bankruptcy and foreclosure), (3) clear rules respecting use of real estate as collateral, (4) financial intermediaries capable of undertaking credit analysis related to collateralized real estate lending, (5) a clear and predictable system of taxation and (6) appropriate financial regulation and supervision. Regardless of whether more complex issues are addressed, putting in place such a framework most likely will enhance financial stability and economic development.

Unfortunately, with respect to most of these issues[108], international agreement on appropriate standards does not exist. Philosophical differences between legal systems and political and cultural variances have prevented

---

[104] Id., p. 61.

[105] "Price distortions in mortgage and bond markets, such as interest-rate controls and subsidies, inhibit bond/MBS market development. They should be used only minimally or, better yet, eliminated." Id.

[106] Id., p. 62.

[107] See S. Gannon, "The Use of Securitization to Mobilize Liquidity and in Particular the Use of Specialized Mortgage Corporations", in M. Giovanoli and G. Heinrich (eds), *International Bank Insolvencies: A Central Bank Perspective* (London: Kluwer, 1999).

[108] The exceptions are the factors of credit analysis and financial regulation and supervision. International efforts have dealt with both of these issues extensively in order to encourage financial stability.

international consensus in the context of property rights, despite their importance in economic development in a market-based system. Further, these barriers have discouraged international and regional development institutions such as the World Bank, Asian Development Bank and European Bank for Reconstruction and Development from pursuing reform programs in these areas.[109] This issue clearly merits more attention and research.

With the development of an appropriate legal and institutional framework supporting real estate finance, the next level of objectives focus on the development of domestic bond markets. Major issues in this respect include the establishment of a benchmark yield curve through the issuance of government securities and the creation of the infrastructure necessary for a market in government securities.[110] Once a market for government securities has been established, the framework can be extended to mortgage-backed securities and corporate debt.

With the establishment of a benchmark yield curve, mortgage securitization is the next focus in the process of capital market development. Issues which need to be addressed include: (1) modification of land and collateral laws to support the transfer of mortgages, (2) development of laws supporting use of intangibles as collateral, (3) establishment of a government-supported mortgage institution (focusing on both insurance and purchase), (4) modification of corporation and/or trust laws to support the creation of SPVs and (5) establishment of credit rating agencies or credit agencies.

In this context, capital adequacy rules and lending limits have had a significant impact upon the development of securitization internationally. The Basel II Capital Accord, discussed in Chapter Six, provides guidance for countries seeking to put in place the requisite elements to support securitization.[111] Specifically, countries seeking to establish appropriate legal infrastructure to support securitization (perhaps through a law on securitization and/or modifications to bankruptcy and collateral laws) can look to the specific requirements necessary for capital adequacy purposes in order to guide legal

---

[109] Perhaps because of these difficulties, these institutions have placed more focus on collateral as opposed to movables. See generally J. Simpson and J. Menze, "Ten years of secured transactions", Law in Transition 20 (Aut. 2000); N. de la Pena, H. Fleisig and P. Wellons, "Secured Transactions Law Reform in Asia: Unleashing the Potential of Collateral", in *Law and Policy Reform at the Asian Development Bank 2000*, vol. 2 (Manila: Asian Development Bank, 2000); J. Norton and M. Andenas (eds), *Emerging Financial Markets and Secured Transactions* (London: Kluwer, 1999).

[110] These issues are discussed in Chapter Four in the context of market functioning.

[111] See Basel Committee, *International Convergence of Capital Measurement and Capital Standards: A Revised Framework – Comprehensive Version*, Jun. 2006 ("Basel II").

reforms.[112] Clearly, government efforts must focus on the necessary legal infrastructure to fulfill the minimum internationally acceptable operational requirements with respect to securitization and capital relief for banks. In addition, certain requirements apply to credit enhancements.[113]

Through domestic implementation, the Basel II structure is likely to provide incentives for banks to securitize both residential mortgages and commercial property mortgages in order to reduce associated capital charges. As a result of the risk-weighting structure of Basel II, governments around the world are likely to focus increasingly on developing appropriate legal infrastructure to support mortgage securitization. Further, the reliance on ratings of Basel II should encourage the development of ratings agencies and services, especially in emerging economies, with the requirements of rating agencies acting as a further incentive to government reforms. Nonetheless, the experience in the United States and Europe suggests that even with the existence of the necessary supporting elements, market development requires a significant amount of time, perhaps in the neighborhood of ten years.

**Derivatives.** Developing derivatives markets has received less attention that debt and equity market development. To some extent, this is a result of the newer and less understood nature of the market. Likewise, derivatives by their nature depend upon the existence of underlying markets in order to develop. Nonetheless, because of both the wide usefulness of and the risks inherent in these instruments and markets, it is important to consider ways in which to develop domestic derivatives markets, especially in the context of volatile exchange and interest rates.

Banks and other financial intermediaries need to have access to advanced risk reduction and hedging techniques, especially as currencies move closer to full convertibility. During the both the Mexican crisis of 1994–95 and the east Asian crisis of 1997–98, the lack of access to risk sharing and hedging techniques contributed to the severity of the impact of the crisis on the domestic financial system. In this regard, domestic derivatives markets should be developed, albeit very carefully, due to the complexities and potential dangers of these sorts of financial instruments. Recent standards by IOSCO are instructive in this regard, as is the wealth of work done by the International Swaps and Derivatives Association (ISDA).[114]

---

[112] Id. Basel II identifies three fundamental elements composing the minimum capital requirements: a definition of regulatory capital, risk-weighted assets, and the minimum ratio of capital to risk-weighted assets.

[113] Id. Additional special requirements may apply in certain contexts, but these are outside the scope of the present analysis.

[114] See www.isda.org.

## 7.2. INSURANCE

Like securities regulation, insurance supervision has historically not received the attention given to that of banking. With the growth of financial conglomerates and the consequent spread of potential systemic risks throughout the financial system and with the development of significant insurance company assets available for investment, insurance regulation is an area of increasing concern for regulators as well as a potential source of systemic risk in financial systems.[115]

Insurance is important for financial development and economic growth. While analysts have identified a correlation between the economic development of a country and the deepening of its insurance sector, no cause-and-effect link has been established but it seems evident that growing, vibrant economies all have insurance sectors. Udaibur Das, Nigel Davies and Richard Podpiera conclude[116]:

> A resilient and well-regulated insurance industry can significantly contribute to economic growth and efficient resource allocation through transfer of risk and mobilization of savings. In addition, it can enhance financial system efficiency by reducing transaction costs, creating liquidity, and facilitating economies of scale in investment.

As such, the insurance sector in any economy can play an important role in its economic growth, with insurance companies playing an important role in risk management. At the same time, as the insurance industry develops, it acquires long-term liabilities with a consequent need for long-term investments. In support of these obligations and investment requirements, insurance companies also take on the role of institutional investors and, as such, they can become important players in the provision of long-term finance.

Research also supports the importance of the development of contractual savings firms (e.g., pension funds and life insurance companies) in supporting securities market development, in addition to providing sufficient, sustainable and affordable benefits for old age.[117] Das, Davies and Podpiera summarize conclusions[118]: First, institutionalization of savings leads to the deepening of equity and debt markets. Second, the impact on securities market depth is nonlinear: it is stronger in countries where corporate information is more transparent.

---

[115] See U. Das, N. Davies and R. Podpiera, "Insurance and Issues in Financial Soundness", IMF Working Paper WP/03/138 (Jul. 2003), pp. 3, 14–16.

[116] Id., p. 3. See pp. 7–9 for discussion.

[117] See C. Impavido, A. Musalem and T. Tressel, "The Impact of Contractual Savings Institutions on Securities Markets", World Bank Policy Research Working Paper 2948 (Jan. 2003).

[118] Das, Davies and Podpiera, op. cit., n. 115, pp. 3–4, 16.

Third, there are significant differences among countries and contractual savings have a stronger impact on securities markets in countries where: (1) the financial system is market based, (2) pension fund contributions are mandatory and (3) international transactions in securities are lower. Fourth, the impact of contractual savings on securities markets is not explained by other characteristics such as the overall level of development, openness to trade, the legal environment, and the demographic structure, therefore suggesting that policy decisions that shape the evolution of contractual savings firms do matter and that the impact of contractual savings on securities markets is not due solely to slow-moving factors.

In looking at insurance development first through the lens of financial stability, the starting point is the key guidance identified by the FSF.

### 7.2.1. *Financial Stability Forum Key Standard: Insurance Core Principles*

The International Association of Insurance Supervisors (IAIS) has published Insurance Supervisory Principles to serve as guidelines for the regulation and supervision of insurance markets and is in the process of developing guidelines or standards in the areas of licensing, use of derivatives, on-site inspections, solvency, reinsurance, market conduct and investment policies.[119] Released in September 1997 and revised in October 2000, the Insurance Supervisory Principles comprise essential principles that need to be in place for an insurance supervisory system to be effective. These principles set out the framework for insurance supervision, identify subject areas that should be addressed in legislation or regulation in each jurisdiction and provide a framework for the IAIS on which to develop more detailed international standards. The IAIS also has enunciated general principles that identify subject areas that should be addressed in the laws of each jurisdiction, with further guidance specifically tailored to the needs of emerging economies.[120]

In 2003, the IAIS released a comprehensive revised set of principles and related methodology: the Insurance Core Principles.[121]

At the outset, the IAIS lays out the objective as follows[122]:

> To contribute to economic growth, efficiently allocate resources, manage risk, and mobilize long-term savings, the insurance sector must operate on a

[119] International Association of Insurance Supervisors (IAIS), *Insurance Supervisory Principles*, Sep. 1997, updated Oct. 2000.

[120] IAIS, *Guidance on Insurance Regulation and Supervision for Emerging Market Economies*, Sep. 1997.

[121] IAIS, *Insurance Core Principles and Methodology*, Oct. 2003.

[122] Id., p. 4.

financially sound basis. A well-developed insurance sector also helps to
enhance overall efficiency of the financial system by reducing transaction
costs, creating liquidity, and facilitating economies of scale in investment.
A sound regulatory and supervisory system is necessary for maintaining efficient, safe, fair and stable insurance markets and for promoting growth and
competition in the sector. Such markets benefit and protect policyholders.

As such, the Insurance Core Principles address the usual concerns of systemic
stability, consumer protection and market efficiency but also go further to
include financial development as an objective.

In pursuing these objectives, the Insurance Core Principles (ICPs) include
twenty-eight principles grouped under seven headings:

(1) ICP 1 addresses conditions for effective insurance supervision;
(2) ICP 2 through 5 deal with the supervisory system;
(3) ICP 6 through 10 address the supervised entity;
(4) ICP 11 through 17 address requirements for on-going supervision;
(5) ICP 18 through 23 deal with prudential requirements;
(6) ICP 24 through 27 address markets and consumers; and
(7) ICP 28 deals with money laundering and terrorist financing.

**Conditions for Effective Insurance Supervision.** Insurance Core Principle 1
provides the counterpart to the Basel Core Principles "preconditions", stating
that insurance supervision (and likewise development) rely upon: (1) a policy, institutional and legal framework for financial sector supervision; (2) a
well-developed and effective financial market infrastructure; and (3) efficient
financial markets.

Given that insurance is a business of contracts and therefore highly dependent upon enforcement, Principle 1 highlights specifically the need for the
legal system to provide support in honouring and enforcing insurance contracts.[123] In addition, it highlights the importance of financial information
and "broad-based, liquid and well-functioning money and securities markets",
emphasising the institutional complexity required to be in place for development and stability.

**Supervisory System and Supervision.** In relation to the supervisory system,
the Insurance Core Principles address the usual issues: supervisory objectives
(ICP 2), authority (ICP 3), supervisory process (ICP 4) and supervisory cooperation and information sharing (ICP 5).

---

[123] Id., p. 7.

In relation to on-going supervision, the Insurance Core Principles require systems for market analysis (ICP 11), reporting to supervisors and off-site monitoring (ICP 12), on-site inspection (ICP 13), preventive and corrective measures (ICP 14), enforcement and sanctions (ICP 15), winding-up and exit from the market (ICP 16) and group-wide supervision (ICP 17).

While largely similar to the 1997 Basel Core Principles, the ICPs go beyond in one important respect: winding-up and exit. Experience has indicated a pressing need for an effective system for dealing with insolvent insurance companies, including provisions relating to bankruptcy and liquidation. This system should recognize and protect the special status of policyholders as creditors of an insurance company. The system should delineate clearly the circumstances that will attract intervention by the supervisor, indicate the nature of the intervention and outline the means by which it will be invoked.

**Insurance Entities and Activities.** In relation to the supervised entity, the Insurance Core Principles set requirements for licensing (ICP 6), suitability of persons involved (ICP 7), changes in control and portfolio transfers (ICP 8), corporate governance (ICP 9) and internal controls (ICP 10). In addition, they deal with a variety of prudential operational requirements, including risk assessment and management (ICP 18), insurance activities (ICP 19), liabilities (ICP 20), investments (ICP 21), derivatives and similar commitments (ICP 22), and capital adequacy and solvency (ICP 23). Principle 24 addresses requirements for intermediary operations and supervision.

**Consumer Protection and Integrity.** Principle 25 deals with consumer protection, focusing on information disclosure, while Principle 26 relates to money laundering and terrorist financing.

### 7.2.2. *Other Financial Stability Forum Standards*

In addition to the Insurance Core Principles, the FSF Compendium – similar to the sections addressing banking and securities – includes a range of other guidance. Specifically, it includes standards in five subcategories: (1) general supervision, (2) capital adequacy, (3) cross-border supervision, (4) disclosure and transparency and (5) risk management.

In addition to the Insurance Core Principles, general supervision includes guidance regarding fit and proper standards[124], group coordination[125], the 2000

---

[124] IAIS, *Guidance Paper on Fit and Proper Principles*, Oct. 2000.
[125] IAIS, *Supervisory Standard on Group Coordination*, Oct. 2000.

principles methodology[126], insurance activities on the internet[127], conduct of insurance business[128], on-site inspections[129], licensing[130] and emerging market economies.[131] Capital adequacy is addressed by a single set of principles.[132] Cross-border supervision standards cover exchange of information[133], international insurance companies[134] and model MoUs.[135] Standards relating to disclosure and transparency address public disclosure[136] and money laundering.[137] Risk management guidance includes evaluation of reinsurance cover[138], asset management by insurance companies[139] and derivatives.[140]

### 7.2.3. *Implementation*

At the end of 2002, the IMF and the World Bank conducted a review of FSAP/ROSC experiences to date.[141] In the area of insurance supervision[142], assessments began in 1999; by December 2002, forty-five assessments had been undertaken under the FSAP. Some of these were under the 1997 Insurance Supervisory Principles, with the remainder under the 2000 Principles. These concerns therefore were taken into account in the revised 2003 Insurance Core Principles. A number of conclusions emerged from the reviews, of which two are most significant for present purposes:

First, satisfactory observance was generally seen in a number of areas, including financial reporting, cross-border business operations, capital adequacy and solvency, sanctions, prudential rules, liabilities, and confidentiality.

Second, common weaknesses included: (1) weak organization of the supervisor, (2) no clear criteria for denying changes in control, (3) weaknesses in

---

[126] IAIS, *Insurance Core Principles Methodology*, Oct. 2000.

[127] IAIS, *Principles on the Supervision of Insurance Activities on the Internet*, Oct. 2000.

[128] IAIS, *Principles for the Conduct of Insurance Business*, Oct. 2000.

[129] IAIS, *Supervisory Standard on On-Site Inspectors*, Oct. 1998.

[130] IAIS, *Supervisory Standard on Licensing*, Oct. 1998.

[131] IAIS, *Guidance on Insurance Regulation and Supervision for Emerging Market Economies*, Sep. 1997.

[132] IAIS, *Principles on Capital Adequacy and Solvency*, Jan. 2002.

[133] IAIS, *Supervisory Standard on Exchange of Information*, Jan. 2002.

[134] IAIS, *Principles Applicable to the Supervision of International Insurers and Insurance Groups and their Cross-border Operation*, Dec. 1999 revised.

[135] IAIS, *Model Memorandum of Understanding (MoU)*, Sep. 1997.

[136] IAIS, *Guidance Paper on Public Disclosure*, Jan. 2002.

[137] IAIS, *Anti-money Laundering Guidance Notes*, Jan. 2002.

[138] IAIS, *Supervisory Standard on Evaluation of Reinsurance Cover*, Jan. 2002.

[139] IAIS, *Supervisory Standard on Asset Management by Insurance Companies*, Dec. 1999.

[140] IAIS, *Supervisory Standard on Derivatives*, Oct. 1998.

[141] IMF and World Bank, *Analytical Tools of the FSAP*, op. cit., n. 42.

[142] Id., pp. 26–7; IMF and World Bank, *Experience with the Insurance Core Principles Assessments Under the Financial Sector Assessment Program*, Aug. 2001.

corporate governance and internal controls, (4) weak prudential rules on investment and exposure limits, (5) inadequate supervisory power to review or set standards for the use of reinsurance, (6) inadequate market conduct and complaint handling systems and (7) weak rules for use of derivatives and related disclosures.

As of January 2007, the IMF and World Bank had published insurance FSAP/ROSCs for forty-six countries.[143]

### 7.2.4. *Other International Standards*

In addition to the work of the IAIS, the OECD has also been active in relation to insurance, focusing especially on reinsurance[144]; governance[145]; mitigation and compensation of large-scale risks, including terrorism risks[146]; monitoring of insurance markets and related regulatory frameworks[147]; and development of insurance in emerging[148] and transition economies.[149]

### 7.2.5. *Developing Insurance*

According to Donald McIsaac[150], the process of development of the insurance sector in a developing, emerging or transition economy follows a predictable path, and usually begins with the participation of the public in certain obligatory classes of insurance, such as third-party liability coverage for operators of motor vehicles. This type of coverage is made mandatory in order to protect innocent victims who may suffer injury or loss as a result of an accident. The

---

[143] Australia, Austria, Bahrain, Barbados, Belgium, Bulgaria, Cameroon, Canada, Croatia, Cyprus, Czech Republic, Denmark, Estonia, Finland, France, Gabon, Georgia, Germany, Ghana, Greece, Hong Kong, Hungary, Iceland, Ireland, Italy, Japan, Latvia, Lithuania, Luxembourg, Malta, Mexico, Morocco, The Netherlands, Norway, Poland, Portugal, Russia, Singapore, Slovakia, Slovenia, South Korea, Spain, Sweden, Switzerland, Tunisia, United Kingdom.

[144] OECD, *Decision of the Council on the Exchange of Information on Reinsurers*, Oct. 2002; idem, *Recommendation of the Council on the Assessment of Insurance Companies*, Mar. 1998.

[145] OECD, *OECD Guidelines for Insurers' Governance*, Apr. 2005.

[146] OECD, *Guidelines for Good Practice of Insurance Claim Management*, Nov. 2004; idem, *OECD Check-List of Criteria to Define Terrorism for the Purpose of Compensation*, Dec. 2004.

[147] OECD, *Selected Principles for the Regulation of Investments by Insurance Companies and Pension Funds*, Jan. 1998.

[148] OECD, *Twenty Guidelines for Insurance Regulation and Supervision in Emerging Economies*, Jan. 1997; idem, *Detailed Principles for the Regulation and Supervision of Insurance Markets in Emerging Market Economies*, Jan. 1997.

[149] OECD, *Insurance Guidelines for Economies in Transition*, Apr. 1997.

[150] This section draws from D. Arner, D. McIsaac, K. Reed and C. Kang, *Consultation Document: Financial Sector Blueprint 2006–15* (Cambodia: National Bank of Cambodia / Ministry of Economy and Finance / Ministry of Commerce / Asian Development Bank, Aug. 2006). Special thanks to Donald McIsaac for these insights.

next step occurs when lenders, such as banks, begin to insist that collateral provided in support of loans be insured. A related step requires insurance on the life and health of the borrower.

Life insurance sales usually begin when employers seek to offer their workers a package of benefits that might include a death benefit to the surviving family members upon the untimely death of a worker. A major impetus for life insurance business growth often comes when either employers, or the government, launch programs for providing retirement income to workers. Life insurance in such circumstances often serves as a guarantee of support in the event a worker does not live to retirement although, in some cases, it can also be used as a funding vehicle for pension benefits.

While the initial insurance products that appear relate to mandatory coverages, the insurance industry does not experience rapid growth until such time as voluntary purchases of insurance begin. For example, the logical progression for insurance of motor vehicles is to combine the mandatory coverage for third-party liability with a comprehensive form of cover that protects the owner of the vehicle from loss in the event of an accident, a fire or even theft. Accumulation of assets under life insurance policies only assumes substantial proportions once consumers begin to appreciate its usefulness in personal financial planning and saving for retirement or for any family need, such as education of children.[151] Growth in the insurance sector depends upon the availability of discretionary, disposable income and personal choice.

A number of factors contribute to consumer confidence in insurance as a service.

First and foremost is a need for public understanding of the business of insurance and the services it can provide. It is also important that the business be conducted in as transparent a manner as possible. Claims filed by policyholders should be dealt with promptly by the company. Settlement of claims must always be in conformity with the terms of the policy, but must also be perceived to be fair and reasonable in the circumstances.

Governments can contribute to the development of the insurance sector by:

(1) Establishing an insurance regulatory system which ensures that only soundly financed and prudently managed insurance companies are authorized to write business.

---

[151] There is little asset accumulation in support of employee group life insurance or through the sale of term life insurance policies of short duration.

(2) Implementing an effective and efficient supervisory system to ensure continual monitoring of the financial strength and market conduct of companies.

(3) Empowering the supervisor with all the tools and authority required to deal with situations of noncompliance, and applying those rules across the market.

(4) Ensuring that rules applied to the operations of insurance companies, such as rules that govern their investment powers, are not unduly restrictive. The same standards must be applied to all companies in the marketplace.

(5) Providing protection against systemic risks. If an insurance company becomes insolvent the government should take appropriate steps to protect the interests of policy holders.

(6) Raising public awareness about insurance.

(7) Providing training to increase professionalism.

(8) Protecting consumers by encouraging disclosure requirements, ensuring that information given by insurance companies is accurate.

As noted earlier, life insurance policies are longer-term contracts, and therefore require an effective system of contract enforcement and commercial dispute resolution (discussed in Chapter Three). In addition, development of sound life insurance markets requires: (1) functioning capital markets offering an appropriate diversity of investment opportunities offering attractive yields with a satisfactory degree of security; (2) fully transparent accounting systems; (3) clear policy language that is uniformly adopted, along with adequate public understanding; (4) reasonable tax treatment for savings through life insurance; and (5) policy terms and values supported by sound actuarial advice.

## 7.3. PENSIONS

In looking at pensions, the focus is twofold: providing sufficient, sustainable and affordable benefits for old age; and supporting securities market development.[152]

In this context, the World Bank released a groundbreaking study in 1994, raising the issue of demographic transformation trends and the possibility

---

[152] See G. Impavido, A. Musalem and T. Tressel, "The Impact of Contractual Savings Institutions on Securities Markets", World Bank Policy Research Working Paper 2948 (Jan. 2003).

of an impending "old age crisis".[153] In the 1994 study, the Bank identified three functions of old age financial security systems: redistribution, saving and insurance. In order to support both old age provision and economic growth, the Bank recommended the adoption of "three pillar" pension systems, comprising: (1) a publicly managed system with mandatory participation and the limited goal of reducing poverty among the old (Pillar I); (2) privately managed, mandatory savings systems (Pillar II); and (3) voluntary savings (Pillar III).

Following ten years of implementation and study, in 2005, the World Bank released a new study, revisiting its 1994 conclusions.[154] In its 2005 review, the Bank recommends a flexible multi-pillar design, comprising five basic elements:

(1) a noncontributory demogrant or social pension providing a minimal level of protection (Pillar 0);

(2) a contributory system that is linked to varying degrees of earnings and seeks to replace some portion of income (Pillar I);

(3) a mandatory individual savings account (Pillar II);

(4) voluntary arrangements of a variety of forms, including individual and employer sponsored plans (Pillar III); and

(5) informal intra-family or inter-generational sources.

The first step therefore is to design an overall pensions system appropriate to the needs and individual circumstances of the economy concerned. At the same time, development of Pillar I, II and III pensions systems rely heavily on other aspects of the financial sector. In this respect, preconditions for the development of Pillar I, II and III pensions markets include the following[155]: sound macroeconomic policies, the existence of a core of efficient and sound banking and insurance intermediaries, and a lasting commitment for the creation

---

[153] World Bank, *Averting the Old Age Crisis: Policies to Protect the Old and Promote Growth*, 1994.

[154] R. Holzman and R. Hinz, *Old Age Income Support in the 21st Century: An International Perspective on Pension Systems and Reform* (Washington, DC: World Bank, 2005).

[155] Impavido, Musalem and Tressel, op. cit., n. 152, p. 5, citing G. Impavido, A. Musalem and D. Vittas, "Contractual Savings, Capital Markets, and Firms' Financing Choices" in S. Devarajan and F. Rogers (eds), *World Economists' Forum* (Washington, DC: World Bank, 2002), vol. II; D. Vittas, "Policies to Promote Saving for Retirement – A Synthetic Overview", World Bank Policy Research Paper 2801 (2002); D. Vittas, "Pension Reform and Financial Markets", Harvard Institute for International Development Development Discussion Paper 697 (1999).

of an effective regulatory and supervisory agency and reform of the capital markets.

In looking at these sorts of systems, the focus of international standards has been largely on Pillar II and III.

### 7.3.1. *International Standards*

The FSF does not include any standards directly related to pensions. However, for a number of years, the OECD has been active in this area, under the auspices of its Working Party on Private Pensions. In addition, the International Organization of Pension Supervisors (IOPS) was formed in 2004 to formalize the efforts begun through the International Network of Pensions Regulators (INPRS). The purpose of the IOPS is to[156]:

(1) serve as the standard-setting body on pension supervisory matters and regulatory issues related to pension supervision;
(2) promote international cooperation on pension supervision;
(3) provide a worldwide forum for policy dialogue and exchange of information on pension supervision;
(4) participate in the work of relevant international bodies in the area of pensions; and
(5) promote research, collection and dissemination relating to pensions.

In December 2005, IOPS approved the *IOPS Principles of Private Pension Supervision*.[157] According to the IOPS, the main objective of private pension supervision is "to promote the stability, security and good governance of pension funds and plans, and to protect the interests of pension fund members and beneficiaries."[158] To achieve this objective, the IOPS has established ten principles:

(1) National laws should assign clear and explicit objectives to pension supervisory authorities (Principle 1).
(2) Pension supervisory authorities should have operational independence, meaning that day-to-day operations and decision making are under the autonomous control of the supervisor (Principle 2).
(3) Pension supervisory authorities require adequate financial, human and other resources (Principle 3).

---

[156] See www.iopsweb.org.
[157] IOPS, *IOPS Principles of Private Pension Supervision* (OECD, Dec. 2005).
[158] Id., p. 2.

(4) Pension supervisory authorities should be endowed with the investigatory and enforcement powers necessary to fulfill their functions and achieve their objectives (Principle 4).

(5) Pension supervision should seek to mitigate the greatest potential risks to the pension system (Principle 5).

(6) Pension supervisory authorities should ensure that investigatory and enforcement requirements are proportional to the risks being mitigated and that their actions are consistent (Principle 6).

(7) Pension supervisory authorities should consult with the bodies they are overseeing and cooperate with other supervisory authorities (Principle 7).

(8) Pension supervisory authorities should treat confidential information appropriately (Principle 8).

(9) Pension supervisory authorities should conduct their operations in a transparent manner (Principle 9).

(10) The supervisory authority should adhere to its own governance code and should be accountable (Principle 10).

In addition, the IOPS is currently working on a number of related principles and standards projects, including core elements of a risk-based approach to pension supervision and strategic planning (with the World Bank), and guidelines for compliance with the licensing of pension funds (with the OECD).[159]

As mentioned earlier, in addition to the IOPS, the OECD has been active in this area for a more extended period, focusing on private pension schemes.

In 2001, the OECD, working with the INPRS, released the first set of principles dealing with regulation of private occupational pension schemes[160], which set out fifteen principles addressing: (1) adequate regulatory framework, (2) appropriate regulation of financial markets, (3) rights of beneficiaries, (4) adequacy of private schemes, (5) regulatory system and separation, (6) funding, (7) calculation techniques, (8) supervisory structures, (9) self-supervision, (10) fair competition, (11) investment, (12) insurance mechanisms, (13) winding up, (14) disclosure and education and (15) corporate governance.

In 2004, the OECD and the INPRS agreed upon core principles for occupational pensions and a supporting methodology, updating the 2001 principles.[161] The 2004 OECD occupational pensions core principles address seven areas: (1) conditions for effective regulation and supervision (Principle 1);

---

[159] See www.iopsweb.org.

[160] OECD, *Fifteen Principles for the Regulation of Private Occupational Pension Schemes*, Jan. 2001.

[161] OECD, *OECD Recommendation on Core Principles of Occupational Pension Regulation*, Jul. 2004.

(2) establishment of pension plans, pension funds and pension fund managing companies (Principle 2); (3) pension plan liabilities, funding rules, winding up and insurance (Principle 3); (4) asset management (Principle 4); (5) rights of members and beneficiaries and adequacy of benefits (Principle 5); and (6) supervision (Principle 6).

In addition, the OECD has released additional guidance in relation to certain specific aspects of these core principles, including protection of rights of members and beneficiaries[162], pension fund governance[163], asset management[164] and, most recently, funding and benefit security.[165]

### 7.3.2. *Developing Pensions*

In looking at pensions development, two aspects stand out: first, the need for coherent policy planning in the design of the overall system; and second, a need to focus on the environment in which pensions develop.

In relation to the second, the best guidance is provided by the first OECD occupational core principle, addressing conditions for effective regulation and supervision (and the counterpart of the Basel Core Principles preconditions and IAIS Core Principle 1). Under this framework, the objective of the regulatory framework for private pensions is ensuring: (1) the protection of pension plan members and beneficiaries (consumer protection), (2) the soundness of pensions plans and funds (prudential concerns), and (3) the stability of the economy as a whole (financial stability). Such systems require well-functioning capital markets and financial intermediaries, and the development of advance-funded pensions systems must occur alongside strengthening of the foundations of finance and financial regulation generally.

### 7.4. OTHER FORMS OF NONBANK FINANCE: MICROFINANCE AND RELATED ACTIVITIES

Following the success of a number of initiatives such as the Grameen Bank in Bangladesh, microfinance has become quite topical in financial development circles over the past five years or so.

While not addressed in the context of the FSF framework, the Consultative Group to Assist the Poor (CGAP) has developed a set of *Key Principles of*

---

[162] OECD, *OECD Guidelines for the Protection of Rights of Members and Beneficiaries in Occupational Pension Plans*, Dec. 2004.

[163] OECD, *OECD Guidelines for Pension Fund Governance*, Apr. 2005.

[164] OECD, *OECD Guidelines on Pension Fund Asset Management*, Mar. 2006.

[165] OECD Directorate for Financial and Enterprise Affairs, *OECD Guidelines on Funding and Benefit Security*, Jul. 2006.

*Microfinance*[166] which were endorsed by the Group of Eight[167] members at their Sea Island Summit on 10 June 2004. The eleven principles are:

(1) Poor people need a variety of convenient, flexible and affordable financial services, including loans, savings, insurance and cash transfer services (CGAP Principle 1).

(2) Microfinance is a powerful tool to fight poverty (CGAP Principle 2).

(3) Microfinance means building financial systems that serve the poor, integrating microfinance into the financial sector (CGAP Principle 3).

(4) Microfinance can pay for itself and must do so if it is to reach very large numbers of poor people: financially sustainable providers can improve services and increase access to financial services (CGAP Principle 4).

(5) Microfinance is about building permanent financial intermediaries, attracting savings, making loans, providing other financial services, and building financial sustainability as institutions and financial markets improve (CGAP Principle 5).

(6) Microcredit is not always the best tool, especially when dealing with the destitute (CGAP Principle 6).

(7) Interest rate ceilings hurt poor people by making it harder for them to get credit (CGAP Principle 7).

(8) The role of government is to enable financial services, not to provide them directly. In this respect, government should set policies to stimulate financial services for the poor while protecting customers. Macroeconomic stability, avoidance of interest rate caps, subsidized government lending, reduction of corruption and improving the environment for microbusinesses are the objectives (CGAP Principle 8).

(9) Donor funds should complement private capital, not compete with it (CGAP Principle 9).

(10) The key bottleneck is the shortage of strong intermediaries and personnel (CGAP Principle 10).

(11) Microfinance works best when it measures and discloses its performance (CGAP Principle 11).

---

[166] CGAP, *Key Principles of Microfinance*, available at www.cgap.org. See B. Nelms, *Access for All: Building Inclusive Financial Systems* (Washington, DC: CGAP / World Bank, 2006).

[167] The G-7 plus Russia. Interestingly, all other financial standards initiatives have emanated from the G-7.

# 8

## Financial Liberalization, Financial Conglomerates and Financial Regulatory Structure

Beyond central concerns relating to banking and nonbank finance, as financial systems develop, additional issues arise. These issues, as a general matter, need to be dealt with according to the general principles outlined in previous chapters and focusing on two sets of concerns: (1) financial stability and (2) financial development. Under this framework, the approach to general cross-sectoral considerations should address possible risks to financial stability as the first-order concern while at the same time supporting financial development and innovation.

Four primary considerations arise: (1) financial liberalization, (2) competition, (3) financial conglomerates and (4) financial regulatory structure.

Liberalization and competition bring important economic benefits in the context of supporting financial development, and economic growth. Research and experience suggest that a liberalized and competitive financial sector supports increased economic growth. At the same time, financial sector liberalization brings with it certain risks that need to be addressed appropriately. Most importantly, financial liberalization without appropriate sequencing and development of a legal and regulatory framework to reduce risks actually can increase the risk of financial crisis. As such, the concerns addressed in previous chapters regarding foundations of finance, banking and nonbank finance are all of special significance as financial sectors liberalize and develop.

In looking at liberalization, international best practice suggests that in building a competitive financial sector, countries can use international and regional arrangements to reinforce progress and encourage competition. Beyond international and regional financial sector and related commitments, it is also necessary to consider the context of domestic competition and the development of a competition law and related policy and institutional framework. Such a framework should address the special concerns which arise in relation to the financial sector, especially those related to banking and banks, and should be designed to support continued competition in the financial sector while at the same time dealing with risks as they arise in a pragmatic and market-oriented manner.

As financial product and service innovation and financial intermediary activities develop and increase in sophistication, countries around the world must address second-level considerations relating to the financial conglomerates and the overall structure of financial regulation and supervision.

## 8.1. FINANCIAL LIBERALIZATION AND FINANCIAL DEVELOPMENT

Financial innovation is integral to financial development and therefore should be supported and encouraged in the context of maintaining financial stability through appropriately addressing risks that may arise. In looking at financial systems around the world, we find two main approaches to financial innovation: permissive and restrictive. The permissive approach essentially allows financial innovation unless it is otherwise barred but always in the context of addressing risks that arise. This approach is found in the world's most developed financial systems. The restrictive approach essentially bars financial innovation unless it is specifically allowed. This approach tends to be found in less developed financial systems around the world.

Financial innovation typically takes a number of forms: (1) new financial intermediaries, (2) new financial products and services and (3) financial intermediary activities and financial conglomerates.

### 8.1.1. *New Financial Intermediaries*

In the spirit of supporting domestic and foreign competition in the financial sector, new financial intermediaries should be allowed to establish so long as they meet appropriate requirements (based on international and regional standards) for licensing, authorization and operations in respect to the specific financial services which they intend to provide. For example, new banks or insurance companies (whether foreign or domestic) should be allowed to establish so long as they meet the requirements for licensing, authorization and operations relating to banks or insurance companies, as appropriate. In addition, new forms of financial intermediary (for example, pensions firms) should be allowed to establish once the appropriate legal and regulatory framework and institutional structure are in place.

## 8.1.2. *Financial Products and Services*

Financial product and service innovation is vital for financial development. At the same time, new financial products and services may bring risks to financial stability which must be carefully addressed as products and services develop.

As a general matter, financial intermediaries should be allowed to develop new financial products and services which fall within their existing areas of business (i.e., banking, securities, insurance etc.), so long as the financial intermediary concerned is otherwise already performing satisfactorily from a supervisory standpoint. Financial intermediaries seeking to provide financial products and services in another sector (for example, banks selling insurance) are discussed subsequently in the context of financial intermediary activities and financial conglomerates.

As new products arise, regulators and supervisors should seek to understand these products and any risks which they might present to the financial intermediary concerned, potential customers and the financial system as a whole. Financial intermediaries should have in place appropriate systems to support new products and appropriate consumer and systemic protection mechanisms should be put in place as necessary. At the same time, in some cases, development of the legal and/or regulatory framework may be necessary for some financial products or services, and financial regulators should support necessary legal and regulatory development to support financial innovation in the context of appropriately addressing risks.

## 8.2. FOREIGN AND DOMESTIC PARTICIPATION AND COMPETITION

Competition in the financial sector, as in other segments of a market economy, is important for proper market functioning and efficiency of resource allocation. Unlike many other markets, however, financial markets (especially those related to banking), as noted throughout this volume, carry a number of externalities, both positive and negative. One role of regulation therefore is to limit participation in some circumstances to qualified intermediaries and individuals. As a result, financial regulation deals, inter alia, with qualifications for financial intermediaries and their management, and thus presents barriers to entry. Nonetheless, competition remains important and there is a need to balance prudential concerns with developmental concerns.

Generally, competition issues in the financial sector arise in three contexts: domestic competition, competition between state-owned and private-sector participants, and foreign competition. To date, insufficient account has been taken of these issues in international financial standards.

### 8.2.1. *The Domestic Context*

As noted, there is a need to balance prudential concerns with competition concerns in the financial sector. Unfortunately, domestic interests often act to prevent new entrants, with many economies strictly limiting new entrants, whether domestic or foreign. In some cases, this resulted from decisions taken with respect to financial structure and economic organization; in others, from purely anticompetitive behaviour by entrenched interests. On the other hand, a number of countries have experienced severe problems as a result of not sufficiently limiting new entrants into the financial system. Examples can be seen in Russia with respect to banks and in Albania with respect to collective investment schemes.

As a result, countries should have clear transparent prudential limitations on entry, reflecting the international standards discussed in previous chapters. At the same time however they should not otherwise place limits on market entry in the financial sector; rather, they should focus on on-going supervision and preparations for potential financial intermediary exit. After all, failure is the ultimate competitive sanction and, as in other areas of the economy, financial intermediaries need to be allowed to fail or otherwise exit from the system. These sorts of ideas can and should be incorporated across the system of standards during the review and revision process.

### 8.2.2. *State Ownership in the Financial Sector*

In addition, state ownership of financial intermediaries can impact on both efficiency and competition in financial systems. State-owned financial inter-mediaries or implicit or explicit state guarantees of financial intermediaries can have a significant impact on both competition and efficiency. As a result, many commentators recommend eliminating state-ownership through privatization of financial intermediaries. At the least, state-owned financial intermediaries should be required to operate on market principles; otherwise, private-sector participants will be disadvantaged, usually with eventual implications for the general health of a country's economy. Examples of these sorts of distortions and their eventual consequences can be seen in the problems facing the financial systems of both Germany and Japan during the 1990s. Once again, the role of state ownership in the financial sector should be taken explicitly into account in the various international financial standards.

### 8.2.3. *Foreign Competition*

Financial systems generally benefit from foreign participation and competition. At the same time, however, open capital markets can also have negative consequences if a proper institutional framework does not exist. Nonetheless, one of the best ways to generate competition is to allow foreign participation. Empirical research supports the idea that foreign financial intermediaries have a positive role in financial stability and development.[1] In addition, among other issues, clear rules governing foreign investment and public-private partnerships (concession law) must be established to enable foreign investment and participation.[2] Without clear rules on foreign investment, foreign capital and expertise will not enter an economy. Clear rules discourage corruption and enhance respect for the rule of law as well as aiding in the transfer of funds and technology necessary to transition and development. Public-private partnership arrangements require a legal infrastructure that recognizes the legitimate needs and expectations of the parties.

However, in addition to risks, foreign participation also often raises a number of difficult political issues in many economies, historically often resulting in efforts to block such participation. Today, foreign participation is dealt with largely through bilateral, regional and international negotiations, with the latter centred on the World Trade Organization (WTO). Specifically, on 1 January 1995, the Marrakesh Agreement Establishing the WTO (WTO Agreement) entered into force, with its annexes, including, inter alia, the General Agreement on Tariffs and Trade 1994 (GATT), and the General Agreement on Trade in Services (GATS). The main legal components affecting international trade in financial services include: (1) GATS[3], (2) Annex on Financial Services, (3) Second Annex on Financial Services, (4) Understanding on Commitments in Financial Services, (5) Second Protocol to the GATS, (5) Fifth Protocol to the GATS, (6) Decisions and (7) Understanding on Rules and Procedures Governing the Settlement of Disputes (DSU)

These components contain a number of general obligations respecting trade and financial services contained in the various agreements, including

---

[1]  See R. de Hass and I. Van Lelyveld, "Foreign Banks and Credit Stability in Central and Eastern Europe: A Panel Data Analysis", DNB Staff Reports no. 109/2003 (Nov. 2003).

[2]  See J. Taylor and F. April, "Fostering Investment Law in Transitional Economies: A Case for Refocusing Institutional Reform", 4 Parker Sch. J. E. Eur. L. 1 (1997).

[3]  According to the Results of the Uruguay Round of Multilateral Trade Negotiation, the GATS is composed of four parts: (1) the main text of the Agreement (The General Agreement on Trade in Services), (2) eight Annexes, (3) Schedules of specific commitments (4) List of Art. II Exemptions. The GATS Text refers to only the first part.

most-favoured nation (MFN) treatment[4], transparency[5], and the effect of domestic regulation, discussed further in the following section. The GATS covers all sectors of services[6], including financial services. In addition, the Annex on Financial Services and the Second Annex on Financial Services, as part of the GATS, directly relate to financial services. The Understanding on Commitments in Financial Services, as part of the Final Act, stipulates higher requirements for financial liberalization for those members that have adopted it. The so-called Financial Services Agreement and its scheduled commitments, in contrast to the financial services commitments undertaken in the Uruguay Round and in the 1995 interim agreement, are not temporary, but permanent, until the WTO members conclude a new agreement through negotiations. The Fifth Protocol to the GATS entered into force on 1 March 1999, and at the same time, those schedules of specific commitments and lists of MFN exemptions annexed to the Fifth Protocol replaced those undertaken in the 1995 interim agreement or in the Uruguay Round. These commitments form the basis for future financial services negotiations.

The WTO framework therefore provides the international framework for foreign participation in financial services. However, unlike other areas, in the area of financial services, commitments made by members are exclusive rather than inclusive, as in the area of trade in goods, and therefore liberalization is at the discretion of individual WTO members and remains quite limited in most cases. The framework is therefore an important starting point in supporting foreign competition in financial services, but needs to be extended through further negotiations in order to provide greater benefits. It also should be explicitly incorporated into the system of international financial standards. At the same time, it needs to be carefully considered in the context of the relationship between financial liberalization and financial stability – an issue which is addressed in the following section.

---

[4] GATS Article II (Most-Favoured-Nation Treatment) is composed of three paragraphs, applicable to all services sectors. Paragraph 1 is the core rule identifying the MFN obligation with respect to trade in services. It requires that each member accord to services and service suppliers of any other member treatment no less favourable than that it accords to like services and service suppliers of any other country.

[5] The obligation of transparency provided by GATS Article III can be divided into three categories. The first is the obligation of publication of all relevant measures or international agreements pertaining to or affecting trade in services. The second is the obligation of notification to the WTO (the Council for Trade in Services) of any new laws (or any changes to existing laws) significantly affecting trade in services. The third is the obligation of responsiveness to requests by other WTO Members for information through the establishment of enquiry points.

[6] GATS Art. I: 3(b): "'services' includes any service in any sector except services supplied in the exercise of governmental authority."

8.3. FINANCIAL LIBERALIZATION AND FINANCIAL STABILITY

This section discusses the risks of liberalization and links the financial stability framework to their reduction.

### 8.3.1. *Risks of Liberalization*

Following financial crises in the 1990s, attention primarily focused on domestic institutional weaknesses and international contagion. The response has been the series of standards and codes outlined in Chapter Two. The crises also generated significant research on other aspects of financial crises. One important result has been to link financial liberalization with financial crises. At the same time, however, there is an important link between financial liberalization, and especially competition, and financial sector development and economic growth. It is important therefore to consider how countries should go about achieving the benefits of liberalization and competition, while at the same time reducing risks of financial crisis.[7] The focus therefore is increasingly on the concept of sequencing. Sequencing looks to the process of liberalization and the process of institutional strengthening and asks which order is best to secure financial development while at the same time minimizing financial crises.

Several studies explore the link between financial services liberalization and financial crises.[8] Research by the Bank for International Settlements (BIS) and the International Monetary Fund (IMF) concludes that financial liberalization is a key leading indicator of financial crises in countries around the world over the past century. This is the case in developed countries (e.g., the United States and Europe), in developing and emerging economies (Latin America, east Asia), and in transition countries (Russia). Analyses of financial crises during the 1990s suggest that weak domestic financial systems are a significant underlying cause of crisis when coupled with liberalization without appropriate prior and/or concurrent restructuring. Recent research indicates that financial liberalization is followed by more pronounced boom-bust cycles in the short run; however, financial liberalization leads to more stable markets in the long run.[9] While the literature is generally incomplete and inconclusive

---

[7] For a highly readable treatment, see F. Mishkin, *The Next Great Globalization: How Disadvantaged Nations Can Harness Their Financial Systems to Get Rich* (Princeton, NJ: Princeton University Press, 2006).

[8] M. Goldstein and P. Turner, "Banking Crises in Emerging Economies: Origins and Policy Options", BIS Economic Paper no. 46 (Oct. 1996); W. White, "What Have We Learned from Recent Financial Crises and Policy Responses?", BIS Working Paper no. 84 (Jan. 2000).

[9] G. Kaminsky and S. Schmukler, "Short-Run Pain, Long-Run Gain: The Effects of Financial Liberalization", IMF Working Paper WP/03/34 (Feb. 2003).

to date, there is some positive effect of capital account liberalization on growth, especially for developing countries[10], though crises seem to be larger in emerging economies if the capital market opens first, rather than the domestic financial sector.[11] Further, equity market liberalization appears to decrease both output and consumption growth volatility, indicating that equity market liberalization is good for both global markets and individual markets.[12] Finally, insurance liberalization also correlates with financial instability: "most life-insurance company failures occurred after financial deregulation, economic expansion, and a large price fluctuation."[13]

Graciela Kaminsky and Sergio Schmukler have provided the most comprehensive analysis of the issue[14], concluding that financial liberalization is a leading indicator of financial crisis in the short run, but that financial liberalization leads to more stable and developed markets in the long run. In a review of the literature, they suggest that there are two main streams, one indicating that financial liberalization supports financial development[15] and another indicating that financial crises are triggered by financial liberalization.[16] Kaminsky and Schmukler, in analysing the issues, focus on the definition of liberalization and the time periods involved.

In relation to liberalization, they look at a number of criteria to identify twenty-eight countries' financial systems as "fully liberalized", "partially liberalized" or "repressed" in each of three main areas over the period 1973–99[17]:

(1) capital account liberalization. regulations on offshore borrowing by domestic financial intermediaries, offshore borrowing by nonfinancial corporations, multiple exchange rate markets, and controls on capital outflows;

(2) domestic financial liberalization: regulations on deposit interest rates, lending interest rates, allocation of credit, foreign currency deposits, and reserve requirements;

---

[10] H. Edison, M. Klein, L. Ricci and T. Sloek, "Capital Account Liberalization and Economic Performance: Survey and Synthesis", NBER Working Paper no. 9100 (2002).

[11] Id., p. 24.

[12] G. Bekaert, C. Harvey and C. Lundblad, "Does Financial Liberalization Spur Growth?", NBER Working Paper no. 8245 (2001).

[13] U. Das, N. Davies and R. Podpiera, "Insurance and Issues in Financial Soundness", IMF Working Paper WP/03/138 (Jul. 2003), pp. 3, 17–18.

[14] Kaminsky and Schmukler, op. cit., n. 9.

[15] See F. Mishkin, "Financial Policies and Prevention of Financial Crises in Emerging Market Countries," NBER Working Paper no. 8087 (2001); Bekaert, Harvey and Lundblad, op. cit., n. 12.

[16] See sources cited earlier.

[17] Kaminsky and Schmukler, op. cit., n. 9, pp. 8–9 and related tables.

(3) liberalization of securities markets: regulations on acquisition of shares in the domestic securities market by foreigners, repatriation of capital, and repatriation of interest and dividends.

Their analysis produced a number of interesting results, including:

(1) At present, mature financial markets are on average less regulated than emerging economies, but there is a pattern of gradual liberalization across all regions and markets.
(2)  Liberalization in developed economies has been uninterrupted while liberalization in emerging economies reversed following the 1980s debt crisis before resuming in the 1990s.
(3) Securities markets in developed economies were liberalized first, beginning in the 1970s, though the domestic financial sector and capital account tended to be repressed until the 1980s, with liberalization of the domestic financial sector (by the mid-1980s) typically preceding liberalization of the capital account (at the beginning of the 1990s).
(4) In emerging economies, reform waves occur in the late 1970s and late 1980s, with the 1970s reforms focusing only on the capital account and domestic sector, with securities markets universalized, while in the second wave, domestic sector and securities market joint deregulation preceded capital account liberalization in the 1990s.
(5) Liberalization increases the effects of financial crisis in the short run, especially in emerging economies, with development increased over the long term.
(6) Financial crises in emerging economies are more likely when the capital account is liberalized first.
(7) Institutional reforms tend to occur after initial liberalization, with partial liberalization supporting further institutional reforms.
(8) Improvements in the legal system improve market stability.

They leave unanswered the question of whether countries can deregulate financial systems without becoming vulnerable to financial crisis.[18]

David Beim and Charles Calomiris use financial liberalization as the definition and objective of the move from a developing or transition economy to an

---

[18]  Id., p. 37.

emerging economy, arguing the essential role of law in successful financial and economic development.[19] They define repression in terms of six aspects[20]:

(1) interest rate ceilings on bank deposits;
(2) high bank reserve requirements;
(3) government credit and direction of bank credit;
(4) government ownership and micromanagement of banks;
(5) restrictions on foreign bank and domestic non-bank entry; and
(6) restrictions on capital flows.

Likewise, they define liberalization in terms of six aspects[21]:

(1) elimination of interest rate controls,
(2) lowering of bank reserve requirements,
(3) reduction of government interference in banks' lending decisions,
(4) privatization of nationalized banks,
(5) introduction of foreign bank competition and
(6) facilitation and encouragement of capital inflows.

They conclude that while liberalization is destabilizing and related to financial crises, with proper institutional strengthening, the benefits can be secured.

### 8.3.2. *The World Trade Organization and Financial Liberalization*

A related question is the relationship between WTO financial services liberalization and financial crises. One aspect of WTO membership is financial services liberalization under the GATS. The potential danger inherent in financial liberalization under the WTO has also been pointed out and the lack of linkage between the WTO framework and international financial standards has been noted, though, to date, not developed in significant detail.[22]

Nico Valckx has analysed this issue and concludes[23]: (1) commitments tend to relate to economic growth, current account balances, banking sector development, policy restrictiveness and peer group behaviour; and (2) more liberal commitments may be associated with greater vulnerability to financial crisis in

---

[19] D. Beim and C. Calomiris, *Emerging Financial Markets* (New York: McGraw-Hill, 2001).
[20] Id., p. 47.
[21] Id., p. 119.
[22] J. Norton, "International Financial Law, An Increasingly Important Component of 'International Economic Law'", 20 Mich. J. Int'l L. 133 (1999).
[23] N. Valckx, "WTO Financial Services Commitments: Determinants and Impact on Financial Stability", IMF Working Paper WP/02/214 (Dec. 2002).

the short term, though this risk can be reduced by sound domestic policies and regulation. Alexei Kireyev has taken the analysis further, focusing on the very limited nature of WTO financial services commitments as one small segment of wider financial liberalization, concluding that WTO-mandated liberalization, because of its limited focus on competition, has led to financial stability in the longer term.[24]

However, no explicit link has been developed between financial services liberalization under the GATS and the development of a robust financial system through implementation of international financial standards. As noted earlier, the central issue appears to be sequencing, and the Beim and Calomiris framework appears to provide an appropriate ordering (though it does not expressly do so), supporting the view that WTO financial services liberalization (which only takes place as steps 5 and 6) should be beneficial, so long as it is done as part of a broader process of reform. It is worth noting that China appears to be following this trajectory. Beim and Calomiris do suggest a sequence for privatization[25]:

(1) create legal structures for property rights, corporations and contracts (building legal foundations);
(2) restructure state-owned enterprises in corporate form (corporatization);
(3) introduce competition (by allowing market entry, both domestic and foreign);
(4) eliminate government barriers to price setting;
(5) introduce modern accounting and auditing; and
(6) determine and apply privatization process.

While they have not linked this to financial development and transition, a logical step would be the following sequence:

(1) privatize industry according to the steps just given and
(2) liberalize the financial sector according to the steps listed.

At the end of the day, one should have an emerging economy with a financial system to support growth and reduce the likelihood and impact of financial crises.

---

[24] A. Kireyev, "Liberalization of Trade in Financial Services and Financial Sector Stability (Analytical Approach)", IMF Working Paper WP/02/138 (Aug. 2002); idem, "Liberalization of Trade in Financial Services and Financial Sector Stability (Empirical Approach)", IMF Working Paper WP/02/139 (Aug. 2002).

[25] Beim and Calomiris, op. cit., n. 19, pp. 105–6.

In addition to the process of liberalization in individual economies, a related question relates to the role of international organizations in encouraging and supporting the process of liberalization and institution building. These questions become especially important when one considers the role of the IMF and World Bank vis-à-vis the WTO.

In fact, the IMF, WTO and other interested actors have begun to specifically address the question of the relationship of their various mandates and roles in the financial sector. As one example, following the 4th WTO Ministerial Conference in Doha in November 2001, the membership of the WTO mandated it to look into issues of trade, debt and finance.[26] As a result of this decision, a working group involving, inter alia, the IMF, OECD, United Nations and World Bank was established to look into (1) financing of trade, (2) trade and debt and (3) coherence.[27] Individual reports were produced on each of the themes, with only that on trade and debt publicly available[28], and initial findings were reported to the WTO General Council. Further results are expected in the near future. In addition to the WTO working group, the IMF has devoted some attention to these issues.[29]

### 8.3.3. *The World Trade Organization and Domestic Regulation*

As mentioned earlier, the WTO legal framework for financial services addresses the interaction between financial services liberalization commitments and the role of prudential regulation. This section discusses the main elements of this framework and its meaning.

---

[26] See WTO, *Ministerial Declaration adopted on 14 November 2001*, WTO Ministerial Conference, Fourth Session, Doha, 9–14 Nov. 2001, WT/MIN(01)/DEC/1 (20 Nov. 2001), para. 36, p. 8:

> We agreed to an examination, in a Working Group under the auspices of the General Council, of the relationship between trade, debt and finance, and of any possible recommendations on steps that might be taken within the mandate and competence of the WTO to enhance the capacity of the multilateral trading system to contribute to a durable solution to the problem of external indebtedness of developing and least-developed countries, and to strengthen the coherence of international trade and financial policies, with a view to safeguarding the multilateral trading system from the effects of financial and monetary instability.

[27] WTO Working Group on Trade, Debt and Finance, *Report to the General Council*, WT/WBTDF/2 (11 Jul. 2003).

[28] WTO Working Group on Trade, Debt and Finance, *Improving the Availability of Trade Financing: Report of Preliminary Work*, WT/WGTDF/W/23 (25 Mar. 2004).

[29] In relation to trade finance, see IMF, *Trade Finance in Financial Crises: Assessment of Key Issues*, Dec. 2003 (showing a relationship between financial crises and loss of trade via loss of trade finance).

The GATS does not prohibit members' domestic regulation of trade in services, but it does establish certain limitations on such regulation in order to prevent members from avoiding their obligations by way of domestic regulation. First, paragraph 1 of Article VI requires that all measures be administered in a "reasonable, objective and impartial" manner. Second, paragraph 2 requires that members have judicial, arbitral or administrative tribunals (or procedures) to review and provide remedies for administrative decisions affecting trade in services. The third requirement concerning domestic regulation is that an applicant must receive a prompt decision from a competent authority of a member respecting any application. The fourth requirement is related to the effect of domestic regulation on trade in services, meaning that licensing and qualification requirements, as well as technical standards, may not be applied simply as a means to nullify or impair specific commitments made by members. To this end, and pending the establishment of multilateral disciplines relating to qualifications and technical standards, members must ensure that national requirements in these areas are based on objective and transparent criteria, are not more burdensome than necessary to ensure the quality of the service, and licensing procedures should not result in a restriction on the supply of the service.[30]

**The World Trade Organization Prudential Carve-out.** Given the significance of financial regulation, WTO members included a special rule relating to domestic prudential regulation of financial services. In particular, paragraph 2(a) of the Annex on Financial Services states:

> Notwithstanding any other provisions of the Agreement, a Member shall not be prevented from taking measures for *prudential reasons*, including for the protection of investors, depositors, policy holders or persons to whom a fiduciary duty is owed by a financial service supplier, or to ensure the integrity and stability of the financial system. Where such measures do not conform with the provisions of the Agreement, they shall not be used as a means of avoiding the Member's commitments or obligations under the Agreement. (emphasis added)

This rule is generally called the "prudential carve-out".[31] Pursuant to the prudential carve-out, a member may take discriminatory measures against foreign financial services and financial service suppliers in order to protect domestic "investors, depositors, policy holders" etc. or to ensure "the integrity and

---

[30]  See GATS Art. VI:4 and VI:5.
[31]  See generally S. Key, "Trade Liberalization and Prudential Regulation: The International Framework for Financial Services", 75 Int'l Affairs 61 (1999). See also R. Kampf, "Liberalization of Financial Services in the GATS and Domestic Regulation", 3 Int'l Trade L. Rev. 155 (1997).

stability of the financial system". Many members view the prudential carve-out to be of such significance that "inclusion of financial services in the GATS would be unacceptable without a specific exception for prudential regulation and supervision."[32]

The first sentence of paragraph 2(a) entitles a member to take prudential regulatory measures related to financial services trade.[33] The second sentence is a trade-off of the first sentence, providing that such measures (prudential measures provided by the first sentence) shall not be used as means of avoiding the member's commitments or obligations under the GATS agreement. The GATS text and other provisions of the Annex on Financial Services do not resolve the question of relationship between the first sentence and the second sentence, that is, to what extent does the second sentence narrow down the scope of power provided by the first sentence? For example, in a member's Schedule of Specific Commitments, if the column of limitations on market access and national treatment is "none" (full commitments), can a member take a limitation measure on market access or national treatment in the name of the prudential carve-out? If the answer is no, then what is the meaning of prudential carve-out?

**The Scope of the Prudential Carve-out.** The essence of the second sentence is that prudential measures shall not be used as a means of "avoiding the Member's commitments or obligations under the Agreement". This sentence implies that prudential measures should not aim intentionally to avoid a member's commitments and obligations, one of which is the national treatment obligation under GATS Article XVII. Logically, it means that the prudential carve-out should not be used to derogate from the national treatment obligation, but this conclusion seems to be in contradiction to the first sentence which describes the scope of the prudential carve-out with the wording "[n]otwithstanding any other provisions of the Agreement". In a word, the scope of the prudential carve-out is unclear.[34]

The scope of the prudential carve-out depends on the distance between prudential measures and GATS obligations: the longer the distance, the broader the scope of the carve-out, and vice versa. To identify the scope of the prudential carve-out is, in essence, to identify the distance of GATS obligations and prudential measures, or to strike a balance between the two. Paragraph 2(a)

---

[32] Key, op. cit., n. 31, p. 67.

[33] See WTO Secretariat, *Guide to the Uruguay Round Agreements* (London: Kluwer, 1999), p. 176.

[34] K. Nicolaidis and J. Trachtman, "From Policed Regulation to Managed Recognition in GATS", in P. Sauve and R. Stern (eds), *GATS 2000: New Directions in Services Trade Liberalization* (Washington, DC: Brookings Institution Press, 2000), p. 255.

does not define the concept of prudential carve-out, or clearly identify the distance between the carve-out and GATS obligations, so there is much room for members to maneuver. So far, no international prudential standards with binding force exist. For example, the principles issued by the Basel Committee on Banking Supervision, the International Organization of Securities Commissions (IOSCO) and the like are all largely voluntary in nature.

### 8.3.4. *The World Trade Organization and International Financial Regulatory Standards*

It can be argued that there should be a direct relationship between international financial regulatory standards and financial services liberalization via the prudential carve-out. For instance, GATS Article VII:5 states:

> Wherever appropriate, recognition should be based on multilaterally agreed criteria. In appropriate cases, Members shall work in cooperation with relevant intergovernmental and non-governmental organizations towards the establishment and adoption of common *international standards and criteria* for recognition and common *international standards* for the practice of relevant services trades and professions. (emphases added)

It must be noted that the role of international standards in the aforementioned provision should not be exaggerated to be as important as international standards directly applicable to the service trade. GATS Article VII:5 only provides members shall make efforts "towards the establishment and adoption of common international standards and criteria". Therefore, international standards, if any, cannot be directly applied to trade in services under the legal framework of the GATS. There must be a process of "establishment and adoption", which means it is necessary to have multilateral negotiations on the application of international standards in the GATS. Even if GATS VII:5 generally applies to the Annex on Financial Services, there is no legal position of international standards in determining whether a measure is prudential or not.

Some may invoke GATS VI:5(b) as supporting the legal authority of international standards in service trade. It reads[35]:

> In determining whether a Member is in conformity with the obligation under paragraph 5 (a), account shall be taken of international standards of relevant international organizations applied by that Member.

---

[35] The footnote of this paragraph states that "relevant international organizations" refers to international bodies whose membership is open to the relevant bodies of at least all members of the WTO.

This paragraph indeed emphasises the role of international standards in domestic regulation related to trade in services and it seems also to be a general obligation because it is in Part II of the GATS (General Obligations and Disciplines).

Overall, therefore, there is no clear legal basis for relating international financial standards and the WTO agreements. Further, so far, many members think that there is no need to define the prudential carve-out contained in the Annex on Financial Services.[36] The result is that, at present, the exact scope of the prudential carve-out and its relation (if any) to international financial standards remain unclear and subject to on-going discussion.

## 8.4. FINANCIAL INTERMEDIARY ACTIVITIES AND FINANCIAL CONGLOMERATES

As an economy's financial sector develops and its banks and other financial intermediaries develop in sophistication, inevitably questions will arise concerning cross-sectoral financial activities and financial conglomerates.

Financial conglomerates, common throughout emerging, transition and developing as well as developed (since the United States abandoned strict separation under the Glass-Steagall banking legislation in 1999) economies (a notable exception is China, where such entities are currently prohibited), present special concerns due to their conjunction of banking, securities and insurance activities and the differing regulatory rationales for each.

### 8.4.1. *International Standards*

The Joint Forum on Financial Conglomerates (Joint Forum), in which the Basel Committee, IOSCO and International Association of Insurance Supervisors (IAIS) participate, is presently developing a framework for the supervision of financial conglomerates and for the exchange of supervisory information.

The Joint Forum was established in early 1996 under the aegis of the Basel Committee, IOSCO and IAIS to take forward the work of the Tripartite Group, whose report was released in July 1995. The Joint Forum is composed of bank, insurance and securities supervisors from thirteen countries[37]; the European Commission participates as an observer.

Currently, the Joint Forum has developed the following principles, which form a compendium[38]: Capital Adequacy Principles, Fit and Proper Principles,

---

[36] See S/FIN/W/16, para.4, 3 Nov. 2000.

[37] Australia, Belgium, Canada, France, Germany, Italy, Japan, The Netherlands, Spain, Sweden, Switzerland, United Kingdom, United States.

[38] Joint Forum on Financial Conglomerates (Joint Forum), *Supervision of Financial Conglomerates*, Feb. 1999 as updated.

Framework for Supervisory Information Sharing, Principles for Supervisory Information Sharing, Coordinator Guidance, Risk Concentrations Principles, and Intra-group Transactions and Exposures Principles.

These requirements will be relevant to most economies (developed, emerging, developing and transition), given the general trend towards legislation permitting universal banking and the provision of a range of financial services, a development connected to common legal attributes of many EU Member States and aspirants and increasingly to developments in the United States.

The Financial Stability Forum (FSF) framework does not include a key standard addressing regulation and supervision of financial conglomerates, however, the FSF Compendium does include a number of other standards in this area. These are grouped under two subheadings: (1) general supervision and (2) risk management. General supervision includes one standard[39], while risk management addresses intra-group transactions and exposures[40] and risk concentration.[41]

### 8.4.2. *Addressing Financial Conglomerates*

As a general matter, countries around the world have adopted four primary structures for addressing cross-sectoral financial intermediary activities and financial conglomerates: (1) universal banking, (2) strict sectoral separation, (3) financial holding companies or (4) parent/subsidiary structure.

Under the universal banking structure, financial intermediaries are allowed to conduct any sort of financial activity without any need for separately capitalized and/or regulated subsidiaries. Under the strict sectoral separation model, financial intermediaries are only allowed to undertake financial activities within the sector in which they are authorized: banks and banking, insurance, and so on. Cross-sectoral activities are not permitted. Under a financial holding company model, an umbrella company – a financial holding company – may be established which, in turn, may own subsidiary financial intermediaries which undertake activities within individual financial sectors. The financial holding company is a separate company from the individual subsidiaries and does not undertake financial activities directly. Under the parent/subsidiary model, a parent financial intermediary (for example, a bank or an insurance company) may establish separate subsidiaries to undertake financial activities in other sectors.

---

[39] Id.
[40] Joint Forum, *Intra-Group Transactions and Exposure Principles*, Dec. 1999.
[41] Joint Forum, *Risk Concentration Principles*, Dec. 1999.

At this time, there is no general consensus concerning which model is the best. Likewise, there is a direct relationship between the model chosen for financial intermediaries and financial conglomerates and a given country's financial regulatory structure.

In addition to cross-sectoral financial activities and intermediary structure, a second question arises as to whether financial intermediaries should be permitted to undertake nonfinancial business. For example:

- Should banks be allowed to undertake nonfinancial business other than banking business? Should universal banks be allowed to undertake nonfinancial business as well as financial business?
- Should financial holding companies be allowed to have nonfinancial subsidiaries as well as financial intermediary subsidiaries?
- Should holding companies be allowed to own financial holding companies as well as other nonfinancial business?

At present, there is no general international consensus concerning whether or not financial intermediaries and financial holding companies should be restricted to financial business. At the same time, there is no general consensus regarding whether nonfinancial companies should be able to own financial intermediaries or financial holding companies.

The main considerations that arise in this context are therefore a country's regulatory structure and supervisory capacity, as well as the level of sophistication within its financial sector.

## 8.5. FINANCIAL REGULATORY STRUCTURE

As financial product and service innovation and financial intermediary activities develop and increase in sophistication, countries around the world must address a second level consideration relating to the overall structure of financial regulation and supervision.

This second concern relates to regulatory structure – one which links directly to financial structure. Around the world, in recent years, there has been a growing concern regarding financial regulatory structure in individual economies and especially in regard to the appropriateness of existing arrangements in the face of globalization, the development of financial conglomerates and the blurring of lines among traditional financial sectors (banking, insurance and securities) and products.

Two sets of events have brought these concerns into the limelight. First, the new Labour government in the United Kingdom, immediately after coming to power in 1997, announced two major changes: formalizing the independence of the Bank of England in setting monetary policy and establishing a single financial regulatory authority, the Financial Services Authority (FSA), including removal of responsibility for banking regulation from the Bank of England. Second, in the wake of the Asian financial crisis in 1997–98, a number of countries, notably South Korea and Japan, have reviewed their financial regulatory systems and structures in order to avoid similar situations in the future. In addition, a variety of other countries have reorganized their regulatory structures in order to address the challenges of the changing financial landscape, including Australia, Germany, France and China.

In most countries, the financial sector has undergone major changes in recent years. Deregulation, liberalization and rapid technological innovation have allowed financial intermediaries to offer an increasing variety of financial products and services, blurring the traditional frontiers among banking, securities and insurance sectors. Moreover, in order to remain competitive in the global marketplace, financial intermediaries have acquired or merged with other domestic or foreign financial intermediaries, giving rise to a large number of financial conglomerates. These developments in the financial services industry pose enormous challenges to national supervisory authorities, since risks have become more difficult to monitor, not just because financial intermediaries tend to be larger and more complex, but also because they operate in an increasing number of national jurisdictions.

In response to these challenges, countries are exploring ways to ensure adequate regulation and supervision of financial conglomerates (discussed earlier). As part of the efforts to improve the supervision of financial conglomerates, an increasing number of countries are adopting integrated supervision either by creating a single regulator for the entire financial sector industry or by merging two of the main supervisory authorities (such as banking with insurance or, alternatively, banking with securities). In addition, other countries have made changes to address the growth of financial conglomerates, for example, the United States, while retaining traditional sectoral regulatory structures.

This section aims to outline the challenges posed by the changing nature of financial markets and the growing importance of financial conglomerates and the implications for rules and supervisory arrangements. The section neither favours nor discourages integrated regulatory structures. Integrated supervision may work well in some countries, but not in others. Specifically, this section reflects useful lessons for countries exploring the possibility of restructuring and/or unifying their regulatory agencies in the future, analysing the advantages and disadvantages of merging supervisory agencies and the challenges faced by policy makers.[42]

Overall, a number of lessons have emerged. First, countries must examine carefully the advantages and disadvantages of any possible change, including the risks inherent in the change process itself. Second, a number of basic models or structures are possible: the traditional sectoral model (with separate regulators for each financial sector, namely banking, securities and insurance, often combined with strict separation or holding company structures for financial conglomerates); the functional model (with separate regulators for each regulatory function – for example, financial stability, prudential, market conduct and competition regulation – catering to financial conglomerates and product innovation); and the integrated structure (with one or more sectors and/or functions combined in a single agency, often combined with a universal banking model for financial services provision). It cannot be taken for granted that a model is, per se, better than any other; it depends very much on the particular circumstances of the country concerned. The third lesson is that there is an important relationship among regulatory structure (and attendant financial and human resources), financial structure (the relative importance of banking, insurance and capital markets and the level of financial development or repression) and the structure of financial intermediaries (e.g., strict separation of financial sectors versus universal banking).

A number of conclusions may be suggested. First, financial regulatory structure is an important issue. However, the first order of consideration must be to develop the underlying infrastructure (legal and otherwise) necessary to support the development of finance and to develop regulatory and supervisory capacity in line with international standards and within a system of clear objectives, independence and accountability.

With this in mind, the second clear conclusion is that regulatory structure must be designed to coincide with an economy's financial structure. There must be full coverage of the intermediaries (especially financial conglomerates), functions and risks inherent in a given financial system and done in a manner that coincides with the history, culture and legal system of that economy. An additional risk involves financial structure and regulatory design ("financial and regulatory mismatch"). In this respect, the risk is that a jurisdiction's financial regulatory structure will not equate with the structure of its financial sector, that is, financial intermediaries will be organized on a basis

---

[42] See generally D. Arner and J. Lin (eds), *Financial Regulation: A Guide to Structural Reform* (Hong Kong: Sweet & Maxwell Asia, 2003).

which is not appropriately addressed by the regulatory structure. In such circumstances, it is possible that significant risks may develop through financial intermediary operations which are not supervised by the existing structure. For example, in a strict separation financial system, informal financial groups may develop, which in turn are not regulated on a group basis, but only on a sectoral institutional basis, leaving the financial system exposed to the risks of the "group".

Further, coordination and cooperation are essential among all of the various authorities in an economy responsible for financial regulation. The final conclusion is that the restructuring process itself carries risks and must be carefully considered and conducted in order to avoid worsening the existing situation.

As a general matter, countries around the world have adopted four general structures of financial regulation and supervision: (1) single regulator, (2) sectoral regulation, (3) functional regulation or (4) institutional regulation.

Under the single regulator structure, a country has a single financial regulator responsible for all aspects of the financial system and financial supervision. This model works well with universal banking but can also work with other structures of financial intermediary activities and financial conglomerates.

Under the sectoral regulation model, a country has separate regulators for each financial sector (typically, banking, securities and insurance). This model works best with a system of strict sectoral separation of financial intermediary activities. It is also often used in countries which have adopted the financial holding company model or the parent/subsidiary model. It does not work well with universal banking models.

Under the functional regulation model, a country has separate regulators responsible for major regulatory functions. The purest example requires separate regulators responsible for (1) financial stability regulation, (2) prudential regulation of financial intermediary safety and soundness, (3) financial market conduct and (4) competition. Today, financial stability regulation and prudential regulation are often combined in a single agency, with a separate agency responsible for financial market conduct (the "twin peaks" approach). This model can work with any model of financial intermediary activities and financial conglomerates.

Under the institutional regulation model, all activities of a given type of financial intermediary are regulated by one regulator. In the most common structure resulting from the special systemic risks posed by banks and banking, all activities of banks, whether financial or nonfinancial, whether cross-sectoral or not, are regulated by the banking regulator. In most cases, this will be extended to the context of any company owning a bank, so for instance, if an insurance company owns a bank, then the banking regulator would then regulate all activities of the insurance company as well.

Once again, there is no general consensus as this time which model is best. The fundamental issue is tailoring a country's financial regulatory structure to its own circumstances and especially its structure for addressing financial intermediary activities and financial conglomerates.

In looking at financial regulatory structure, the emphasis is therefore on appropriately structured regulators and supervisors – regardless of the overall structure implemented in a given context. Recent research supports the importance of appropriate governance structures in this respect. Specifically, Udaibur Das, Marc Quintyn and Kina Chenard have shown[43]:

> [R]egulatory governance has a significant influence on financial system soundness, along with … macroeconomic conditions, the structure of the banking system, and the quality of political institutions and public sector governance. The results also indicate that good public sector governance amplifies the impact of regulatory governance on financial soundness.

### 8.5.1. *International Standards*

Governments, in addition to the agency responsible for monetary policy (the central bank for purposes of the IMF's Monetary and Financial Policy [MFP] Transparency Code [discussed previously in Chapter Four]), also include one or more agencies responsible for other financial policies[44], defined in the Code as "financial agencies", which refers to[45]:

> … the institutional arrangements for the regulation, supervision, and oversight of the financial and payment systems, including markets and institutions, with the view to promoting financial stability, market efficiency, and client-asset and consumer protection.

This terminology therefore governs both the agency responsible for financial stability at the macro level (which this author argues should be the central

---

[43] U. Das, M. Quintyn and K. Chenard, "Does Regulatory Governance Matter for Financial System Stability? An Empirical Analysis", IMF Working Paper WP/04/89 (May 2004), p. 1.

[44] "Financial policies" are defined as "policies related to the regulation, supervision, and oversight of the financial and payment systems, including markets and institutions, with the view to promoting financial stability, market efficiency, and client-asset and consumer protection." IMF, *Code of Good Practices on Transparency in Monetary and Financial Policies*, Jul. 1999 ("MFP Transparency Code"), p. 18.

[45] Id.

bank) as well as any other financial regulatory and/or supervisory authorities (which may or may not be within the central bank; these issues are discussed further in Chapter Ten). In addition, the MFP Transparency Code is relevant for other agencies responsible for financial sector policies not specifically addressed, perhaps including the ministry of finance or other agency responsible for financial development policy.[46]

Similar to the guidance for central bank transparency in monetary policy, the MFP Transparency Code addresses four areas of good transparency practices for financial policies by financial agencies: (1) clarity of roles, responsibilities and objectives (Part V); (2) process for formulating and reporting financial policies (Part VI); (3) public availability of information on financial policies (Part VIII); and (4) accountability and assurances of integrity (Part VIII).

In respect to clarity of roles, responsibilities and objectives, the broad objective(s) and institutional framework of financial agencies should be clearly defined, preferably through legislation or regulation (section 5.1). Relationships between financial agencies should be publicly disclosed (section 5.2)[47], especially with respect to payment systems (section 5.3) and self-regulatory agencies (elsewhere usually described as self-regulatory organizations or SROs) (section 5.4), with any such SROs guided by the same practices as financial agencies (section 5.5).

With respect to formulation and reporting of financial policies, conduct should be transparent and compatible with confidentiality and effectiveness considerations (section 6.1), with significant changes announced and explained (section 6.2), performance in meeting objectives reported (section 6.3) and the public consulted with respect to regulatory changes (section 6.4).

With respect to public availability of information, financial agencies should issue periodic public reports on major developments (section 7.1) and financial agency financial condition (section 7.3), as part of a public information service (section 7.4). In addition to consultation, directives and guidelines should be publicly available (section 7.5). Further, information on client and consumer protection arrangements should be publicly disclosed (sections 7.6 and 7.7).

With respect to accountability and integrity, financial agency officials should appear before a designated public authority (section 8.1). In addition, financial agencies should publish audited financial statements if applicable (sections 8.2

---

[46] IMF, *Supporting Document to the Code of Good Practices on Transparency in Monetary and Financial Policies*, Jul. 2000, part 1, p. 9.

[47] The wider term appears more relevant here in that relationships between financial regulatory authorities and other financial agencies should be clear.

and 8.3). Integrity standards and any legal protections for financial agency officials and staff should be publicly disclosed (section 8.4).

## 8.5.2. *Developing Effective Financial Authorities*

As noted earlier, regulatory and supervisory authorities need to have an adequate degree of operational autonomy, different government agencies must understand their respective roles in the financial regulatory system, there should exist arrangements for these agencies to coordinate and cooperate effectively, and they need to have the necessary tools to use.

In general, there are a number of essential prerequisites which any financial authority should meet if it is to have a reasonable likelihood of success.[48] The following is an indicative set of features that constitute an effective structure[49]: (1) clear objectives[50], (2) independence and accountability[51], (3) adequate resources, (4) effective enforcement powers[52], (5) comprehensiveness[53], (6) cost efficient regulation[54], and (7) effectiveness criteria and industry structure.[55]

Institutional design of a system of financial authorities requires careful consideration. All functions could be placed in a single institution (i.e., the ministry of finance or the central bank). More usually, however, various functions are divided among several authorities.

When a single organization performs all of the safety-net functions, the smooth resolution of potential tensions is dependent on clarity of mandates and an adequate accountability regime among the relevant departments. However, when the functions are assigned to different organizations, issues related to information sharing, allocation of powers and responsibilities, and coordination of actions among the different functions are more complex and need to be addressed clearly and explicitly.[56]

In respect to the actual roles of the various financial authorities, as a general principle, the more the roles can be kept pure and kept apart, the better it is. They need their scarce supervisory resources and expertise to exercise strong

---

[48] R. Abrams and M. Taylor, "Issues in the Unification of Financial Sector Supervision", IMF Working Paper WP/oo/213 (Dec. 2000), p. 5 (citing Basel Core Principle 1 & IMF, MFP Transparency Code).

[49] See id., pp. 6–9.

[50] See IMF, MFP Transparency Code, op. cit., n. 44, Part V.

[51] Id., Part VIII.

[52] Abrams and Taylor, op. cit., n. 48, p. 7.

[53] Id., p. 8.

[54] Id.

[55] Id.

[56] FSF, *Guidance for Developing Effective Deposit Insurance Systems*, Sep. 2001, p. 45.

supervision – and this is particularly needed in a systemic crisis situation. The central bank should focus on its functions of monetary and financial stability, especially providing liquidity, including lender of last resort, and on ensuring that large value payment systems function without problems. In all those cases when taxpayers' money is put at risk, there should be a governmental decision because only the government may tax, with the recommendation under the remit of the ministry of finance or equivalent. Practical considerations may also lead to the establishment of a separate financial intermediary (most common in the context of banks) support authority, because it may be deemed efficient to have this function outside the ministry of finance, the central bank and the supervisory authority.

**Financial Regulator(s) and Supervisor(s).** Institutional structure of financial sector supervision is a second order issue, to be considered once the various conditions for effective regulation are in place.[57] To be effective, the structure of the regulatory system needs to reflect the structure of the markets that are regulated.[58]

Theory and practice are converging on the view that independent regulatory agencies offer the most adequate solution to the need for good regulatory governance.[59] As a general matter, whether the regulator/supervisor is located within the central bank or elsewhere depends upon individual country circumstances. Regardless, however, it should be "autonomous" – financially, operationally, and so on; accountable; transparent; and efficient (qualified efficacy) in respect to both regulation and supervision, although regulation – essentially regulation of general application – can (should) be shared with the central bank and other appropriate agencies.

Sufficiently flexible powers are necessary in order to effect an efficient resolution of problems in financial intermediaries. Where problems are remediable, supervisors will normally seek to identify and implement solutions that fully address their concerns; where they are not, the prompt and orderly exit of intermediaries that are no longer able to meet supervisory requirements is a necessary part of an efficient financial system.[60]

These powers should include, as a minimum, the ability to require information from regulated firms, to assess the competence and probity of senior

---

[57] Abrams and Taylor, op. cit., n. 48, p. 3.
[58] Id.
[59] M. Quintyn and M. Taylor, "Regulatory and Supervisory Independence and Financial Stability", IMF Working Paper WP/02/46 (Mar. 2002), p. 8.
[60] Basel Committee on Banking Supervision, *Core Principles for Effective Banking Supervision*, Sep. 1997, p. 12.

management and the owners of the intermediary, and to take appropriate graduated sanctions against failure to comply with regulatory rules, including having
the ultimate power to intervene in the intermediary if necessary. Ideally, the
regulatory authority should have the ability to revoke licenses to conduct financial services business. However, in some countries, this may not be compatible
with constitutional provisions that require a strict separation of executive and
judicial functions. In the latter case, the authority should have the ability to
make recommendations on the revocation of licenses, with the decision taker
required to give reasons in the event that the authority's recommendation is
not adopted. Enforcement powers are likely to remain more effective if the
regulator has the ability to amend them quickly: for this reason, it is generally
preferable to set out only the broad framework of the regulatory agency's powers in legislation, leaving the details to be filled in by directives and guidelines
that can be issued and amended by the regulatory agency itself.[61]

Decisions respecting intervention should be independent yet accountable
and reviewable (in most cases ex post, with damages as the appropriate remedy).

Decisions regarding restructuring (individual cases) versus resolution (based
on viability) and decisions regarding specific form of resolution (based on the
principle of least cost resolution in the context of minimizing systemic implications) should both be taken at the consumer protection agency with participation of the ministry of finance, central bank, relevant financial supervisor(s)
and depositor protection agency.

The supervisor can be involved in resolutions that require a takeover by
or merger with a healthier intermediary. When all other measures fail, the
supervisor should have the ability to close or assist in the closing of an
unhealthy intermediary in order to protect the overall stability of the financial
system.[62]

The supervisory agency should be responsible for, or assist in, the orderly
exit of problem financial intermediaries (in coordination with any applicable deposit insurance agency or other authority responsible for consumer
protection).[63]

### 8.5.3. *Coordination Among Financial Authorities*

In systems with more than one financial authority, the supervisor will need
to coordinate actions with other authorities, for example, the government, the

---

[61] Abrams and Taylor, op. cit., n. 48, p. 7.
[62] Basel Committee, op. cit., n. 60, p. 39.
[63] Id., p. 12.

central bank, operators of payment and settlement systems, deposit insurers and other domestic supervisory agencies and their foreign counterparts.[64] On the domestic level, there should be a legal basis for the information exchange with other agencies. Similarly, on the international level, regulators should be able to receive and exchange information with foreign counterparts. Ideally, the terms of such understandings should be laid down in a reciprocal arrangement between the regulators, for example, in the form of a memorandum of understanding or an exchange of letters. Under the principles of consolidated supervision, information tends to flow from the host supervisor to the home supervisor and not in the opposite direction. Host supervisors, however, also have a right to be kept informed on matters affecting particular intermediaries with an office in the host territory and will also wish to be notified by the home supervisor of significant matters affecting a parent firm or head office. If a home supervisor intends to take action to protect the interests of customers, such action should be coordinated with the host supervisors of the intermediary's foreign establishments to the extent possible.[65]

### 8.5.4. *Access to Reliable and Current Information*

Financial reporting is the Achilles' heel of the financial supervisor. Without adequate information about a financial intermediary's noncompliance with prudential standards, the supervisor will not be able to order corrective action as and when needed. In addition, market discipline depends on timely and adequate reports on the financial condition of financial intermediaries.

It is a primary role of the supervisor to constantly obtain accurate and current information from the entities subject to its supervision. Once problems in a financial intermediary come to the supervisor's attention, the first issue will be to determine the facts concerning the financial position of the intermediary concerned. To this end, the supervisor must have the necessary information to make informed decisions on the appropriate strategy to deal with the problem at hand. Auditing requirements, along with a variety of reporting obligations both of financial intermediaries and their auditors, should ensure that the regulator is well-informed at all times. In addition, the supervisor must have the right to access all information and have the power to conduct unscheduled on-site examinations or investigations or to have third parties, for example,

---

[64] See Basel Committee, *Supervisory Guidance for Dealing with Weak Banks*, Mar. 2002, ss. 100–1.
[65] See Basel Committee, *Information Flows Between Banking Supervisory Authorities (Supplement to the Concordat)*, Apr. 1990.

auditing firms, conduct on-site examinations. Regulators should have unfettered access to reports and all other documents issued by the internal control and audit functions. Supervisors should have the legal power to require financial intermediaries to report all relevant data, with sanctions available to punish deficient, incorrect or late submissions of returns.[66] In addition to financial information, the supervisor must have rapid access to a wide range of relevant nonfinancial information about the financial intermediary, including organization and legal structure and information regarding participation in the payments system. The supervisor may have an understanding with intermediaries that information subject to frequent change be kept at the intermediary, but at all times accessible to the supervisor.

---

[66] Basel Committee, op. cit., n. 64, s. 47.

# PART FOUR

# LOOKING FORWARD

# 9

# The International Financial Architecture

This volume began with a question: how can economies prevent financial crises and support financial development and economic growth? The preceding parts and chapters have looked at the international response to this question: the system of international standards for financial stability which has become an important component of the international financial architecture. The volume has sought to show that law is important for financial stability and development. The preceding pages have also sought to draw in recent research on the role of law and institutions in order to highlight how economies can work towards not only financial stability but also financial development, both in order to support economic growth. This part looks to issues which remain and recommends approaches to address financial stability and development at the domestic, regional and international levels.

The part begins by looking at the international financial architecture in Chapter Nine, focusing on the twin objectives of financial stability and financial development to support economic growth.

First, we turn to the system of international financial standards. While the system is definitely a major step in the development of the international financial architecture, certain issues remain unaddressed. First, the existing framework focuses on financial stability. As this volume has sought to demonstrate, the system should address both financial stability and financial development. In addition to including certain other specific areas (noted in the preceding chapters), in order to better address the needs of emerging, transition and developing economies, both the standards themselves and the supporting framework for implementation and monitoring should incorporate development issues explicitly. This probably has the greatest relevance for the World Bank and the regional development banks. Second, the system of standards should also include guidance on competition in the financial sector, both domestic and foreign. Foreign competition is already addressed by the World Trade Organization (WTO) financial services framework and should be integrated into the existing system.

Following this analysis of the system of international financial standards, Chapter Ten turns to the international financial architecture and asks whether the existing structures are appropriate to the changed needs of the international financial system. First, as noted in Chapter Two, the international financial architecture as it currently exists does not yet deal with the issue of crisis resolution. This is an area which merits further attention. Second, as noted previously, the international financial architecture as designed does not integrate its various components in as coherent a manner as the Bretton Woods system. This is an important issue, especially given the link between financial crises and financial liberalization and also the link between finance and trade. The international financial architecture should focus on the issue of integration into the global financial markets and related sequencing. The experience of the European Union is instructive in this regard and is discussed in further detail in Chapter Ten in the context of regional financial stability and development.

## 9.1. INTERNATIONAL STANDARDS AND CODES

In the second chapter, this volume introduced the primary international response to the financial crises around the world at the end of the twentieth century: the system of international standards for sound financial systems. The following chapters have looked in more detail at the standards themselves. This system of standards is perhaps the only major development in the international financial architecture to result from the many discussions of whether there is a need for a "new international financial architecture". The system of international financial standards is certainly an important development and one that has many implications for individual economies, regional arrangements and the international financial architecture. Nonetheless, though significant, a number of weaknesses remain in the existing system. A number of these have already been noted in Chapter Two (e.g., enhancement of the role of the Financial Stability Forum [FSF], improvement of the quality of the FSF Compendium, and formalizing the standard selection and setting process); others have been noted in the intervening chapters (e.g., addressing foundations and underpinnings, as well as certain additional areas such as corruption). This section highlights these issues along with one specific area that merits greater attention in the entire system of standards, namely financial development and economic growth.

### 9.1.1. *International Standards and Codes and Financial Stability*

In 2005, the International Monetary Fund (IMF) and the World Bank released a comprehensive assessment of their experiences with international standards and codes.[1] This review concluded, first, that there were many benefits from the initiative, especially for member authorities; and second, that there was no strong reason to modify or expand coverage beyond the twelve existing areas but that certain improvements could be made in other aspects. Specifically, the Bank and the Fund proposed to:

(1) focus efforts on helping members to strengthen institutions and use the initiative to inform other work;
(2) encourage country participation;
(3) adopt a flexible approach to updates, basically following a five-year cycle;
(4) include a clear executive summary, a principle-by-principle summary of observance and a prioritized list of main recommendations in each Report on the Observance of Standards and Codes (ROSC); and
(5) collect information on observance of standards more systematically to facilitate prioritization of assessments, management of progress towards observance of standards, and cross-country analysis.

Further, the Fund is to institute a process to identify areas of macroeconomic relevance and enhance mechanisms to reflect recommendations into technical assistance prioritization, while the Bank is to implement a multi-step plan to enhance ROSC follow-up. In respect to the latter, the Bank will develop detailed follow-up actions plans, including technical assistance needs, assigning responsibility to coordinate responsibility for assimilating recommendations into work programs, helping members identify and arrange necessary implementation assistance, and implementing a process for monitoring progress.[2]

In addition to the joint report, in 2006, the Fund released an evaluation of the Financial Sector Assessment Program (FSAP) by its Independent Evaluation Office (IEO)[3], and the Bank released a similar evaluation by its Independent Evaluation Group (IEG).[4]

---

[1] IMF and World Bank, *The Standards and Codes Initiative – Is It Effective? And How Can It Be Improved?* Jul. 2005; see IMF, *The Standards and Codes Initiative – Is It Effective? And How Can It Be Improved?: Background Paper*, Jul. 2005.

[2] Id., p. 30.

[3] IMF IEO, *Report on the Evaluation of the Financial Sector Assessment Program*, Jan. 2006.

[4] World Bank IEG, *Financial Sector Assessment Program: IEG Review of the Joint World Bank and IMF Initiative*, May 2006.

Overall, the Fund IEO concluded the FSAP was significant and effective in the context of the Fund's mandate, and made seven recommendations focusing on three themes: (1) reconsidering incentives for participation, clarifying priorities and strengthening the links with surveillance; (2) steps to maintain and strengthen further the quality of the FSAP and organizational changes within the IMF; and (3) the working of the joint IMF-World Bank approach.

Recommendations included prioritizing and strengthening financial sector surveillance, including the FSAP, mainstreaming FSAPs and follow-up work into regular IMF surveillance activities, maintaining the joint approach but giving the Bank the lead in cases in which financial sector development issues predominate with the Fund leading where significant domestic or global financial stability issues exist, and establishing a clearer mechanism for follow-up technical assistance coordination involving the Bank and other providers.

Significantly, these recommendations were supported in the context of the Fund's Medium-Term Strategy.[5]

Similar to the Fund's IEO, the Bank's IEG concluded, overall:

(1) The quality of the diagnostics has been good, although uneven across sectors.
(2) Country authorities have found the FSAP useful.
(3) FSAP recommendations need to be better integrated into Bank programs.
(4) Country selection needs to better reflect surveillance priorities and the likelihood of financial sector reform.
(5) The scope of assessment must be more tailored to the specific needs of the country.
(6) The program must do a better job of keeping the Executive Board informed in a timely manner, as well as coordinating with other partners.

Unfortunately, it is unclear at present whether or how these conclusions and recommendations will be implemented into World Bank work although there appears to be a strong need and valid rationale for so doing.

### 9.1.2. *Integrating Development with Financial Stability*

The first two chapters of this volume sought to demonstrate the significance of the financial sector for economic growth. Specifically, the financial sector can have both a positive and a negative impact on economic development. First,

---

[5] IMF, *Standards and Codes – Implementing the Fund's Medium-Term Strategy and the Recommendations of the 2005 Review of the Initiative*, Jun. 2006.

financial crises around the world have had devastating effects on economic growth in developed, emerging, transition and developing economies. The system of international standards for sound financial systems is a direct response to the destructiveness of financial crises. Second, the financial sector supports economic growth through facilitating allocation of financial resources, with finance providing the support for the exploitation of technology and human capital. Therefore, the financial sector can have a very positive role to play both in economic growth and in facilitating economic development. Significant research has now been done both on this general relationship and also on a number of specific elements across the financial sector. However, at present, the system of international financial standards, while beginning to do so, has not yet taken sufficient account of development needs and opportunities.[6]

In looking at development issues today, the consensus view is expressed through the Millennium Development Goals (MDGs).[7] All the various international institutions have, to some extent, taken account of these goals in pursuing their respective mandates. In addition, these goals have begun to filter through to the system of international financial standards. Specifically, the IMF has already taken steps to incorporate many of the indicators in the Special Data Dissemination Standard and the General Data Dissemination System. In addition, due to their focus on poverty alleviation, the World Bank and the Asian Development Bank consider these issues across their various activities, including in the financial sector. The World Bank also is beginning to use the FSAP/ROSC process to highlight developmental needs and to support its overall efforts in the financial sector.

This sort of activity needs to be increased. In addition, beyond financial stability issues, the standards and their evaluation process need to further incorporate developmental issues. At present, neither the standards nor the evaluation process is designed with developmental issues in mind. As standards are revised, greater account should be taken of their use in development. Further, the evaluation process should be extended beyond assessment of financial stability to assessment of financial stability and development. This sort of assessment would logically fall to the World Bank. However, it should also incorporate the various regional development banks and involve the bilateral aid agencies. If this were to take place, financial sector development assessments could play a

---

[6] See IMF and World Bank, *Development Issues in the FSAP*, Feb. 2003.

[7] United Nations, *United Nations Millennium Declaration*, General Assembly Resolution 55/2, 8 Sep. 2000. See UN General Assembly, Fifty-sixth Session, *Road Map Towards the Implementation of the United Nations Millennium Declaration: Report of the Secretary General*, A/56/326, 6 Sep. 2001. See also www.developmentgoals.org.

major role in directing the efforts of individual economies and the multilateral and bilateral aid providers to greater effectiveness in the financial sector.

## 9.2. IMPROVING THE INTERNATIONAL FINANCIAL ARCHITECTURE

The second chapter discussed the basic components of the international financial architecture as designed under Bretton Woods, as it operated in practice and the major changes that have taken place since the fiftieth anniversary of the IMF and World Bank in 1994. While some of these changes are significant (i.e., the system of international standards for financial stability), the discussions about whether there is a need for a new international financial architecture to deal with the changed nature of the international financial and economic system have not produced any real results (except for the development of international standards for financial stability and the creation of the WTO in 1994, which predated discussions of the "new international financial architecture" and was essentially an independent development, stemming originally from the Bretton Woods idea of the International Trade Organization).

Unfortunately, the (non-)system that has emerged, while detailing the supporting institutional components necessary for financial stability, is not a coherent structure, designed to meet clear overriding objectives, in the manner of Bretton Woods or the single market project of the European Union (discussed in Chapter Ten). Further, it neither addresses the risks inherent in the liberalization process under the WTO/General Agreement on Trade in Services (GATS)/financial services process nor the resolution of financial crises.

### 9.2.1. *International Institutions, Financial Stability and Financial Development*

At the political level (represented by the various "Group of..." or Gs such as the G-7, G-10, G-20, etc.), the clearest need is to improve the representativeness of the most influential grouping, the G-7/G-8, by bringing in the major emerging economies. In this context, the logical additions would be China, Brazil, India and South Africa. Significantly, the creation of the G-20 largely reflects this objective. Importantly, the G-20 is beginning to take more active leadership role in financial sector issues (reflecting its financially focused composition). With luck, future chairs of the G-20 will continue this trend, possibly with the eventual result of the G-20 largely supplanting the G-7 and G-10 in international financial matters. Further, the G-20 parallels the wider technocratic membership of the FSF, providing a natural political parallel to the technocratic role of the FSF while at the same time making up a majority of the voting quotas of the IMF and World Bank (and thereby ensuring implementation of G-20 decisions in at both the technocratic standard setting level and the multilateral institution implementation and monitoring level).

In relation to the international financial institutions (IMF, World Bank and regional development banks) as well as related international institutions (such as the WTO[8] and UN agencies), there is a need to improve coordination and focus, in many ways along the lines suggested for regulatory structure discussed in the previous chapter, with clear objectives and responsibilities. In this regard, it would make sense to bring the WTO (at least as far as its responsibilities for GATS/financial services) into the G-20 and FSF membership. The following sections look to other components of the system of international standards, of which the IMF, World Bank and multilateral development banks are the most significant, with possible suggestions on enhancing their respective roles.

**International Monetary Fund.** In 2005, the IMF published its Medium-Term Strategy, a document considering the future direction of the IMF in light of economic globalization.[9] The IMF concluded that the emergence of new economic powers (e.g., China and India), integrated financial markets, unprecedented capital flows, and new ideas to promote economic development required an updated interpretation of the Fund's mandate as the steward of international financial cooperation and stability. From this basis, the IMF's strategic direction includes the following four main aspects:

(1) making surveillance more effective, focusing on globalization, regional aspects, and standards and codes assessments focused on "macro-criticality";
(2) adapting to new challenges and needs in different members, with differentiated roles in more advanced and less advanced members;
(3) improving internal institutional aspects of the IMF, such as capacity building, organization and budgeting; and
(4) addressing IMF governance issues, especially in relation to quotas.

In relation to differential roles depending on the level of development of members, several aspects are noteworthy. In emerging economies, the focus will be on (1) crisis prevention, (2) crisis resolution and (3) financing

---

[8] The role of the WTO is was discussed in greater detail in the previous chapter in the context of financial liberalization.

[9] IMF, *The Managing Director's Report on the Fund's Medium-Term Strategy*, Sep. 2005.

arrangements. In developing economies, the Fund will focus on macroeco-nomic stability, emphasizing the MDGs, and focused financing instruments, leaving coordination and harmonization to other agencies. In addition, the Fund will expand its work on managing capital account liberalization, focus-ing on sequencing, and on capacity building and institutional reform.

In 2006, the IMF released a report from Rodrigo Rato addressing plans for the IMF's medium-term development, addressing concrete proposals in relation to each area of the Medium-Term Strategy.[10] In addition, the IMF is currently discussing ways in which to improve its representativeness of economic power through changes to quota and related voting structures.

Overall, the IMF should focus on financial stability (as well as monetary stability), leaving financial development issues to the World Bank and regional development banks. Significantly, the Fund appears to be gradually arriving at the same conclusion.

**World Bank.**    In 2006, the World Bank IEG released a major synthesis of evalu-ations of the World Bank's financial sector work from 1993–2005.[11] The report is a synthesis of three underlying evaluations addressing lending[12], technical assis-tance[13] and the FSAP.[14] In addition, findings from a similar report addressing pensions are included where relevant.[15] Overall, the IEG concluded:[16]

> The evaluations found that Bank assistance to the financial sector, both in its lending and nonlending, has contributed to the development of the financial sectors in client countries. The FSAP advanced dialogue with client gov-ernments and provided useful advice and recommendations. Lending has helped to bring about positive changes in governance, regulatory framework, market structure, and efficiency. Overall, and with the important exception of Bank support for [lines of credit], the Bank's presence has helped to catalyze changes in the right direction in the depth and access to credit of financial systems. Nevertheless, financial sectors remain shallow, with narrow access to credit in many, if not most, Bank client countries, and there is room for improvement in the quality and impact of Bank assistance.

---

[10]    IMF, *The Managing Director's Report on Implementing the Fund's Medium-Term Strategy*, Apr. 2006.

[11]    World Bank IEG, *World Bank Assistance to the Financial Sector: A Synthesis of IEG Evaluations*, May 2006.

[12]    World Bank IEG, *World Bank Lending for Lines of Credit: An IEG Evaluation*, May 2006.

[13]    World Bank IEG, *IEG Review of World Bank Assistance for Financial Sector Reform*, Mar. 2006.

[14]    World Bank IEG, *FSAP*, op. cit., n. 4.

[15]    World Bank IEG, *Pension Reform and the Development of Pension Systems: An Evaluation of World Bank Assistance*, Feb. 2006.

[16]    World Bank IEG, *Synthesis*, op. cit., n. 11, p. 29.

In respect to improvements, the report made a number of useful suggestions:

(1) The Bank should focus more on the nonbanking sector (leaving the banking sector to the IMF) and on identifying constraints to credit access through a range of activities, including lending and diagnostic work such as investment climate surveys, poverty assessments and other economic work that could include assessments of access to various types of finance.[17] In other words, the Bank should focus on financial sector development.

(2) Internal Bank guidelines should be prepared for dealing with financial crises, with triggers for actions and clear lines of responsibility (following an unimplemented conclusion following the Mexican financial crisis).[18] Given the decentralized nature of the Bank's organization and work, this would ensure it would be better prepared to deal with emergency situations in a more effective manner.

(3) The overall coherence of Bank work in the financial sector should be improved, with the Financial Sector Network (an internal cross-department virtual group) ensuring that: (a) country strategies incorporate, where relevant, a coherent strategy for the financial sector that draws on the FSAP or other relevant diagnostic work; (2) the sector strategy carries through to lending and nonlending; and (3) quality control exists for lending and nonlending assistance to the financial sector.[19] In other words, the Bank should have a more organized approach to its financial development work, based on the FSAP/ROSC framework.

Overall, these conclusions make complete sense: the World Bank should take the leading role in relation to financial development, working closely with the Fund in the context of the FSAP/ROSC, but taking an expanded, development-focused role. At the same time however the Bank at present is suffering from a lack of direction generally, but especially in regard to its financial sector work. To some extent, this is being alleviated with the International Finance Corporation (the Bank's private sector development arm) increasingly taking on financial sector assistance efforts while leaving research to the Bank.

**Regional Development Banks and UN Agencies.** The regional development banks and UN agencies such as UNCTAD (United Nation Committee on

---

[17] Id., p. viii.

[18] Id.

[19] Id., p. ix.

Trade and Development) and UNDP (United Nations Development Program) have been less involved to date in the FSAP/ROSC process but have and continue to play a significant role in supporting financial development and economic growth. In this context, their efforts should be more closely coordinated with those of the World Bank especially, with a general focus on financial development based on the FSAP/ROSC framework.

### 9.2.2. *Integrating the International Financial Architecture*

This section suggests that the liberalization framework (provided at an international level through the WTO) should be more explicitly linked to the financial stability framework, though at present it is not. Although these issues have not been explicitly linked at the international level, they have, in fact, been so linked through the EU single financial market project (discussed in Chapter Ten), which may, in turn, provide a model for other regional efforts, as well as perhaps for the international financial architecture.

As noted, the international financial architecture today is not integrated to meet the needs of the international financial system. This is most explicit in the context of the relationship between the WTO, IMF and World Bank. In this context, the three would benefit from the creation of a joint committee to deal with issues of common concern (modeled on the original Bretton Woods design and currently operating in the form of the joint IMF-World Bank International Financial and Monetary Committee and Development Committee). There are also lingering, unresolved issues concerning the relationship of the IMF and the World Bank. Perhaps the area where this is clearest today is in the context of financial liberalization and integration.

As can clearly be seen from the preceding pages, law reform cannot be looked at solely in terms of the municipal situation and needs of any given state, whether one of the developed economies or the emerging, transition and developing economies. Today, investment flows to and from all corners of the world with amazing speed and with sometimes dangerous results.[20] In order to acquire the capital necessary for development, countries must look to what can only be described as international or global financial markets

As one aspect of accession to or membership in the WTO and the implementation of the GATS and its annexes respecting financial services, members make numerous commitments with respect to financial services liberalization, addressing, inter alia, banking, securities and insurance activities

---

[20]  See generally D. Arner, "The Mexican Peso Crisis of 1994–95: Implications for the Regulation of Financial Markets", 2 L. & Bus. Rev. Americas 28 (1996).

and intermediaries. Significantly, financial liberalization without appropriate regard for sequencing and adequate prudential safeguards has been a significant precursor to financial crises in economies (developed, emerging, developing and transition) around the world over the past century – and a dominant factor in the last fifteen years. A further central conclusion to emerge from analysis of recent crises is the fundamental role played by institutions, especially law, financial regulation and legal infrastructure, in reducing the risks inherent in financial liberalization.

Therefore, a goal of the international financial architecture should focus on the increased integration of developing, emerging and transition economics into the international financial system. However, integration into the international financial system is not without its dangers and must be based on coherent sequencing of liberalization preceded by the development of an effectively functioning financial system in each country as a necessary first stage.

## 9.3. DEBT AND LIQUIDITY CRISES AND THEIR RESOLUTION

This volume has focused on crisis prevention primarily at the domestic level, albeit as informed by regional and international efforts. It has not dealt with the issue of resolving financial crises when they do occur or with domestic, regional or international efforts to do so. This section briefly mentions one aspect where the international financial architecture requires further adjustment in order to deal with the new type of crisis which is occurring today. While the first strand of discussions of the international financial architecture has focused on crisis prevention, the second major strand of discussion concerning the international financial architecture has focused on the issue of crisis resolution. Unfortunately, while consensus has largely developed in relation to domestic reforms to support financial stability, centred on the system of international standards, similar consensus has not been reached in respect to arrangements to deal with crises which do occur.

### 9.3.1. *Crisis Resolution: An On-Going Debate*

Although it profoundly affects the international financial order and the domestic economy of the country experiencing problems, a debt crisis is simply a breakdown in contractual relations between two parties, namely a debtor and its creditors. If a debtor economy has liquidity problems and cannot meet its debt obligations, the debtor has a number of options, including default, printing money (if the debts are denominated in domestic currency), or restructuring or rescheduling the specific terms of the debt involved. Further, a sovereign debtor usually needs to borrow in order to maintain debt payments and on-going financial operations, even in cases in which debt is rescheduled.[21] In addition, unlike in the context of private parties, insolvency procedures are not available in the sovereign context. The result is that sovereign debt problems differ considerably from those involving only nonsovereign parties.

Debt crises are not new phenomena: in the eighteenth and nineteenth centuries, such crises were relatively common.[22] Debt crises arrive in different ways: in the 1994 Mexican crisis, the local currency was suddenly massively devalued against the US dollar[23], while the 1982 developing country debt crisis was caused by rising interest rates causing the external debt burden to be more expensive while falling commodity prices reduced foreign currency reserves from export earnings.[24] Debt crises may be the result of liquidity crises[25], as well as the result of factors beyond the countries' control, such as the various oil shocks of the 1970s and 1980s.[26]

In circumstances such as the Mexican and Asian financial crises, in which financial markets essentially cease to function in terms of access, markets cannot be relied on to provide necessary liquidity, and for this reason, an international response is probably necessary for the stability of the international and domestic financial systems. During both the Mexican and Asian financial crises, countries were faced with temporary liquidity crises due to a large number of intertwined factors, some the under the control of the country concerned and others not. As a result of these crises and the perceived need to protect the international financial system, some efforts have since been made to address future liquidity crises and attempt to prevent them from causing long-term negative consequences.

An economy can respond to a current account deficit in a number of ways, including: (1) attracting more foreign capital; (2) allowing its currency to depreciate, thus making imports more expensive and exports cheaper; (3) tightening

---

[21] R. Macmillan, "Towards a Sovereign Debt Work-out System", 16 NW. J. Int'l L. & Bus. 57 (1995), ("Macmillan II"), p. 104.

[22] See F. Dawson, *The First Latin American Debt Crisis: The City of London and the 1822–25 Loan Bubble* (New Haven, Yale University Press, 1990), p. 197.

[23] By the end of March 1995, the new peso had fallen by almost 50 per cent in foreign currency terms since the exchange rate was allowed to float in December 1994. IMF, *World Economic Outlook*, Oct. 1995.

[24] See W. Cline, *International Debt Reexamined* (Washington, DC: Institute for International Economics, 1995).

[25] When a country's foreign reserves run low or the cost of its debt increases, debt payments become more difficult. As the problem becomes more serious, lenders become less willing to lend, thereby exacerbating the situation. See Macmillan II, op. cit., n. 21, p. 62.

[26] See Cline, op. cit., n. 24.

monetary/or fiscal policy to reduce the demand for all goods, including imports; and (4) using foreign exchange reserves to cover the deficit. If an economy is unable to correct its current account problems, a liquidity crisis will result in which the country has insufficient reserves to make necessary external payments.

Nations with liquidity problems require new money in order to bridge the problem period and avoid the transition from a temporary liquidity crisis to a more serious debt crisis. There are two obvious sources of new money: first, official sources (such as the other governments and the IMF); and second, private sources, such as investors and banks. During the Mexican and Asian crises, a number of countries tapped official sources, including the United States and the IMF; however, using such sources as the main resource for liquidity is both unsustainable and expensive. New debt issues are unlikely in the climate of a financial crisis, and in fact Mexico was not able to access such sources until six months after the onset of the crisis, and only then because it already had the official backing of the United States and IMF. A six-month delay, however, turns a liquidity crisis into a debt crisis, and makes additional issues even more unlikely than previously.

Finally, commercial banks will lend only if there is some indication that they will, in fact, be repaid by what is, by the very nature of the crisis situation, a risky debtor. If the new money takes priority over the old money, however, commercial banks might, in fact, be induced to lend.[27] The problem, then, is getting creditors to agree to subordinate their outstanding debt to the new money necessary to provide the liquidity to make payments flow again on the outstanding debt. For this reason, some commentators argue that if the underlying problems of debt rescheduling were solved, the necessary requirements for the provision of new money would fall into place, thereby using the solution to potential debt crises to avert future liquidity crises.[28] The suggestion is that rescheduling agreements would be promoted because lenders would be "waiting in the wings to lend".[29]

Three basic changes in the financial environment that have some bearing on the character of potential future sovereign liquidity crises.[30] First, the

---

[27] Macmillan II, op. cit., n. 21, p. 105.

[28] This solution seems to be supported by the G-10. If an agreement to this effect could not be reached, say within 6 months, Macmillan suggests that perhaps legislation of creditor countries could be amended to provide that following a debt rescheduling agreement new debt would take priority over old. Id., p. 106.

[29] Id.

[30] G-10, Group of Ten Working Party, *The Resolution of Sovereign Liquidity Crises*, May 1996, p. 1 ("G-10 Sovereign Crises"), Executive Summary, para. 3.

broader and stronger linkages among domestic and international financial market mean that crises can erupt much more quickly in today's markets and can be far larger in scope than in the past. Second, flows of capital to emerging, transition and even developing economies in the form of purchases of securities have increased greatly in size over the years, especially during the 1990s, substituting for traditional bank lending. At the same time, foreign direct investment (FDI) has increased dramatically in significance over the past fifteen years and will add a new characteristic to future financial crises. Third, when a crisis occurs, new finance is unlikely to be forthcoming from those who provided the original lending, at least in the short term, although private sector capital flows are likely to resume when (or if) confidence returns. At the same time, given the significance of private capital flows, financing available from official sources is less likely to be sufficient to enable a sovereign debtor experiencing a crisis to meet fully its external financing obligations.[31] At the same time, provision of official funds to limit private losses raises serious moral hazard risks and could, in fact, interfere with market discipline.[32] Nonetheless, official financing provided in an effective manner may be sufficient to allow private sector (domestic and international) confidence to return.

Given this background, the next sections provide a brief overview of international responses to the threat of future liquidity crises.

**The IMF Response: Liquidity and Disclosure.** As noted in Chapter Two, principally as a reaction to the sudden and overwhelming nature of the Mexican crisis, world leaders agreed to enhance the emergency funds of the IMF[33], increasing the official lending power of the IMF and enhancing the IMF's capacity as a sort of lender of last resort but at the same time raising moral hazard concerns. As a second response, as noted in Chapters Two and Four, the IMF initiated the SDDS and GDDS for the provision of economic and financial statistics to the public by member countries, especially those countries that participate in the international capital markets or aspire to do so, and including both industrial and emerging economies.[34]

**The International Response.** Following an invitation by the G-7 to the G-10 in Halifax in June 1995, the Deputies of the G-10 established a Working Party

---

[31]  Id.

[32]  Id.

[33]  R. Choate, G. Graham and J. Gapper, "IMF Set to Get More Crisis Cash", Financial Times, 9 Oct. 1995.

[34]  See IMF, "IMF Executive Board Approves the Special Data Dissemination Standard", IMF Press Release No. 96/18 (16 Apr. 1996).

to consider the issues arising with respect to the orderly resolution of sovereign liquidity crises.[35] On 22 April 1996, the G-10 released a communiqué on international financial emergencies, based on and endorsing the Working Party report.[36]

**The G-10 Communiqué.** In its Communiqué, the G-10 noted the on-going discussion between the G-10 countries and other countries aimed at developing new financing arrangements which would double the supplementary resources available to IMF under the GAB for coping with these sorts of international financial emergencies.[37] The G-10 affirmed that, given the need to contain moral hazard and the desirability of equitable burden-sharing, first, neither the debtor countries nor their private creditors should expect to be insulated from any adverse financial consequences of their financial decisions by the provision of large-scale official financing in the event of a crisis, and second, there should be no presumption that any type of debt would be exempt from payments suspensions or restructurings in any future sovereign liquidity crisis.[38] As noted in Chapter Two, importantly, the G-10 stated that the existing flexible, case-by-case practices and procedures, as developed over the years, are an appropriate starting point for considering how to respond to future sovereign liquidity crises, that improvements should continue to evolve to meet the needs of specific crises, and stressed that improvements should be led by private sector groups in developing any new contractual arrangements.[39] Further, they affirmed that the official community's primary role in the resolution of sovereign liquidity crises should remain centred on "the promotion of strong and effective adjustment by debtor countries in the context of IMF-supported programs"[40], thereby indicating the continued importance of IMF conditionality and structural adjustment programs.

**The Working Party Report.** In carrying out its work, the Working Party sought to give the highest priority to measures that would help prevent crises from occurring, sought to endorse efforts already underway in other forums to improve market discipline and strengthen the surveillance of sovereign borrowers' economic performance, and attached particular importance to the

---

[35] G-10 Sovereign Crises (1996), op. cit., n. 30.
[36] G-10, *Communiqué of Ministers and Governors of the Group of Ten Nations on International Financial Emergencies*, 22 Apr. 1996.
[37] Id., para. 1.
[38] Id., para. 3. This latter statement seems directly aimed at holders of sovereign bonds.
[39] Id., para. 4.
[40] Id.

need for sovereign borrowers to make "timely changes" in their economic policies if conditions change in ways that may lead to reductions in capital inflows.[41]

In considering the means to deal with future sovereign liquidity crises, the Working Party concluded that no pre-set procedure could be suitable to all cases; however, it did identify a broad set of desirable principles and features that provide a framework for the development of procedures for handling sovereign liquidity crises in a flexible, case-by-case approach.[42] Any such procedure should have the following features[43]: (1) foster sound economic policies by all debtors; (2) minimize moral hazard for both creditors and debtors; (3) rely on market forces and not interfere with the efficient operation of secondary markets in relevant debt instruments; (4) limit contagion from one debtor's problems to other countries; (5) support credible and sustainable actions and not impose excessive social, political, or economic costs on the debtor; (6) seek to ensure that burdens associated with the provision of exceptional financing are allocated fairly and within and across different classes of creditors; (7) strengthen the ability of governments to resist pressures to assume responsibility for the external liabilities of their private sectors; (8) be suitable for quick and flexible use in a variety of different cases; (9) be cooperative and nonconfrontational, and promote the adoption by debtors and creditors of arrangements to facilitate resolution of liquidity crises; (10) build on existing contractual or other arrangements that facilitate the resolution of crises; and (11) make use of existing practices and institutions. In terms of policy, the official community's interest in containing systemic risk and its role as a lender to sovereign borrowers means that the official community has a stake, and therefore a role to play, in fostering cooperative efforts by debtors and creditors to contend with unexpected payments problems.[44]

The Working Party reached seven broad conclusions in its report.[45] First, it is essential as a basic principle to maintain the terms and conditions of all debt contracts which are to be met in full and market discipline must be preserved.[46] In exceptional cases, however, a temporary suspension of debt payments by the debtor may be unavoidable as a part of the process of crisis resolution and as a

---

[41] G-10 Sovereign Crises (1996), op. cit., n. 30, para. 1.
[42] Id., para. 4. This approach should be taken in light of the conditions prevailing at the time, the nature and intensity of the crisis, and the circumstances of the debtor. Id.
[43] Id.
[44] Id., para. 5.
[45] Id., para. 2.
[46] Id.

way of gaining time to put in place a credible adjustment program.[47] Second, neither debtor countries nor their creditors should expect to be insulated from adverse financial consequences by the provision of large-scale official financing in the event of a crisis[48], as markets are equipped to assess the risks involved in lending to sovereign borrowers and to set the prices and other terms of the instruments accordingly, and no type of debt will be exempt from future problems and solutions.[49] Third, current practices and procedures emphasizing the importance of adjustment efforts of the debtor country and placing primary responsibilities for work-outs on the private participants are an appropriate starting point, and improvements should be evolutionary.[50] The practices are based on the implementation of an IMF-supported sustainable adjustment program as a major precondition for the cooperative resolution of any crisis.[51] Fourth, international bankruptcy procedures do not appear to provide, either currently or in the foreseeable future, "a feasible or appropriate way" of dealing with sovereign liquidity crises.[52] Fifth, further consideration should be given in "appropriate forums"[53] to ways in which the financial systems in emerging market economies could be strengthened in order to reduce the risks they might pose in the event of a sovereign liquidity crisis.[54] The Working Party recognized that structural weaknesses in the banking systems of debtor countries could seriously aggravate liquidity crises and might pose difficulties for

---

[47] Id. The Working Party did not consider that it would be feasible to operate any formal mechanism for signaling the official community's approval of a suspension of payments by the debtor. Id., para. 9.

[48] The Working Party concluded, however, that it is not possible or desirable to preclude official involvement altogether in the event of a serious crisis, albeit short of the creation of an international bankruptcy forum. Id., para. 5.

[49] Id., para. 2.

[50] Id. According to the Working Party, current practices were developed over the course of the past few decades to contend with real world problems in a pragmatic and flexible manner. Further, they are voluntary and make use of market information and market forces. These practices recognize the distinct perspectives of the three main actors involved in a crisis, that is, the official community, private creditors, and the sovereign debtor, as well as their common interest in the orderly resolution of any crisis. The practices involve national authorities and multilateral institutions but place principal responsibility on the individual debtor and its creditors. Id., para. 6.

[51] Id.

[52] Id. The Working Party did note that further study by "private sector entities" may be warranted. Id. According to the Working Party, sovereign debtors have not in the past had a strong need for legal protection against creditors, and moreover, they could not be forced to submit to the jurisdiction of a bankruptcy forum. Id., para. 5.

[53] This would presumably mean, at a minimum, the Basel Committee, IOSCO and the IMF.

[54] Id., para. 2.

financial systems in lender countries.[55] Sixth, a market-led process to develop for inclusion in sovereign debt instruments contractual provisions that facilitate consultation and cooperation between debtors and their private creditors, as well as within the creditor community, in the event of a crisis would be desirable.[56] Seventh, it would be advisable for the IMF to review existing policy in regard to lending support prior to full and final resolution of sovereign borrower arrears to private creditors and to consider whether the scope of its application should be extended to other forms of debt not now covered, "while remaining mindful of the need for prudence and the maintenance of strict conditionality."[57] According to the Working Party, such lending can both signal confidence in the debtor country's policies and longer-term prospects and indicate to unpaid creditors that their interests would be best served by quickly reaching an agreement with the debtor.[58]

The Working Party reached the overall conclusion that there was no need to change existing procedures for official bilateral credits and long-term bank claims.[59] It did, however, recognize that there is a need for the principles and procedures for handling sovereign liquidity crises to take into account the new importance of debt in the form of securities and the growing likelihood that some such debt may have to be subject to renegotiation in the future.[60] As for the official community, while it may be able to facilitate dialogue and assist in

---

[55]  Id., para. 7.

[56]  Id., para. 2. Such market initiatives would deserve "official support" as "appropriate". Id. The Working Party took the view that certain contractual provisions governing debt contracts can facilitate the resolution of a crisis by fostering dialogue and consultation between the sovereign debtor and its creditors and among creditors, and by reducing the incentive for, or ability of, a small number of dissident creditors to disrupt, delay, or prevent arrangements to support a credible adjustment program that is acceptable to the vast majority of concerned parties. Such provisions include, inter alia, those that (1) provide for the collective representation of debt holders in the event of crisis, (2) allow for qualified majority voting to alter the terms and conditions of debt contracts, and (3) require the sharing among creditors of assets received from the debtor. The Working Party noted that in fact such clauses have been employed in a limited number of contracts. Id., para. 8.

[57]  Id., para. 2 Although the Working Party rejected any formal international approval of a suspension of debt payments, it concluded that it would be advisable for the IMF Executive Board to consider extending the scope of its current policy of lending, in exceptional circumstances, to a country that faces the prospect of continuing to accumulate arrears on some of its contractual debt-service obligations to private sector creditors, in cases where the country is undertaking a strong adjustment program and making reasonable efforts to negotiate with its creditors. Id., para. 9.

[58]  Id.

[59]  Id., para. 10.

[60]  Id.

data collection, the Working Party concluded that market participants should take any decisions regarding any innovations in contractual provisions[61]:

> The official community's primary role in the resolution of sovereign liquidity crises should remain centred on the promotion of strong and effective adjustment by debtor countries in the context of IMF-supported programs, which would need to take into account any recourse to temporary suspensions of payments.

These arrangements have largely governed resolution of subsequent sovereign liquidity and debt crises. However, following experiences in Russia, Brazil, Turkey and (especially) Argentina, these issues are once again being revisited, though with no clear resolution.

### 9.3.2. *Contemporary International Lending*

The circumstances under which cross-border financing takes place today are significantly different from cross-border financial activities twenty years ago. One consequence of this is that the resolution of future sovereign financial problems will be very different from the methods used to resolve the 1980s debt crisis, as has been clearly demonstrated by more recent crises in Argentina, Russia and Turkey. The integration of the world's financial systems over the last twenty years is perhaps the single most important change in cross-border finance, with money flowing into and out of economies with astonishing speed, as graphically demonstrated by the series of financial crises over the past fifteen years. Any diminution in investor confidence can be reflected in massive and immediate shifts of capital, to the detriment of individual economies. In this era of quickly moving capital, borrowers and lenders are expected to internalize these lessons, at least in theory; however, in practice, both tend to have short memories.[62]

Historical cycles of cross-border finance have not all been alike. A number of factors illustrate the differences between the current cross-border capital flows and those occurring in the 1970s. Factors include differences in the nature of investors, instruments, borrowers, interest rate bases, use of proceeds, economic reforms, available information, remedies, and disclosure.[63] Most finance to

---

[61] Id.

[62] L. Buchheit, "Cross-Border Lending: What's Different This Time?" 16 NW. J. Int'l L. & Bus. 44 (1995) ("Buchheit I"), p. 55.

[63] See id., pp. 47–54.

developing countries during the 1970s took the form of syndicated commercial bank loans, with banks intermediating petrodollars and flight capital between euromarket depositors and the ultimate sovereign borrowers, many of whom funded the flow of petrodollars in the first place. In contrast, cross-border finance during the 1990s was characterized by the leading role of the international bond markets.[64] More recently, foreign direct investment has come to be increasingly significant, as has equity investment facilitated through privatization. In contrast to the systemic consequences of sovereign defaults on commercial bank debt in the 1980s, in contemporary markets, when borrowers cannot meet their obligations, the full weight of the problem will not fall on banks, their regulators and their government-sponsored deposit insurance agencies.[65]

Further, until the middle of the twentieth century, a lender extending credit to a foreign sovereign did so with no expectation that repayment of the debt could be compelled by legal means due to the general prevalence of theories of general sovereign immunity. Today, most Western creditor countries recognize a restrictive theory of sovereign immunity under which sovereigns engaged in commercial activity abroad may be sued in the national courts of other countries.[66] Moreover, drafters of credit agreements and bond indentures for sovereign borrowers and government-owned enterprises routinely include express waivers of any immunities to which the borrowers may be entitled.[67] While lenders could have attempted to sue their way out of the 1980s debt crisis, this was not the solution chosen.[68] At the same time, resort to the courts

---

[64]  Id., p. 47; Macmillan II, op. cit., n. 21, p. 80.

[65]  See Buchheit I, op. cit., n. 62, p. 48.

[66]  For example, in the United States, the restrictive theory of sovereign immunity is codified in the Foreign Sovereign Immunities Act of 1976; it also is codified in the United Kingdom, in the State Immunity Act 1978.

[67]  See Macmillan II, op. cit., n. 21, p. 72.

[68]  See "Avoiding the Nightmare Solution", Int'l Fin'l L. Rev., Aug. 1992, p. 19. Several reasons have been advanced to explain this forbearance: the brotherhood of bankers, the fear of prompting a raised eyebrow of disapproval by one's regulator, and a recognition that any widespread resort to lawsuits would jeopardize the renegotiation process and force borrowers into a "bunker" mentality. Buchheit I, op. cit., n. 62, p. 53. Legally, the banks could have brought suits over their loans: New York or English law usually controlled the agreements, and neither of these jurisdictions apply foreign sovereign immunity to sovereign bonds. See *Republic of Argentina v. Weltover, Inc.*, 504 US 607, 617–19 (1992); see also, G. Delaume, "The Foreign Sovereign Immunities Act and Public Debt Litigation: Some Fifteen Years Later", 88 Am. J. Int'l L. 257 (1994); idem, "Sovereign Immunity and Public Debt", 23 Int'l Law. 811 (1989). The nature of syndicated lending further hindered banks from suing on the debt because it is very difficult for member banks to take unilateral action due to contractual provisions, such as sharing clauses generally contained in the agreements. See L. Buchheit, "The Sharing Clause as a Litigation Shield", Int'l Fin'l L. Rev. (Oct. 1990), p. 15.

following the 2002 crisis in Argentina have not been as successful as had been predicted. At the same time, it is clear that when sovereign financial problems recur in the future, negotiated settlements cannot be pursued without the threat of harassing litigation by some creditors.[69]

### 9.3.3. *Proposed Solutions*

Three factors have made financial restructuring more difficult in situations such as the Argentine and Russian crises.[70] First, the systemic threat experienced by the international banking industry has not been repeated in a form that would produce sufficient pressures on creditors. Second, bondholders at least initially have some hope that official sources will provide the necessary liquidity to enable their bonds to be paid in full without restructuring. Third, maverick bondholders seeking redress in court have caused problems.[71]

According to Rory Macmillan, however, in future sovereign financial crises, restructurings are inevitable simply because there is no alternative.[72] While in some cases, official sources may organize a successful rescue package to deal with liquidity problems as in Mexico and South Korea, in other cases, the problems may be more in relation to solvency, as in Russia and Argentina in 2002. In cases where international assistance bridges a liquidity crisis, private finance is likely to return quite quickly. At the same time, in situations involving sovereign solvency problems, international finance is unlikely to return until there has been a credible economic improvement in the economy concerned (i.e., a return of confidence). In some cases, however, confidence will not return quickly (e.g., Indonesia) and private financing will continue to be unavailable.[73] These ideas have been borne out by recent experiences. Given

---

[69] Overall, the arguments against "pressing the button", while other opportunities to recover the debt remain unexplored, are probably persuasive. "Latin American Debt Obligations in the 1990s: Risk Strategies: Remedies and Judicial Enforcement", 16 NW. J. Int'l L. & Bus. 5 (1995), pp. 7–8.

[70] See Macmillan II, op. cit., n. 21, pp. 71–2.

[71] Bondholders can expect to obtain judgements in US and/or UK courts. See R. Macmillan, "The Next Sovereign Debt Crisis", 31 Stan. J. Int'l L. 305 (1995) ("Macmillan I"). This, in fact, has started to occur and is likely to increase in frequency. Id.

[72] Macmillan II, op. cit., n. 21, p. 59. Banks are unlikely to lend to sovereigns experiencing problems after their experiences following the 1980s debt crisis. Id. This was demonstrated in the 1994 Mexican crisis when commercial banks were asked by the US government to participate in the rescue plan, but their portion never materialized. See R. Waters and L. Crawford, "Banks Pull Out of $3bn Role in Mexican Rescue", Financial Times (23 Mar. 1995), p. 20; T. O'Brien, "Prospects Look Dim for Bank Loan to Mexico", Wall Street Journal (13 Feb. 1995), p. A3.

[73] Mexico was unable to return to international capital markets for 6 months after the onset of the crisis, with the first issue of Mexican sovereign debt not coming until July 1995. L. Crawford,

these realities, the current legal and institutional framework for handling a sovereign financial crisis has been described as "embarrassingly unprepared" to handle the "enormous amount of bonds spread across a vast international market of different types of investors."[74] This latter situation has been vividly highlighted by experiences involving Argentina.

A number of proposals have emerged for a workable solution to future sovereign financial crises.[75] One suggestion has come from Jeffrey Sachs who has suggested that governments set up a sort of international bankruptcy regime for debtor governments.[76] This approach has subsequently also been endorsed by the IMF[77] but continued discussions appear to have stalled for the present (probably until the next major financial crisis). Under Sachs' proposal, such a system would give the IMF legal powers analogous to a bankruptcy judge in US Chapter 11 proceedings. The IMF would have the legal authority to declare a moratorium on debt payments, stop legal proceedings and organize debt workouts.[78] Such a system would reapportion losses to the market, providing a less expensive solution to governments than publicly funded IMF bailouts, and the problems of leadership, coordination and solidarity could all be solved and imposed by the IMF.[79] The problem with the Sachs/IMF proposals, as noted by the G-10, is they look to the international institutions as an answer: while such a solution seems like the obvious starting point, such a solution threatens the sovereignty of countries by giving the IMF the power to decide when a country would declare a moratorium on its debt.[80] Further, giving the IMF such legal powers would also revolutionize international financial law, with debt instruments governed by New York or English law suddenly being subject to the uncertainties of the international political order, as the IMF

---

"Mexican Bonds Welcomed", Financial Times (11 Jul 1995), p. 3. See also D. Dombey, "Mexico to Restructure Debt Through $500m Bond Issue", Financial Times (26 Jul. 1995), p. 4.

74   Macmillan II, op. cit., n. 21, pp. 59–60.

75   See S. Schwarcz, "'Idiot's Guide' to Sovereign Debt Restructuring", 53 Emory L. J. 1189 (2004).

76   See id., p. 76 (citing Jeffrey Sachs, "Do We Need an International Lender of Last Resort?" [1995, mimeographed]).

77   IMF, *A New Approach to Sovereign Debt Restructuring*, Apr. 2002. See H. Scott, "A Bankruptcy Procedure for Sovereign Debt", 37 Int'l Law. 103 (2003).

78   This was not the first time this idea had been suggested. See B. Cohen, "A Global Chapter 11", 75 For. Pol'y 109 (1989); C. Oechsli, "Note: Procedural Guidelines for Renegotiating LDC Debt: An Analogy to Chapter 11 of the US Bankruptcy Reform Act", 21 Va. J. Int'l L. 305 (1981); S. Bainbridge, "Comity and Sovereign Debt Litigation: A Bankruptcy Analogy", 10 Md. J. Int'l L. & Tr. 1 (1986); R. Sklar, "Note: Renegotiation of External Debt: The Allied Bank Cases and the Chapter 11 Analogy", 17 U. Miami Inter-Am. L. Rev. 59 (1984).

79   Macmillan II, op. cit., n. 21, p. 77.

80   Id., pp. 77–8. For this reason, Macmillan suggests that IMF's role should be limited to providing temporary liquidity and conditional structural adjustment programs. Id., p. 78.

may be subject to unpredictable political influence at the hands of its member governments.

A second proposal (initially from James Hurlock) argues that the problems of leadership and coordination are not significant because corporate debt work-outs are largely "self-executing in that creditors, in concert with the debtor, collectively determine the economic terms upon which the enterprise will be restructured", and that insolvency judges, in fact, play a peripheral role in reorganizations.[81] He argues that a debt work-out system does not necessarily require any international institution to play a central role because the difficulties consist of fundamental mechanical problems which do not need governmental supervision, and that, in fact, debtors and creditors can reach restructuring agreements successfully without official intervention. The real problem, then, is solidarity – that is, the danger of the maverick bondholder disrupting the negotiations by suing – and Hurlock suggests that this problem could be dealt with by closing the courts to such investors through the amending of sovereign immunity laws so that a sovereign debtor would be immune from law suits in the midst of a negotiated work-out. Such an approach has been criticized for two reasons:[82] first, the problems of leadership and coordination are probably much more serious than Hurlock suggests, given the complexity of sovereign debt crises today; and second, amending sovereign immunities laws in this fashion could create serious moral hazard problems as it could foreseeably bring about a return to the pattern of defaults seen during the nineteenth and early twentieth centuries.

A third proposal has been put forth by Barry Eichengreen and Richard Portes, which has been endorsed by the G-10 and also by the United States. Eichengreen and Portes suggest a three-pronged work-out system.[83] First, in order to address the problem of coordination, they endorse the idea of creating one or more bondholder councils which, with the help of a mediation or conciliation service, would negotiate debt reschedulings on behalf of bondholders. Second, they suggest that the lack of solidarity could be solved by an ex ante solution: if the legal provisions of future bonds allowed a majority of bondholders to negotiate changes in the essential terms of the bonds, for example, maturity date, coupon payment date, principal and interest amounts, and the like, then bondholder councils could negotiate effectively with the sovereign debtor.[84] Third,

---

[81] J. Hurlock, "The Way Ahead for Sovereign Debt", Euromoney (Aug. 1995), pp. 78–9.
[82] See Macmillan II, op. cit., n. 21, p. 79.
[83] B. Eichengreen and R. Portes (eds), *Crisis, What Crisis? Orderly Workouts for Sovereign Debtors* (London: Centre for Economic Policy Research, Sep. 1995).
[84] To make this fair to dissenting minority creditors, they suggest that such creditors have access to an arbitration tribunal if they do not like the solution negotiated by the majority bondholders.

they endorse strengthening the IMF's ability to provide emergency financing and encourage it to play a legitimizing role for countries wishing to renegotiate their debts.[85]

Based on the experiences with bondholder councils in the nineteenth and early twentieth centuries, Rory Macmillan suggests another, based on proposals for US and UK legislation to provide for leadership and coordination.[86] Under his proposal, indenture trustees would be allowed for sovereign issues, thereby gaining the benefits provided by the lead banks during the debt crisis of the 1980s. Further, to deal with the coordination problem, national bondholder councils would be set up in the major issuing jurisdictions, namely the United States and the United Kingdom, funded by fees form the issuing of bonds and from rescheduling efforts. Finally, to deal with the solidarity problem, Macmillan suggests, inter alia, that rather than granting complete immunity to debtors as in the Hurlock proposal, legislation might be used to vest bondholder rights collectively and exclusively in the bondholder council, but only during debt crises officially declared by either the country of IMF.[87] Overall, Macmillan's proposal is well thought out, but nonetheless seems to require intelligent and coordinated action by the major creditor country legislators – something that may or may not be possible; however, it nonetheless seems largely in line with the thinking of the G-10.

### 9.3.4. *Private Lending and Investment*

Investors since the early 1990s have had a preference for private sector borrowers and investment, and the balance of payments financings for sovereign borrowers that characterized the late 1970s are no longer favoured. Private sector borrowers, however, are likely to be caught in any problems that their sovereign experiences, and accessing assets located abroad may not be as easy as it may appear at first glance. A private sector entity, particularly one that has its own reliable source of foreign currency earnings, may be perfectly creditworthy when viewed in isolation; however, the company may find itself in a predicament as a result of its location in a country whose aggregate foreign exchange inflows are insufficient to pay for the country's necessary imports and external debt service. As a consequence, even the most solvent private

---

[85] Coupled with stronger conditionality, countries which are afraid to default because of the negative effect on their access to international capital markets would be enabled to do so with approval from IMF.

[86] Macmillan II, op. cit., n. 21, pp. 86–94. See also R. Macmillan, "New Lease on Life for Bondholder Councils", Financial Times (15 Aug. 1995), p. 11.

[87] Macmillan II, op. cit., n. 21, pp. 94–104.

sector company may find itself drawn into its government's external financial difficulties, despite its own best efforts.

Unlike the predominantly syndicated bank lending of the late 1970s, directed mostly to sovereign and state-owned or guaranteed enterprises, private sector firms were the principal beneficiaries of private capital flows over the past fifteen years. For this reason, the external debt position of private sector borrowers is a centrepiece of concern in sovereign financial problems today.[88] In such circumstances, the fate of private sector borrowers is not clear, for several reasons.[89] First, the stock of private sector debt is far larger today, both in nominal terms and as a percentage of the overall credit exposure of most countries. Second, the special circumstances that induced the governments of the debtor countries to assume or guarantee private sector debt in the 1980s probably will not be replicated in the future. Third, today's lenders (bondholders) and investors (both portfolio and direct) will respond differently to the financial problems of their counterparts than did the lenders of the 1970s and 1980s (principally commercial banks).

While the problems of restructuring private sector obligations are not so difficult on a practical level as those facing sovereign debt, they are nonetheless significant, and include, inter alia, consensual out-of-court restructurings with their bondholders or local bankruptcy proceedings. The implications, however, bear more on the need for prevention and solution of liquidity crises, the need to strengthen domestic banking systems, the need to provide for hedging opportunities, and the need to maintain and increase investor confidence in domestic financial systems in order to encourage the provision of the needed capital to prevent unpleasant long-term impacts on the domestic private sector, as well as possibly the interests of large holders of corporate bonds.

### 9.3.5. *The International Financial Architecture and Crisis Resolution*

In looking at crisis resolution and the international financial architecture, the primary point of analysis is the role of the IMF. In this context, a useful

---

[88]  L. Buchheit and R. Reisner, "Latin American Debt in the 1990s: A New Scenario for Creditors and Debtors", 16 NW. J. Int'l L. & Bus. 1 (1995), p. 2. Oddly enough, private sector borrowers during the debt crisis of the 1980s did not really have to worry about this problem. In many of the countries undergoing a generalized debt rescheduling during the 1980s, formal programs were established pursuant to which the host government agreed to assume the outstanding indebtedness of private sector borrowers in return for payment of the local currency equivalent of the amount due to the central bank or other monetary authority. Over time, these programs operated to transform most private sector debt into sovereign debt.

[89]  See id., p. 3.

framework is that for the financial safety net developed in Chapter Four: (1) contingency planning, (2) lender of last resort, (3) financial regulation and supervision, (4) systems for addressing financial resolution and insolvency, and (5) depositor and consumer protection mechanisms.

Looking at the international financial architecture (especially the IMF) in relation to each and in the context of the guidance developed in Chapter Four, clearly, contingency planning is a necessary step at the international level in assessing how to deal with potential crises which could affect financial stability at both the international and domestic level. This is an area which now receives significant attention from the IMF (through its various financial stability reports), through other international organizations (such as the Basel Committee, BIS and OECD) and domestic/regional authorities (such as the Bank of England and European Central Bank).

In relation to the lender of last resort function, as discussed in the context of Chapter Four, a central aspect is in rebuilding confidence in order to prevent liquidity problems evolving into solvency problems. As highlighted previously in this chapter, confidence is as important in the international financial system and for individual economies as it is for domestic financial intermediaries. Therefore, even the IMF does not have the potential to provide unlimited liquidity, it does have the potential to provide sufficient liquidity to address immediate problems, therefore preventing the evolution from liquidity to solvency crisis. At the same time, the IMF also has the ability to join its emergency liquidity provision with conditions which can serve to reinforce and/or rebuild confidence in a given economy or financial system. Clearly, this sort of mechanism must be responsible to the general requirements of lender of last resort support, especially those relating to speed and lending only in cases of illiquidity and not insolvency.

As discussed in Chapter Four, the requirement to provide lender of last resort support only in the context of a liquidity (and not a solvency) crisis, in the domestic context, raises the need for banking regulation and supervision. Likewise, at the international level, a similar problem arising, with the necessary tool kit having already been developed through the system of international standards and the related implementation and monitoring framework of the IMF and World Bank FSAP/ROSC framework. As noted above, the Fund should take a leading role in the financial stability aspects of FSAP/ROSC work, with these integrated into its regular surveillance processes, while the Bank should lead on the development aspects.

Investor protection should be dealt with essentially through transparency, as reflected throughout this volume and reinforced by the IMF's SDDS and GDDS.

This leaves the most difficult situation: mechanisms for dealing with financial restructuring and insolvency. As discussed above, economies (unlike firms) cannot be placed in insolvency administration (at least not since the end of gunboat diplomacy in the nineteenth century). At the same time, the combination of mechanisms discussed in the preceding paragraphs should address the most significant aspects: (1) crisis prevention and (2) liquidity crisis resolution. In this author's view, if these are effective, then situations of insolvency should be immediately identifiable to the IMF, clearly flagged to investors (who will also know that such cases do not merit an IMF rescue package, hence minimizing moral hazard through transparency) and known to economies concerned. Thus, such situations should be left to those involved for resolution, similar to the case with the crisis in Argentina and the restructuring and resolution of related obligations which continues today.

## 9.4. CONCLUSION

This chapter has looked to issues of financial stability and development which merit further attention. First, it has suggested that the international standards framework should be expanded and modified to explicitly incorporate development goals in addition to stability. While financial stability is a central goal, financial development should merit the same attention. Second, in looking at the international standards framework, issues of competition and financial liberalization and their role in both financial stability and development should also be covered.

Third, beyond the standards initiative, the international financial architecture deserves further attention, if not a full Bretton Woods–style review, then at least to take into account the WTO and related financial services framework and to address financial crisis resolution in a more coherent manner. In respect to the first, the experiences of the European Union (discussed in the final chapter) provide a useful example and possible model, not only for the international financial architecture but also for other regional financial arrangements as they seek to achieve the twin goals of financial stability and development across a given region. The final chapter concludes with the suggestion that individual countries, as well as regional arrangements and international stability and development efforts, should recognize the role of institutional design as an extension of the agreed role of law and institutions in financial stability and development and economic growth and development.

# 10

# Reforming Financial Systems

If law and institutions are important for stable and effective financial systems, how can countries take advantage of research and best practices in their own economies and what can development professionals do to assist? This chapter concludes with a discussion of financial sector design and a suggestion that countries should coherently address the legal and institutional framework of their financial and economic systems on a holistic basis in order to achieve the desired results of financial stability and development.

This final chapter seeks to synthesize the lessons and ideas of the preceding parts and chapters into a set of recommendations for individual economies in respect to supporting economic growth through financial sector development in the context of financial stability. Specifically, it suggests that countries should work actively on these issues themselves. The system of international standards process is a very useful starting point. In addition, however, countries need to carefully consider their own levels of financial and economic structure and development. Appropriate legal and institutional choices should be made on this basis. It then extends the discussion to regional financial arrangements, focusing on the experience of the European Union and its lessons for other regional financial development initiatives.

## 10.1. SUPPORTING FINANCIAL DEVELOPMENT

Countries may consider a variety of models for domestic financial development. In order to approach this subject properly, one should have an understanding of five interrelated underlying issues: (1) the importance of law and other institutions to economic development, (2) the significance of the financial sector, (3) the risks inherent in liberalization and their interaction with World Trade Organization (WTO) financial services commitments, (4) the role of regulation in reducing the risks of liberalization while achieving the goals development and stability and (5) the importance of appropriate legal and institutional design to the financial sector. The preceding chapters have sought to lay these foundations.

This background provides the most appropriate approach through which to analyse financial regulation generally and to seek to achieve the goals of (1) strengthening the legal and regulatory framework for the financial system, (2) identifying legislation that is clearly in conflict with the development of the financial sector, and (3) developing legislation that is consistent with financial stability and economic development. Within this context, the strategy in the financial sector should be to: (1) establish a progressive policy and institutional framework, (2) improve the legal and regulatory environment, (3) enable the financial sector to play an important role in supporting economic development, and (4) facilitate integration into the global financial system. The application of this approach produces a methodology designed to assist in devising an appropriate legal and regulatory institutional framework to meet the goal of financial sector development in the context of maintaining financial stability and supporting economic growth and development.

Are there models for countries to follow in seeking to develop financial systems? On a general level, law reform efforts in developing, emerging and transition economies (as well as developed) must now be seen in terms of a large number of interconnected factors, loosely broken down into international, domestic and regional factors.[1]

## 10.2. THE ROLE OF THE INTERNATIONAL ARCHITECTURE

On an international level, the development, promulgation, implementation and monitoring of international standards are significant developments. These efforts, although technically a form of soft law[2], are becoming ingrained into both domestic and regional financial market law reform efforts in developed and developing, transition and emerging economies alike. While these standards do not necessarily represent the final word on international best practices for financial market law reform, they are certainly of great importance in encouraging development and implementation of international best practices and in the overall process of integrating domestic and regional financial systems into the international financial system.

---

[1] For analysis of the development of banking supervision in terms of this sort of developmental model, see J. Norton, *Devising International Bank Supervisory Standards* (Dordrecht: Martinus Nijhoff, 1995).

[2] See id., pp. 255–62.

Unfortunately, the framework of international financial standards does not explicitly address development. The preceding chapters have sought to show, however, that there is much useful experience for countries to look to in their efforts. Further, while they are useful in respect to individual areas (as discussed in the preceding chapters) they are not truly organized into a coherent structure or plan upon which countries can draw, other than in a somewhat piecemeal fashion. At the same time, some of the limitations of the international architecture may be addressed through regional arrangements, discussed subsequently.

## 10.3. DOMESTIC MODELS

On the basis of the most recent wave of theory relating to the role of law and development, one can describe a complex interaction between law, the economy and development.

### 10.3.1. *The Regulated Market Economy*

At the end of the twentieth century battle of ideas between economic systems based on central-planning and state-ownership and control and those based laissez-faire capitalism, we have emerged with something in between the two: the regulated market economy, a form of societal organization in which resources are allocated primarily through market mechanisms. These market mechanisms, however, function within a complex regulatory framework addressing government, individuals and enterprises, based on law and the institutional framework.

As such, the current model of economic organization appears to be a regulated market economy.[3] In a regulated market economy, there are a number of overriding issues of concern. First is the role of the government in the society and the economy: how much control, influence and/or participation are proper and/or culturally preferable? Second, the role of government tends to change with changing societal expectations. Examples include welfare and democracy. Third, regulatory states tend towards complexity: how much complexity may exist before it begins to become ineffective? Fourth, regulatory states take a range of forms: there are competing models of regulated market economy. This is the focus of the new comparative economics, discussed in

---

[3] For a discussion of the development of the "regulatory state", see E. Glaeser and A. Shleifer, "The Rise of the Regulatory State", J. Econ. Lit. (Jun. 2003).

the first chapter. Fifth is the question of how one pays for it all – this relates to fiscal policy and especially taxation (discussed in Chapter Three).

The model of a regulated market economy suggests that the government should step back from the economy and instead focus on the provision of "public goods". Classic public goods include defence, political stability and economic policy. A wide range of other roles have also been called public goods, including public utilities, education, justice / dispute settlement, social welfare, and environmental issues. There is a continuing and vigorous debate over many of these around the world. In addition, Garry Schinasi and others have argued that "financial stability" constitutes a public good; others have argued that property rights are also a fundamental public good.[1]

Generally speaking, in economies today, law and regulation address all aspects of the economy and business, including enterprise establishment, management and operation, finance, and closure. In relation to establishment, partnerships and companies both require action of law in order to be effective. In relation to management and operation, a wide range of regulations must be dealt with, including competition (both as to participation and behaviour), consumer protection (including both information requirements and standards/rules), employee protection, corporate governance and accounting/auditing.

In relation to finance, law plays a fundamental role in establishing fundamental property rights, general economic conditions, infrastructure necessary for the functioning of complex financial markets, basic rules of the game, and prudential standards. Law and institutions play a variety of important roles in a financial system. First, they provide the fundamental "rules of the game". Second, they support availability of information. Third, they support fairness in markets. Fourth, they assist with the operation of monetary policy. Fifth, they act to reduce and manage systemic risk. Overall, law and institutions play a central role in supporting confidence in the financial system and its constituents. Finally, law plays an important role in respect to exit, in the operation of bankruptcy and insolvency systems and their role in allocating residual values to stakeholders.

### 10.3.2. *Financial Structure*

A major design issue to be considered is an economy's financial structure, with the primary focus being the allocation and governance model. Corporate governance can be looked in at two ways: at the microeconomic or firm

---

[4] These ideas were discussed in Chapter Two.

level (discussed in Chapter Five) and at the macroeconomic level. This section looks to the latter and its implications for financial system design and planning.

One of the reasons for the debate on corporate governance in recent years has been the simple fact that historically there has been no single dominant structure in successful developed economies. The corporate governance world today subdivides into rival systems of dispersed and concentrated ownership, with different corporate governance structures characterizing each.[5] The major macro-models include:

(1) government-dominated financial system (the traditional model in most of the former centrally planned economies and the People's Republic of China, the limitations of which have been exposed as a result of the collapse of the Soviet bloc);

(2) bank-dominated financial system (the traditional model in Germany – with limitations being exposed through Germany's economic stagnation in the 1990s);

(3) government/bank-dominated financial system (the traditional model in Japan, South Korea and France, the limitations of which have been exposed as a result of the east Asian financial crises);

(4) family-dominated systems (prevalent in Asia and much of continental Europe); and

(5) securities-based financial systems, with widely dispersed ownership (the Anglo-American or Berle and Means model, which has been receiving new scrutiny following the collapse of Enron).

The promotion of efficiency and effective corporate governance should guide policy choices relating to financial structure. However, efficiency and corporate governance, while both valuable for different reasons, may, in fact, point to divergent solutions[6]: in highly liquid markets, control tends to be dispersed, thus reducing the governance functions of the equity market.[7] On the other hand, when control is concentrated, thus facilitating corporate governance by larger shareholders, conflicts of interest between different types

---

[5] B. Cheffins, "Does Law Matter? The Separation of Ownership and Control in the United Kingdom", 30 J. Legal Stud. 459 (2001).

[6] See B. Steil, *The European Equity Markets: The State of the Union and an Agenda for the Millennium* (London: Royal Institute of International Affairs, 1996), pp. 147–84.

[7] This has traditionally been the case in markets characterized by broad-based equity ownership, namely the United States and the United Kingdom. See id., pp. 1–58.

of shareholders may arise and liquidity tends to be lacking.[8] To some extent, however, with the globally growing significance of institutional investors, such as pension and mutual funds, as major shareholders of corporations and users of the securities markets, this traditional dichotomy of market forms may be gradually losing some of its importance, to the extent that these institutional investors desire not only liquidity, but also some measure of control over management and impact on enterprise decisions.[9] Nonetheless, the choice of a model of corporate governance and its relationship to corporate finance in a given country are very important from the standpoint of policy makers.

While specific market and corporate governance structures have become entrenched in each economy as a result of its particular historical experience, the developing, emerging and transition economies are in a position to influence their developmental path and to learn from previous experiences and mistakes.

While the debate in the 1980s and early 1990s focused on which macrostructure was most efficient, as a result of privatization and financial market liberalization, the collapse of the Soviet bloc, the economic stagnation of Germany and Japan, and the string of financial crises during the 1990s, it is now generally agreed (as originally suggested by Berle and Means) that the Anglo-American structure of widely dispersed ownership and dominant securities markets is the most effective and efficient structure (though this has not gone unchallenged following the collapse of Enron). It is worth noting in this context that during almost two decades of rapid post–World War II growth and modernization, two successful capitalist nations – France and Japan – relied on financial systems that did not allocate capital in an open market simply or even essentially by price.[10] This may indicate that a system based on valuation and resource allocation through open financial markets is possibly not a *conditio sine qua non* of development.

Nonetheless, as a result of this general consensus in respect to the value of the development of securities markets and widely dispersed ownership, in recent years attention has focused on mechanisms through which this objective

---

[8] This situation has traditionally been the case in markets characterized by dominant financial institutions, such as banks, with a large role in both enterprise funding and control. See id., pp. 147–84.

[9] See id.

[10] See generally S. Cohen, *Credit Policy and Industrial Policy in France, Monetary Policy, Selective Credit Policy, and Industrial Policy in France, Britain, West Germany, and Sweden*, Staff Paper Prepared for the Use of the Joint Economic Committee, US Congress, U.S. GPO No. 77 744 O (1981); see also J. Zysman, *Governments, Markets and Growth* (Ithaca, NY: Cornell University Press, 1983).

may be achieved. Much of the recent debate has focused on the idea that a given economy's legal system and structure are significant factors underpinning the development of the Anglo-American structure. Research suggests that the degree of protection a country's legal system provides for outside investors has a significant effect on its corporate governance regime, with stronger legal protection for minority shareholders associated with a larger number of listed companies, more valuable stock markets, lower private benefits of control, and more diffuse share ownership.[11] In other words, a country's legal system can impact the development of the Berle and Means corporation, now widely agreed as the most efficient model.

At the same time, however, the Anglo-American model requires the most sophisticated institutional environment of all the alternative systems in order to function properly. According to Rajan and Zingales, "[t]he relationship system [i.e., bank-based] differs from a market-based [i.e., arm's-length] system on two important attributes: *transparency* and *access*"[12] – both of which are strongly related to the underlying institutional framework. As a result, countries with less sophisticated levels of institutional development should look to other models to meet their own circumstances, while at the same time working to put in place the necessary institutional supports for the Berle and Means model. In this regard, Eric Friedman, Simon Johnson and Todd Mitton suggest that firms may issue more debt to counteract the effects of weak country and firm-level investor protection, helping to explain why developing and emerging economies with weak institutions sometimes grow rapidly and why they are subject to frequent economic and financial crises.[13]

This view is supported by Thorsten Beck, Asli Demirguc-Kunt and Vojislav Maksimovic, who find[14]:

> Firms in less developed systems substitute alternative forms of external financing for those used more prevalently in developed countries: Thus, for equity and bank loans they substitute trade credit and what we term "other" or

---

[11] See e.g. K. Scott, "Corporate Governance and East Asia", in A. Harwood, R. Litan and M. Pomerleano (eds), *Financial Markets and Development: The Crisis in Emerging Markets* (Washington, DC: Brookings Institution Press, 1999), p. 335; B. Black, "The Legal and Institutional Preconditions for Strong Securities Markets: The Nontriviality of Securities Law", 44 Bus. Law. 1565 (2000); R. La Porta, F. Lopez-de-Silanes, A. Shleifer and R. Vishny, "Investor Protection and Corporate Governance", 58 J. Fin. Econ. 3 (2000).

[12] R. Rajan and L. Zingales, *Saving Capitalism from the Capitalists: Unleashing the Power of Financial Markets to Create Wealth and Spread Opportunity* (New York: Crown Business, 2003), p. 249.

[13] E. Friedman, S. Johnson and T. Mitton, Propping and Tunneling (15 Aug. 2002, mimeographed).

[14] T. Beck, A. Demirguc-Kunt and V. Maksimovic, "Financing Patterns around the World: The Role of Institutions", World Bank Policy Research Working Paper 2905 (Oct. 2002), pp. 3–4.

residual sources of finance, that is funding from miscellaneous sources such as government, development banks and informal sources. Financial and legal institutions do significantly affect the type of external financing that firms obtain.... Firms in common law countries have greater access to bank and equity finance.... Firms in countries with better-developed banking systems are less likely to use equity finance. Developed legal systems increase the proportion of bank finance and lower the proportion of residual financing form other sources in the financing mix of firms. We also see that these other sources and trade credit play a larger role in the financing of investment in countries with less developed institutions.... Our results also suggest that firms in less developed financial systems and civil law countries substitute less efficient forms of external finance, trade credit and other sources of funds, for bank loans and equity.

Banks therefore have an important role to play in the process of financial development, especially in weaker institutional environments. Further, Macro Da Rin and Thomas Hellman have shown that banks can act as a catalyst for industrialization, provided they are sufficiently large to mobilize a critical mass of firms and possess sufficient market power to make profits from coordination, with universal banks better able to fulfill this role, though perhaps at the cost of concentration in the industrial sector.[15] Their research follows on the theoretical frameworks developed by Joseph Schumpeter[16] and Alexander Gerschenkron[17], and has important implications for governments seeking to support economic development.

### 10.3.3. *Domestic Financial Development*

On a domestic level, countries must look to lessons from a large number of policy choices and experiences elsewhere in attempting to find the path that best suits their particular situation and needs. Countries tend to look first to the experiences of the developed countries, often focusing on the leading economy at any given point in time. As a result, during some periods, Britain and France have served as models (especially to their former colonies); during others, the focus has been on Germany and Japan. At present, the focus tends to be on the United States. Unfortunately, experience shows that no one single model or piece of legislation is appropriate for every situation or every individual state. This may be especially true of the US experience – which is often convoluted

---

[15] M. Da Rin and T. Hellman, Banks as Catalysts for Industrialization (Oct. 2001, mimeographed).
[16] J. Schumpeter, *The Theory of Economic Development* (Cambridge, MA: Harvard University Press, 1934).
[17] A. Gerschenkron, *Economic Backwardness in Historical Perspective* (Cambridge, MA: Harvard University Press, 1962).

and complicated because of the nature of the U.S. political system. As a result, it would be useful if countries could draw on internationally agreed lessons and experiences.

In the context of the United States, Mark Roe has analysed the significance of the impact of law and legal structures on financial system structure[18] and has applied a similar framework to Germany and Japan.[19] In addition, recent work has drawn links between legal structures and corporate governance structures.[20] While the debate on the exact role of law continues, it is generally agreed that the legal structures in place have an impact on the structure of domestic financial systems. Further, while the experiences of others can provide guidance, those experiences must be applied in each individual context – by nature *sui generis*. According to North[21]:

> Path dependence means that history matters. We cannot understand today's choices (and define them in the modeling of economic performance) without tracing the incremental evolution of institutions.

Most developing, emerging and transition economies have made substantial progress (albeit at different rates) in establishing the basic legal framework for the operation of a market economy. The next level of development to be attained has a dual focus. The first goal is to effectively develop a framework which will both achieve financial stability and support economic growth. The preceding chapters have presented the current state of knowledge in this regard. This section discusses how countries should work to achieve the best results. It is in this respect that the continuing work of the Financial Stability Forum and the various international financial organizations must be seen as being of significant value. Despite these efforts, however, it is the responsibility of individual countries to take the initiative to put in place the necessary legal infrastructure necessary to support financial sector development.

In achieving such a goal, the following framework is suggested. First, a country needs to establish a centre for coordination of the overall work program (typically the central bank, finance ministry or specialized financial policy arm of the government). This will take responsibility for coordination of the

---

[18]  M. Roe, "A Political Theory of American Corporate Finance", 91 Colum. L. Rev. 10 (1991).

[19]  M. Roe, "Some Differences in Corporate Structure in Germany, Japan, and the United States", 102 Yale L. J. 1927 (1993).

[20]  J. Coffee, "The Future as History: The Prospects for Global Convergence in Corporate Governance and its Implications", NW. U. L. Rev. 641 (1999); L. Bebchuk and M. Roe, "A Theory of Path Dependence in Corporate Ownership and Control", 52 Stan. L. Rev. 127 (1999).

[21]  D. North, *Institutions, Institutional Change and Economic Performance* (Cambridge: Cambridge University Press, 1990), p. 100.

work program, mobilization of funding, use of any consultants, and review of implementation. Second, a plan must be developed that looks at the financial sector as a whole. Questions to be addressed include: What is the current status of the financial sector? What are its strengths and weaknesses? Are there any significant failures? What are the needs for the coming years? The idea is that the financial sector should not be looked at piecemeal, but rather as part of a coordinated plan to establish coherent and meaningful rules for participants and regulators in order to secure its future development. It should be noted, however, that this is not a plan for how the sector should function but rather to formalize the rules of the game so that development in the context of stability can take place and move the country toward the overall goal of an open, effectively functioning financial system. Third, the legislation and regulations governing the market and its participants must be analysed vis-à-vis international standards and best practices and any gaps addressed in a coherent and effective manner. It is especially important to secure coordination of authorities and establishment of independence and clear objectives, while at the same time being forward looking (e.g., the interaction with an economy's WTO, regional and other commitments) and noninterventionist. This must be seen as no small task and one that may require time, but one that will pay dividends in financial and overall economic growth and development in the future.

Overall, financial liberalization provides important support for financial and economic development. At the same time, liberalization of financial services is a leading indicator of financial crises. A robust financial system reduces the likelihood of crises and the severity of crises that do occur. A robust financial system is based upon key international standards for a sound financial system implemented through an appropriate and effective legal and regulatory framework. The choices made in implementing international standards through the legal and regulatory framework, in turn, are central determinants of financial structure. In addition, as discussed previously, financial systems today have the added complication of their interaction with one another. As a result, in addition to domestic design, countries must consider issues with respect to interactions with global and regional financial markets. Regrettably, the current system of financial standards does not address the important issue of the relationship between financial liberalization and financial stability at a global level. This relationship has been addressed at a regional level by the more formal structure of the European Union, which may provide a model for both international and other regional arrangements. Unfortunately, even coherent design faces the problem of evaluation, especially given that many questions regarding the optimum institutional design for financial markets remain unanswered.

## 10.4. THE ROLE OF REGIONAL ARRANGEMENTS

On a regional level, efforts such as those of the European Union, North American Free Trade Agreement (NAFTA), Mercosur and Association of Southeast Asian Nations (ASEAN) now have an increasing significance for those countries wishing to become involved with these various sorts of regional efforts. For EU aspirants especially, its regional model has been of major significance given the nature of the accession process. As a result of its successes, the European Union is increasingly serving as a model for other regional integration exercises. These sorts of regional factors, then, cannot be ignored in the process of domestic law reform. Further, European financial markets rules provide an excellent second level of detail to international financial standards, because European directives and similar instruments have been carefully developed in order to deal with issues across a variety of institutional structures.

### 10.4.1. *The European Experience*

The experiences of the European Union show how, in one context, liberalization and regulation have been formally related. The EU experience shows that regional integration can play a role in promoting the adoption of sound principles and practices in economies and in supporting their implementation. The fundamental principle of mutual recognition and a system of a single license ensure that these directives provide a set of minimum norms while at the same time avoiding the creation of obstacles to competition among financial institutions.

**Creation of the Internal Market and Single Market for Financial Services.** A study of capital markets by the European Economic Community in 1966 addressed impediments to the effective functioning of national markets and their availability to foreign borrowers. The Segré Report[22] found that national markets in Europe discriminated in favor of domestic borrowers, especially national governments, as against foreign, primarily through regulations governing the investment of funds of savings banks and insurance companies. In addition, few European securities were listed on exchanges outside the domicile of the issuing company. As a result of practical governmental needs (combined with the forces of harmonization, access deregulation, and prudential

---

[22] European Economic Community (EEC), *The Development of a European Capital Market* ("Segre Report"), 1966. See C. Kindleberger, *A Financial History of Western Europe*, 2nd ed. (Oxford: Oxford University Press, 1993), pp. 438–9.

re-regulation inherent in the process of market liberalization developed the "Maastricht" objective of free movement of capital), national financial regulation in Europe has developed significantly in recent years. Prior to the 1990s, however, financial regulation in western Europe was virtually nonexistent outside of the United Kingdom, especially in the area of securities.[23]

The EU framework for financial services provides minimum standards for banks and other financial institutions, securities regulation, accounting and auditing, company law, and regulation of institutional investors, all based on the premise of universal banking and an open internal market. It should be borne in mind, however, that this framework is not complete. Since its purpose is to ensure the harmonization of the laws of the Member States to common minimum standards, insofar as this is necessary for the achievement of a single market, and to fill gaps relating to cross-border activities, it builds on the existing national systems of laws, rather than trying to replace them with a complete, new system. The purpose of this chapter is not to evaluate the specific provisions of the EU framework; however, a general appreciation of the key elements of the EU framework is necessary to understand the development of European financial market regulation and the way in which it integrates liberalization and regulation.

The EU legislative framework for financial markets seems to be grounded in a concept that can be thought of as a search for equivalence among disparate regulatory and legal systems, while taking into account the continuing reality of separate and distinct national legal and regulatory regimes as the basis of any overall EU initiatives.[24] Initially, efforts focused on harmonization of rules across Member States, however, this proved impossible in many areas, and in the 1980s, efforts moved to the development of mutual recognition based upon common minimum standards. The key principles were outlined in the European Commission's 1985 White Paper[25] and enshrined in the 1986 Single European Act[26], implementing the common internal market on the basis of "mutual recognition", based on common minimum standards applicable in all Member States through European Directives and implemented through domestic legislation.[27] According to this methodology, all Member States agree to recognize the validity of one another's laws, regulations and standards, thereby

---

[23]  See M. Warren, "Global Harmonization of Securities Laws: The Achievements of the European Communities", 31 Harv. Int'l L. J. 185 (1990).

[24]  See Steil, op. cit., n. 6, p. 113.

[25]  European Commission, *Completing the Internal Market: White Paper from the European Commission to the European Council*, 1985, Com(85)310 final.

[26]  *Single European Act*, 1987 OJ (L 169) 1 (1987) (effective 1 Jul. 1987).

[27]  Id.

facilitating free trade in goods and services without the need for prior harmonization[28], while limiting the scope for competition among rules by mandating Member State conformity with a "floor" of essential, minimum European requirements. As such, financial services regulation in the European Union seeks to avoid the problem of competitive deregulation and regulatory arbitrage that may undermine the legitimacy and efficiency of financial markets.[29]

The single market is rooted in basic tenets of the Treaty of Rome respecting the free movement of capital, establishment and services, and is manifested in the various single "passport" directives.[30] Under the concept of the "single" passport, an EU firm authorized in one Member State (its "home state") and wishing to operate in other Member States ("host states") will generally be able to choose to supply services through branches or to supply services on a cross-border basis without having a permanent physical presence in the host state.[31] The intended benefit of the passport is that it should increase competition by opening markets to a wider range of participants and by allowing firms to choose the most cost-effective means of supplying services to a particular market.[32] The passport directives in the financial services area have of number of common aspects: each defines its scope in terms of the type of intermediary and the activities that it will carry out (though perhaps with reference to particular instruments); each requires firms to be authorized and sets out the conditions a firm must satisfy for initial and continuing authorization; each sets the division of responsibility between the home state and the host state in various areas[33]; and each addresses the issue of relations with non-EU Member States.[34]

**The Accession Process.** While the work of international financial forums forge globally accepted core principles, EU requirements relating to financial services are more directly relevant for those countries aspiring to accede to the

---

[28]  See Steil, op. cit., n. 6.
[29]  See Warren, op. cit., n. 23.
[30]  The passport directives in the financial services area include: (1) the First and Second Banking Coordination Directives (1BCD and 2BCD) (banking), (2) the Investment Services Directive (ISD) (investment firms and securities markets), (3) the UCITS Directive (collective investment schemes); (4) the First, Second and Third Life Assurance Directives (life assurance), (5) the First, Second and Third Non-Life Insurance Directives (non-life insurance) and (6) the proposed First Pension Funds Directive (pension funds).
[31]  See "The EC Single Market in Financial Services", Bank of Eng. Q. Bull. 92 (Feb. 1993).
[32]  Id.
[33]  As a general rule, the home state will have responsibility for the prudential supervision of a firm and all its branches as well as the "fitness and properness" of its managers and major shareholders, while the host state will be responsible for the conduct of a firm's business with its customers in the host state. Id., p. 93.
[34]  Id.

European Union. Given the composition of many of the international bodies concerned with promoting effective regulation and supervision of financial markets, it is not surprising that EU requirements relating to financial services have influenced the content of the emerging international standards and reflect their content. Nonetheless, EU standards have been more immediately relevant for countries in the region seeking EU membership.[35]

The accession process involved Europe Agreements with the European Union[36] which obliged applicants to take on board the *acquis communautaire*. A primary obligation of an accession state is the approximation of existing and future state legislation in the financial services sector to that of the European Union. Moreover, under existing Europe Agreements, EU financial companies have the right to operate on the territory of the respective accession candidate country prior to accession. Accordingly, the accession state must have in place a fully EU-compatible system of financial services regulation by the date of accession.

As an aid to this process of incorporation of the *acquis*, in April 1995 the European Commission issued a White Paper identifying the key measures required to undertaken in each sector of the internal market. The White Paper proposed a sequence under which the accession candidates should seek to approximate their domestic legislation to that of the European Union, including that European rules in the financial services area should be adopted in two stages: the first involved the introduction of the basic principles for the establishment of financial intermediaries, and the second (although some elements are important for the first stage) aimed to strengthen prudential supervision of financial firms in order to bring them up to international standards. This second stage of the Commission framework for the accession candidates focused on the various European provisions for free movement of capital and services in the financial sphere. The EU accession process thus provides a possible model for sequencing of financial reform and liberalization, as well as for integrating liberalization and regulation.

**Economic and Monetary Union (EMU).** On 1 January 1999, the individual currencies of the eleven EU Member States that met the relevant criteria and accepted the relevant obligations of the Maastricht Treaty (Austria, Belgium,

---

[35] For details, see C. Hadjiemmanuil, "Central Bankers' 'Club' Law and Transitional Economies: Banking Reform and the Reception of the Basel Standards of Prudential Supervision in Eastern Europe and the Former Soviet Union", in J. Norton and M. Andenas (eds), *Emerging Financial Markets and the Role of International Financial Organizations* (London: Kluwer, 1996).

[36] Bulgaria, Cyprus, Czech Republic, Estonia, Hungary, Latvia, Lithuania, Malta, Poland, Romania, Slovakia and Slovenia. All have, as of Jan. 2007, become EU member states.

Denmark, France, Germany, Ireland, Italy, Luxembourg, The Netherlands, Portugal, and Spain) became permanently fixed in exchange rate and ceased to exist, thereby creating a single European currency, the "euro", and European Economic and Monetary Union (EMU). From 1 January 2001, the twelve (Greece has since been added) different sets of notes and coins were quickly replaced by a single physical currency. While significant differences still exist in European financial markets, with the introduction of the euro, information has begun to become comparable. This shift is beginning to produce, when combined with the painfully developed financial regulatory framework discussed in the previous sections, the development of a unified European financial market for the first time.

Prior to the signing of the Maastricht Treaty in 1992, there existed little impetus for Member States to actively implement the various financial services directives. However, with the entry into force of the Treaty in 1994, and its requirements for adoption and implementation of the framework supporting freedom of capital movements necessary to underpin EMU, Continental Member States adopted and implemented legislation quite foreign to the financial markets of their domestic systems. The result has been an increased awareness of the use of financial markets and the realization that the legislative changes, when combined with the advent of the single currency, will change (and have already changed) the nature of finance throughout the European Union, but most especially in the euro-13 members (Slovenia became the first former Soviet Bloc country to adopt the euro in 2007).

While the ultimate result is yet to be seen, significant movements have already taken place with the significant and continuing development of domestic financial markets in the European Union. Further, new initiatives are coming rapidly, seeking to take advantage of new opportunities and to place competitors at an advantage in the European markets that are, in all likelihood, to arrive in short order. Although numerous impediments to such developments remain (most notably in the area of taxation), activity is set to continue increasing at a rapid pace, putting pressure on the barriers that remain. Other issues related to the need to differentiate between wholesale and retail financial services.[37] One example of the recognition of continuing impediments and the pressure to remove them is the establishment of financial services committees to review aspects of EU financial markets and to develop proposals to remove remaining barriers to the creation of a single European financial market.

---

[37] C. Jordan and G. Majnoni, "Financial Regulatory Harmonization and the Globalization of Finance", World Bank Policy Research Working Paper 2919 (Oct. 2002), p. 9.

### 10.4.2. *Implications for Other Regional Arrangements*

It is this "real world" experience of the countries of the European Union and their moves to develop a single regional financial market that indicates the real advantages of the multilateral path that may lie ahead in the globalization of financial markets. The development of European financial markets, and other countries' nervousness respecting the same, has provided impetus to international organizations, such as the International Organization of Securities Commissions (IOSCO) and the International Accounting Standards Borad (IASB) (and their previously recalcitrant members, such as the United States).

Jordan and Majnoni suggest that two lessons can be drawn from the European experience with financial integration:[38]

> First, the principle of minimum harmonization together with mutual recognition principles underlines the potential for leaving integration to market forces once national legal and regulatory frameworks share common minimum standards. Secondarily, in a financially integrated world, size matters both for regulated entities and for the regulators and the same set of rules may not be efficient and equitable for both large and small players.

While the EU experience is definitely instructive to both the international financial architecture and other regional arrangements, the reality is that the EU process will not be politically acceptable in most other environments due to its impact on sovereignty.

### 10.5. CONCLUSION

Through analysis of the series of financial crises which have occurred during the 1990s, this volume has sought to draw a number of lessons from those experiences, not only for the economies concerned and for those similarly situated, but also for the international institutions and actors and to inform the debate concerning the international financial architecture. First, in order to become full participants in the international financial system while at the same time maintaining both domestic and international financial stability requires careful domestic restructuring as part of any process of financial liberalization. Financial liberalization without appropriate restructuring has been followed by financial crisis, and those crises have often had international or even global impact. Second, the policies and systems advocated by the Bretton Woods and other international financial organizations during the 1990s did not

---

[38] Id., pp. 9–10.

adequately take into account the risks inherent in financial sector liberalization and likewise provided insufficient guidance on the requirements necessary to implement domestically in the context of restructuring. Third, developments in one country are no longer restricted to its own borders in today's increasingly globalized financial markets and therefore there is an imperative need to readdress the Bretton Woods system and to design an appropriate international financial architecture in much the same way that was done originally at Bretton Woods in 1944. Fourth, all of these systems, whether domestic or international, need to be based upon transparent, rule-based structures, that is, upon the rule of law. The lesson then is that if these lessons are not addressed, financial crises similar to those common in the past fifteen years (and in fact in likewise in the nineteenth century) will continue to be commonplace in the twenty-first.

Overall, the development of the financial systems in emerging, developing and transition economies should respond to two overriding requirements: (1) the need to expand the size and increase the depth and availability of finance; and (2) integration into the international financial system. More fundamentally, legislation and implementation must ensure stability and confidence, since these are the primary factors upon which the success of every financial system depends.

The importance of law and law reform to financial and economic development has been underlined by financial crises over the past fifteen years. One generally agreed conclusion of the many analyses that have followed on these events is that an underlying cause of these crises, or at least an exacerbating factor, was weaknesses in domestic financial sectors and improper sequencing of the liberalization of international capital flows. This is especially significant in the context of developing, emerging and transition economies where development of an effective financial sector has been (and continues to be) one of the greatest challenges. In this respect, attention to legal reform is essential to financial stability in that it not only underlies efforts to develop financial systems but moreover can strengthen such systems in order to reduce potential vulnerabilities to financial crises. Legal reform can also help countries weather possible international economic contagion (pressure stemming from adverse investor "herd" behaviour) from financial crises elsewhere which can be extremely dangerous to the development of financial systems.

The financial stability and viability, and hence development, of an economy depend on two fundamental sets of factors. The first is the macroeconomic and structural conditions in the real economy which impact financial decisions and form the environment within which the financial system operates. The second factor is the robustness of the financial system itself, comprising the financial markets, intermediaries, and arrangements through which financial transactions are carried out. By their nature, the component elements that comprise a robust financial system depend on legal structures and institutions.

Legal structures and institutions serve as the underlying framework for the operation of modern financial systems and are important elements underpinning their development. Today, legal structures and institutions are seen as necessary both to establish and maintain the rules by which participants in the financial sector must play and to build confidence in the financial environment and thereby encourage finance and investment. Further, an effective legal system enables financial commitments to be created and honored and also governs the conduct of the market in which the underlying transactions occur. Vibrant financial systems require not only that appropriate legal rules exist but that they operate in an environment where they are effective. While the phrase "rule of law" has been often repeated, until recently, the meaning of the idea and its effective implementation received very little practical attention; for that reason, financial sector development was seen as the field of economists and the role of law was viewed as largely irrelevant. Difficulties and set-backs during the 1990s have caused focus to shift somewhat to the rule of law and related institution building.[39]

The development of appropriate regulation of finance and the creation of effective financial legislation promote financial development and stability in two fashions. First, prudential regulation protects depositors and investors and strengthens their confidence in the financial system as a whole, thereby encouraging savings, investment and the development of effective financial intermediaries. Developing a functioning financial sector has become a key goal, necessary to the development of an effectively functioning market economy. Second, a clear and effective legal infrastructure promotes reliance on and respect for contracts that underpin financial dealing. While the rule of law has often been thought of as an amorphous goal, the development of a functioning legal system is now strongly emphasized, as understanding has developed of the role of law in encouraging business activity generally and in reducing the dangers of corruption and other governance problems. Law therefore must be seen to play a central role in creating and promoting the development of a decentralized, noncorrupt financial system. Additionally, weaknesses in the banking system, capital markets or insurance sector (or combination thereof) of a country can threaten financial stability and development, both in individual countries and internationally, through contagious failures in market

---

[39] For an overview of progress, difficulties and transition generally since 1989, see European Bank for Reconstruction and Development, *Transition Report 1999: Ten Years of Transition*, 1999.

confidence. Thus, there has been growing international attention to methods to strengthen financial systems, with various international bodies increasingly acting to develop principles to underlie such efforts at reform. In order to be meaningful, such international principles must be implemented through legal reform, encompassing broad legislative, institutional and cultural changes.

What, then, are the most significant principles underlying financial market stability and development and how is a robust supporting legal system to be developed? This volume has attempted to answer these questions, arguing that the minimum content of the requisite financial laws and the necessary elements of the legal system that makes those laws effective can be discerned through analysis of the demands of the rule of law in the context of the financial sector and through recognizing that internationally acceptable minimum financial standards can be distilled from a developing consensus regarding underlying principles necessary to support the requisite elements of financial systems.

It must be noted, however, that these international principles and standards are just that: minimum internationally agreed guidelines that leave wide latitude in their implementation and effectiveness. Despite their increasing importance, the mere adoption of such standards by any given country will not assure the viability, stability and development of its financial system. Rather, the question arises as to how to implement these general principles into the legal and institutional framework of a given country. Nonetheless, these principles for the first time do give guidance concerning the minimum requirements necessary to develop in a country's financial system to prepare it for participation in international financial markets. As has been most clearly demonstrated by the on-going volatility of international capital flows, such participation is not without its dangers. Individual countries are therefore increasingly interested in developing effective regulatory and other legal mechanisms that can provide their own financial systems some measure of protection from such outward capital movements, while at the same time encouraging investment flows to their economies. Such efforts must be seen to be especially significant in the context of the recent development of the financial services liberalization provisions of the WTO.[40]

More importantly, the development of an international consensus on the requisite elements of a stable and robust financial system is extremely significant. Different countries have pursued different models, based on the theories of different academics, consultants, and international and domestic bureaucracies. A constant, however, is the need to develop functioning market-based

---

[40] See J. Norton, "International Financial Law and International Economic Law: Implications for Emerging and Transition Economies", Law in Transition 2 (Spr. 1999).

financial systems. Prior to the development of this emerging consensus on principles underlying stable and robust financial systems, financial sector development had to be viewed as, at best, a haphazard process. While today there is still certainly no single road-map to successful financial sector development, at least for the first time, there exists now general agreement as to the goals to be achieved. This can only be viewed as a very significant step forward and one that is long overdue.

In the final analysis, however, appropriate legal design is not sufficient. While legal and institutional structures are fundamental for debt market development and securitization, neither appropriate laws on the books nor effective institutions are sufficient in themselves for development.[41]

While financial laws and regulations and their enforcement are fundamental to the development and functioning of sound financial systems, the question remains as to what are the legal and regulatory arrangements toward which the developing, emerging and transition countries should be moving. Just as there is no archetype for a market economy, there historically has been no unique set of laws and regulations and mechanisms for their enforcement that underpin sound finance: indeed, there is wide variation in these institutional arrangements and practices in market economies world-wide. From this diversity, though, has come a range of experiences and many valuable lessons. These standards serve as a mechanism for harmonization of legal and regulatory systems in an increasingly globalized and integrated financial system that expands the potential for jurisdictions with stronger systems to attract financial activity away from those with weaker arrangements.

When questions of development and transition were being analysed prior to the 1990s, law was not seen as significant to financial development; rather, emphasis was placed on various policy-based models, with the theory being that appropriate structures would develop naturally as part of the development and transition process. In the event, this has not been the case; rather, without attention to the institutional fabric, including law, development and transition have not generally proceeded as successfully as more gradual processes integrating development of supporting institutions. As a result, increasing

---

[41] Pistor, Raiser and Gelfer sum up the situation well:

In their analysis of law and finance around the world, [La Porta, Lopez-de-Silanes, Shleifer and Vishny] show that effective law enforcement is not a substitute for poor laws on the books. The experience of transition economies suggests that the reverse is also true: Good laws cannot substitute for weak institutions.

K. Pistor, R. Raiser and Gelfer, "Law and Finance in Transition Economies", EBRD Working Paper no. 48 (2000), p. 25 (citing R. La Porta, F. Lopez-de-Silanes, A. Shleifer and R. Vishny, "Law and Finance", 106 J. Pol. Econ. 1113 [1998]).

attention is devoted to supporting institutions and the development of the rule of law; unfortunately, until recently, there has been no general consensus regarding which factors are significant, especially in respect to financial sector development. This volume has sought to review, integrate and highlight these, to analyse continuing areas of concern and to suggest directions for future consideration and development.

# Index